**ON
TO
CIVVY
STREET**

ON TO CIVVY STREET

Canada's Rehabilitation Program for Veterans of the Second World War

Peter Neary

McGILL-QUEEN'S UNIVERSITY PRESS   Montreal & Kingston • London • Ithaca

© McGill-Queen's University Press 2011

ISBN 978-0-7735-3913-6 (cloth)
ISBN 978-0-7735-3927-3 (paper)

Legal deposit fourth quarter 2011
Bibliothèque nationale du Québec

Printed in Canada on acid-free paper that is 100% ancient forest free (100% post-consumer recycled), processed chlorine free

This book has been published with the help of a grant from the Canadian Federation for the Humanities and Social Sciences, through the Aid to Scholarly Publications Program, using funds provided by the Social Sciences and Humanities Research Council of Canada. Funding has also been received from the J.B. Smallman Publication Fund, Faculty of Social Science, The University of Western Ontario.

McGill-Queen's University Press acknowledges the support of the Canada Council for the Arts for our publishing program. We also acknowledge the financial support of the Government of Canada through the Canada Book Fund for our publishing activities.

Library and Archives Canada Cataloguing in Publication

Neary, Peter, 1938–
On to Civvy Street : Canada's rehabilitation program for veterans of the Second World War / Peter Neary.

Includes bibliographical references and index.
ISBN 978-0-7735-3913-6 (bnd)
ISBN 978-0-7735-3927-3 (pbk)

1. Veterans Charter (Canada). 2. Veterans—Legal status, laws, etc.—Canada. 3. World War, 1939–1945—Veterans—Canada. 4. Veterans—Government policy—Canada. I. Title.

UB359.C3N43 2011   362.86'80971   C2011-903524-3

Designed and typeset by studio oneonone in New Baskerville 10.2/13

Frontispiece: Illustration from C.N. Senior, *When the Boys Come Home*, 1944, front cover

In Memory of
Christopher Perrin Beatty (1984–2008)
and for
Eleanor and Colin

Contents

List of Illustrations ix

List of Tables xiii

List of Abbreviations xv

Preface xvii

1 Origins 3
2 Depression Divide 25
3 PC7633 60
4 Program Development 88
5 Ready for Release 117
6 Golden Future Time 159
7 Building and Rebuilding 216
8 Conclusion 275

Appendix: Tables 291

Notes 301

Bibliography 339

Index 349

Illustrations

Zennosuke Inouye in his Great War uniform   21
Ian Alistair Mackenzie   58
Walter Sainsbury Woods   58
Harold French McDonald   64
Robert England   65
Alex Walker   71
Gordon Murchison   89
The Inouye family   99
George Moir Weir   107
Sperrin Noah Fulton Chant   132
Emerson Baker Reid   134
Advertisement on planning   134
Back to Civil Life   135
Olive Ruth Russell   139
Harold Williams Jamieson   144
E.L.M. Burns   163
Marching Home to What?   163
After Discharge "What"?   168
Cartoonist's summary of the postwar situation   168
A newspaper voice for Canadian veterans   168
The YMCA welcomes veterans   168
When the Boys Come Home   170
Citizens' Rehabilitation Council of Greater Vancouver   170
The promise of a better tomorrow   173
DVA's office in London, Ontario   174
Discussing plans at Montreal Rehabilitation Centre   174
Canadian business welcomed the self-help approach of the Veterans Charter   177
Bank of Montreal poster   180
Department of Labour reminder to business   180
War service gratuity form   189
The re-establishment credit   189

Simpson's primer on re-establishment credits   194
Cautionary words for veterans   195
One of the many beneficiaries   199
Veterans at a commercial class   199
Veterans in class, London, Ontario   199
Instructor Gordon Duncan explains use of the mitre box   200
Norman and Jacqueline Haddow opened a laundry for dogs   200
A graduate of the CVT barbering school at work   200
Bill Vaughan, John Cleary, and Bob Alexander at the CVT School of Electronics   201
Float of Canning District Board of Trade   201
Veteran Peter Omond setting up tent accommodation   204
Ross Bates at the University of Saskatchewan   206
Army huts at the University of British Columbia   206
Mary Dinsmore Salter   221
Ex-service women at the 1948 Canadian Legion convention   223
Wilfred Parsons Warner   227
Ray F. Scott, first patient at Sunnybrook Hospital   230
Edward Arunah Dunlop   233
Walter Woods, Ian Mackenzie, Eddie Baker, William Dies, and James Melville   234
John Gibbons Counsell   237
Harry Botterell   237
Albin Theophile Jousse with Viscount Alexander   237
Publicity to help disabled veterans find employment   238
DVA pamphlet on behalf of tuberculous veterans   239
Margaret Stevens, Hamilton's Queen of the Fair, discusses exhibit to help disabled veterans   239
Paraplegic veterans in Vancouver playing a football game they invented   240
Amputee William Graham making artificial hands   240
Skating champion Barbara Ann Scott signing a veteran's cast   240
Cartoonist Jack Boothe on the postwar housing crisis   245
Advertisement used in DVA's 1945 housing campaign   245
Thomas John Rutherford   249
Ken and Susan Inkster on their VLA smallholding   251
Walter and Molly Penrose on their VLA dairy farm   251
Milton Fowler Gregg   259
Howard Cameron   276

ILLUSTRATIONS

Campbell and William Eaton   276
André Gadbois, with his mother and grandmother   276
Dante Lenardon   277
Nonie Ketchum   277
Leslie Harrison Porter   279
Susanne Day   279
Donald M. Thompson   279
Arthur Patrick Bates   280
On to Civvy Street   298

Tables

1 Number of recipients and cost of DPNH relief/unemployment assistance, 1927–28 to 1939–40 / 36
2 Distribution of disabled veterans according to primary disability / 235
3 Distribution of disabled veterans according to rehabilitation status / 235
A1 First World War pensions in force at the end of fiscal years 1918 to 1955 / 291
A2 Second World War pensions in force at the end of fiscal years 1941 to 1955 / 292
A3 Number of veterans approved for the receipt of an allowance under the Veterans Rehabilitation Act, fiscal years 1941–42 to 1951–52 / 293
A4 Activity under the Veterans' Business and Professional Loans Act, to 13 March 1951 / 294
A5 Application for qualification under the Veterans' Land Act, to 31 March 1955 / 295
A6 Hospitals operated by DVA during the fiscal year 1946–47 / 297
A7 Walter Woods's 1953 table of benefits / 299

Abbreviations

CCF Co-operative Commonwealth Federation
CCL Canadian Congress of Labour
CEF Canadian Expeditionary Force
CMA Canadian Medical Association
CMHC Central Mortgage and Housing Corporation
CNIB Canadian National Institute for the Blind
CVT Canadian Vocational Training
CWAC Canadian Women's Army Corps
DND Department of National Defence
DPNH Department of Pensions and National Health
DSCR Department of Soldiers' Civil Re-establishment
DVA Department of Veterans Affairs
GACDR General Advisory Committee on Demobilization and Rehabilitation
GWVA Great War Veterans' Association of Canada (and, in context, Newfoundland)
JCNM Japanese Canadian National Museum (Burnaby, British Columbia)
LAC Library and Archives Canada (Ottawa)
NCCU National Conference of Canadian Universities
NHA National Housing Act, 1944
NRMA National Resources Mobilization Act, 1940
RAF Royal Air Force
RCAF(WD) Royal Canadian Air Force Women's Division
TLC Trades and Labor Congress
UAW United Auto Workers
UIC Unemployment Insurance Commission
VAC Veterans Affairs Canada
VLA Veterans' Land Act, 1942
WAAF Women's Auxiliary Air Force (UK)
WRCNS Women's Royal Canadian Naval Service

Preface

In writing this book I have been assisted by family, friends, colleagues, and institutions. At Veterans Affairs Canada I was helped by many officials, Ken Hawkes and Terry Tobin especially, and I thank them all most sincerely for their interest in my work. At Library and Archives Canada, Ottawa, I owe much to Paul Marsden and George de Zwaan, to whom I also extend my grateful thanks. Although I no longer teach in the Department of History at the University of Western Ontario, I was given expert technical help by Lana Williams, Chris Speed, and Paula Nopper of that department, and I thank them most sincerely. As always, the estimable Alan Noon kindly assisted me with photographs. I also acknowledge special help with illustrations from Barry Arnott and Theresa Regnier of the University of Western Ontario Archives (*London Free Press* collection) and from Denny Russell of the Calgary Highlanders Museum and Archives. The list of scholars who helped and encouraged me is long. I thank them one and all and extend particular thanks to Melvin Baker, Sam Clark, Michael DeKay, Keith Fleming, J.L. Granatstein, Robert Hawkins, A.M.J. Hyatt, Laurence Mussio, Patricia Roy, Renée Silberman, Michael Stevenson, James Struthers, Jonathan Vance, Robert Wardhaugh, Martin Westmacott, and Robert Young. I salute, with gratitude, the research accomplishments of the late Shaun Brown and Mary Tremblay. My knowledge of the career of Zennosuke Inouye owes much to my fruitful interaction with the late Beverley Inouye, and my understanding of the history of Newfoundland veterans to the many courtesies extended to me by the late G. Campbell Eaton. I am very pleased indeed to record here my gratitude to them both. I am most grateful to Janet Leith of Coventry, England, for sharing with me her exemplary research into the history of the Woods family. For aid and counsel at McGill-Queen's I thank especially Jonathan Crago, Joan McGilvray, John Zucchi, and my distinguished former undergraduate student Philip Cercone, executive director. I am likewise most grateful to my editor and fellow Londoner, Carlotta Lemieux, for her constructive advice and help. Her commitment to scholarship and her command of the Queen's English have been an inspiration to me over many years. At every turn my efforts have been supported by my kind, considerate, and informed brother-in-law, Jock Bates of Victoria, British Columbia. Thank you, Jock. And thank you, dearest Hilary, for your indispensable research assistance and for your unfailing advice and support.

I trace my interest in the subject of this book to my Newfoundland beginnings. My father, for whom I am named, trained in St John's with the Royal Naval Reserve before 1914 and joined up for active service on the day Great Britain entered the 1914–18 war. I grew up hearing his stories of his service overseas and learning the names of faraway places such as Devonport, Kirkwall, Scapa Flow, and Jutland. The medals he earned are among my family's most prized possessions. He was not by nature a joiner (he was, in any case, too busy working) but was active in the affairs of the Bell Island, Newfoundland, branch of the Great War Veterans' Association. A deeply patriotic Newfoundlander, he opposed the 1949 union of his country with Canada and never fully adjusted to the disappearance of his beloved GWVA into the Canadian Legion. He nevertheless benefited in later life from Ottawa's veterans' affairs programs and died in 1970 in a hospital that received funding from the federal government's Department of Veterans Affairs. A Legion honour party came to his funeral, and we were all deeply touched by that. From my mother, ever on the lookout for unfairness in society, I learned that governments had not always given veterans the justice they deserved. All historical writing has autobiographical elements, and I was certainly aware of this in writing the following account of a major episode in Canadian history. My book brings together, in a master narrative, some research findings that I have published elsewhere, but it adds much more and tells a complete story. For enabling me to proceed in this fashion, I thank Breakwater Books, McGill-Queen's University Press, Nelson Education, the University of Toronto Press, and the British Association for Canadian Studies. My study is set in the context of war, but my interest is in benefits rather than bullets. My purpose will be served if the Veterans Charter lives on in the teaching of Canadian history in the same way that the G.I. Bill of Rights does in the teaching of American history. Our veterans deserve to be remembered not only for what they achieved in war but for what they then accomplished in peace.

**ON
TO
CIVVY
STREET**

1 Origins

Late one evening in December 1918, a few weeks after the armistice that ended the Great War of 1914–18, a group of six soldiers arrived from overseas at the railway station in Calgary. There was no welcoming party to meet them, and the men quickly parted company and went their separate ways from the station and into the night. One of the returnees was Private Cecil John Kinross, who had won the Victoria Cross, the British Empire's highest military decoration, for his gallantry in assaulting an enemy machine-gun position at Passchendaele. Another was Walter Sainsbury Woods, who in later life became a principal architect of Canada's program for the veterans of the Second World War – a conflict rooted in the terrible war just ended.[1]

Born in Frome, Somerset, England, on 16 July 1884, and named Walter Edwin Sainsbury, Woods was the seventh child in a family of twelve – eight sons and four daughters. His parents were Elizabeth Barnes and William Sainsbury Woods, a schoolmaster. Sometime before their last child was born and when their two eldest offspring were fifteen and fourteen, William (to use Walter's own word) was "lost" to the family. To support herself and her children, Elizabeth, who also was a qualified teacher, looked to the classroom, moving to Holmpton, Yorkshire, in 1896 with eight of the children, including Walter, who remained at home. In 1899 the family moved to Hull, Yorkshire, where, at age fifteen, Walter was apprenticed to the firm of Brown, Atkinson and Son, shipowners and brokers. Completing his apprenticeship in 1903, he went to London, where he worked in Bishopsgate, the hub of the shipping industry. There, his interest was piqued by immigration advertising extolling the attractions of life in the British dominions, and he decided to go to Canada, then a booming country and a magnet for British immigrants. In August 1905, at age twenty-one, having saved his passage money, he travelled for fourteen days by steerage aboard the ss *Sardinian* and landed at Quebec City. He chose Canada over the other destinations he considered – South Africa, Australia, and New Zealand – because pictures of its "lush fields, big red barns, towering forests and leaping fish of impossible size" made it seem more attractive. But his decision was also based on the fact – and here was a practicality that never left him – that Canada was the nearest of the dominions and therefore the least expensive to reach.

From Quebec, Woods made his way to Toronto and then to Milton, Ontario, where his brother Ben (who had come to Canada the year before) was working as a farm labourer. Walter was taken on by the same farmer, and so began his Canadian working life as a hired hand. At the end of the 1905 harvest season, the two brothers moved to Toronto, where they rented a room on Jarvis Street and began to look for work. Walter soon found a job as a shipper with Keith, Fitzsimmons Company, a plumbing and lighting supplies business on King Street. In the spring of 1906, feeling the pull of the burgeoning Prairie West, the brothers moved to Winnipeg, travelling by train in colonist coaches, along with young men who were heading out to help with the planting. In Winnipeg the two English adventurers stayed in an immigration hall but soon moved on to Brandon, where they found work on separate farms. When the harvest was in, Walter worked with a railway section gang, and this in turn led him into prospecting for gravel, which was needed for railway construction and maintenance. Thereafter, based in Stockton, Manitoba, he did clerical work for a gravel pit that was opened up in the area. When this enterprise was shut down, he worked at a signal station at Oak Point, near Winnipeg, and from there went to Portage la Prairie, where he again did clerical work. A succession of better paid and more responsible railway administrative positions soon came his way in Winnipeg, but in 1908 he returned to outdoor work, taking charge of a Grand Trunk Pacific Railway section gang that was working on the track at Meighen (now Viking) in the new province of Alberta. In 1909 he supervised the laying of Grand Trunk Pacific track from Melville to Canora, Saskatchewan.

As a boy in England, living for much of the time with a single parent working hard to make do, Woods had learned well that success in life comes to those who help themselves. He likewise always remembered the lesson "that to get money we had to earn it."[2] In Canada, he applied this philosophy to advantage, and by dint of self-discipline, thrift, and enterprise, quickly established himself in the country. He greatly admired both the individualist ethos and the hospitable spirit of the developing West, where opportunity abounded, people helped one another, and work was the key to success. All this was exemplified in the dominion government's homesteading system, which was giving thousands of people the chance to become landowners through self-help and the careful husbanding of resources. The state was providing opportunity, and individuals were seizing it to become property owners. This was the Canadian way, and it was a good recipe for getting ahead in life. Woods succeeded in Canada, became deeply attached to the Prairie West, and was very much a self-made man – an optimist about both his own future and that of the country he had chosen. He knew how to make a living and prided himself on his adaptability, resourcefulness, and sturdy independence. In Canada he dropped the name Edwin, delinked Sainsbury from his surname while keeping it as a middle name, and became plain Walter Woods – an adjustment that, he believed, was in keeping with the spirit of the country. Canadians "didn't have hyphenated names."[3]

When war began in August 1914, Woods was living in Edmonton and was by then a widower with two small sons, one born in January 1913 and the other in December of the same year (their English mother, whose given names were Rose Nancy, had died on the second child's birth).[4] Although his personal circumstances were manifestly complex, Walter immediately enlisted, turning over one child each to the care of two of his Canadian sisters-in-law (the wives of his brothers Ben and William, the latter having immigrated to "the man-hungry West" in 1911).[5] Woods's response to the outbreak of fighting typified the outlook of the British-born men in the country. From then to the introduction of conscription in 1917, almost half of those who enlisted in Canada for service in the Great War were British born, many of them living on the Prairies, which had been such a magnet for emigration from the United Kingdom during the boom years of the early twentieth century. In fighting for his adopted country, Woods would also be defending his native land, where he had family members still living, where his character had been formed, and to which he felt a strong tie. Venturesome in some respects, Woods was deeply conservative in others and rationalized "the apparent abandonment" of his children with "the conviction that I could not take care of them myself anyway."[6]

Now aged thirty, he volunteered for the 19th Alberta Dragoons and was soon on his way to Valcartier, Quebec, where the Canadian Expeditionary Force (CEF, originally Canadian Over-Seas Expeditionary Force) was in training. There, on 24 September 1914, he signed the attestation paper required of a recruit. He gave his occupation as "automobile salesman" (he was working at the time as secretary-treasurer of the Scott Motor Co.) and named his brother Frank as his next-of-kin.[7] He also indicated that he had served previously for three years in the Royal Garrison Artillery. He was given the regimental number 2068. His squadron – men and horses – left Quebec City aboard the Cunard liner *Arcadian* on 3 October 1914 and arrived at Devonport eleven days later. The *Arcadian* sailed in a convoy of thirty ships, which transported the First Canadian Contingent, and Woods was therefore among the first Canadian troops to arrive in the United Kingdom. A period of training followed, but he was also able to visit his mother, five of whose sons served during the war in France and Belgium.

On 2 February 1915, Woods and his Canadian fellow cavalrymen embarked for France and eventually took up a position at the Belgian town of Poperinghe in the Ypres salient (from September of that year the units of the CEF that served in France and Belgium were known as the Canadian Corps). During his first months at the front Woods was treated at the British Ophthalmic Centre for an eye injury, and in 1916 he was admitted to No. 2 Australian General Hospital "suffering from a foot injury which had cut an artery, a chest condition and general debility."[8] From there he went to a hospital in Sheffield, England, and after that to a convalescent hospital on the estate of the Duke of Devonshire. In March 1917 he went back to France, where he served with field artillery, running dispatches – sometimes under fire – to Brigade Headquarters. In February 1918 he went on furlough to Canada but was soon back in England, travelling there on a ship carrying men conscripted under the controversial Military Service Act of 1917. Following a period in quarantine, he went to the artillery base at Borden (Sittingbourne, Kent), where he contracted influenza. He recovered from this but was still at Borden when the war ended. His memory of that event was one of sadness: "I was consumed with a sickness of soul. Try as I would to forget I was overwhelmed by memories of comrades with whom I had come from Canada, who had been killed, grievously wounded or were missing."[9] Gunner Woods himself had been through much, but he was fortunate, unlike so many others who had volunteered, to be sound in mind and body. Above all, he was anxious to go home for good to pick up the pieces of a life that had veered far from its expected course. From Borden, he went to Rhyl in North Wales, where Canadian troops were assembled for repatriation, and thence to Liverpool and Halifax. From Halifax he travelled by train to Calgary, meeting "wonderful receptions" en route "with bands playing and refreshment and cigarettes distributed."[10]

And then came the jolt of arrival. As they disembarked in Calgary and said their goodbyes, Woods and his fellow passengers faced the complex process of readjusting to civilian life, a transition now being experienced by tens of thousands of Canadians as the country pushed forward the complex and at times messy process of demobilization. After the hard years of war, this changeover was both welcome and full of perils – individually and collectively. In Woods's case, re-establishment meant deciding where to live, finding work, and, above all, reconnecting with children he hardly knew, who had lived separate lives. Like many others leaving uniform, he faced the prospect before him with mixed emotions: he was glad to be back in Canada, but he had "no job, no home and no future mapped out."[11] From the train, he made his way to the hall of the Great War Veterans' Association of Canada, an increasingly influential and militant mutual aid organization, founded in Winnipeg in 1917. There he was given directions to find a room for the night. His life had manifestly entered a new and decidedly unpredictable phase. Much would obviously depend on his own imagination, initiative, and perseverance – but much also on how the government of the day responded to the re-establishment needs of those who had enlisted. War had strained Canada's resources, and peace was about to do the same.

In politics, the period immediately following the Great War was a disturbed time in the history of Canada. In 1917 the Liberal opposition in the House of Commons, led by former prime minister Sir Wilfrid Laurier, divided over the issue of conscription for overseas service, and a Union government, which brought together Conservatives and Liberals in favour of conscription, was subsequently formed. The new government was led by the Conservative Sir Robert Borden, a Nova Scotian, who had been prime minister since 1911. The Union government won a bitterly contested election in December 1917, but in the aftermath of the war, Borden's administration had to deal with many daunting challenges. In July 1920, Borden was succeeded as prime minister by Manitoba MP Arthur Meighen, one of the principal architects of conscription and Union government, but Meighen's administration was swept from office in the election of 6 December 1921, which not only brought the Liberals to power but gave the largest number of seats on the opposition side of the House to members elected by the newly formed National Progressive Party. William Lyon Mackenzie King, who had become leader of the Liberal Party in August 1919, became prime minister – but at the head of the country's first minority government. A notable development of the period was a wave of strikes that swept the dominion in 1919. The biggest confrontation was the general strike in Winnipeg (where veterans were a volatile element), which evoked a harsh response from the authorities. Prices had spiked immediately after the war, but this development was followed by a collapse in the agricultural economy in the early 1920s. Adding to the stress and tension of the times was widespread public resentment over big business profiteering in wartime, along with a rising tide of nativist sentiment that fed on competition for jobs, and a corrosive Red scare triggered by the 1917 Bolshevik Revolution in Russia. In 1919 a farmer-labour government took power in Ontario, and in 1921 and 1922 farmer governments were also elected in Alberta and Manitoba. This postwar political, social, and economic upheaval had no precedent in the history of Canada and formed the backdrop for the civil re-establishment of members of the CEF.

More than 600,000 Canadians had enlisted during the Great War (the population of the country in 1911 was 7.2 million), and of this number more than 424,000 had served overseas.[12] Discharges during the war numbered about 168,000, and at the time of the armistice there were 300,000 men and 38,000 dependants overseas to be brought home. Added to these were 73,000 on duty in Canada, now also ready and anxious to leave uniform. These were sobering numbers that commanded priority attention in Ottawa. But in practice, demobilization was poorly planned and lurched from crisis to crisis. There was rioting with loss of life at Rhyl among Canadian servicemen waiting to ship out, and more than a year elapsed following the armistice before the last of those who had gone overseas arrived back. Repatriation was a messy operation and it left a bitter aftertaste in Canada. The end of the Great War was remembered by those who lived through it for hard lessons that stood as a warning to future governments. Canada was on the winning side, but for many who had served their country, the aftermath of victory brought disappointment and a lingering sense of betrayal as they struggled to have their service duly recognized in tangible benefits. In the words of Desmond Morton and Glenn Wright, veterans had to fight a "second battle" after 1918, this one for social and economic justice.[13]

In this battle the Great War Veterans' Association, the most vocal and important of the many veterans organizations that emerged from the Great War, was at the fore. When it was incorporated on 9 October 1918, it listed thirteen "aims and objects."[14] Prominent among its many goals, it sought to "perpetuate the close and kindly ties of mutual service in the Great War," "preserve the memory and records of those who suffered and died for the nation," "see to the erection of monuments to their valour, the provision of suitable burial places, and the establishment of an annual memorial day," and "ensure ... proper provision ... for the due care of the sick, wounded and needy among those who ... [had] served." Specifically, the association wanted "reasonable pensions, employment for such as are capable, soldiers' homes, medical care and equitable provision for dependent families of enlisted men." Its brief was written in blood, and in keeping with its emphasis on solidarity, members called one another "Comrade." The association was well organized, grew quickly, and in short order became a considerable force in national public life. A militant new interest group, with a deep sense of entitlement and with membership that cut across existing societal divisions (social, economic, religious, ethnic, racial, etc.), had been born out of the bitter experience of war. Its perspective mixed radicalism and conservatism, and while it trumpeted loyalty to established authority, it could also push hard against it. At its 10–12 April 1917 founding convention in the Manitoba capital, the Great War Veterans' Association demanded sweeping action against enemy aliens, the replacement of all physically fit men of military age in public service jobs (federal, provincial, and municipal) by qualified returned soldiers, and the appropriation for settlement by veterans of arable land on Indian reserves held under lease for stock grazing or otherwise readily available.[15] The land scheme proposed would be jointly administered by the government and the veterans' organization itself.

If veterans were quick to mobilize, it was also the case that the dominion government had made solemn promises to them. These promises had been duly noted and would now have to be honoured. In a June 1917 address to the CEF after the battle of Vimy Ridge, Prime Minister Borden had committed the country to show "just appreciation" of the contributions of those who served.[16] This would be the "first duty" of the dominion, he said, and nobody would have "cause to reproach the government for having broken with the men who won and the men who died." Later the same year, in the campaign leading to the general election, the Unionist party made another sweeping pledge: "The men by whose sacrifice and endurance the free institutions of Canada will be preserved must be re-educated where necessary and re-established on the land or in such pursuits as they may desire to follow. The maimed and the broken will be protected, the widow and the orphan will be helped and cherished. Duty and decency demand that those who are saving democracy shall not find democracy a house of privilege, or a school of poverty and hardship."[17] There had never before been a social welfare commitment of this magnitude in Canada, but there had never been times like these either. Behind the patriotic rhetoric of honour and gratitude attached to veterans, there lurked the possibility – events in Winnipeg in 1919 were indicative of this – of social disorder and perhaps even revolt. Ottawa acknowledged an obligation but in reality had no choice but to act – and act it did. The dominion government had by definition been responsible for the mobilization for war. By extension, it assumed full responsibility for veterans' benefits, even when the administration of these – in the fields of health and education, for example – fell within what was normally provincial jurisdiction. War and veterans' benefits not only led Ottawa into many new activities but in the process transformed constitutional practice.

How did the dominion government, swept along by events, actually attempt to keep its promises to veterans of the Great War and maintain social peace during the tumultuous years of their return to civil life? The answer to this question is complex and involves a series of interrelated – and expensive – policy initiatives that broke new ground in Canadian public administration. Pensions – to support the families of those who had lost their lives and to sustain those who were injured and their family members – were fundamental. Going into the war, Canada had a system of military pensions deriving from the Militia Pension Act of 1901 and administered by the Pensions and Claims Board within the Department of Militia.[18] From 1907 the pay and allowances regulations of this department provided a pension of $150 annually for a private who was "rendered totally incapable of earning a livelihood as a result of wounds received in action."[19] On 1 September 1914, these regulations were amended to take account of the outbreak of war, and by two orders-in-council issued in April 1915, pension payments were authorized to members of the CEF.[20] These arrangements, however, were soon overtaken by events. During the course of the Great War, 59,726 men and 43 women who enlisted were killed and 138,166 others were wounded, including 3,500 who suffered amputations and 196 who were blinded.[21] In the 1916 Battle of the Somme alone, Canada suffered 27,000 casualties, and by the end of 1916 total Canadian casualties stood at 70,000.[22] In 1917, when about 5 per cent of the country's population was in uniform, monthly casualty numbers exceeded recruiting figures.[23] This was carnage and misery of truly shocking and totally unexpected magnitude, and it forced sweeping changes in a system of pension administration rooted in the past and under military control.

The instrument of reform was a special committee of the House of Commons (the first of many such to deal with veterans' issues) appointed on 14 March 1916 to investigate and report upon the particular pension requirements of the CEF. The bipartisan committee, chaired by Naval Affairs Minister J.D. Hazen, submitted a unanimous report on 10 May.[24] The key recommendations were that the dominion government pay for "all pensions, expenses for appliances – such as artificial limbs – and for vocational training, or other advantages awarded to members of the Canadian Expeditionary Force, or their dependents" and that a Board of Pension Commissioners be appointed. The proposed board would have three members, appointed for ten years, and its decisions would be final. The committee further recommended that the new system apply retroactively from 4 August 1914 (the first day of the war), that an improved scale of payments be introduced, and that pensions be safeguarded from being "assigned, charged, attached, anticipated, or commuted." Under the proposed rules, account would be taken of the obligation of a man to support his wife and children (and, to a lesser extent, dependent parents and other close relatives), the degree of medically determined and service-related disability, and his rank while in uniform.

Pensions would be determined by the applicant's disability without regard to his pre-enlistment occupation, and a man would have two years from becoming disabled to make a claim. Payments would be made according to five classes of disability, with class 1 defined as total or 100 per cent disability, and classes 2 to 5 set, in order, at 80, 60, 40, and 20 per cent disability. Class 6 would cover disability under 20 per cent. The examples given in the committee report of class 1 disabilities were: "Loss of both eyes. Loss of both hands, or all fingers and thumbs. Incurable tuberculosis. Loss of both legs, at or above knee joint. Permanent extreme leakage of valves of heart." Class 6 disabilities were exemplified by "partial deafness in one ear. Partial deafness in both. Loss of index or other finger." For 100 per cent disability, payments would range from $480 annually for rank-and-file former members of the CEF (the existing rate was $264) up to $2,700 annually for a former member with the rank of brigadier-general, with varying sums for thirteen other ranks in between. Payments in classes 2 to 5 would be proportionate to class 1 according to the percentage involved. Class 6 recipients (below 20 per cent disability) would not be paid a pension at all, but would receive a gratuity of up to $100. Pensions would be subject to review a year after being granted, except when a disability was "obviously permanent." If a pension was being "improvidently expended," a "reputable person" could be assigned to its administration by the board. For anyone up to and including the rank of lieutenant who, besides being totally disabled, was "totally helpless," the commission could make an additional grant of not more than $250 annually. To "encourage industry and adaptability," there would be no deduction from a pension because a recipient had "undertaken work or perfected himself in some form of industry." Here the thinking of the committee was as follows: "The welfare of the State demands that so far as possible those who are at all able should endeavour to augment their pension allowance. If the pension granted were subject to reduction owing to the recipient having remunerative work ... a premium would be put on shiftlessness and indifference." This was to be avoided.

The recommendations regarding payments to dependants were likewise complex and hierarchical, but covered – here was evidence of an underlying social reality brought to the surface by the war – both married and unmarried couples and their families. If a man was killed in action or died "as the result of injuries received, or disease contracted or aggravated while on active service," either his widow or a woman "publicly ... represented" by him as his wife for "a reasonable time" before enlistment would qualify for a personal pension at the class 2 equivalent rate. On the death of a class 1 or class 2 pensioner, either the widow or common-law spouse would likewise be eligible for a pension, but at class 2 and class 3 equivalent rates, respectively. Payments for dependent children would also be on a sliding scale according to the father's rank and would normally end at age sixteen for boys and age seventeen for girls. In the case of a widower or an unmarried man without dependent children, a dependent widowed mother, stepmother, grandmother, or father might qualify for payments. On remarriage, a woman receiving a personal pension would automatically lose her entitlement but would be given a gratuity equal to one year of pension payout. A woman who married a pensioner after he qualified for a pension would not thereby herself acquire any personal pension right. The purpose here was to prevent the appearance in Canada of the American "pension widow" – a woman who married into pension entitlement, which, if she was young and her husband old at the time of their nuptials, could literally drag on into another era. There would be no such costly abuse in Canada, where only a woman married to, or in a recognized wifely relationship with, a man at the time he was killed or injured would qualify for a pension.

The recommendations of the special committee were accepted by the government, the Board of Pension Commissioners was duly appointed, and the new scale of pensions was introduced. During parliamentary debate on the committee report, Hazen explained that the thinking behind the creation of the pension board was to have pension decisions made by a body "entirely removed from all considerations of a political character."[25] "It is desired," he optimistically asserted, "that there should be a finality with regard to the board's decisions, and that no impression shall be allowed to get abroad in the country that a man's claim to a pension can be influenced in the slightest degree by pull or influence of any kind. Every claim will be considered on its merits, and no one will have any influence whatever on the matter except the Board of Commissioners, who will adjudicate upon the claim."

Effective 1 April 1917, the annual pension for 100 per cent disability was raised from $480 to $600 for rank-and-file soldiers and for naval ratings below the rank of petty officer.[26] Then, on 3 March 1919, another special Commons committee on pensions was formed, this one chaired by Ontario MP and president of the Privy Council N.W. Rowell. It recommended further payment increases and brought forward a draft bill to consolidate in statutory form a pension system that had developed through order-in-council. In the Commons debate that followed, one contentious matter was the use in the bill of the term "unmarried wives" to describe women eligible for pensions on the basis of co-habitation rather than marriage. Kingston, Ontario, MP W.F. Nickle, who took responsibility for coining the phrase, defended this language on the grounds that the country had to face up to "conditions as they were disclosed by the war."[27] The reality was that there were many women who found themselves in the situation captured by the phrase, and not to acknowledge their equal access to pensions would be unjust and impractical. Ultimately, the offending words were dropped, but the meaning they conveyed was retained. On 7 July 1919 the Pension Act received assent.[28] As of 31 March of that year, Canada had 44,726 disability pensioners and, excluding children, 16,888 dependent pensioners.[29] These figures produced a total annual liability for the government of more than $17.1 million, a figure that the 1919 special committee forecast would grow over the next year to $30 million.[30] Through the exigencies of war, Canada had acquired a substantial income-support program, the terms, conditions, and administration of which were a leading concern of the influential and ever-vigilant Great War Veterans' Association.

Another important government initiative on behalf of veterans began on 21 February 1918 when Alberta Senator James Lougheed, government leader in the upper house and minister without portfolio since 1911, was appointed minister of soldiers' civil re-establishment. Previously, Lougheed had been running the Military Hospitals Commission which, following its formation in 1915, had expanded operations rapidly to meet the urgent medical need. In 1918 the military and veterans' services functions of the commission were separated, with activities on behalf of those still in uniform hived off to the Department of Militia and Defence.[31] The reconstituted organization was then named the Invalided Soldiers' Commission, and this body was in turn absorbed into the new Department of Soldiers' Civil Re-establishment (DSCR). The act establishing this department received assent on 24 May 1918 and assigned to the minister "the management and control of all matters relating to the re-establishment in civil life" of everyone who had served in the war, but without affecting the powers and duties of the Board of Pension Commissioners.[32] The department inherited substantial medical and rehabilitation operations and attempted to coordinate activities across a broad and expanding front. Between May 1918 and 31 December 1919, DSCR directly ran forty-four hospitals and sanatoriums, partially ran six, had agreements for beds with fifty-four other hospitals, and was responsible for 6,520 in-patients and 1,634 out-patients.[33] To manage its caseload it had separate directors of medical services (Dr E.G. Davis) and orthopaedic and surgical appliances (R.W. Coulthard), the latter based in Toronto, where the production of artificial limbs was concentrated.[34] As of 31 December 1919, DSCR had a staff of 8,131 across Canada, 55.5 per cent of whom had served in the forces and 46.4 per cent of whom were returned soldiers who had served in France.[35] Among the male staff members, not counting men who had been exempted or rejected from service or had been too young or too old to serve, fully 95 per cent had served in the CEF – 83.5 per cent in France, 10.4 per cent in England, and 6.1 per cent in Canada.[36] From its inception, priority to the employment of veterans was given in the administration of veterans' affairs in Canada.

The rehabilitation effort of DSCR also continued work started by the Military Hospitals Commission. Lougheed favoured "a centrally directed" system of vocational training, and to this end T.B. Kidner, director of technical education in Calgary, toured the provinces in March 1916 seeking cooperation and help.[37] As a result of his work, voluntary committees, with membership drawn from a variety of interests, were formed in each province, and arrangements were made to borrow staff members of provincial departments of education. One provincial organization, the Ontario Soldiers' Aid Commission, agreed to provide training and be paid by Ottawa for its services. In June 1916 a system of pay and allowances was authorized for men continuing training after discharge. W.E. Segsworth of Toronto became director of vocational education in July 1917 and was succeeded in 1919 by N.F. Parkinson. In August 1918 the vocational training branch of DSCR created a separate section for the care of soldiers who had been blinded in service.[38] This unit was directed by Captain Edwin Albert (Eddie) Baker, winner of the Military Cross and the Croix de Guerre, who had lost his own sight in the war.[39] As of 31 December 1919, DSCR had on strength 27,602 men for vocational training and listed 380 occupations, ranging alphabetically from agriculture to X-ray operating, for which it either had provided or was then providing instruction. To assist veterans to move from training to employment, the department, in January 1919, created an Information and Service Branch, which immediately distributed questionnaires to all soldiers overseas. The first director of this unit, which shared facilities across the country with the newly created Employment Service of Canada (a general employment agency and itself the product of postwar economic necessity), was Major

L.L. Arthnes, chairman of the Toronto branch of the Canadian Manufacturers' Association.

Unquestionably, DSCR broke new ground in vocational education in Canada and fostered a more enlightened approach to disability. But despite the department's sweeping legislative mandate, its programs were limited in scope. In particular, only disabled veterans and those who had enlisted under the age of eighteen were eligible for the department's rehabilitation program. Ultimately, 52,603 men, including 8,338 minors, undertook rehabilitation training, of whom 43,357 completed their courses.[40] According to one estimate, 64 per cent of those trained found jobs appropriate to what they had learned, while another 25 per cent found work but not in occupations for which they had been specifically prepared.[41] Training apparently worked, but it was not an option available to the general veteran population, which numbered in the hundreds of thousands.

To help re-establish the great mass of veterans who were able bodied and did not qualify for pensions, the government depended on a one-time payment scheme and various opportunities for self-help. On leaving the forces, a man was allowed to keep his uniform and was given a clothing allowance of $35. More substantially, in December 1918, most of those who had served and been honourably discharged became eligible for a war-service gratuity, paid on a sliding scale that took account of duration and location of service (whether overseas or at home) and marital status.[42] For three years of service, including time overseas, an ex-soldier was entitled to a gratuity equivalent to pay and allowances for 183 days, or about $420. A year of service with time overseas produced entitlement equivalent to 122 days of pay and allowances, while service in Canada produced entitlement of 92 days of pay and allowances for three years of service, 61 days for two years, and 31 days for one year. In practice, approximately 429,000 veterans received the gratuity, a total that included about 14,500 members of the imperial forces who had been domiciled in Canada before the war and about 14,500 dependants of soldiers who had died while enlisted.[43] The average gratuity was $240, and the highest possible payment to a private, if married, was capped at $600.[44] Expenditure on the scheme was approximately $165 million, most of it paid out in 1919 and early 1920.[45] Although veterans got badly needed cash, there was no further obligation or commitment on the part of the government.

Subgroups within the general veteran population, however, were able to take advantage of other limited opportunities provided by Ottawa. From 1918 all honourably discharged veterans with overseas service enjoyed a preference in appointments to the civil service. In 1919 this de facto affirmative action program was extended to the widows of men who had died on active service or as a result of injuries attributable to such service. Two years later, pensioners were given special consideration within the existing preference arrangement. The effect of this whole initiative, the first of its kind in Canada, was substantial, though the numbers involved constituted only a small percentage of all veterans. Between 1 September 1918 and 31 December 1934, of 26,349 permanent and seasonal civil service appointments made (excluding postmasters), 1,897 went to disability pensioners, 10,681 to men with overseas active service, and 42 either to women with overseas active service or to war widows. In the same period, again excluding postmasters, 82,025 temporary civil service appointments were made, of which 1,922 went to disability pensioners, 28,916 to male veterans with overseas active service, and 55 to women with overseas active service and war widows. Of 7,962 permanent and seasonal postmasters appointed in the same years, 187 were disability pensioners, 1,373 were duly qualified male veterans, and 16 were either duly qualified female veterans or war widows.[46]

Many veterans also bought life insurance under a plan the government introduced for them in 1920.[47] This plan featured preferred rates on policies ranging in value from $500 to $5,000, and its objective was to encourage veterans to provide for their dependants. Policies could not be used as collateral for loans, and benefit was payable only on "the death or total and permanent disablement of the insured."[48] So focused was the scheme on traditional family life that a single man who got insurance had to name his "future wife" as the beneficiary of his policy. At first, the insurance was available only to 1 September 1922, but the deadline for applications was subsequently extended by one year. In 1928 a new round of applications was authorized, and policies were then issued until 31 August 1933. On 31 March 1935, 26,933 policies were in effect with a face value of $57,903,586. To the same date, 262 death benefits to a value of $202,971 and 33 disability benefits to a value of $12,200 had been paid out, and there had been 844 cash surrenders to a value of $323,632. This small-scale plan to bolster family security had produced worthy but limited and predictable results.

A much more risky benefit offered to selected ex-servicemen after the war was land settlement, "the only provision of government aid for the physically fit veteran."[49] Rewarding soldiers with land had a long tradition in Canada and elsewhere, and in a young country agricultural settlement was still thought of as a principal answer to the problem of getting started in life; or, in the case of veterans, restarted. The generation that fought the war – Walter Woods exemplified all this – had witnessed the opening of the Prairie West, was close to the soil, and was imbued with the pioneer spirit. Providing an opportunity for veterans to acquire and work land accorded with the economic realities of the country, and was an obvious way for the government to help ex-servicemen help themselves. Homesteading was a proven Canadian road to economic security, and the dominion government was experienced in its administration. Connecting veterans' unemployment needs to further agricultural development was therefore a natural linkage for Canadian policy makers, and on 29 August 1917 the Act to Assist Returned Soldiers in Settling upon the Land and to Increase Agricultural Production received assent.[50] It provided for a Soldier Settlement Board, the reservation of government-owned land for soldier settlement, loans for agricultural purposes of up to $2,500 at 5 per cent interest, and an instruction program for settlers.[51] On 11 February 1919, after it was found that there was not enough suitable dominion-owned land near railways to accommodate many settlers, the board was authorized to buy land in any province for resale.[52] This power was then put in statutory form by the Act to Assist Returned Soldiers in Settling upon the Land, which received assent on 7 July 1919.[53]

Under this legislation the board could lend up to $7,500 to a qualified settler buying land through its auspices – up to $4,500 for the purchase of land, $2,000 for stock and equipment, and $1,000 for buildings and other permanent works. Settlers on dominion-owned land could likewise qualify for loans of up to $3,000. By the same token, settlers who already owned land could be advanced up to $3,500 to get rid of encumbrances, as well as additional funds, to a combined maximum of $5,000, to assist operations. Interest on loans was again set at 5 per cent, and land costs were amortized over twenty-five years. Under the 1919 act, the Soldier Settlement Board was also authorized to acquire land by compulsory purchase, and if land was "being retarded from cultivation" in a locality, to declare it a "settlement area."[54] To administer the act, local agricultural qualification committees were empowered to receive applications from returned soldiers. If an applicant was "sincere in his desire to engage in farm work" and possessed "the necessary experience and aptitude" for the job, the committee could "grant him a certificate to farm forthwith."[55] If an applicant lacked experience but was otherwise judged suitable, the committee could recommend him for training. To ensure that settlers got value for money in the purchase of land, a local loan committee, "composed of men who understood farm values," vetted every loan application.⁵⁶ Only when the board was assured through appraisal that land proposed for purchase was suitable for farming and that the price being asked was fair was a loan granted.

Not surprisingly, the prospect of becoming independent proprietors, in a country where the ownership of land largely defined economic success for many, proved attractive to veterans. Between March 1919 and March 1921, 180,000 of them inquired about land settlement and nearly 60,000 actually applied to the board.⁵⁷ Of these, over 43,000 were deemed qualified, of whom 25,017 (including 224 First Nations Veterans) were ultimately issued loans to the value of $100,034,331. In short order, Ottawa took on yet another substantial commitment with long-term financial and administrative implications. In the process, much good land in western Canada previously controlled by First Nations passed out of their hands through questionable proceedings, which have been well documented by historian Sarah Carter.⁵⁸

One successful applicant to the Soldier Settlement Board was Zennosuke Inouye, one of 222 Japanese Canadians who served in the Canadian army in the Great War, 54 of whom gave up their lives for their country.⁵⁹ Born on 13 September 1884 in Asagun, Hiroshima, Japan, an agricultural region, he came to British Columbia in 1900. There he worked in logging and mining and for Saiki and Co., a Vancouver real estate and brokerage firm. He was naturalized in 1914 and in 1916 trained with the Canadian Japanese Volunteer Corps and received the medallion of that organization. After the dominion authorities declined the services of this corps, Inouye, who was single at the time, enlisted in the CEF on 6 June 1916 in Calgary and was given the service number 228458. In July 1916 he arrived overseas with the 13th Battalion of the Canadian Mounted Rifles and eventually served with the Princess Patricia's Canadian Light Infantry in France. There, in July 1917, he was wounded in the upper left arm during fighting on the Somme. He was treated first at No. 20 General Hospital, Camiers (near Calais), and then at Admiral Beaufort War Hospital in Bristol, England. After passing through the Canadian repatriation camp at Rhyl, he arrived back in Canada in May 1919. Then, following a stay at the DSCR-administered Shaughnessy Hospital, Vancouver, he was honourably discharged on 31 July.

On 20 September 1919, Inouye made an agreement with the Soldier Settlement Board whereby he was lent $3,200 for the purchase of an 80-acre parcel of land in Surrey, British Columbia. Following an initial payment to the board of $320, the balance of this loan was to be paid back in twenty-five annual instalments, beginning in 1920 and ending in 1944, due on 1 October each year. In two separate agreements on that date, he obtained additional loans from the board to start operations, and on 1 December he borrowed another $125 to purchase feed. On 17 May 1920 Inouye married Hatsuno Morikawa of Vancouver, and in July a writer for the New Westminster *British Columbian* offered this positive (albeit casually racist) account of Inouye's progress on his recently acquired property: "There is a comfortable little house on the land – not a mansion but not a shack – it has a plentiful supply of good water from a nearby pump and well. Around the house is such a garden as the city man dreams and but few countrymen get ... 'A Jap can start on uncleared land and be independent in five years,' say the old-timers. Inouye despite his very heavy handicaps, will do it in less than that."[60] To develop his farm, which eventually featured berry, fruit, and vegetable growing and pastureland, Inouye had to build a road, clear brush, and install drainage. This was daunting, but the Inouyes worked hard and were entrepreneurial and resourceful. They made a living and were independent and thereby realized the objective of the soldier settlement scheme. Through military service, Zennosuke Inouye had earned a new place in Canadian society, and his success was indicative of the fact that veteran status cut across existing social cleavages.

Walter Woods's re-establishment – he was living at the YMCA in Calgary when he was discharged on 7 February 1919 – was very different. He received minimal assistance from Ottawa's benefit package and did not forget this: "Ninety-five percent of those who had served (amongst whom was the writer) found themselves eligible for the clothing allowance of $35, the gratuity, in my case $420 (the balance of $180 being paid to the foster parents of my children), and a chance to borrow money to settle on the land. I did not want to settle on the land and my assets were therefore $455 with which to start anew."[61] Nevertheless, he was soon back on his feet. Before being discharged, he found a temporary job assisting the secretary of the Calgary branch of the Great War Veterans' Association (GWVA), which enrolled more than 6,000 members immediately after the war. He eventually served as president of the branch, and on 16 July 1919 married Elene Lucille Fawk, an Oregonian of English descent whose family had moved to an Alberta farm from Salem, Oregon. They met at a party for veterans where she was a hostess. "When I was introduced ," he wrote towards the end of his life, "I was immediately attracted by her freshness, vivacity and courage. She was auburn-haired, blue-eyed and slender, and packed full of the quality I most lacked, a keen interest in living. She was the daughter of an early pioneer Oregon family, and I soon realized that with her at my side, we could go places together, pick up loose ends, and as her forebears had done, start to build."[62] Remarriage allowed him to be reunited with his children. By this time, he was working as assistant superintendent in the Calgary office of the Soldier Settlement Board under the Great War amputee Tom Smith. In short order, Woods had found his way back to family life and full employment – and had moved from veterans' advocate to veterans' affairs official.

Not all ex-servicemen were this fortunate, and relations between the GWVA and the government mirrored the rocky road travelled by many. The GWVA at first welcomed the government's announcement in December 1918 of the war service gratuity. It was, Secretary-Treasurer R.M. Stewart publicly stated, "a generous action"; the payment would put returning men "in an independent position for a sufficient length of time after their discharge to enable them to find the employment for which they are most suited, and which is most suitable to them."[63] The ex-soldier would "not be a supplicant for labour, forced to accept unsuitable employment at low wages ... to ward off privation" but could choose properly remunerated work that suited his ability. Canada was giving "every soldier a splendid opportunity" and treating veterans "more generously than any other nation." "No one," Stewart further ventured, "can complain of unfairness. The allowance is in fact more generous than we ever anticipated it would be." Within a few months, however, the GWVA was running a noisy campaign calling for a dominion government bonus to supplement the gratuity. According to a resolution passed on 2 July 1919 at the GWVA convention in Vancouver, this further payment was needed to place soldiers as close as possible on the same footing as those whose careers or earning power had not been interrupted by military service.[64] The bonus should be paid on "an equality basis ... limited only by the country's ability to pay" and administered under a system "to be agreed and decided upon by a joint Parliamentary and G.W.V.A. Commission." The government disagreed. The gratuity, Borden told the association on 27 August 1919, was "more liberal ... than that granted in any other country" and could not be improved upon.[65] In fact, through pension, re-establishment, and other expenditures, the government was facing "a very serious financial situation" that called for "rigid economy and careful retrenchment." On 5 November, speaking during the debate on the report of the Special Committee on Soldiers' Civil Re-establishment which he had chaired, Saskatchewan MP James Calder, the immigration and colonization minister, told the House of Commons that if Parliament ever supported "a further general distribution of grants and gratuities to all of the ex-members of the forces," the government would have no choice but

Zennosuke Inouye in his
Great War uniform
(Courtesy of Beverley Inouye)

to resign.⁶⁶ He also dismissed as impractical a variety of other ideas – support to establish small businesses, help with mortgage payments, etc. – which the GWVA had floated before the committee. These, too, were beyond the means of the country.

The government was able to hold the line on the bonus agitation, but it nevertheless incurred other substantial costs in this period to keep the peace with veterans. In late 1919 an emergency appropriation of $50 million was authorized by Parliament to meet various pressing veterans' needs, and during the winter of 1919–20, $4,991,474 of this was spent on direct relief.⁶⁷ Payments were made through the Canadian Patriotic Fund, the country's principal wartime charity, and the first help was given at the beginning of Christmas week 1919. Normally in Canada, relief of the unemployed – to the extent that it was provided at all – was a municipal or private charitable responsibility; Ottawa became involved in 1919 only because of the emergency conditions. But once engaged, the government found it difficult to pull back, though in January 1921 relief to veterans, now the responsibility of the Department of Soldiers' Civil Re-establishment, was limited mainly to unemployed pensioners and for the period January–March of that year only. In making this change, the government was careful to assert (this was fundamental) that it was in no way "responsible for the employment of former members of the Forces who have been returned to civil life."[68] In 1922, with Mackenzie King's Liberals now in office, relief payments were again made to needy pensioners for the same months of the year, but at reduced rates. A further rate reduction was made later the same year, but seasonal payments were then continued through the 1920s at this level. Typically, the pensioners who received winter relief through DSCR were at the low end of the disability scale and therefore had small pensions. The purpose of the additional assistance given them (in kind) was to supplement their pensions to subsistence level.

The land scheme for veterans, begun with such enthusiasm and promise, soon presented the government with yet another set of problems. The soldier settlers, many of whom were on the Prairies, had got started when land and commodity prices were still high, but in 1920–21 they were overtaken by the big depression that struck the agricultural economy. Many did not survive this reverse. In the words of Kent Fedorowich, who has written the fullest account of soldier settlement schemes in the British Empire after the Great War, the "cost-price squeeze," brought on by falling prices for farm products, especially wheat, "ushered in a period of failure, foreclosure, abandonment and indebtedness which haunted soldier settlers and politicians alike throughout the interwar period."[69] By March 1923, fully 14.5 per cent of the soldier settlers had given up farming, and a year later this figure had jumped to 21.5 per cent.[70] The mounting crisis forced the government to grant interest exemption of $10,269,109 in June 1922, reduce the original price of livestock by $2,927,810 in June 1925, and reduce by $7,479,345 the value of soldier settlement land in 1927.[71] These actions helped to keep many farmers afloat financially, but for many other veterans land settlement turned out to be a dead end.

Pension administration likewise encountered heavy weather. Far from keeping the administration above politics as its architects had hoped, the Board of Pension Commissioners became mired in controversy, both with individual veterans unhappy about application outcomes and with the GWVA, unhappy about the interpretation of legislation and what it saw as an overly bureaucratic and high-handed approach. In 1922 this tangled history, well surveyed by Desmond Morton and Glenn Wright in *Winning the Second Battle: Canadian Veterans and the Return to Civilian Life, 1915–1930*, led to the appointment of the Royal Commission on Pensions and Re-establishment. Chaired by Col. J.L. Ralston of Nova Scotia, this body was given a broad mandate to investigate various charges made by the

GWVA against the pension board and to assess the progress of re-establishment and make recommendations for improvements. The royal commission produced four reports,[72] the first of which dealt with the GWVA's specific complaints. Its work was ameliorative and led to the introduction of a limited right of appeal against the pension board's decisions to a newly constituted Federal Appeal Board.[73] This acknowledged one of the principal grievances of veterans, but controversy about pension decisions and rules and regulations dragged on. In truth, a system that by definition produced winners and losers and concentrated pensioners at the low end of the disability scale (there were twenty categories from 1919, ranging at 5 per cent intervals from 5 to 100 per cent) was made for trouble, and this persisted. In the twenty years after 1919, the Pension Act was amended sixteen times.[74]

What the royal commission clearly showed was that organized veterans had become a force to be reckoned with in national politics. They found new strength in the election year of 1925, when the GWVA and a number of smaller veterans' organizations came together at a unity conference in Winnipeg in November to form the Canadian Legion of the British Empire Service League. In its constitution, the Legion declared that it would be non-sectarian and would "not be affiliated to, or connected directly or indirectly with, any political party or organization."[75] It also promised to "stand for strong and united comradeship among all those who have served in His Majesty's forces throughout the Empire, so that neither their rights nor their interests shall be forgotten, and so that their welfare and that of the dependents of the disabled and the fallen may be safeguarded." The Legion continued the traditions of the GWVA, and members were kept in touch with the affairs of the organization by the *Legionary*, published in Ottawa. The Legion had a "Dominion Command," provincial commands, and a national network of branches that made the Legion Hall a familiar institution across the country. Emblazoned on its stationery were the words of former Canadian Corps commander General Sir Arthur Currie, "They served till death! Why not we?"

In 1919 imperial veterans in Canada had formed their own association, which had received a dominion charter in 1923. From 1929 this association, known as Imperial Veterans in Canada, functioned as the imperial division of the Legion while retaining its charter and separate identity. This arrangement was indicative of the fact that veterans in Canada did not speak with one voice. Working alongside the Legion were a number of other ex-service organizations, most notably the Sir Arthur Pearson Club for Blinded Sailors and Soldiers, the War Amputations of Canada, the Tubercular Veterans' Association, the Army and Navy Veterans in

Canada, and the Canadian Pensioners' Association of the Great War. From 1934, moreover, the Legion faced stiff competition from the Canadian Corps Association, formed on the initiative of a group of NCOs following the first Corps reunion, held the same year in Toronto.[76]

On the government side, there was an important change in 1928 when, during Mackenzie King's second administration (1926–30), the continuing work of the DSCR was rolled into a new department, originally conceived of as the Department of National Health and Veterans' Welfare but ultimately named the Department of Pensions and National Health.[77] In its first year of operation, the new department ran eight hospitals across the country, supported the treatment of veterans in many other institutions, ran sheltered workshops for pensioners who were not fit for regular employment, provided relief during the winter of 1927–28 to 4,182 men, and administered the returned soldiers' insurance scheme. The first minister of pensions and national health was British Columbia MP J.H. King, who had previously presided over DSCR, and the first deputy minister was J.A. Amyot. Both men were medical doctors. The secretary of the new department was Ernest H. Scammell, an influential policy voice since the days of the Military Hospital Commission.

Ten years after the end of the Great War, in a period of economic revival and high employment, the conduct of veterans' affairs in Canada had settled into fairly predictable patterns. The main programs were in place, the basic administrative structure was entrenched, and the principal interlocutor of the government – the Canadian Legion – was well established in its role. At the same time, though, there was continuing discontent. In March 1930 Sir Arthur Currie told a House of Commons special committee on pensions and returned soldiers' problems that the good intentions of the Canadian people towards the veterans of the Great War were not being "fulfilled as they should be" and that more needed to be done.[78] The government of the day responded positively to this call for improvement (preparatory work had already been completed at the Department of Pensions and National Health). But as the Great Depression unfolded, Ottawa resisted a sustained Legion campaign for a sweeping redefinition of what the country owed those who had served in 1914–18, pensioners and non-pensioners alike. In these formative events lay the genesis of the rehabilitation program eventually worked out for veterans of the Second World War.

2 Depression Divide

In the United States, the sharp economic downturn that began with the Wall Street crash of October 1929 led to a dramatic confrontation between Great War veterans and the government in Washington.[1] In 1924 Congress had promised a bonus to these veterans, payable in 1945, but in 1932 a "Bonus Army" descended on the US capital demanding that the payment be made forthwith.[2] The veterans set themselves up in a tent city on the Anacostia Flats, but their protest ended badly when troops, led by General Douglas MacArthur (himself a Great War veteran), were used against them. For an already very unpopular President Herbert Hoover, this use of force, which he had not authorized, was a shattering political blow. Nothing comparable happened to Canadian veterans in the 1930s, and in fact the decade began on an improving trend as the government acted quickly on the recommendations of the special committee before which General Currie appeared. In 1930, while Mackenzie King was still in office, Parliament passed the War Veterans' Allowance Act,[3] it extended to 31 August 1933 the deadline for applications for insurance, improved pension administration, and provided additional support for soldier settlers. These changes, lobbied hard for by a combination of the Canadian Legion and the smaller veterans' organizations, were well received. Indeed, according to a May 1930 circular from the Legion's president, Lieutenant-Colonel Léo Richer LaFlèche, veterans were "so generously" dealt with by these improvements that it would be "ungracious" and "extremely dangerous" for them to seek further concessions in the immediate future.

The purpose of the War Veterans' Allowance Act was to assist certain elderly and permanently unemployable veterans. To be eligible for the new allowance, an individual had to be sixty years old and be either a pensioner or a veteran of a theatre of war. Veterans under age sixty in the same categories were eligible for the benefit if "found to be permanently unemployable by reason of physical and mental disability." The amount of the monthly allowance would vary according to individual circumstances, but the maximum payment was set at $20 for a single person and

$40 for a married person with dependent children. Provision was also made for payment of the allowance to a widow for one year after her husband's death. Administration was by the War Veterans' Allowance Committee, which had three members, including a chair, and functioned as an independent unit within the Department of Pensions and National Health (DPNH). Investigations on behalf of the committee into the circumstances of individual applicants were carried out by either departmental or soldier settlement officials. The first chair was Woods, whose career with the Soldier Settlement Board had taken him to Saskatchewan (where he had served as superintendent in Saskatoon) and then back to Calgary (where he became superintendent for southern Alberta). He was now very well known in veterans' circles, had proven administrative ability, and had served on a fact-finding committee, appointed by the minister of pensions and national health, which had proposed the creation of the War Veterans' Allowance.[4] As of the fiscal year 1934–35, the "burnt-out pension," as the allowance was dubbed, was being provided, at a cost of $2,017,075, to 7,289 persons: 5,061 veterans over the age of sixty, 2,125 veterans under sixty, and 103 widows or other dependants. Canada had acquired yet another income support program, and in the process Woods, whose new job brought him to Ottawa, positioned himself well for further opportunity.

The change made to pension administration in 1930 involved the creation of an itinerant pension tribunal to work alongside the Board of Pension Commissioners, a Veterans' Bureau (to help veterans prepare applications), and a Pension Appeal Court.[5] The bureau, a venture that got the government into the business of facilitating claims which it might ultimately have to pay, offered the services of lawyers, known as pension advocates. In 1933, faced with further administrative difficulty and continuing complaints from veterans, the government abolished both the Board of Pension Commissioners and the new tribunal, and replaced them with the Canadian Pension Commission, while retaining the Veterans' Bureau and the Appeal Court.[6] The first chairman of the new pension commission, which operated until 1995, was Colonel John Thompson, who had chaired the Board of Pension Commissioners since 1919. His appointment, which represented continuity rather than change, was controversial among veterans and came in the same year that the exemption of pension payments from income tax was cancelled as a Depression cost-saving measure. On the other side of the ledger, in 1933 and again in 1935 the government had to provide additional aid to soldier settlers, most of whom were in the hard-hit Prairie West. So great was the failure rate among the settlers that by 31 March 1935 the number with loans outstanding had been reduced to 10,828.[7] Obviously, as the Great Depression took hold, LaFlèche's rosy forecast of May 1930 was quickly overtaken by events.

Ottawa had sponsored soldier settlement and was tied directly to the scheme. Likewise, by instituting the War Veterans' Allowance it acknowledged a responsibility to provide long-term income support to one highly vulnerable group of veterans. But what was owed to those ex-servicemen – pensioners and non-pensioners alike – who were able to work but, through no fault of their own, became unemployed? As the Depression deepened and mass unemployment overtook veterans along with other Canadians, this became a persistent and unavoidable policy question for the Conservative government of R.B. Bennett, which took office in August 1930. DPNH was, of course, already in the business of providing direct relief to some needy pensioners, and in 1929–30 expenditure on this began to rise dramatically (see table 1, page 36).

The department responded to the surge by contemplating the possibility of cutting off support altogether. The provision of unemployment relief, argued deputy minister Amyot in an April 1932 memorandum, was "fundamentally a provincial and municipal responsibility" and DPNH should respect this arrangement.[8] "The question of unemployment amongst ex-service men," he wrote, "has not been assumed by legislation as a responsibility of the Federal Government." By law, Ottawa's obligation to veterans was "to award adequate pension for disabilities, to provide hospitalization for men with war disabilities, and to provide a living allowance for the aged or totally incapacitated." Paying unemployment relief to pensioners was both wasteful and inefficient, and the department should get out of the business. The existing unemployment crisis in the country was not attributable to the Great War, and all Canadians, including the pensioners who were accustomed to receiving seasonal relief from DPNH, should be treated the same in the distribution of help. Indeed, to act otherwise would be to deny pensioners their full rights of citizenship: "It is assumed that by the payment of pension a pensioner is placed economically in the same position as a non-pensioner, in that he is compensated for the loss or lessening of earning power. He has the right to consider himself a citizen of Canada, being taxed as any other citizen; therefore, he should enjoy any benefits which are available to the people of Canada as a whole." In the case of unemployment relief, this meant that pensioners should not be Ottawa's responsibility but should be covered by the system of municipal relief that operated generally in the country. (Relief varied from place to place and was subject to local residency requirements.) Yet another argument in favour of this approach, Amyot ventured, was that the local authorities had the trained social workers required to assess need. For DPNH to attempt to build up its own relief machinery would only duplicate existing municipal efforts. Furthermore, DPNH relief efforts often worked against the interest of veterans by encouraging municipalities to deny them work on relief projects on the grounds that Ottawa alone was responsible for their welfare.

Not surprisingly, organized veterans rejected the prevailing logic at DPNH about relief and unemployment. From their perspective, the setback of the Depression called for not less involvement by Ottawa in the affairs of veterans forced to seek relief but for a renewed commitment to help them, pensioners and non-pensioners alike. Veterans were especially incensed that some of their comrades were ending up in the relief camps for single men which the Department of National Defence had opened in 1932. Although the residents of these camps were housed and fed, they were paid only a pittance – twenty cents each per day. In a scathing letter dated 14 January 1935 and addressed to Prime Minister Bennett and all members of Parliament, A.L. Brereton, the secretary-treasurer of the Unemployed Ex-Servicemen's Association, accused Ottawa of parsimony and neglect. On behalf of his grassroots Alberta organization, which had branches in Calgary, Lethbridge, and Drumheller, he called for a new deal for out-of-work veterans:

> You will realize that certain definite promises were made to the troops during the Great War, by the Government of ... Canada, which promises as yet have not been carried out, although nearly every other country has made and are making definite strides to alleviate suffering amongst ex-servicemen, who, a short while ago, were laying down their all in an effort to safeguard their future economic existence. We won the war, we are told, but at this date we as the victors, are suffering the toils of the vanquished. Ex Service-men, grown prematurely old through effects of the terrible conditions which they were forced to endure, men, who at the time of demobilization felt that they were fit to take up the reins of life and "carry on" to build a country "fit for heroes to live in," today they find that they were mistaken, they did not realize to what degree of havoc four years of slime, mud, and gore would do in their later years, and who today are wandering like animals around the country in search of food and a reason for living; men who are forced to see their families deprived of the proper care, men who are relegated to slave-camps and soup kitchens; men working for 20c a day. Is this, we ask you, the fruits of victory? Are you prepared to grapple with the sit-

uation as it exists, and see that legislation is enacted, whereby all ex-servicemen and their dependents are guaranteed a decent standard of living? Or, are you still going to wink at the distress amongst the men who fought for you and yours.[9]

Promises had been made to those who had served in 1914–18, and these should not be treated as just "another 'Scrap of paper.'" The dominion government owed all unemployed veterans decent living allowances and should launch "special works programs" that would ensure them "a standard of living equal to that enjoyed by regular Govt. employees." All ex-servicemen should "be immediately placed on the basis of a 5% pensioner" and, if unemployed, paid an allowance (minimally $30 per month for a single man and $45 per month for a married couple, with additional specified payouts on behalf of children).

Just how desperate the situation was for one especially needy group of veterans – single unemployed men living on municipal relief – was highlighted in a June 1937 report by a Legion official in Manitoba:

> He is usually a much older man than the general class in that category, and if he is in any way disabled the existing conditions can only result in a final breaking down. So very often he is of the type who cannot hold employment when he does obtain it, and he wanders around the country from place to place, a transient outcast remaining in a town or city only as long as the municipal relief regulations will permit him to stay, but hoping always that he may eventually find some place where he can settle down. There is something inexpressibly sad in the circumstances of these men, and the fact that they who sacrificed their youth for this country can be considered transients in any part of it only reveals that, generous as Canada has been in many ways, there are instances where a very slight consideration would change the whole outlook on life. As it is, one can only express admiration for their fortitude and steadfast loyalty to the Constitution, exposed as they have been to urgings of agitators of every color and often subjected to indignities which would have caused revolt in persons less loyal. The very least that should be done for these men is to segregate them and treat them as a class entirely apart from single recipients of municipal relief; they should be all taken under the care of the Dominion Government until suitable employment can be found for those of them able to take it and action should be taken with a view to taking the remainder off the labour market entirely.[10]

Obviously, the veterans had a powerful case, but within DPNH resistance to change that would extend entitlement was strong. In a lengthy memorandum, departmental secretary Scammell dismissed Brereton's claim that promises had been made to soldiers but not kept.[11] Brereton had not specified what these promises were and had ignored all that the government had done in addition to what had been promised: various pension increases, the war service gratuity, soldier settlement, returned soldiers' insurance, the War Veterans' Allowance, and the relief paid to unemployed pensioners. When these and other benefits were taken into account, observed Scammell, it was clear that Canada had been both a pioneer and a leader in the field of veterans' benefits. As for the proposal to pay allowances to all unemployed veterans, the cost of this would be "enormous" and would "place these men permanently on the unemployed list as there would be no incentive whatever for them to secure work."

This dismissive attitude was not possible, of course, in dealings with Legion leaders, who had behind them a national organization and tens of thousands of members. Nationally, the Legion turned its attention to the mounting crisis of unemployment and relief in June 1931, when its Dominion Council, following up an initiative in Saskatchewan, decided to survey the situation in each province in preparation for forming a Special Unemployment Committee at the Legion's Fourth Dominion Convention in Niagara Falls, Ontario, between 31 August and 3 September.[12] To this end, the provincial commands were asked to set up their own special committees to gather the information which the larger committee would need once it was established. They were also requested to each select a delegate to the national committee, which would be chaired by the dominion chairman, A.E. Moore. The outcome of the unemployment committee's deliberations was a report to the convention that did not try to "set out or deal with fundamental causes or make specific suggestions for permanent solution" but attempted to address the "emergency treatment" that the economic downturn required.[13] At the same time, the committee sought to inform the public that veterans were "not entirely disregarding the larger issues in favour of their own particular interests." What a "permanent solution" to the economic crisis required was "the wholehearted exercise of co-operation between Governments, Capital, Labour, [and] Leaders of business, finance and economic thought," along with the modification of "cherished ideas and privileges," change in "established methods," and "the practice of a vigorous personal discipline" – all "forms of sacrifice" well known to veterans of the Great War. The committee also stressed that while remaining "steadfast in loyalty to King, Empire, and to the constituted authority" of the country, veterans must make their voices heard on the federal, provincial, and municipal bodies that were attempting to deal with the bad times that had descended on Canadians.

With a view to increasing employment opportunities for disabled and other needy veterans, the special committee called on provincial commands to review the operation within their jurisdictions of the vetcraft factories run by DPNH under its sheltered employment appropriation. Recommendations flowing from these inquiries should form the basis of a proposal to the dominion government for an improved system. By the same token, the committee called for government action to stimulate employment in the coal industry, in part by controlling oil imports. Under the heading "Measures to ensure the preferential treatment of veterans," it proposed that in awarding government contracts, provision be made to employ "a definite percentage of veterans," and that no ex-serviceman lose a government job until all unnaturalized alien employees, no matter what their seniority, had been laid off. Other changes called for were an "emergency measure" to urge industry "to reduce hours rather than reduce staff" while maintaining existing wages; the end of "dual employment" (i.e., husband and wife), in the interest of supporting as many families as possible; employment preference "for the breadwinner of a deceased or totally disabled non-pensioned veteran's family"; the extension by one year of the age limit for the payment of allowances to the children of pensioners; and a wage system for relief work that ensured that no veteran would work for less than DPNH paid to its relief recipients.

In a circular letter dated 18 September 1931, the Legion's general secretary J.R. (Reg) Bowler, a Great War amputee, informed the provincial commands that copies of the report had been given to Labour Minister Gideon Robertson and that a "formal presentation" to the federal government would follow.[14] At the same time he urged Legion action at the provincial level on behalf of veterans in connection with the administration of the Unemployment and Farm Relief Act, 1931.

Against this backdrop of developing advocacy and concern, the Legion reacted forcefully in July 1932 when DPNH reduced Ottawa's commitment to pensioners by slashing its relief budget for them by one-third.[15] So drastic was this action that it left some pensioners in the position of receiving less relief than was being supplied by their municipalities. Dominion president John S. Roper, a Halifax lawyer, businessman, and recipient of the Military Cross, was on his way from the Nova Scotia capital to Ottawa when, on 17 July, Legion headquarters received word of this action. On arriving in the capital and accompanied by Bowler and the Ontario Command president F.J. Picking, Roper immediately confronted the minister of pensions and national health, Murray MacLaren, himself a veteran.[16] In a follow-up letter, Roper told MacLaren that the government's decision had "caused a storm of protest from every Branch of the Canadian Legion from Coast to Coast."[17] As a result, a march on Ottawa – contemplated "by various returned soldiers" but so far "held in check" – was again being considered and threatened to disrupt the imperial economic conference soon to be hosted by Canada. The Legion did not "wish to witness in Ottawa a repetition of what had occurred in Washington," Roper said, but had been operating on the clear understanding that the government would not cut relief without consultation. This trust had now been broken. For his part, MacLaren denied that such a commitment had been given. Rather, the government had promised to inform the Legion of any pending change in relief rates, and this had been done. Moreover, the minister insisted, previous practice had been to give little or no relief during the summer, with 1931 being an exception. More skirmishing over relief rates, followed, and in August 1933 the Legion pressed DPNH to end the practice of forcing single unemployed pensioners, under threat of losing their pensions, into the relief camps run by the Department of National Defence (DND).[18]

In July 1934, Dr Ross Millar, director of medical services for DPNH, reported that pensioners receiving relief, especially those in western Canada, were a source of growing difficulty for chief medical officers and district administrators alike.[19] He attributed this situation to the division in relief administration between the department and the municipalities. Pensioners receiving relief from DPNH expected the same range of medical services for their families as the municipalities in which they lived were providing to the families of their own relief recipients. But the department was not authorized to provide this, and the municipalities were refusing to pick up the slack. A similar problem existed in municipalities that ran shops offering relief recipients discount prices. Recipients of DPNH relief were being refused the use of these stores. By the same token, pensioners who received clothing for themselves from the department often found that municipalities and voluntary associations would not then provide clothing for their dependants as was being done for the dependants of other relief recipients. Millar's conclusion, which challenged established departmental wisdom, was that there should be "one uniform authority" to "issue relief to all unemployed on an equal basis." This was acute, but it was also a solution that the Government of Canada, though faced with rocketing relief expenditures across the country and a growing crisis in municipal finance, categorically rejected.

In his presidential address to the Legion's Fifth Dominion Convention, held in Ottawa on 12–15 March 1934, Roper praised the many veterans who, having exhausted their own resources, had been forced onto relief. These ex-servicemen had experienced "severe trial and hardship" but had shown "marvellous self-restraint and patience" and through their example had "steadied all classes of the Canadian people during a time of economic chaos."[20] They had been "a bulwark in defence of constituted authority," in preserving law and order, and in maintaining "the British principles of freedom and justice." Despite "hunger and want," they had "withstood the temptation to join those who, with plausible tongue and devious methods," had attempted to use them to subvert the principles that the country held dear. The Canadian people, said Roper, should remember all this and resist "the tendency to regard the ex-service man as one who seeks to prey upon his countrymen." The ex-soldier did "not expect a lifelong bed of roses" but had a right to "fair recognition and decent treatment," including the opportunity to "earn a livelihood in his own Country." Of the problems confronting the Legion during his term of office, Roper reported, unemployment had "caused greatest concern and … presented the greatest difficulties." The Legion had taken many ameliorative actions, had worked hard to maintain the veterans' preference enshrined in law, and had pushed for "more adequate recognition for ex-servicemen, and indeed for all Canadian and British born, in respect to seniority rights, as against foreign born persons on the Canadian Railways." Alas, despite its many efforts, both locally and nationally, it had not been able to accomplish "overmuch" on behalf of those out of work, and unemployment remained a burning issue for the organization. Given the existing state of affairs, Roper commended to his convention comrades the words that General Currie had written not long before his death on 30 November 1933:

> Whither are we leading? Are we drifting from one desolation into another? Are the sacrifices made by those who fought that civilization might be preserved, to be wasted? Are the lives which were so freely offered to have been given in vain? It is to our national leaders and to our world leaders that we must turn at this time and it is in

them that we must put our faith, and to them we must render all the assistance in our power. God forbid that they should fail in their task. The Legion, and indeed all our Comrades cannot but have a deep and abiding concern in these matters. Our men have paid the price of present day civilization with their flesh and blood and with their lives. Who, more than ourselves, have a right to be assured that we have not greatly overpaid the price, and that all will be well? The Legion waits in expectation of better things and is ever ready to assist in bringing them about.[21]

Roper's successor was Brigadier-General Alexander Ross, judge of the District Court in Yorkton, Saskatchewan, who had been mentioned seven times in dispatches and was from the province hardest hit by the Great Depression. Under his energetic leadership, the Legion lost no time in advancing its brief on unemployment; on 30 November 1934, acting president Colonel William Wasbrough Foster (Croix de Guerre winner, businessman, former member of the BC legislature, and chief constable of a Vancouver 1935–39) sent a memorandum to Prime Minister Bennett explaining the organization's point of view on the impact of the Depression. A supplementary submission, which drew upon a survey the Legion had undertaken on instruction from the 1934 convention, was then sent to the government in January 1935 by Ross himself. The Legion's position was that while the unemployment now faced by many veterans was part of a larger national problem brought on by world economic conditions, it also constituted a special case within the general crisis and would be unlikely to disappear, even in normal times, because of factors relating to age, disability, and lost opportunities.[22] Overcoming the unique disadvantages that veterans faced in the job market would require extraordinary measures. This did not mean "any permanent system of doles or 'handouts'" but adopting an approach that would allow men who had served the country "to work to the extent of their capacity" and raise families "without the stigma of pauperism." It was a matter of principle, the Legion asserted, "that a man who answered his country's call and saw service should be entitled, as a right, to remunerative employment, and failing such remuneration to adequate maintenance, providing he has the will to work." What the Legion wanted, in short, was "rehabilitation rather than relief."[23]

This was a tall order, and the government responded by appointing a committee of inquiry to investigate "the existing facilities in connection with unemployment of Ex-Service Men, and care and maintenance while unemployed, and to report thereon with such suggestions and recommendations as may be deemed advisable."[24] The members were Justice J.D. Hyndman, president of the Pensions Court (chair), Colonel C.B. (Basil) Price of Montreal, and W.B. Woods of Toronto. The experienced Scammell was secretary. The committee held sessions in Ottawa, Toronto, Montreal, and Verdun, received briefs, heard from a long list of witnesses, and submitted its report on 23 May 1935. The report began by noting that to 31 December 1934, federal benefits expenditures for Great War veterans had been $1,131,722,638. This large sum was "incontrovertible evidence" that the country had not been parsimonious in its attitude towards those who had served.[25] Nevertheless, there were undoubtedly unemployed veterans who, though not eligible for pensions, had been handicapped by their war service. These men were "entitled to sympathetic consideration" from the government.[26] According to the committee's estimate, of the roughly 225,000 non-pensioned veterans then residing in Canada, about 29,500, or 13 per cent, were receiving municipal relief. At the same time, some 8,500 of the 74,500 pensioners were receiving DPNH relief. With respect to finding jobs for out-of-work veterans, the committee concluded that "no single scheme would be suitable for the whole body of the unemployed."[27] This being the case, a Veterans' Assistance Commission should be appointed to make a thorough survey of the problems faced by veterans in the labour market and to launch selected job creation projects. The proposed commission would operate for about eighteen months but would have the option of submitting to the government a report with suggestions and recommendations for "some permanent machinery" to continue its work.

With respect to the administration of DPNH relief, the Hyndman committee made sixteen recommendations.[28] These called for a higher scale of payments, the end of the existing voucher system (departmental relief was still given in kind), substituting the term "unemployment assistance" for "relief," a more permissive attitude towards certain casual earnings, greater cooperation with the municipalities, the hiring of more administrative staff, and periodic visits by members of the committee administering the War Veterans' Allowance to various centres across the country. The purpose of these visits would be to interview applicants for the War Veterans' Allowance under age sixty who were not permanently unemployable from a medical point of view, but had become so "from an industrial standpoint."

Most of what Hyndman and his colleagues had to say about relief could be, and was, readily accommodated by DPNH, while keeping the number of veterans receiving help and the cost of assisting them within manageable limits. As table 1 below shows, in the 1930s the peak year for the number on relief was 1932–33 and for expenditure was 1936–37.

TABLE 1

Number of recipients and cost of DPNH relief/unemployment assistance, 1927–28/1939–40

Year	Recipients	Cost in dollars
1927–28	4,182	390,004
1928–29	4,647	367,231
1929–30	5,548	517,947
1930–31	8,811	907,010
1931–32	12,303	2,082,052
1932–33	14,368	1,978,285
1933–34	12,735	1,912,563
1934–35	11,541	2,042,355
1935–36	12,083	2,365,579
1936–37	12,322	2,435,285
1937–38	11,179	2,232,398
1938–39	10,732	2,186,683
1939–40	8,907	1,847,229

Source: *Report of the Work of the Department of Pensions and National Health,* 1931–40

In July 1935, as suggested, the term "relief" was dropped and a scale of "unemployment assistance" was introduced that supplemented the pension and other income of an out-of-work pensioner to a monthly maximum of $18.75, with additional payments for dependants.[29] This was diplomatic, but one of the committee's recommendations – the seventh in the list of fifteen – was flatly rejected by the department. It called on the government to supplement, as required, municipal relief payments to non-pensioners in specified classes up to the DPNH unemployment assistance rate for pensioners. The classes of potential beneficiaries would be former members of the Canadian forces who had served either "in a theatre of actual war, or in the British Isles" and non-pensioned ex-members of the imperial forces who had been domiciled in Canada before 1 January 1935. What led an essentially cautious and conservative committee to make recommendation no. 7 was the shocking distress it found among many unemployed ex-servicemen in the country and the manifest inability of the municipalities to cope with the situation. A hard reality was explained in a chilling section of the report as follows:

> Due to the limited time at our disposal it was not possible to hold sittings in all parts of Canada, but the city of Verdun was selected as a typical centre where municipal relief is on a lower scale than

departmental relief. It was stated by witnesses that there were from 700 to 750 ex-soldiers on relief in the city, apart from pensioners. A majority of those who appeared before us were in that class. It was obvious that these men were undernourished to the point where many would be unable to undertake manual labour, even were this available.

While it is recognized that there must be a dividing line in so far as responsibility is concerned the present situation is that an ex-soldier who saw service in Canada or England only, and who suffered possibly an aggravation of a pre-war disability for which he is in receipt of pension, is eligible to receive departmental relief, while another ex-soldier who spent four years in a theatre of war and underwent rigours and hardships of front line service is ineligible because he is not in receipt of a pension.

The yardstick by which municipalities are expected to measure the amount of relief issued is the minimum sum on which it is possible for the recipient and his family to provide the bare necessities of life. Unfortunately, in many municipalities another yardstick has to be applied, viz., the financial ability of the municipality. In those cases the amount issued in relief is less than is absolutely necessary for a proper minimum standard of living ...

We are satisfied from all we have seen and heard that something should be done to ameliorate the situation in which many of the non-pensioned veterans find themselves, in various parts of Canada, due to inadequacy of the municipal relief measures in operation. Our considered opinion is, after seeing many of these men and hearing what they and others had to say in connection with their condition, that in places where relief is less than the maximum basic rate of the department, the Federal Government should assume and implement, in cash, the amount of difference between such rates, in the case of veterans who served overseas.[30]

Predictably, this call for Ottawa to play a bigger role in relief administration met a frosty reception at DPNH, which was determined to keep down costs and limit obligations. "For the Dominion Government to pay cash unemployment relief to ex-soldiers whose service did not disable them," it was argued in one departmental analysis, "would be a radical departure from Canada's policy in providing for her veterans."[31] No other country had done what the committee envisaged, and the cost of such a scheme would be prohibitive. This was because to pay part of the relief of a non-pensioned veteran would "ultimately result in pressure ...

to carry the entire burden." Out-of-work able-bodied veterans were "part and parcel of the unemployment situation as a whole"; they were therefore, by definition, a municipal responsibility. In practice, this view of recommendation no. 7 prevailed, as the government sought to appease veterans without conceding too much by way of expensive long-term obligations.[32] This approach was facilitated by the existence of the War Veterans' Allowance, which allowed Ottawa to offer additional help by changing eligibility criteria, but at the same time keeping numbers down and costs within predictable limits. By extending established assistance to some, the government was able to avoid an expensive new program for many more. In short, some would be helped so that many could be denied.

By contrast, the Legion endorsed the analysis and recommendations of the Hyndman Report. On 5 June the members of the unemployment committee of its executive council met in Ottawa and, having examined the document, concluded that it was "an adequate and sufficient basis" for government action on behalf of unemployed ex-servicemen.[33] Accordingly, the Legion called the same day for the appointment of a parliamentary committee (the established and preferred way of dealing with veterans' affairs issues because of its non-partisan flavour) to get on with the job. Ross and his committee colleagues were invited to meet Prime Minister Bennett and the cabinet on 7 June, but were told now that, because of the wide-ranging nature of the report, it would not be possible to give it proper consideration in the last days of the current parliamentary session (the country was due for an election, and Parliament was in fact dissolved on 15 August). The government wanted the report to go to a parliamentary committee, but because of the pressure of business this was impractical for the moment. The Legion delegation asked for time to consider this response and ventured that another possible way forward might be "by mutual co-operation of the Parties."[34] To this end, Ross suggested that he and his colleagues meet with the leaders of the opposition parties, and this approach was welcomed by the government. Following the meeting with cabinet, Ross told the minister of pensions and national health, Donald Sutherland, who was a fellow veteran, that the "irreducible minimum of assistance" required by the Legion was the quick establishment of the proposed Veterans' Assistance Commission, introduction of the changes recommended in unemployment assistance, and liberalization of the terms of the War Veterans' Allowance Act, a measure that the Hyndman committee had considered but not recommended.[35] (Its reasoning on the War Veterans' Allowance was as follows: "To enact that a man who is out of work at the age of 50 or 55 is permanently unemployable would be to depart from the intention of the Act and would virtually convert any benefits under that Act into general service pensions ... We ... are constrained to the view that it would be unwise to disturb the principle upon which the War Veterans' Allowance Act was based.")

In subsequent meetings with opposition leader Mackenzie King – who was accompanied by Liberal members J.L. Ralston (elected MP in 1926) and Ian Alistair Mackenzie and, on one occasion, by Alfred Speakman of the Co-operative Commonwealth Federation – they found the same reluctance as that of the government to act on the full report in a dying Parliament and the same preference for ultimately referring the document to a parliamentary committee to remove it from "political controversy."[36] At the same time, however, they found all parties "willing to co-operate in an endeavour to implement the Report, insofar as it is possible, by mutual agreement and without making it a matter of controversy." In the circumstances and to avoid "action which would embarrass Parliament in ... very difficult times," the Legion negotiators concluded that a two-step process would best serve the interest of veterans: dealing with the more outstanding problems by mutual agreement during the current session and planning for the formation of a parliamentary committee early in the next session. All this was explained to Legion branches in a circular sent by Ross on 13 June.[37] The Hyndman Report, he asserted, justified the Legion's representations on behalf of unemployed veterans, highlighted the need for work rather than relief, and acknowledged the need for improved support to those who were out of work during the transition to employment. These were the key considerations, and the important thing now was to move forward while avoiding party strife. In July, when the House of Commons approved a supplementary estimate of $500,000 to DPNH for unemployment relief, Sutherland told MPs that almost all of this sum would be used to implement the Hyndman recommendations.[38] The Legion had made limited but substantial progress, and now, crucially, it also had a blueprint for further change. In September, Bowler instructed the provincial secretaries to send the Hyndman Report and Ross's circular of 13 June to all candidates in the election, asking them to state their attitude "in regard thereto."[39]

In the general election held on 14 October 1935 the Bennett government was soundly defeated, and on 23 October Mackenzie King again became prime minister. The new cabinet included three prominent veterans and Legion members: Ian Alistair Mackenzie as minister of national defence, Norman Rogers as labour minister, and Charles Gavan (Chubby) Power as pensions and national health minister. Power, twice wounded in France, had been awarded the Military Cross and had been MP for Quebec South since 1917. Much was expected of these ministers by their fellow veterans, especially of Power, and soon after the election Bowler came away from a meeting with the Quebecer convinced of his "desire to extend to The Legion the greatest possible co-operation."[40] The new minister was "fully convinced as to the existence of the problems under discussion, particularly that of unemployment" and "proposed to examine remedial measures without delay." On 25 November, Power, who had given up his disability pension of $62 a month on taking office,[41] addressed 1,200 people at a banquet in Ottawa to mark the tenth anniversary of the Legion. His speech was broadcast coast to coast, and he "again made clear his sympathetic appreciation of the problems of ex-service men."[42] On 30 November, Ross convened a subgroup of the Dominion Council, which then met with Power. At this "most harmonious" gathering, the Hyndman Report was reviewed "in detail," and the minister again showed himself to be "highly sympathetic" to Legion concerns.[43] The Legion followed up with a series of memorandums to Power, calling for the lowering of the age limit for the War Veterans' Allowance and for various improvements relating to pensions and medical treatment. The Legion, it seemed, had caught a tailwind.

Deeds followed words during the first session of the new Parliament, and on 16 March 1936 the House of Commons special committee that had been agreed to the previous year was finally established.[44] Known as the Special Committee on Pensions and Returned Soldiers' Problems, it had twenty-eight members (many of them veterans), was chaired by Power, began meeting on 1 April (timed to follow the sixth convention of the Legion, held in Vancouver on 23–25 March), made four reports to Parliament, and had referred to it for consideration three bills: one to amend the Pension Act, another to amend the War Veterans' Allowance Act, and the third, "An Act to Assist Towards the Employment of Former Members of the Forces," to create the Veterans' Assistance Commission recommended in the Hyndman Report.[45] The committee held 34 meetings, examined 32 witnesses, and heard from 11 veterans' groups (the Legion had hoped for one presentation on behalf of veterans but was unable to achieve this). In addition, it received communications or briefs from Dominion Command, five other Legion bodies, and 22 other parties, along with many individual representations. It was also able to draw on the knowledge of representatives in attendance from DPNH, the Canadian Pension Commission, the Pension Appeal Court, the Veterans' Bureau, and the War Veterans' Allowance Committee, as well as on the expertise of superintendent of insurance G.D. Finlayson. At the end of the day, the committee made unanimous recommendations to Parliament and had printed in amended form the three bills sent to it for consideration (they all received assent on 23 June). Its minutes and proceedings were published daily in English and French and ultimately collected into a single volume.[46]

The Pension Act amendments set pension application deadlines for Great War veterans, simplified application procedure, and provided "for a more thorough preparation of claims."[47] The legislation amending the War Veterans' Allowance Act changed the name of the administering body from War Veterans' Allowance Committee to War Veterans' Allowance Board and clarified the authority of that body. It also extended eligibility for the allowance to veterans aged 55 to 60 who had served in a theatre of actual war and, though not meeting existing medical disability criteria for inclusion, were nevertheless "permanently unemployable."[48] The Legion had wanted a blanket inclusion of the 55 to 60 age group, but having noted "general satisfaction" with current practice, the committee expressed itself "reluctant to recommend any far-reaching change in the existing legislation that would tend to change its character."[49] The act creating the Veterans' Assistance Commission provided for a three-member commission with a broad mandate to investigate and report upon the number, circumstances, needs, and prospects of unemployed veterans and to promote job opportunities for them.[50] To assist in this work, the commission was authorized to appoint honorary local committees.

Ross's assessment of the work of the committee was generally favourable. It had conducted "an extremely thorough investigation into every phase of Veteran problems," and while the Legion had not prevailed on every matter and was not entirely "satisfied with the progress made," its position was now well understood and respected.[51] The organization had been given every opportunity to present its case; nothing had been left undone that could have been done, nothing unsaid that should have been said. Moreover, because the committee's report was unanimous, the legislation it endorsed represented the most that could be secured for the moment. The Legion's purpose had been to make unemployment the committee's main concern, and although other matters had drawn attention away from this, important progress had been made on the issue. While the unemployed might feel that "adequate consideration" had not been given to their needs, the foundation had been laid for "a constructive policy for the future." In addressing the unemployment issue before the committee, the Legion had advanced three objectives: to reduce the age of eligibility for the War Veterans' Allowance to 55 and make decisions on applications for the allowance contingent on "general fitness for employment" rather than on "medical fitness"; to get the federal government to assume "some measure of responsibility" for unemployed ex-servicemen who were not pensioners and to achieve "constructive action" in this regard; and to get the Veterans' Assistance Commission established in a fashion that would acknowledge the "necessity of adequate maintenance" for unemployed veterans and the need to develop means to provide employment and remove the stigma of the dole. With respect to the War Veterans' Allowance, the Legion had not managed to get the age of eligibility reduced across the board to 55, but the amended act did give the administering body "very wide powers," which, practically speaking, achieved this objective in the case of applicants who "by reason of pre-aging or general unfitness" were unlikely ever to find work again. Moreover, the commission soon to be appointed was specifically instructed to study the needs of this particular group in more detail and make recommendations to the minister. Overall, the way forward in dealing with unemployment among veterans was through "a combination of Government assistance and voluntary aid by veteran and civilian organizations." What the Legion should do next, therefore, was facilitate the work of the Veterans' Assistance Commission and secure "the co-operation of the unemployed." While it was a disappointment that the outcome of the special committee was "not immediate relief of conditions in connection with unemployment ..., substantial progress ... [had] been made" and the Legion could "face the future with some degree of confidence."

At the urging of the executive council, Ross allowed himself to be nominated for appointment to the new commission. Alhough concerned about his already busy schedule and worried that his presence on the commission might "expose the Legion to adverse criticism," he nevertheless believed that this was the right thing to do.[52] Since the Legion had pushed for the commission, it was duty-bound to do all that it could to make it work. By serving, he could apply the knowledge he had acquired during his two and a half years as president and thereby "render invaluable assistance."[53] Power's initial preference had been for a commission that had an independent chairman, a French Canadian member, and a representative of the "other ranks."[54] But he deferred to the Legion's wishes, and Ross was duly appointed, along with Lieutenant-Colonel Hugues Le Moyne de Martigny and Colonel John Grant Rattray, who was named chairman.[55] By early July the commissioners were hard at work, with Ross insisting that the first item of business be the preparation of a questionnaire to be distributed across the country to determine the exact nature and extent of the unemployment problem among veterans.

With this project launched and a tentative schedule worked out for public sessions, Ross left for Europe as a leading member of the Vimy Pilgrimage, which brought hundreds of Canadian veterans back to the blood-stained and hallowed ground in France that had become synonymous with the heroism and sacrifice of the Great War. There, on 26 July 1936, Edward VIII unveiled an enormous and stunning memorial to the Canadian fallen, designed by the Canadian sculptor and architect Walter Seymour Allward. Back in Ottawa on 13 August and now exhausted by his many responsibilities, Ross was disappointed at the progress made by the commission in his absence and pushed for the start of public hearings, which began in Montreal on 14 September. When the commission reached Toronto soon afterwards, his condition had deteriorated to such an extent that, following a medical examination, he was advised to take a three-month break from all work to avoid a complete breakdown. This led to his resignation from the commission and his replacement, on 7 October, by Robert Macnicol, secretary of the British Columbia Command. Ross welcomed the appointment on the grounds that Macnicol came from a region of high unemployment, was from the "other ranks," and therefore fitted in with the minister's original plan for membership on the commission; and as he but was not an elected officer of the Legion, the organization could not be blamed for his actions as commissioner. Macnicol's appointment assured "sound Legion representation" without the "entanglements" that might have resulted from Ross's continued service.[56]

On 11 January 1937, having resumed his duties as dominion president of the Legion, Ross met in Ottawa with Rattray, who now told him that 32,000 questionnaires had been returned to the commission, which expected to have the results tabulated by the end of the month. But when Ross asked when an interim report might be expected, the chairman replied that no formal report would be forthcoming until the honorary committees which the commission had established across the country were working. Ross vigorously objected to this, telling Rattray that the unemployment question "had been investigated so long, and action ... delayed so long, that there was general unrest among the unemployed and a general impression that the commission was simply devised to fend off the evil day, and was not intended to be a genuine effort to meet the situation."[57] The next day he told the chairman in writing that the delivery of an interim report was "imperative" in the interest of moving along to "some degree of finality."[58] In the same spirit, on 19 January British Columbia Conservative MP and Great War veteran Howard Green opposed the adoption of the pension estimates by the House of Commons until the commission was heard from.[59] Three days later, Ross pressed his case at a meeting with Power but was unable to persuade the minister of the need for a full-scale report at this juncture.

On 23 January, Ross submitted a lengthy memorandum to the Legion's executive council, summarizing recent developments on the unemployment question. While acknowledging a "demand for immediate action" among veterans, Ross cautioned that it would be "absolutely suicidal" to push the government for relief when the Legion had not yet figured out what this should be.[60] This was a work in progress and "time must be given to examine cases ... individually and determine the extent of the problem and the nature of it." With the limited information available, the Legion could do nothing more than ask for a service pension, which would be refused. "We can make a demonstration and impress the veterans with our sincerity," he wrote, "but the point is that we will not be able to secure action; on the contrary, we will probably produce the opposite effect, and by precipitate action delay the possibility of securing any effective remedy." In sum, the Legion should look to the local committees now operating across the country to benefit the unemployed while an "effective remedy" was worked out for the "unabsorbable residue" among them. Ultimately, whatever answer was found for the latter group would have to "be fair both to the man and to the State."

The meeting rejected this advice and instead, responding to dissatisfaction across the country with the "long delays" in dealing with the unemployment issue, passed two blunt resolutions.[61] The first of these called on the government to immediately grant relief to all unemployed ex-servicemen who had served in France, according to the scale of payments for DPNH unemployment assistance recommended in the report of the Hyndman committee (i.e., the equivalent of a 25 per cent pension for a single man without dependants, and the equivalent of a 30 per cent pension for a married male veteran with dependants). Having heard that an interim report would soon be coming from the Veterans' Assistance Commission after all, the council further called on the government to introduce legislation based on its preliminary findings and its final report during the session of Parliament then in progress, with provision for action by order-in-council if the full report was received after Parliament had prorogued. When Mackenzie, Labour Minister Rogers, and Finance Minister J.L. Ilsley met with a committee of the executive council on this occasion, they were told that "a feeling of dissatisfaction was growing among ex-service men," who increasingly believed that both the old and new government "were endeavouring to postpone recognition of their claims." To many it seemed that "government after government ... [had]

appointed commission after commission" but "refused to meet the actual situation."⁶² This was unacceptable.

In the wake of these developments, Ross acted to counter internal criticism that the Veterans' Assistance Commission was "simply designed to delay" matters and that the Legion itself was at fault because it was responsible for the commission's operation.⁶³ In its efforts on behalf of the unemployed, he explained in a circular, the Legion had always acted on the assumption "that simple relief was not what was desired, and that no policy was sufficient unless it embodied some provision for securing work for those ... able to work."⁶⁴ This explained the Legion's support for an approach that emphasized local initiative and responsibility: "After examining all the proposals available, it seemed to us that it would be quite impossible to evolve any one scheme which would put all the unemployed in Canada to work, and that as our men in many cases presented problems, the situation would have to be dealt with locally, and there we felt that local organizations, working in co-operation with veteran organizations, presented the best medium for assisting employment." The Legion was cooperating with the Veterans' Assistance Commission, but this did not make it responsible for what the government was now attempting on behalf of veterans, and it could not therefore be held accountable if that effort failed.

In February Ross sent another circular challenging the revival in the country of the postwar campaign for payment of a bonus by the federal government to former members of the CEF and reporting on an anti-bonus resolution passed by the executive council. The bonus cause, he stated, was being pursued "by persons interested in embarrassing the established Government and developing agitation" and was "unalterably opposed" by the Legion.⁶⁵ The responsibility of the government was not to pay a bonus to everyone who had served but to provide adequately "only for those disabled as a result of war service, their dependents, and the dependents of the fallen, and to assure adequate assistance for those who saw service in a theatre of war and ... [were] now, by reason of economic conditions ... [and] their disabilities – tangible and intangible, resulting from war service – unable, through no fault of their own, to secure employment." Unemployed veterans might find the idea of a bonus attractive, but such a payment would in reality work against their long-term interest by diverting assistance to those who did not need it at the expense of those who did. Having spent their bonuses, unemployed veterans would be no better off than before. Yet "the resources of the country would have been so impaired" that the Legion would find it impossible to obtain benefits for them "in their declining years." The Legion believed in targeting resources to real need and promoting economic independence. Its policy was to make every effort possible to use national resources for rehabilitation of the unemployed and adequate care of the unemployable. "We should concentrate upon these policies," Ross argued, "rather than approve of a payment which would, in the long run, make achievement of our aims impossible. In our view, our primary object must be to secure the welfare of those who have been unfortunate and that we should ask for nothing which will result in benefits for those who are not in need of such benefits. For this reason, therefore, we ask that our Branches will give no assistance to this [Bonus] movement but will cooperate with us in every way, in our endeavours to place the unemployed veterans in a position of some security for the rest of their lives."

On 12 March, having received word that the commission's interim report would be available within three days, Ross sought to prepare Legion branches for the possibility of limited gains. The Legion had "lost no opportunity," he wrote, to impress on the minister the need for immediate action once the report was released.[66] Unfortunately, Parliament was again approaching prorogation, and this might prevent the Legion from obtaining maximum results. If this happened, blame "must rest with those having the final responsibility" – in other words, the government. The Legion had done everything it could to get action on unemployment and had argued that it was "a National Problem" that required a national solution. Unemployed men were understandably "impatient," but "hasty and ill-considered schemes" would have adverse consequences for them. The Legion needed to maintain its "sense of proportion" and seek solutions along "sound lines" so as to achieve "maximum benefit with the elimination of any suggestion of pauperization or charity." If the Legion could not secure its "maximum objective" during the current session of Parliament, it could position itself to advance its cause when Parliament resumed sitting.

The interim report of the commission, dated 27 January, was tabled by Power in the House of Commons on 15 March 1937.[67] Before tabling the document, the government sought additional information from the commission and worked out its response to the recommendations made. First and foremost, the commission reported that it had "met with insistent requests that the Dominion Government assume responsibility for payment of unemployment relief to all unemployed veterans, whether ... on the pension roll or not."[68] The commission was sympathetic to this point of view, noting that the difference between the situation of unemployed veterans who were not pensioners and those who were, even on the lowest rung of the pension scale, was indeed striking: "In the case of a pensioner, if single, he receives for a 5% disability, $3.75 per month pension, and if unemployed, an extra $15.00 unemployment assistance from the Department of Pensions and National Health, besides free medical treatment and hospitalization if suffering from a pensionable or non-pensionable disability. The non-pensioner who may have a disability, that he cannot prove is due to war service, has to take his chance on Municipal, City or Provincial relief, which in amount, is very often less than the Department of Pensions & National Health rate. If ill, the veteran without pension has to take treatment in the pauper ward of the nearest hospital."[69] As a result of the desperate circumstances of their lives, the "outlook of many unemployed veterans" had become tragic: "Continued unemployment has had its effect. Men who were ready to risk their all for Canada and the Empire, now find themselves on the bread line, existing, not living. They see others, more fortunate than themselves, able to provide some of the decencies of life for their families, while they, the veterans, have to augment their clothing supplies and extra nourishment for their children, the best they can. Remembering the speeches of many statesmen of war days, no doubt made in all sincerity at that time, but never fulfilled, it is difficult to blame these veterans for harbouring bitter feelings on some occasions."[70] Accordingly, noted the report, the time had come for the government to take some responsibility for all veterans who had seen "real service," including imperial veterans who had come to Canada after the war (mainly from the United Kingdom) and were denied either British or Canadian benefits.[71] The imperials had come to Canada in good faith (many drawn by immigration schemes), and the country had a "moral responsibility" towards them.[72] Through the War Veterans' Allowance, the government had acknowledged that some men who had served overseas, though not eligible for pensions, might have suffered "intangible disabilities" leading to permanent incapacity. By extension, it was now "reasonable to suppose" that others who had been there had been "handicapped" in facing the existing economic situation."[73] Given the continuing plight of non-pensioned veterans who were on public relief and the fact that its own efforts would take time to mature, the commission recommended that the government immediately consider trying "to relieve temporarily the acute distress of ageing unemployed veterans, particularly those who saw service in a war zone." [74]

When Power asked the commission to put a dollar figure on this recommendation and give details of the number of veterans to be helped, he heard back that 16,268 veterans (12,056 married and 4,212 single) who had served in a theatre of war were now on relief and that the monthly cost of the proposed assistance would be $141,620.[75] In nine cities, however, including Toronto and Montreal, the local relief rate equalled that of DPNH and further assistance might not be needed. Assuming this was the case and that 4,000 of the married veterans then on relief would not need additional help, the monthly cost would be about $101,620. Of the more than 16,000 veterans on municipal, city, or provincial relief, 3,250 were aged 35–39, 4,693 aged 40–44, 3,428 aged 45–49, 2,950 aged 50–54, and 1,950 aged 55–59. This information was accompanied by a formal recommendation that the government bring local relief payments for veterans who had served "in a theatre of actual war" and former members of the imperial forces domiciled in Canada before 1930 up to the relief scale of DPNH by granting unemployment assistance of up to $10 a month for married veterans with dependants and up to $5 a month for the unmarried.[76] But the recommendation to do this was submitted by Martigny and Macnicol only, Rattray dissenting on the grounds that the proposed scheme was designed "not ... to relieve specific cases" but to create a "permanent benefit"; in effect, "a Permanent Service Pension, not based in disability, age or employability."[77] As such, it would create "virtually a new class of pensioner," awarded pensions "not on the basis of injury or disability incurred on war service, or presumption thereof, but ... service only." For their part, Martigny and Macnicol rejected this claim, arguing that if a permanent pension had been intended, their recommendation would have covered everyone who had served overseas. In fact it covered "a comparatively small group of unemployed ex-service men ... in distressed circumstances" and needing a supplementary relief payment to render the public assistance they were receiving "at least equal" to the basic rate that DPNH paid its relief recipients.[78]

On the same day that the interim report of the Veterans' Assistance Commission and the supplementary correspondence between the minister and members of the commission was put before the Commons, Ross and Lieutenant-Colonel B.W. Roscoe, the Legion's second vice-president, addressed a memorandum to Power commenting favourably on the recommendations made and calling for immediate action on them.[79] This memorandum was also circulated to the soldier MPs, and a meeting was held with them, at which Ross offered a further explanation of the Legion's position. On 16 March, after he and Roscoe had met with Power again, Ross told Legion branches that for the moment everything that could be done in Ottawa by their organization had been done and that the matter was now with Parliament, where "a great responsibility" rested.[80] When no immediate action was forthcoming, Bowler wrote to Power on 5 April on behalf of the Dominion Council, telling him that "much apprehension and alarm" had arisen from the fact that no consideration had been given to the interim report, though Parliament seemed likely to be prorogued soon.[81] The Legion, Bowler warned, was counting on "full and complete" discussion of the report in the current session, as well as the implementation of whatever was decided upon. Power had committed himself to this, and the Legion would welcome "a re-assuring statement" about his intention.

The government finally showed its hand two days later, when the House considered estimates relating to the commission's report. Power led the debate and, to the consternation of the Legion, flatly rejected the key recommendation that local relief payments to unemployed veterans with overseas service be augmented, as required, to the relief scale of DPNH. Since the end of the war, he noted, whatever the party in power, government after government had wisely "drawn a very broad line of distinction between the man who suffered a disability and the man who did not": that is to say, between the pensioner and the non-pensioner.[82] The tradition of the country was that service alone did not "establish a claim on the Canadian people for special treatment beyond that given to ordinary civilians."[83] But this was exactly what was now recommended, there being no difference between putting non-pensioned ex-service men "on relief and giving them service pensions."[84] "Long experience in dealing with returned soldiers' problems," stated Power, had shown that once the door was opened there was no closing it.[85] Inevitably, unemployed veterans on local relief who did not require the proposed supplementary payment would also expect something from Ottawa, and this in turn would escalate into the demand that all veterans "be made the wards of the federal government."[86] In the long run, the recommended relief scheme meant "something equivalent to a pension or payment of some kind for every man who wore a uniform simply because he served in the Canadian army and not because he incurred any disability during that service."[87] This was unacceptable, announced Power, and "it would be the height of folly to set up an entirely new direct relief agency."[88] Nor would offering temporary relief be a proper solution. Once the government got into the relief business for non-pensioned veterans, politicians would find it impossible ever to pull back, so great would be the pressure on them to continue payments and even augment them. And if Ottawa began supplementing relief payments for some veterans, local governments could be expected to claim that it should carry the whole burden, and so on and so on. A scheme whose estimated cost was less than $1 million annually could end up costing the country $10 to 12 million annually. As for Imperial veterans living in Canada, the country had "no responsibility whatever" to those who had arrived "long after the war," and it would be "the acme of imperialistic jingoism now to take them on as wards of the Canadian people."[89] They were treated equally with other Canadians and "should look to their own government" for any additional assistance they required.[90] Instead of "handouts from the public treasury" and "assistance for doing nothing," stated Power, the government favoured – and wanted Parliament to fund – the continuation of the efforts underway through the Veterans' Assistance Commission and the honorary committees to find employment for out-of-work veterans.[91] There were signs that this approach was working and that the country was coming out of the worst of the Depression.

As part of the estimates, the government sought and obtained a vote of $250,000 for a probational training scheme to assist younger unemployed veterans (a group the commission had identified as constituting a special problem) to find their way back to work. As for the non-pensioned unemployed veterans who were truly unemployable – those the Legion had described as constituting an "unabsorbable residue" – Power said that the government would consult with the veterans' organizations to see what could be done to help.

The Legion had lost an important round, but Ross immediately told Power that the organization could not accept his judgment and would continue its "vigorous representations" on behalf of the unemployed.[92] During the summer and fall of 1937, the Legion sought to assist the efforts of the Veterans' Assistance Commission and facilitate the operation of the training scheme Power had announced in April, which in effect subsidized wages for three months to encourage employers to offer work. Then, in December 1937, with a Legion convention scheduled for 31 January to 3 February at Fort William, Ontario, the commission submitted its long-awaited final report which, in printed form, ran to 175 pages.[93] The report was in five sections and had seven appendices, one of which gave individual reports on the work of the fifteen honorary committees (elite local groups that brought together regional business and ex-service leaders to promote employment opportunities). Following a summary of its own activities and an analysis of the results of the survey it had conducted, the commission moved on to a searching narrative that elaborated on the themes of its interim report and called for a permanent national scheme of financial support for unemployed non-pensioned veterans. The federal government, the report concluded, should "assume responsibility for the whole group of veterans who served in a theatre of actual war."[94] The typical veteran did not want "special privileges" but bitterly resented "having to come cap in hand to the Government for benefits that should be within the reach of every citizen of the country."[95] Moreover, Ottawa faced no constitutional problem in acting on behalf of veterans because the provinces and municipalities considered the dominion government responsible for the relief of ex-servicemen in distress. By reaching out to all veterans who had served in a theatre of actual war, Ottawa could "pioneer in social legislation" for all Canadians: "By using the veterans as an experimental group Canada would ... not only requite an obligation of the past but would get for herself valuable experience in the benefits and pitfalls of further social legislation. The veteran would be served; Canada herself would be served. What more could Canada and her veterans ask?"[96] As a country, Canada needed "unemployment insurance, health insurance, and a revision of the Old Age Pension Laws," and it was to be hoped that the recently formed Royal Commission on Dominion-Provincial Relations would find a way of amending the constitution to make all this happen. But veterans could not wait for this development.[97] They needed action straightaway.

Specifically, the commission called for a variety of make-work, preference, and training schemes (on its initiative the Canadian Corps of Commissionaires was reconstituted into a lasting source of employment for veterans and became a familiar and respected institution); for the further expansion of eligibility under the War Veterans' Allowance Act to include unfit veterans of any age who had served in a theatre of war; and, most importantly, for the payment by DPNH of a "provisional economic allowance" to unemployed, non-pensioned veterans.[98] To qualify for this allowance a veteran would have to be indigent, have served in a theatre of actual war, and have been domiciled in Canada at the time of enlistment. Payment would be at the rate for pensioners receiving DPNH relief: namely, $18.75 per month for a single man and $30 per month for a man with a dependent wife. No payment would be made for dependent children, who would remain the responsibility of provincial and municipal authorities. In sum, in its key recommendation the commission advocated the very course of action towards non-pensioned unemployed veterans that Ottawa had already rejected.

Ross responded to the report with a ten-page memorandum to branches, intended to set the stage for discussion at the Fort William conference.[99] The commission, he trumpeted, had produced "a formidable argument" in support of the view that the federal government had an obligation to all veterans who had served in a theatre of actual war because of their disadvantage in the job market arising from "disabilities real and intangible, pre-aging, lack of training in the formative years of life, and loss of opportunity." Their experience in "the conditions of modern warfare, including the incidental long absence from civilian life," had "created special conditions" that put these veterans "in a different category from the ordinary unemployed." The government had acknowledged their particular need by introducing the War Veterans' Allowance Act. Now it must face up to the fact that unemployability arose not only from physical limitations but from these other factors, and must act accordingly to broaden entitlement. Fortunately for all concerned, the commission's statistics showed that the number of unemployed non-pensioned veterans – 34,312, of whom 15,317 had been in a theatre of war – was considerably less than the Legion's original estimate of 50,000. While this did not "minimize the importance of the problem," it clearly eased matters in terms of potential cost to the public treasury. Ross's enthusiasm for the report carried over to the convention, which passed resolutions in favour of a more liberal War Veterans' Allowance system and immediate introduction of the proposed provisional economic allowance. The convention also elected Colonel W.W. Foster (known to his intimates as Billy) to succeed Ross as dominion president. Armed with the Hyndman and Veterans' Assistance Commission reports, it would now be Foster's job to bring to a successful conclusion the cause relating to unemployment that had dominated Ross's troubled time in office.

Following the convention, a Legion delegation headed by Basil Price (now first vice-president) met with Power and presented him with the resolutions that had been passed.[100] In response, on 4 March, Power introduced a bill to amend the War Veterans' Allowance Act by eliminating the age restriction entirely, specially recognizing service at the front, and, while retaining disability criteria, acknowledging "economic handicaps" in deciding on applications.[101] This bill was duly passed, and although the changes made fell short of what the Veterans' Assistance Commission had recommended and what the Legion wanted, the legislation was nonetheless accepted by the veterans' organization as "a substantial advance."[102] However, when the Commons turned to DPNH unemployment assistance estimates (which actually reduced appropriations for local committees and probational training), Power flatly rejected the commission's main recommendation. The government, he said, did not intend to accept "responsibility for the care and maintenance, whether by way of an economic allowance or otherwise, of 100 per cent fit men" and would not provide grants to veterans in this category. Instead, the government would continue its efforts to find work for them.[103] The government likewise reacted negatively in 1938 when the National Employment Commission, appointed in 1936 and chaired by Montreal businessman Arthur Purvis, recommended a national system of unemployment relief. In short, Ottawa's response to veterans was part and parcel of a larger Canadian story: the dominion's rigid and conservative approach to Depression events.

Meeting with another Legion delegation on 21 March, Power not only reaffirmed his opposition to the proposed provisional allowance but questioned whether the Legion convention itself had supported the actual scheme advanced by the commission. Price followed up with a letter making plain that, while changes may have been suggested at Fort William "in the detail of the terms of the Recommendations of the ... Commission," the Legion stood firmly behind "the principle that the Government should take responsibility for all unemployed veterans."[104] This now was the issue, with the need for reform driven by "the varied methods of handling relief by the local authorities in various parts of Canada, involving lack of uniformity, and in certain localities great hardship." Price likewise challenged the minister on the government's proposed expenditures to promote job opportunities for veterans. The Legion agreed, he explained, that jobs to make unemployed veterans "self-supporting and self-respecting members of the community" were fundamental, but the government's own current expenditure plans belied its stated commitment to this goal. If there was to be no allowance, the government would have to increase, not reduce, its expenditures on projects to generate work.

On 7 September 1938, with the government still refusing to budge, Foster and the executive council met with Power and other members of the cabinet. Unemployment, Foster now told the politicians, was "still the matter of paramount importance" to the Legion, which was duty bound to see that unemployed veterans were provided for through the proposed allowance.[105] Different views may have been expressed across the country on the rate of the allowance, but it was the principle behind the payment that was important, and this should be acknowledged by the government forthwith. The government answered on 29 November in a letter from Mackenzie King to Foster. The changes made to the War Veterans' Allowance Act, the prime minister wrote, were "broad enough to embrace unemployed indigent ex-service men of front line experience who, because of tangible or intangible disabilities and handicaps ... [were] incapable of maintaining themselves."[106] The proposed allowance had been "fully discussed" in the Commons during the last session of Parliament but had been ruled out. Moreover, the Legion representations on this subject in September were not strictly in accordance with the resolutions passed at the Fort William convention. The allowance was a non-starter, but in addition to the further benefits provided under the amended War Veterans' Allowance Act, the government would continue the broader program of treatment benefits that was first made available in April 1937. Under this arrangement, non-pensioned veterans with front-line service could obtain limited treatment in departmental hospitals to avoid becoming charity cases.[107]

On 10 December, Foster shot back that the government's approach was greatly disappointing. Two commissions had endorsed the payment of "a living allowance" to out-of-work veterans who had served in a theatre of war, and despite possible differences about the details of the proposal, veterans were "unanimous upon the principle."[108] Nor would the payment called for involve the government "in a new field of expenditure," because, under the War Veterans' Allowance Act, the government had already made a commitment to this class of veterans. With Department of Labour statistics showing that there were now fewer than ten thousand unemployed veterans to whom the allowance would apply, it made economic sense to grant it. And then there was the most compelling reason of all: "justice to those who offered everything they had to give in the service of their country," only to find themselves now, late in life, "without hope."

On 31 January 1939, Foster and the executive council pressed the Legion case again at a meeting in Ottawa with Mackenzie King, Power, Rogers, and Mackenzie.[109] The Legion likewise kept up its efforts with the opposition parties and with ex-soldier MPs. But towards the end of March, when Foster again met with Power, the minister made clear "that he personally could not concede the principle involved in the Legion's request."[110] Foster then appealed again in writing to the prime minister, but while this correspondence was in progress, trouble erupted in the Legion itself. This began when the British Columbia Command launched a loud campaign on behalf of the allowance, criticized national headquarters for the slow pace of events, demanded that all other Legion business be made "subsidiary" to advocacy of this benefit, and called for an immediate push to ensure that another session of Parliament would not be prorogued before action was taken on what was wanted.[111] On 2 May, Price presided over a meeting of those members of the executive council who could get to Ottawa on short notice. This gathering reviewed the whole situation, and as a backup position if needed in negotiations with the government, developed a proposal for supplementing local relief payments. With this plan in hand, the group met with ministers Power, Rogers, and Mackenzie the same day. But Power remained adamant about the government's position: the decision of cabinet was that neither the provisional economic allowance proposal "nor any other plan involving the principle of responsibility of the Dominion Government for the maintenance of the fit ex-service men in whole or in part" could be accepted. On 4 May, in answer to yet another missive from Foster, Power sought to accentuate the positive, pointing out that of the 20,010 current recipients of the War Veterans' Allowance, 7,000 had been granted the benefit in the previous twelve months, 5,100 of them thanks to the amendment to the act made in 1938.[112]

There was reason to be encouraged also, he maintained, in the government's other "constructive and progressively beneficial activities on behalf of ex-soldiers": the new treatment arrangements (to 15 June, 864 non-pensioners had received hospital treatment and 1,050 had received dental care); the support being given to the employment-creating efforts of the honorary committees (to 30 June, permanent work had been found for 4,100, temporary work for 6,841, and casual work for 14,831); the probational training scheme (to 22 July, 1,084 commitments had been made and 797 persons had completed training); the work of the reinvigorated Corps of Commissionaires (by November, eleven units were functioning across the country and providing job opportunities); and the preference being given to veterans in employment under government contracts and in the sale of radio licences.[113] These initiatives, which had led to work being found for many, would be continued and were the way forward. Indeed, statistics now showed that the unemployment rate among veterans was lower than that of the rest of the population. "Your contention," Power told Foster, "that Service alone shall entitle the fit ex-soldier to special legislation to provide for his maintenance, either temporarily or permanently, is one that I cannot accept, and it is with respect to the principle contained therein that we are in disagreement."

Although the Legion would remain committed to the allowance, the high point of the campaign in favour of it had now been reached. In his report to the branches on 19 May about what had happened, Foster reminded Legion members that recent negotiations with the government had been carried on against the backdrop of the developing international crisis, which had distracted attention from "ordinary business." The Legion, "above all organizations," had had to acknowledge this reality, and great care had also been taken "to prevent the principle at issue from becoming a party question."[114] For the moment, Foster explained, the case for the provisional economic allowance was lost. But, he stressed (taking obvious aim at dissident elements within the organization), the Legion must not allow itself to become involved "politically," in violation of its own constitution. Having "forced a decision from the Government upon a question of policy," the Legion of necessity had had to regroup, but it remained resolute in its objectives on behalf of the unemployed. In fact, though, the cause the organization had pursued for so long was soon overtaken by the Second World War, which broke out in September 1939. This had the effect of both mopping up unemployment in the country and setting a new agenda for veterans' affairs. In the end, the proposed provisional economic allowance became an artifact of the 1930s and disappeared along with the Great Depression.

Following the Great War, Canada had acknowledged a range of short-term and long-term obligations to veterans and introduced some innovative programs on their behalf. But the government of the country steadfastly refused to admit that veterans were owed jobs by the state or that able-bodied ex-servicemen who had served overseas had a special claim in relation to the administration of relief. As with unemployed Canadians generally, the dominion sought, as far as possible, to keep responsibility for out-of-work veterans at the local level, in order to control costs and foster the work ethic. At root, policy towards unemployed non-pensioned veterans was inspired by the idea that a national relief system would encourage dependence and pauperism by removing the incentive to work. Avoiding this outcome took priority over everything else. What Ottawa offered instead of more liberal relief administration was broader eligibility for the War Veterans' Allowance and the prospect of a better future through the make-work projects of the Veterans' Assistance Commission.

In refusing the key recommendation of the commission – that a provisional economic allowance be provided on a national basis to all non-pensioned unemployed veterans who had served in a theatre of war – the government had several advantages in its protracted argument with the Legion. Powerful and well organized as the Legion undoubtedly was, it faced internal division and was not the only veterans' organization in the country – weaknesses that were easily exploited. Moreover, the Legion was also constrained by its own conservatism. Seeing itself as a bulwark of authority, it was not always well cast in the role of protest group and was further constrained by its prized political neutrality. The Legion channelled protest and had an interest in heading off upstart groups, but it was torn between its own radical and conservative impulses. All of this strengthened the hand of the government. That Chubby Power, the lead minister in the scuttling of the provisional economic allowance proposal, was himself a distinguished veteran likewise worked against the veterans' organization. Having a veteran say "no" to organized veterans obviously eased the passage of the government, and it was not by accident that four of five ministers of pensions and national health and one acting minister were ex-servicemen who had gone overseas. Again, Legion leaders (Ross especially) were themselves always concerned not to push demands so far as to turn the public against veterans or to undermine the will to work. Like the public servants at DPNH, Legion leaders had their own fears about eroding the work ethic in the country. In the end, the Legion failed to get the politicians to concede an important point of principle – that the government had a lasting economic obligation to non-pensioned veterans with overseas service – and had to satisfy itself with lesser gains (for which, of course, it could also take credit).

The limit on veterans' benefits that was thus set in Canada in the 1930s was well understood by the policy makers who were on the scene when the country again went to war and who had a model before them in the Veterans' Assistance Commission, which emphasized training, self-help, and voluntarism but eschewed the promise of work or long-term income support. Prominent among them were Ian Mackenzie, who was transferred from Defence to Pensions and National Health in a cabinet shuffle on 19 September 1939 (Power moved over to Postmaster General), and Walter Woods – apprentice, immigrant, gunner, and public servant – now one of the country's most experienced administrators in the field of veterans' affairs. Together, they became important builders of post-1945 Canada. Mackenzie and Woods were veterans not only of the Great War but of the Great Depression and had learned lessons from both. From their military experience they well understood the need for early, systematic, and careful planning for demobilization and re-establishment. From their Great Depression experience, they had ingrained in them the need to give priority in veterans' benefits to short-term assistance leading to employment over long-term entitlement leading to dependence.

Born into humble circumstances in Assynt, Sutherlandshire, Scotland, on 27 July 1890, Mackenzie had gone on a scholarship to Edinburgh University and had completed law studies before emigrating to Canada in 1914. He enlisted the next year (giving his address as the University Club, Vancouver), served overseas with the 72nd Battalion of the CEF and as a staff officer for the Canadian Railway Troops, and was mentioned in dispatches.[115] After the war he resumed legal practice in Vancouver, and from 1920 to 1930 served in the British Columbia Legislative Assembly (he was provincial secretary in 1920). He was briefly federal minister of immigration and colonization in 1930 and was returned for the Liberals

Ian Alistair Mackenzie, minister of pensions and national health, 1939–44 (standing fifth from left, under the Union Jack) at a patriotic gathering, Orangeville, Ontario, October 1943 (Library and Archives Canada [LAC], C146002)

Walter Sainsbury Woods, Canada's first deputy minister of veterans affairs, in retirement in Vancouver, where he was working on his book *Rehabilitation (A Combined Operation)*, published in 1953 (*Veterans Affairs*, April–May 1951)

in Vancouver Centre in the federal election of that year. As minister of national defence, 1935–39, he played to mixed reviews; the day before his transfer out of the portfolio, King wrote that Mackenzie was "not an administrator" but a platform performer, whose career had been blighted by drink.[116] Mackenzie had been prominent in the Great War Veterans' Association in the 1920s, and even though he is now most remembered as the leading protagonist for the removal of Japanese Canadians from coastal British Columbia during the Second World War, he had campaigned, unsuccessfully, in the British Columbia legislature to extend the franchise to Japanese Canadian residents of British Columbia who had served in the CEF (this was finally achieved in 1931). He was six feet, two inches tall, had "Scotland forever entrenched upon his tongue," and was well known for his "mastery of the high-flown phrase and the purple passage."[117]

Obviously, he and Woods had much in common: both were British-born, had served overseas, and prided themselves on being veterans. But they were also very different personalities – Mackenzie as mercurial and indulgent as Woods was steady and sober. Nevertheless, in harness together, they eventually formed a productive two-horse team. Woods, of course, had the great advantage of having lived the Canadian veteran experience, both as outsider and insider. He had etched in memory, never to be forgotten, the circumstances of his own return from overseas in 1918 to an uncertain future, and he eventually combined this with an encyclopedic knowledge of how the Canadian system of veterans' benefits worked (or didn't work). He served as secretary of the Vimy Pilgrimage Committee and was present at the 1936 memorial dedication in France, and again on 21 May 1939, when George VI unveiled the National War Memorial in Ottawa in the presence of ten thousand Legionnaires. His self-image was that of a veteran in the service of veterans. As the country mobilized after September 1939 and new possibilities opened up to him, Woods wanted to correct the mistakes of the past and build a better world for a new generation of Canadians in uniform. He soon got his chance.

3 PC7633

According to statistics used by Woods in 1953, during the Second World War 1,081,865 Canadians were enlisted in their country's military forces (the population of Canada recorded in the 1941 census was 11,506,865).[1] In the first months of the war enlistment was voluntary, but this changed following the national election of 26 March 1940, in which the King government won the biggest House of Commons majority seen to that time. By the National Resources Mobilization Act (NRMA), triggered by the fall of France and given assent on 21 June 1940, men could be conscripted for home service (that is to say, for service in Canada or its territorial waters). Thereafter, the Canadian forces consisted of volunteers and conscripts, the latter known popularly as "zombies," an unflattering designation that speaks for itself. The geographical limitation in the NRMA accorded with the promise made by Prime Minister King and the government on more than one occasion (both before and after the start of hostilities) that, in this conflict, men would not be conscripted for overseas service. The rationale for this decision lay in the deep wound that such action had inflicted on the country during the Great War. Conscription, except for the defence of Canada, remained anathema to French Quebec, where King and his ministers enjoyed strong support but where history had fostered a point of view on events in Europe that had much in common with American isolationist sentiment. From the French Canadian perspective, participation alongside Great Britain in war was one thing, but compulsory service overseas in support of British causes quite another. In 1939, in the interest of national unity, the King government promised participation without conscription, but wartime reverses soon forced the retreat given tangible form in the NRMA; this legislation sought to meet a pressing military need while preserving national unity by appealing to the body of sentiment in Quebec that made a clear distinction between protecting Canada and fighting in other people's wars. More backpedalling by Ottawa followed in 1942, when through a national plebiscite the government won release from its previous commitment respecting the methods of raising men for military service. By an amendment to the NRMA that received assent on 1 August 1942, the government was authorized to deploy NRMA conscripts as it saw fit, without geographical limitation. In practice, though, it did not use this authority until November 1944, during the hard fighting that followed the D-day landings, when 12,908 NRMA men were sent overseas. Of these, 2,463 actually joined field units; 315 became casualties, 69 of them fatal.[2]

Canada's 1939–45 mobilization also involved a changed and greatly expanded role for women in the forces. During the Great War, 2,854 women had served with the Canadian Army Medical Corps as nursing sisters, but beginning in July 1941, women's auxiliary forces were formed in the three branches of the forces. These were the Canadian Women's Auxiliary Air Force, authorized by PC4798 of 2 July 1941 and known from February 1942 as the Royal Canadian Air Force Women's Division; the Canadian Women's Army Corps, authorized by PC6289 of 13 August 1941; and the Women's Royal Canadian Naval Service, authorized by PC56/6755 of 31 July 1942. The purpose of the auxiliary units was to free men to fight by releasing them from work that could be done by women. Wartime enlistments by women, including about 5,000 nursing sisters, numbered 50,656; of these, 26,063 were in the army, 17,467 in the air force, and 7,126 in the navy.[3] In November 1942 members of the women's branches began serving overseas in non-combat roles and were eventually stationed in the United Kingdom, Italy, and Northwest Europe.

Demographically, the Second World War Canadian forces were very different from the CEF. In the case of the 1914–18 conflict, more than half of those who served were born outside the country (mainly in the United Kingdom), whereas those who signed attestation papers in 1939–45 were mainly Canadian born. The immigrants who went overseas in the Great War knew Canada as a boom country, "a land of opportunity" that favoured "short term employment by choice" over "long service, seniority and slow gains."[4] Many of them were "relatively unskilled," and according to survey research, 32 per cent of them wanted to return to agricultural work. The enlistees of the Great War came "from the homestead, from the laying of new railroad track, from the building of new towns, from new wheat lands, and from an economy in which an expanding agriculture played a prominent part." Only 5 per cent had worked in the manufacturing sector, 4 per cent in "commercial pursuits," and 2.2 per cent in mining. By contrast, 1941 data about those who began enlisting in 1939 showed that only a small percentage of them had come from agriculture, that they were better educated than their Great War predecessors, and that they came from a wider variety of occupations (many, of course, had been unemployed in the 1930s). Their composition reflected the deep changes that had occurred in the country in the interwar period. As Ian

Mackenzie explained in one review and analysis of the numbers, "Everything is changed – the type of war, the character of the combatant force, the economy of the dominion, the directives of our society, and the world in which we live."[5]

As recruitment began ramping up in the fall of 1939, Ottawa was almost immediately faced with the issue of what to do about a new generation of veterans. Soldiers in training were injured on the day Canada went to war, and soon afterwards one was killed.[6] By September 1940, about ten thousand who had enlisted and served in Canada only had already been discharged, and by December roughly twenty thousand had left uniform, including about a thousand who had returned from overseas.[7] They were the first representatives of the hundreds of thousands of veterans the war would eventually produce. Many of those discharged in the early days of the war were returned to civilian life because they were medically unfit for service. What did the country owe them, and what branch of government would be responsible for administering whatever was decided upon? The second question was quickly answered in favour of the Department of Pensions and National Health (DPNH), which jumped into the policy lead. A clear division of labour was soon worked out between DPNH and the Department of National Defence, whereby a newly created auxiliary service in the latter department ended its involvement when a man "put off his uniform."[8] A moment of rare opportunity had arrived for the administrators who ran DPNH, most of whom were Great War veterans, and they were quick to seize it. History was giving them a second chance: an opening to apply the lessons of the past, both personal and administrative, and to rebuild for a better tomorrow. In practice, this meant dealing with immediate business – the needs of those who left the forces in the first phase of the war – while planning for the long term.

On 13 October 1939, just over a month after the war had started, the chairman of the Canadian Pension Commission, Harold French McDonald, made a powerful case to Mackenzie for the immediate appointment of a committee to study the problems that one day would inevitably arise in connection with repatriation and demobilization.[9] Mackenzie responded positively, and on 30 October wrote to King that although the war effort was just getting underway, attention should be given forthwith to preparing the country for the end of hostilities.[10] King, who had been personally defeated in the 1917 election over the divisive issue of conscription and had become prime minister in the tumultuous aftermath of the Great War, readily agreed, observing that consideration of the "problems of demobilization and the rehabilitation of ex-servicemen into civil life after the war" could not start "too soon."[11] The result of this exchange was the unusually numbered Privy Council order 4068½ (the ½ was a well-established administrative convenience) of 8 December 1939, which created a cabinet committee on demobilization and rehabilitation to inquire into and report on the matters in question. Named to the committee were Mackenzie (convenor), the ministers of public works, national defence, agriculture, and labour, and Minister without Portfolio J.A. MacKinnon. The purpose of the committee was "to procure information respecting and give full consideration to and report regarding the problems which will arise from the demobilization and the discharge from time to time of members of the Forces during and after the conclusion of the present war, and the rehabilitation of such members into civil life."[12]

Mackenzie next formed an interdepartmental committee, with McDonald as chairman and Woods as vice-chairman. On 15 September 1940, Robert England, another prominent and well-connected Great War veteran, began work as executive secretary to this group, which was then enlarged and given terms of reference in PC5421 of 8 October 1940. Under this order-in-council, the membership of what was afterwards referred to as the General Advisory Committee on Demobilization and Rehabilitation (GACDR) was to consist of a chairman and vice-chairman (respectively, the chairman of the Canadian Pension Commission and the chairman of the War Veterans' Allowance Board), the chairman of the Civil Service Commission, the deputy ministers of labour, public works, and pensions and national health, the director of auxiliary services at the Department of National Defence, two members to be nominated by each of the ministers of national defence, agriculture, finance, and pensions and national health, and one member nominated by the minister of trade and commerce. The GACDR was instructed to consider the matters referred to the special committee of the cabinet by PC4068½ and to report and make recommendations thereon. For this purpose, it was authorized to appoint subcommittees, which could draw members from government departments and agencies and include established experts from outside the public service.[13]

McDonald brought to the role of chairman of the GACDR notable personal and administrative qualifications. Born on 22 November 1885 in Fort Qu'Appelle, Saskatchewan, he was a graduate of Upper Canada College and McGill University and a civil engineer by profession. Having served in the militia, he had been commissioned as lieutenant in 1914 and went overseas with the 79th Canadian Highlanders. He was badly wounded at the battle of Passchendaele and suffered the loss of an arm.

Great War amputee Harold French McDonald, first chairman of the General Advisory Committee on Demobilization and Rehabilitation (GACDR) (Department of National Defence/LAC, PA-007485)

In December 1917 he was promoted to the rank of brigadier-general, in 1918 was assigned to the Military Hosptials Commission, and from 1919 to 1922 commanded Military District 13 with headquarters in Calgary. In 1931 he moved from private business to pension administration and in 1936 became chairman of the Canadain Pension Commission. McDonald remembered vividly the aftermath of the Great War and believed that no country engaged in the conflict had done more than Canada in re-establishment effort. The dominion had spent heavily, and it was wrong to characterize its record "as unproductive or wholly unsuccessful, or to blame the succeeding years of comparative distress and unemployment upon either the conception or the implementing of the policies of rehabilitation."[14] International economic conditions had worked against the initiatives undertaken; but without the dominion's actions, the Depression years would have been much worse than they were.

The lesson in all this was that the re-establishment of ex-servicemen was linked to economic reconstruction generally and would not be successful unless considered in this context. At the end of the war now in progress, Canadians could be expected to give priority attention to the needs of those who served, but the public's good intention would need "guidance and direction." This would apply equally to the veterans themselves, McDonald explained, "so that their enthusiastic efforts to

Robert England, secretary of the GACDR, 1940–43 (*Veterans Affairs*, 15 July 1948)

re-establish themselves" would "not be spent in vain and ill-considered directions." For the moment, though, the emphasis must be on planning: "We cannot operate the machinery of war and the machinery of post-war reconstruction simultaneously, but we should be able to study and investigate the opportunity avenues along which we should march when the occasion comes." McDonald wanted change, but his instincts were deeply paternalistic, and he worried that many young men now enlisting had only minimal education and had "been encouraged to remain idle by the relief facilities available to them." To get everyone ready for work would require careful and thorough "study, investigation and forethought," and that was the pressing first job.

Robert England had similar views and brought to his new duties a flair for the king's English.[15] Born in Portadown, County Armagh, Northern Ireland, on 15 September 1894 and the thirteenth of fourteen children, he had come to Canada just before the Great War. He started out doing farm work in Saskatchewan but was soon registered at Queen's University, Kingston, Ontario, as an extramural student in English, Greek, and philosophy. Having been commissioned as an officer with the Saskatchewan Rifles, he went overseas in 1916 with the 203rd Battalion of the CEF. He saw action at Vimy Ridge, Hill 70, and Cambrai, was twice wounded, and was awarded the Military Cross for heroism at Cambrai. When he enlisted, he had described himself as a Methodist and a student for the ministry, but after the war he attended normal school in Saskatoon and then taught at Slawa Rural School, near Hafford, Saskatchewan, in an area of Ukrainian settlement. Thereafter he worked in London, England, and in

Winnipeg for the colonization branch of Canadian National Railways. In 1929 he published *The Central European Immigrant in Canada* and in 1936 *The Colonization of Western Canada: A Study of Contemporary Land Settlement (1896–1934)*. In 1936–37 he was director of extension and associate professor of economics at the University of British Columbia and from 1937 to 1939 was an economic adviser to the Winnipeg Electric Company.

In 1938, alarmed by developments in Europe and anxious to promote national unity in Canada in case of war, England undertook a series of broadcasts, dubbed "Ventures in Citizenship," on the young Canadian Broadcasting Corporation. The programs in the series celebrated the contributions of various groups to Canadian life, and, remarkably, the program honouring the Jewish experience was heard across the country on the night of 9 November, at the very time that the *Kristallnacht* assault on Jews was in progress in Nazi Germany. After war broke out, England went to London as director there of the Canadian Legion Educational Services, a joint endeavour of the veterans' organization and the Canadian Association for Adult Education. Headed by CAAE president Lieutenant-Colonel Wilfrid Bovey, who was director of extra-mural relations at McGill University, it sought to build upon the achievements of the Khaki University in the Great War. England was still in the early stages of his work when the opportunity to be executive secretary to the GACDR came along.

England was a man of parts, whose varied career had given him connections across the country. Those in uniform, he once memorably wrote, must not be made "heroes today and hoboes tomorrow."[16] In his demanding new appointment, he was an influential policy voice and efficiently managed the extensive paperwork of the subcommittees through which the work of the GACDR proceeded. Each subcommittee was chaired by a member of the main group and examined a particular topic related to the larger issue of rehabilitation. In December 1940 seven subcommittees were functioning and examining issues relating to post-discharge pay and service gratuity, vocational and technical training and retraining, the retraining of special casualties, land settlement, the administration of special funds (mainly from the Great War Patriotic Fund and various canteen funds), preference in public service employment, and employment generally.[17] Eventually, seven more subcommittees were added, bringing the total to fourteen. The topics addressed by these were interrupted education, women's rehabilitation, the special problems of ex-service women, demobilization priorities, neuropsychiatric cases, the rehabilitation of the older veteran, and returned soldiers' insurance.[18] By the second year of the war, Canada was well launched into making plans that would shape the lives of its new cohort of veterans. The main architects of all this were four comrades of the Great War – Mackenzie, McDonald, Woods, and England – three of them immigrants to Canada from the United Kingdom and all of them determined to build, through judicious state action, the better tomorrow heralded by the 1914–18 "war to end all wars," but manifestly unrealized thereafter.

While the planning effort was getting underway to devise a long-term program of rehabilitation for those serving in uniform, immediate needs were also being addressed, and indeed actions taken in this regard were influential in shaping the larger enterprise. On 2 September 1939, before Canada entered the war, PC 2491 extended the benefits of the Pension Act to those who soon came forward to serve.[19] This action was timely, but by PC 1971, effective 21 May 1940, the government acted to limit its pension liability. It did so by making a distinction between active service in Canada, which would be governed by the "due to service" principle (eventually known as the "compensation" principle) and service in an actual theatre of war, to which what was called the "insurance" principle applied.[20] Under the "due to service" principle, a pension would be granted only for death or disability attributable to military service as such. By contrast, the insurance principle meant round-the-clock coverage no matter what the cause. It was the latter principle that had applied in the Great War, and it had left Ottawa with a hefty pension bill. In the year ending 31 March 1939 there were 233,470 beneficiaries under the Pension Act, and the total annual liability of the government was more than $40 million.[21] The thinking behind the change made through PC 1971 was subsequently explained by Mackenzie in the House of Commons as follows:

> The chief principle involved in the order in council of May 1940, was a clearer definition of the responsibility of the state, in relation to those whose service occurred in Canada. It was provided that, where the man served in Canada only, the liability for war pension should exist only when disability or death arose as a direct result of the performance of military duties. It will be realized that thousands of the men on active service in Canada are engaged in their military duties for only a limited number of hours per day and that, in the evenings and on week-ends, they are at liberty in very much the same way as the ordinary civil employees of the government ... Actually, many of them are living normal civilian lives except for the hours during which they are on duty. Full protection is given where

death or disability arise as the result of the performance of duty. But a number of cases arose in which men were the victims of accident while away from their military duties and under circumstances in no way associated with their service. It was not considered that any claim for war pension should arise from the consequences of accidents and incidents which come to all of us in the course of our ordinary lives. A special regulation was necessary to meet this set of conditions because the original pension act was based on conditions of the last war, when the assumption was that every man enlisted would proceed as rapidly as possible to a theatre of war.[22]

In short, Canada would honour its pension obligations to those now going into uniform but within a new framework that would keep costs under control. In this matter, as in so much else, the experience of the Great War and its aftermath shaped policy after 1939.

Important choices were also made in 1940 about a rehabilitation benefit package for those already leaving uniform. In July it was decided that men discharged after a short period of service would have to rely on existing facilities and that nothing special should be done for them.[23] But the arrival back in Canada of about eight hundred men who had been overseas and either had now been discharged or were awaiting discharge made this approach unsustainable. This group, Woods noted, had "a stronger sentimental appeal with the Public" than those who, having served in Canada only, had been found unfit for the military.[24] In October, with the need for something to be done becoming increasingly apparent, Woods toured western Canada and met with local committees established under the Veterans' Assistance Commission, superintendents of provincial employment services, youth-training representatives, labour and business leaders, and Canadian Legion officials. His purpose was to explain how the government was going about rehabilitation planning and to build support for its efforts. On his return to Ottawa, he told McDonald that he had been confronted everywhere "with the plight of those now being returned from overseas."[25] Often men were discharged while still being treated in hospital, a circumstance that was pushing many families onto relief, since the pay of a married man stopped when he was demobilized. "The view was advanced everywhere," Woods reported, "that something should be done forthwith with respect to these men, until they are ready to resume work and positions are found for them." On a follow-up trip in November through various centres in Ontario, Quebec, New Brunswick, and Nova Scotia, he again heard much about the "predicament" of men who were being cast adrift.[26] He also had urged on him that, for those being discharged, transportation should be provided back to their original places of residence rather than to their places of enlistment, so that they would not become burdens on the latter. Likewise, he was urged to have any preference given to veterans of the CEF under government contracts extended to former members of the new Canadian Active Service Force who had been overseas.

Not surprisingly, the Canadian Legion had its own views about what should be done for men now being discharged. On 1 September 1939, before the war actually began, the Legion fired its first shot in a trenchant memorandum to the dominion government.[27] In this document the Legion urged that enlisted men should be fully informed about their pension rights, that the medical examination of recruits should leave "no argument as to whether a condition was pre-enlistment or incurred on service," that the procedure for compiling medical histories be overhauled, that company officers be instructed about pension policy and reporting requirements, and that the government give a clear statement of its responsibility for looking after dependants. The Legion likewise made the case that, whether a man was conscripted or volunteered, he made "a certain sacrifice for the state" that merited recognition. If young, he lost "the benefit of the formative years of life"; if established, he lost "the benefit of experience and advancement." These losses, arising from "sacrifice of opportunity," were also "service disabilities" and "should be recognized as such and made the subject of definite Government policy." Specific measures envisaged by the Legion included statutory reinstatement, with full seniority rights, of an able-bodied man in his pre-enlistment employment (assuming it still existed), and assistance to enable a man who had been in business before enlistment to re-establish himself in that enterprise. The Legion took the position that men who had been "untrained or unestablished" when joining up should be kept in the military until employable. Here was a sweeping and controversial proposal for which the organization subsequently pushed hard.

On 13 September 1939, three days after Canada went to war, the Legion's dominion president, W.W. Foster, gave a national radio address in support of the war effort, and later in the month the Dominion Council met in emergency session in Ottawa.[28] This gathering called for an immediate declaration by the government of the use to which those now enlisting would be put, regulation of the cost of living, imposition of "equitable sacrifice upon wealth and industry," and a public role for the Legion in providing war services.[29] The council reiterated the organization's support for compulsory military service (opposed at the time by both government and opposition), but acknowledged the reality that the country would proceed on the basis of voluntary enlistment; for this to meet the military need, there would have to be "proper safeguards as to the family, and personal future of the volunteer."[30] After a meeting between the council and the prime minister and members of the cabinet, the Legion heard back from the government that the first trained division to be formed "would go overseas as soon as required." The Legion was now also invited to submit "its detailed views upon general war services, pensions and re-establishment" and was informed that its offer to provide war services "would be referred to the Minister of Defence for sympathetic consideration."[31] Subsequently, the organization busied itself with the launch of Canadian Legion War Services, Canadian Legion Educational Services, and the Veterans Guard of Canada, a home defence force, the basis for which had been laid in a national survey of ex-service men and women, undertaken early in 1939, which had produced 70,000 registrants.[32] The purpose of the Veterans Guard was to free younger men from home duties for service abroad.

In March 1940, during the campaign leading to the national election of that month, the Legion sent all the party leaders a lengthy statement of its views entitled "Memorandum Concerning the Welfare of Ex-Service Men, Men Now Serving and Their Dependents." Signed by acting dominion president Alex Walker of Calgary and former president Ross (Foster had stepped down after becoming director of auxiliary services at the Department of National Defence), the document invited "due consideration" of its submissions without asking for "specific pledges" of support.[33] This was in keeping with the Legion's "desire to achieve such changes as may be necessary by combined action of all parties and without any suggestion of partiality to any political party." The organization's concern for the servicemen of the current conflict, it was explained, was rooted in its constitution; the Legion would serve the country by making its expertise available to the new generation of enlisted men until they were able to act for themselves. Following an introduction, the text of the memorandum was organized under two headings: "Problems of 1914–1918" and "Problems of the Present War." The Legion had many messages for the politicians, pointedly noting that a new army was being enlisted while "remnants" of the last one remained "objects of public charity" (a recurring phrase in the memorandum). "No corporation or individual," the Legion insisted, should benefit financially from the war. Moreover, "equality of sacrifice" dictated that a man who volunteered should not be disadvantaged in the workplace compared with a man who did not volunteer.

"Fighting Alex" Walker, president of the Canadian Legion, 1940–46 (Royal Canadian Legion, *Report of the 10th Dominion Convention*)

On the crucial issue of "the extent of the Government's responsibility on discharge," the position now enunciated by the veterans' organization was that young men who had not worked and were unable to earn a living should be kept in uniform until they had been trained and absorbed into employment "in an orderly manner."

At the Legion's biennial national convention, held in Montreal from 27 to 30 May 1940, Sergeant Alex Walker was elected president of the organization. Born in Scotland, he had served overseas with the 50th Calgary Battalion and had been wounded on the Somme. In recognition of his outspoken advocacy of ex-service causes, he was known in veterans' circles as "Fighting Alex." He was the first non-commissioned officer to head the Legion and turned out to be its longest-serving president (he remained in office until 1946). He spent much of the war battling the King government on conscription – the limited measure of compulsory service introduced in June 1940 did not satisfy the avowedly conscriptionist Legion – but he also gave high priority to the rehabilitation file and to turning the Legion into the voice of those who were serving in the war. In preparation for the convention, he established a committee on unemployment and rehabilitation, which met for three days and was informed by a lengthy memorandum from Ross entitled "Rehabilitation and Re-establishment of Members of His Majesty's Canadian Active Service Forces."[34]

Ross made the case for "the Government's Responsibility" in no uncertain terms:

> The Canadian Legion has consistently maintained the view that every man serving overseas is in a sense a casualty and therefore, the responsibility of the federal government. If he suffers physical injury the provisions for compensation are as generous as are made by any government in the world and generally speaking more generous, if properly administered. But the disabilities of services are not confined to physical disabilities. Nearly every man who severs his connection with civil life and gives years in the service of his country suffers an economic handicap, as compared to the man who stays at home, and in respect of that disability he is entitled to a like measure of assistance. It must be remembered that very few of the casualties are so injured as to entitle them to an allowance sufficient to enable them to subsist in comfort. The remainder must be rehabilitated, so that within the limits of their physical capacity they may amplify their allowances to ensure subsistence. And those who have escaped physical injury must, by some means, be assured of an opportunity of making a living, which in many cases implies that they be trained in some vocation. Until every man is given an opportunity to train for some vocation for which he is fitted, and until every man is afforded an opportunity to make a living according to his capability, the duty of the government of Canada and the people of Canada has not been discharged. [35]

In keeping with this logic, the committee, which included representatives from across the country, produced a report to the convention that called for a demobilization plan to be put into operation immediately and built up throughout the war. Under the envisaged scheme, all members of the forces would "be kept on the strength for a reasonable period to permit a gradual and economic" return to civilian life.[36] A man who rehabilitated himself quickly would be paid a gratuity "equal to what he would have received had he remained on the strength the full period of time allowed for demobilization, thus setting a premium on a man making his own efforts for re-establishment."

After taking office, Walker pressed the Legion's point of view about discharge and rehabilitation on the government at every opportunity. On 6 November he told Prime Minister King that while there was good reason to be confident that the minister of pensions and national health was making appropriate plans for future rehabilitation needs, the circumstances of the men now returning from overseas called for swift action.[37] As things stood, those returning were eligible for a small clothing allowance only. Most of them were "medically unfit," and it would take time for the Canadian Pension Commission to decide on their pension entitlements. These men should "be automatically taken on the strength of the Department of Pensions and National Health at a rate of pay equivalent to their army pay and allowances and so retained until a decision as to treatment or pension" was given. If a pension was granted but, along with other income, was not enough for a man to support himself, he should automatically become eligible for other DPNH help. Medically unfit men whose pension applications were denied "should be carried on the strength of the Department of Pensions and National Health ... for a time sufficiently long to permit the proper and adequate application of the measures for finding employment" that were being worked out by the department. In the case of "men of lower category," discharge should not take place until a determined effort had been made to see if employment that took account of physical condition could be found for them in the services. In no circumstances, should men be discharged to public relief – something, unfortunately, that was already happening to many of them.

The government responded to the situations thus highlighted by the Legion – and well recognized by its own officials – with a series of measures and announcements. On 18 November 1940, PC 204-6613 authorized DPNH to grant medical treatment to a man subsequent to his discharge and to grant pay allowances to his dependants.[38] The payments were to be made according to National Defence's dependants' allowance scale and would continue until seven days after either the completion of the individual's treatment or a ruling by the pension commission that the condition being treated did not entitle him to a pension. Following this action, on 6 December, Mackenzie gave a lengthy statement in the House of Commons in which he reviewed everything that had happened in rehabilitation and pension policy since the beginning of hostilities and announced that a veterans' welfare division (authorized by PC 6282 of 27 November) would be created in DPNH.[39] The new unit would have a chief administrative officer in Ottawa and representatives (i.e., welfare officers) across the country. Its purpose would be "to interview, advise and assist former members of the forces," facilitate their employment, encourage voluntary effort on their behalf, and "develop favourable public opinion" in relation to their re-establishment, while keeping in touch with veterans' organizations and other bodies interested in rehabilitation.[40] On 19

December, this announcement was followed by PC7521, which provided a rehabilitation grant to anyone discharged from the services with 183 days of continuous service.[41] The amount of the grant was tied to rank and was equal to thirty days' pay, plus dependants' or marriage allowances. Anyone who had been discharged at his own request or by reason of having given false information on enlistment, been sentenced by court martial, or been imprisoned by civil authority was ineligible. Further to this initiative and the reorganization underway at DPNH, Woods was made acting director of the Veterans' Welfare Division and then, in March 1941, associate deputy minister with responsibility for rehabilitation administration and planning. In combination with his role as vice-chairman of the GACDR, the promotion positioned him to play a commanding role in everything that followed. He already had a hand in making rehabilitation policy; now he would be responsible for carrying it out. An ex-soldier who had arrived back in Calgary in 1919 looking to rebuild his own life would now be at the fore in refashioning the prospects of an entire generation.

On 17 January 1941, Mackenzie chaired a meeting in Ottawa with senior officials from the departments responsible for labour and unemployment relief in Ontario, Manitoba, Saskatchewan, Alberta, and British Columbia.[42] He provided a summary of the activities of the GACDR, and McDonald and Woods, respectively, gave explanations of the pension regulations and the work being done nationally and locally by the new Veterans' Welfare Division. The Alberta commissioner of public welfare, Major A.A. Mackenzie, told the meeting that "unemployables" among discharged men with short service were posing problems: "Many were of the agitator type, and because of their being in possession of discharge certificates, public officers had considerable difficulty dealing with them." Major Mackenzie's view was that many of those being released from service should have been kept in uniform and that "in the case of those who were of the agitator type, the machinery of military discipline should have been used to ensure that they carried out their obligations to the country." In the discussion that followed, it was noted "that in no country in the world had there been any obligation assumed by the state for men who had been unable, for various reasons, to serve it" and that "short service" did not bring with it entitlement to "undue preference or consideration." Individuals in this category were "civilian on leaving the army"; by definition, this entitled them "to the privileges of citizens," but "public officers should expect them to live up to their obligations as citizens." Consideration was also given on this occasion to whether men let go because they were "unlikely to become efficient soldiers or because of subversive propaganda" should have this information included on their discharge certificates. According to Major Mackenzie, if Ottawa would assume responsibility for the relief of ex-service men, Alberta could be out of the relief business by the end of the year; but his federal namesake gave no commitment in this regard. The issue of relief, the minister explained, would be addressed in the context of discussion about the recently submitted report of the Royal Commission on Dominion-Provincial Relations. Overall, the provincial representatives promised cooperation with the federal government in the measures it had adopted to assist those leaving the forces.

On 24 February 1941, with the GACDR and its subcommittees busily at work, the Legion in full flight, and the Veterans' Welfare Division of DPNH functioning across the country, a special committee of the House of Commons was formed to consider the Pension and War Veterans' Allowance acts and "such questions connected with pensions and the problems of ex-service men" as the House might specifically refer to it.[43] Thirty-nine members, including Mackenzie, were named to the committee, which was chaired by the MP for Queen's (Prince Edward Island), Cyrus Macmillan, dean of arts and science at McGill University and veteran of the 7th Canadian Siege Battery in the Great War. The committee met from 28 February to 11 June and its *Minutes of Proceedings and Evidence* were printed in English and French in twenty-two separate instalments (with continuous pagination); 1,500 hundred copies of each publication were made available in English and 300 in French. The committee reported on 12 June, and its report, along with its minutes and proceedings, were then bound in a single volume, which remains an indispensable source for understanding wartime developments in the field of veterans' affairs. In the course of its deliberations, the committee held thirty meetings and heard from twenty-nine witnesses "representing soldier organizations and Government Administrative branches."[44] Prominent among them were McDonald, Woods, Walker, Bowler, Legion assistant general secretary J.G.C. (George) Herwig, DPNH medical services director Ross Millar, and Civil Service Commission chairman C.H. Bland. The committee was provided with a brief history of Canadian military pension legislation, and on 3 April was given a summary by Mackenzie of what had happened in relation to demobilization and rehabilitation after the Great War and how the government was now proceeding. The next day, when the committee heard from McDonald and Woods, it was given up-to-date documentation (another invaluable source, printed in two appendices to the minutes and proceedings) on the work of the GACDR and its subcommittees.

Walker appeared before the committee on 6 May 1941 and presented a brief that again made the case for "some form of 'retarded demobilization.'"[45] While there were "obvious objections to the indefinite maintenance of a standing post-war army," he said, the Legion's proposal was workable. The fact that planning for demobilization was already in progress meant that for many there would be an easy transition to work. Moreover, large numbers of enlistees would be able to return to their pre-war jobs. Yet another positive factor was the likelihood that Canada would in future want bigger peacetime armed forces and that many now serving might want to pursue military careers. "One thing," Walker bluntly asserted, "is very certain (providing the individual concerned is willing to work): there should be no period between demobilization and employment during which the ex-service man or his dependents are obliged to have recourse to public charity. The Legion feels very keenly, and it believes it echoes the opinion of the whole Canadian people that public relief as a means of maintenance during the transition period should be ruled out wholly and completely." After the war, the threat of communism might replace that of Nazism, and there was "no more fertile ground for the communist than a large body of unemployed men." Walker noted with satisfaction that the Trades and Labor Congress had reached the same conclusion about demobilization as his own organization; in a brief to the government on 14 March, the congress had argued that, in order to avoid the upheaval that followed the 1914–18 war, at the end of the conflict now in progress members of the armed forces should "be retained on the government payroll" until they could find or be provided with "steady employment."

The Legion's case was persuasive, and in its four-page final report the special committee recommended consideration for "the retaining in the service for a period not exceeding six months after the date on which they would otherwise be discharged, non-pensionable and non-disability members of the forces with no assurance of immediate post-discharge employment, with the object of enabling such members of the forces to obtain employment and to be re-established in civil life."[46] In a circular dated 20 June, Bowler told Legion members that this recommendation was of "outstanding importance" and appeared "to accept the principle of 'retarded demobilization'" advanced by Walker.[47] Bowler praised Mackenzie for his foresight and success in launching the GACDR and concluded that the country was "very far advanced" in its re-establishment planning compared with where matters had stood at the corresponding time during the 1914–18 war. The results of this could not but be advantageous to everyone involved.

The report of the special committee set the stage for decisive action by the government. But when this ultimately came, it was in a measure that flatly rejected the notion of "retarded demobilization" being trumpeted by the Legion. The government's response made it clear that whatever support the Legion may have had – or thought it had – from the Trades and Labor Congress, the veterans' organization had in fact made no significant headway with the country's leaders. Central to the thinking of Ottawa's veterans' affairs planners as events next unfolded was the belief that the payment of the gratuity at the end of the Great War (it had cost Ottawa $164 million to March 1927) had been expensive, wasteful, and inefficient, and was an experience not to be repeated.[48] According to the GACDR Sub-Committee on Post Discharge Pay and War Service Gratuity, the decision to pay the gratuity had been made "in a rush of sentimentality" and three-quarters of the recipients had not needed the money, which would have been better spent re-establishing the quarter that did.[49] Assuming a Second World War military force of 500,000, an equivalent payment would cost about $200 million, an expenditure for which the taxpayer would have "nothing to show ... except an increased national debt and a devalued dollar." Hypothetically, to realize the sum involved, all gainfully employed Canadians would have to work "three days annually for 35 years." This was "equivalent to a sentence of three months hard labour," and was totally unacceptable. No such payment should be made. Although Mackenzie expressed himself less colourfully, he was of like mind. In April 1941 he told the special committee that while gratuity payments may have avoided trouble immediately after the Great War, they had also probably "encouraged undue periods of idleness and minimized rather than maximized the desire to become re-established"; the "emphasis upon monetary grants without corresponding responsibility for use of the leisure afforded by such grants" had been of "doubtful value as a long-run policy."[50] A failed approach must now be eschewed in favour of "more scientific planning."

This particular lesson from the past took practical form on 23 July 1941, when McDonald sent Mackenzie a draft order-in-council incorporating a bold and coordinated scheme of postwar benefits – but without provision for a gratuity. His submission inaugurated a new phase in Ottawa's rehabilitation planning, and a busy round of meetings and interdepartmental discussions followed. The preparation of the draft, McDonald explained, had "commanded the best efforts" of the members of the subcommittees on employment and post-discharge pay as well as senior officials from the

Department of Labour, the Unemployment Insurance Commission, and the Department of Insurance, and it was being sent to the minister before being submitted to the GACDR because of the fundamental importance of what was being proposed.[51] This was the introduction of a sweeping and contributory program of out-of-work and training benefits and the inclusion of everyone who served under the unemployment insurance scheme legislated in 1940 following a constitutional amendment. In combination with what was already being provided for those leaving the forces, these further and very substantial improvements would round out what Canada would need at the end of the war by way of "rehabilitation machinery."

The subsistence allowances to be paid would be in line with those already available under the War Emergency Training Programme and would be sufficient to encourage those whose interest in training and the resumption of interrupted education was genuine, but they would not be so large as "to discourage acceptance of more remunerative employment."[52] Acceptance of the plan now proposed would make plain the government's determination to rehabilitate those who fought for the country, assist recruiting, promote work over dependency, highlight the "common sense fundamentals of personal contribution and responsibility," and undercut the arguments of "radical groups alleging inadequacy of pensions or re-establishment or arguing for some form of social credit dividend." The action called for, McDonald ventured, would enable the government, in the "difficult period of general demobilization," not to buckle under pressure should the Canadian Legion, "backed by provincial and public bodies, and radical groups," make "a drive for bonuses, gratuities and relief." For the moment, actual costs were hard to predict, but "the Government could maintain on training allowances for out-or-work benefit, 100,000 at a cost of $57,200,000, for the full fifty-two weeks of maximum benefit." This sum was large but was only a quarter of the amount spent on rehabilitation training after the Great War. Moreover, keeping 100,000 individuals in uniform until work was available for them – as might happen under the demobilization scheme envisaged variously by the Legion, the Trades and Labor Congress, and the special committee – would be much more costly.

Woods followed up on 25 July with a report to Mackenzie on another trip through the Prairie region, during which he had spoken to Rotary clubs, addressed Legion conventions in all three provinces, and found widespread support for the government's rehabilitation plan and praise for its foresight in seizing the initiative.[53] Given this favourable public response and the progress being made by the GACDR subcommittees,

Woods urged Mackenzie to push forward and, to the extent now possible, complete the development of the government's overall plan for veterans of the war. Acting now would give time "to set up the necessary administrative facilities." Mackenzie agreed, and on 28 July he sent McDonald's submission to the prime minister, whereupon the matter was referred to a cabinet committee.[54] Mackenzie was named chair and had as colleagues the ministers of national defence (there were now three of these, one as such and one each for air and naval services) and the ministers of finance and labour.

In the consideration of the draft order-in-council that followed, two connected issues dominated discussion: whether the proposed benefit package should be contributory and how unemployment insurance could be coordinated with military service. Contributions by those in insurable employment to the unemployment insurance fund began in July 1941, and benefits were scheduled to take effect from 1 February 1942. By definition, this arrangement posed a dilemma in relation to the armed forces. As Robert England trenchantly explained, "The civilian in insured employment who remains in such employment during the war, ignoring his country's need, will accumulate a record of contributions, whilst the service man on discharge will start his civilian working life with a blank page."[55] This would both work against recruitment and foster a deep sense of grievance against the government among those who served. The answer of the draft order-in-council was to put the two groups on an equal footing by having unemployment insurance contributions made on behalf of those in uniform. The contributions would be funded in part by the government and in part by individual payment. In keeping with existing unemployment insurance practice, the daily rate contemplated would be seven cents for the government as employer and five cents for the person covered.[56] Eventually, though, it was decided to have the required contributions made entirely out of public funds, a change dictated by several factors. As a review of events explained,

> To make the contributory arrangement acceptable to the Forces it was felt that refunds would have to be made to those who did not directly benefit, and this seemed also to require partial refunds to those who had not benefited up to the amount of their contributions. Such a scheme would have involved a large amount of pay-staff during the war and difficult adjustments for refunds after the war; notwithstanding the principles of refunds, there would probably be objection from a large proportion of those in the Forces; the contributions of the members of the Forces would provide but a small part

of the benefits in any event, but the Government would probably not get much if any credit for doing anything for the men if they were required to make even a nominal contribution; the contribution might induce demands for additional pay, and, if granted, the situation, from the point of view of costs, would be less favourable to the Government than a non-contributory basis; for those who might become established in insurable employment their war service would have to be counted in computing the rate of unemployment insurance benefit on the contributory basis of 5¢ per day, which would in a substantial proportion of cases result in insurance benefits in excess of the earnings of the insured persons – an unsound position from an insurance point of view; as a recruiting inducement, the order on a contributory basis would lose much of its force; the requirement of contributions would have been perhaps the one point at which criticism might be directed; without contributions it is difficult to see where the scheme is open to any criticism; with benefits of a non-contributory basis, greater administrative freedom is possible than if the benefits were acquired rights on the basis of contributions therefore, i.e. virtually contractual rights.[57]

Whatever the merits of these arguments, the non-contributory option set off alarm bells at the Unemployment Insurance Commission, fearful of an outcome that would undermine the infant program it was administering. The case for a different approach from the one being contemplated was made by the acting chief commissioner and deputy minister of labour, Arthur MacNamara, in a letter dated 9 September to V.C. Phelan, the commission's chief employment officer, who was chairman of the GACDR Sub-Committee on Employment. Writing on behalf of the commission and an interdepartmental committee it had established, MacNamara pointed out a variety of administrative problems posed by the envisaged scheme and offered the opinion "that no one could predict with any degree of accuracy whether or not the payments provided for would be adequate to protect the [unemployment insurance] fund."[58] An alternative plan, MacNamara countered, would be to pay a monthly gratuity (based on duration of service), which would have to be depleted before unemployment insurance benefit could be claimed, with "the cost in respect of insurance credits due to war service to be borne by the Consolidated Revenue Fund."

McDonald struck back forcefully against this wavering. "Am very apprehensive," he told England in a telegram sent from Banff (before the full unemployment commission case had been heard), "of any policies or administrative arrangements that will segregate or separate ex-service men from [the] general structure of post war labour and employment measures."[59] Experience had shown that such "differentiation" could breed trouble arising from "pauperization of [the] individual on [the] one hand and an antagonistic or 'let the government do it' [attitude] on the other as well as encouragement of group sentiment dangerous to public good and social stability generally." The proposals under consideration were "based upon [the] reabsorption of discharged men into [the] civilian attitude of mind as expeditiously as possible," and "questions of administrative convenience or departmental timidity" should not be allowed to block a program "based on broad principles of sound economic and social policy." For his part, England feared that unemployed ex-servicemen, instead of being treated like everyone else in the administration of unemployment insurance, might end up being "thrown upon some form of 'Consolidated Fund' relief siphoned through the Unemployment Insurance Commission."[60]

In practice, backed by the opinion of chief actuary W.D. Watson that the unemployment insurance fund was not at risk – "it can be predicted with certainty," he wrote, "that the provisions of the order will protect the Fund more adequately than the provisions of the Unemployment Insurance Act itself protects that Fund"[61] – the architects of the draft got their way. On 29 September the GACDR voted in favour of the amended document, with the addition of a clause laying out a procedure whereby the unemployment insurance fund could be augmented from the general revenue of the country if adversely affected by the operation of the new benefit package.[62] In an explanatory memorandum prepared in connection with this pivotal meeting, the case for the action taken was reviewed in detail and the argument against the payment of a war service gratuity given full orchestration:

> This method of dealing with re-establishment has been given careful study and rejected. Unconditional and indiscriminate gratuities based only on the period of service differential, payable to everyone, irrespective of need, constitute a bonus to the man who is employed and a dole to the unemployed and too often postpones the urgency of becoming re-established in the minds of ex-service men. Furthermore, there is a tendency to duplication since pensions, training allowances, and relief becomes payable later to those individuals who received gratuities. Furthermore, it would be difficult to decide as to the merits of service in Canada and overseas or in respective areas of danger and in the case of returning civil servants and per-

manent force personnel, the payment of gratuities seems doubtful. The diminished social utility of such gratuities is obvious and they cannot be described as a rehabilitation policy with any purpose or objective in it.[63]

The matter of "reward for war services" should be separated from that of rehabilitation and "dealt with on its own merits," noted the memorandum. Moreover, once the benefit scheme now agreed upon took effect, it would "be difficult to make a case for the payment of large sums of money simply as a reward." By the same token, it "would be extremely unwise" to keep individuals in the armed forces whose services were not needed there. This would not only postpone re-establishment but would hamper the war effort. The best course of action was the one envisaged in the draft order, an alternative the special committee had not had before it when it made its recommendations: to return servicemen "to civilian life" and "face the issues." Indeed, anything else was likely to be rejected by those in uniform. It was imperative that young people who had enlisted before being trained for work or whose education had been interrupted by service should be helped "to get a foothold in civil life." Under the scheme envisaged, the determining factor in making a grant would be its effectiveness in promoting re-establishment based on individual need.

On 1 October 1941, with about 2,000 persons per month now leaving the forces, the order, as finally approved, was issued, pursuant to the War Appropriation Act, 1941, and the versatile and sweeping War Measures Act, as PC 7633, the Post-Discharge Re-establishment Order.[64] In a fundamental break with what had been done at the end of the Great War, when the only universal benefit had been the cash gratuity, the rehabilitation benefits now provided applied theoretically to everyone who served. Specifically, PC 7633 provided out-of-work benefits "to those capable of and available for work but unable to obtain suitable employment," and a variety of grants: to those pursuing technical and vocational training; to those temporarily incapacitated and unable to work or take training; to those "awaiting returns' from agriculture or other individual enterprise; and to those "resuming interrupted education."[65] These benefits would be available following the expiry of the rehabilitation grant of thirty days' pay and allowances already in effect, and war service would be counted for unemployment insurance benefits effective 1 July 1941. The weekly maximum training benefit payable under PC 7633 was nine dollars (the basic pay of an army private) for a single man and thirteen dollars for a married man. These sums were less than the highest payments available under unemployment insurance but accorded with allowances being paid under the War Emergency Training Programme and were purposely set to be "less attractive than wage and salary rates so as to avoid undue expectation of higher rewards on completion of training" and to attract only those genuinely interested in improving themselves.[66] The out-of-work benefit and grant support to be paid to an individual (except for interrupted education) was limited to the period of service to a maximum of fifty-two weeks, and the out-of-work benefit was payable only within eighteen months of discharge.

Within this framework, an ex-serviceman who could not find a job would be supported by the out-of-work benefit until he found work. If his new job was in the category of insurable employment, he would then become eligible for unemployment insurance after fifteen weeks of work in any twelve-month period, and his military service would be taken into account in calculating his benefit (and the Unemployment Insurance Commission reimbursed accordingly). In sum, PC 7633 offered a flexible benefit package that covered many contingencies and gave a boost to recruitment by offering the prospect of a smooth return to civilian life when the war was won. Thanks to the terms of their enlistment, moreover, the advantages on offer would apply to women who went into uniform. In 1942 the future prospects of those serving were made even brighter when Parliament, building on the achievement of PC 7633, passed the Reinstatement in Civil Employment Act, which, to the great satisfaction of the Legion, guaranteed those who gave up their jobs in order to enlist the right to return to their former employment under conditions that would have applied had they not signed up.[67]

In a press statement, Mackenzie said that the purpose of the government's post-discharge plan was "to promote ... orderly re-establishment in civil life" and that PC 7633 was "a basic measure of far-reaching importance in connection with the future welfare of thousands of young sailors, soldiers, and airmen."[68] The government's "primary task" was "to reinstate in and secure employment for men discharged during the war and later upon general demobilization." The "essential basis of rehabilitation" was a job, but emergency assistance was also needed "to avoid any loss of morale, through idleness." Whereas the war service gratuity paid out at the end of the Great War had "been uneconomic both to the individual and the state," Canada's new program was "directly related to employment and security." In a letter the same day he told J.E. Atkinson, publisher of the *Toronto Daily Star*, that Canada was the "first country in the world to adopt any such comprehensive programme for demobilization," and that in comparison with "the non-constructive war service gratuity" paid out at the end of the 1914–1918 conflict, PC 7633 marked "a great stride forward."[69] "On the negative side," he wrote (here was evidence of underlying caution), "this Order-in-Council provides every discharged man with security, but on the positive side, it not only provides an incentive to seek for employment but affords the opportunity for a man to improve his employability through training and education. This is going to be particularly valuable in the case of young men who interrupted their educational courses."

The preliminary response of the Canadian Legion to PC7633 noted that it appeared to incorporate "new principles decidedly in advance of those applying following the last war" in that all might benefit from it, "whether disabled or otherwise."[70] While reserving judgment on the actual payments to be made and making plain that it did not accept that the plan substituted for the gratuity paid following the Great War, the Legion nevertheless commended the minister and his officials on the action taken. As for the Unemployment Insurance Commission, it promised cooperation but stood firm in the view that a preferable outcome would have been a plan through which "the actual cost of benefits due to war services" would be "paid out of a special vote."[71] "We say this," MacNamara explained to McDonald on 6 October, "because ... the Government and the general body of employers and employees who are contributing to the Unemployment Insurance Fund, would know that the actual cost of bringing the Armed Forces into insurable employment in the matter of paying benefits was being paid out of consolidated revenue rather than out of the Unemployment Insurance Fund. The Unemployment Insurance Commission would not be in the position of having to prove that such was the case, which otherwise may be necessary. A further advantage would be that the money required for paying benefits would come out of the appropriations for the years in which the benefits were actually paid."

On 20 October, Woods issued regulations under PC7633 and made known to the circularized officials that application forms and copies of an information leaflet that had been prepared would be distributed soon.[72] Noting that officials would no doubt be asked why the benefits of the order applied only to those discharged after 1 July 1941, he explained the reasoning behind the starting date as follows:

1 The primary object of the Order was to make the benefits of Unemployment Insurance available to men in the Services on the same basis as to other citizens, and the Unemployment Insurance Act only became effective on July 1, 1941
2 Although 30,000 men had been discharged from the Army on

July 1, 1941, only a few hundred of them were recorded as unemployed. One is forced to the conclusion that by far the greatest majority of them have been absorbed as the result of war activity and, for the most part, in insurable employment.

3 This [PC7633] was designed as a post-war measure to meet the great problem at the time of general demobilisation. The service of the great majority of those who have been discharged is fairly short and comparatively uneventful. 30% of those discharged up to July 1st last had served less than ninety days, and over 60% or 18,000 less than six months. Of this group of 18,000, only 106 served Overseas.

Acknowledging the additional burden of administration that PC7633 would bring to district offices, Woods held out the possibility of additional staff if experience showed this to be necessary. In fact, rehabilitation administration would occupy more and more of the resources of DPNH as time went on, and Woods's influence grew accordingly. With this first set of instructions under PC7633, he was well launched into the work that would occupy him for the remainder of his public service career and make him one of the shapers of postwar Canada. In November and December 1941, he and England crossed the country to explain to provincial premiers and university heads the government's new plans for veterans.[73] By nature quiet, dutiful, and unassuming, Woods is now mainly forgotten, but he emerged after 1941 as one of the country's most influential mandarins. When McDonald died in Banff on 2 September 1943, Woods succeeded him as chairman of the GACDR, which reported to the government on 25 September in a document that concisely summarized its 1940–43 work.[74] With this job done, England retired as executive secretary of the group. In 1943 he published, with Macmillan Toronto, *Discharged: A Commentary on Civil Re-establishment of Veterans in Canada* (royalties went to the War Amputations of Canada).[75] His book gave an inside look at the big plans that Mackenzie and Woods, working closely together, were now making operational.

The realization of PC7633 was without doubt a considerable personal achievement for the tight network of officials whose vision of the future it embodied, but their success hinged on the government's need to meet the immediate problem of preventing the introduction of unemployment insurance from affecting recruitment for the armed forces adversely. Remembering well what had happened at the end of the Great War,

Mackenzie King and his ministers had good reason to begin demobilization and re-establishment planning early on in the war that began in 1939, but the specific issue that arose in relation to unemployment insurance forced the government's hand. One government action had the unintended consequence of requiring another (a well-known phenomenon in the history of the Canadian welfare state). In effect, the architects of PC 7633 were able to lever the resolution of the problem posed by unemployment insurance administration into a larger program of benefits that comprehensively addressed the needs that one day would come with mass demobilization. Yet, although PC 7633 opened the door to sizable government spending, the thinking behind it was decidedly conservative (as was the introduction of the "due to service" principle in relation to pensions). The purpose was to spend substantial sums of public money purposefully in the short run to prevent dependency on government in the long term (the work of the Veterans' Assistance Commission was the obvious model). Moreover, while everyone in uniform would be covered by PC 7633 – a strong selling point – not everyone would actually benefit. To get the out-of-work benefit, an individual had to be unemployed; to get the unemployment insurance benefit required at least fifteen weeks of insurable employment; and to get support for training required official approval. At its core, the new program gave priority to cultivating the work ethic and individual responsibility while giving officialdom a strong directive role, thereby avoiding what were thought of as the failings of the no-questions-asked Great War gratuity scheme. While the government would not guarantee veterans work, it would, in the spirit of the Veterans' Assistance Commission of the 1930s, help them get back to work. In short, it would provide "opportunity with security" – a phrase later used by Woods that harked back to his days as a young man in the enterprising Prairie West.[76]

From Ottawa's perspective, this approach had many advantages. The benefits to be provided would show the government's solicitude for those who were enlisting, but would be limited in duration and predictable in cost, and while constituting an investment in the young that commanded widespread public support and promised future returns both individually and collectively, it could be calibrated so to avoid moral hazard, – the undermining of the will to work through the disruption of the market economy (the Great War gratuity scheme was the example to be avoided). Veterans would be helped – but in order to help themselves. This was the Canadian way: enterprise, sturdy self-reliance, and independence; collective action would reinforce individualism. For the government, the scheme launched in PC 7633 also had the advantage of being administered in the first instance for those leaving the military while the war was in progress. This would allow for refinements and improvements to be made in the system before it had to be applied en masse once the war was over. Lessons could be learned and changes made as required – a process facilitated by the decision to proceed by executive fiat. "One of the basic reasons that the General Advisory Committee recommended action by means of Order-in-Council rather than by act of Parliament at this time," McDonald told MacNamara on 16 October 1941, "was that they felt that the whole scheme should be regarded as developmental in character and that any changes or improvements should be facilitated before it was crystallized into final form by actual legislation."[77] Above all perhaps, PC 7633 gave the government a credible means to head off the radical view that those who enlisted should remain in uniform and on the government payroll until they could go directly to civilian jobs. By making an early and innovative but limited commitment, Ottawa secured the high ground in a developing debate over veterans that had explosive potential.

In April 1942 Woods sent Mackenzie an extract from a letter that a nineteen-year-old member of the RCAF serving overseas had written to his father in Montreal. "The boys seem sceptical," this airman wrote, "that the Government will do anything for them except that they will supply them with a good suit and give them their best wishes. You cannot blame them for taking that stand for the present anyway, for they have only to look back and see what the results were in the last war."[78] The government's answer to this scepticism was PC 7633, which transformed veterans' benefits in Canada and gave DPNH and its officials, Woods in particular, a new lease on life. The drafters of PC 7633 would not have thought of themselves as social engineers, but in truth that is what they were.

4 Program Development

In 1942 a scheme of land settlement was added to the multiple benefits provided by PC 7633. In the drafting process, the failings of the soldier settlement opportunity provided for selected Great War veterans were kept front and centre. After its bumpy start in the early 1920s, the soldier settler project had faced continued difficulty, a situation compounded by the advent of the Great Depression and the fact that 70 per cent of the establishments were in the hard-hit Prairie West.[1] The ironic result was more and more spending by Ottawa to rescue a plan designed to promote financial independence. To 31 March 1940, not counting expenditures under the Farmers' Creditors Arrangements Act, 1934, debt relief in connection with soldier settlement had cost the federal government $52,756,982, or 48.4 per cent, of the $109,034,816 advanced under the program (total recoveries a year later were $65,640,518). These numbers were indicative of a heavy human toll. As of 31 March 1941, of the 24,793 veterans who had become soldier settlers (not including 224 First Nations people who also had qualified), 2,750 had paid off their loans and obtained title, 884 had sold their equities, and 8,118 were still on the land but not free and clear. The remainder – 13,041 – had either given up of their own accord or been driven off the land through foreclosure. Of those left on the land but still in debt at the end of 1940, 976 had an equity stake in their properties of less than 25 per cent, the average for this group being 16 per cent. This was a decidedly mixed record and was recognized as such within the government, which had paid a heavy financial and administrative price for an initiative that had been launched with such high hopes. If soldier settlement had brought success to some, its record was also one of foreclosure, broken dreams, and shattered lives.

"My husband ... and I," the wife of one Alberta settler told Mackenzie in 1944, "were established on a lovely farm near Stettler in 1919. We worked hard and tried to meet our payment (We managed the taxes almost to the last), but towards the last few years, when farm conditions were so bad, payments fell woefully behind. Two thousand dollars was paid, but $2,000.00 was still owing ... and lawyers threatened and worried us so that in 1940 my husband took a job in a Hotel to try and meet our

Gordon Murchison, appointed director of soldier settlement, 1938; served as director of the Veterans' Land Act, 1942–47 (Schull, *Veneration for Valour*, 69)

obligations ... I stayed on the farm with the child, had a cow and chickens, and we rented the land out. We rented a house for the winter near his work. Then, we were forced to give up our home of twenty-two years, all the work of our youth and old age home because we could not meet the payments and took a job to do it. We kept a decent place and my husband does not drink. At present he is in the Vets guard of Canada. The farm is in the hands of renters which are turning the place into a shamble, slops pitched out of the kitchen window, trees cut down, the place makes me shudder now."[2] This painful testimonial went to the heart of the troubled soldier settler experience. Obviously, as in so many other aspects of rehabilitation planning, much could be learned from the mistakes of the past.

The task of ensuring a better outcome for veterans of the current war now fell to the land settlement subcommittee of the GACDR, which was chaired by Woods, who had, of course, started his own career in veterans' affairs working on the Prairies in soldier settlement administration. The other members of the committee were drawn from the ranks of government and from businesses with a stake in settlement and agriculture. The leading member of the committee was Gordon Murchison, who had been director of soldier settlement since 1 March 1938. Murchison had been born on a farm at Ripley, Huron County, Ontario, on 12 November 1889.[3] He left school at age 14 when his father died and, beginning in 1909, homesteaded in the Kindersley district of Saskatchewan. He enlisted in the CEF at Valcartier, Quebec, on 21 September 1914, describing his "Trade or Calling" as that of telegraph operator.[4] He went overseas with the 5th

Canadian Infantry Battalion, was injured while on training in England, joined the 19th Alberta Dragoons, Canadian Cavalry Brigade, in France on 13 December 1915, and remained in the field with that regiment until 13 February 1918. Medically unfit for further service, he left the army in London, Ontario, on 14 August 1918 with the rank of corporal. On his discharge certificate it was noted that he had been wounded at the Somme on 27 August 1916 and at Passchendaele on 12 November 1917. Murchison left the military with a slight limp, with ankles that were painful, and with feet that were "aggravated by wet, cold weather" and that swelled up and throbbed.[5] He passed the civil service examination grade C in February 1919 in Regina and on 22 July applied for the position of loan inspector with the board that was now busily administering the Soldier Settlement Act.

In his letter of application, Murchison wrote that he had "personally experienced all the trials and hardships of homesteading and farm developing," had been in debt, knew "the follies of overloading," and could "distinguish between good land and bad."[6] "I have studied the Returned Soldier problem," he ventured, "and realize that the successful back-to-the-land movement is going to mean the making of thousands of returned men. While desiring to give a Soldier all possible assistance in regards to recommending his loan, I fully realize that the future administration of the Soldier Settlement Act can only be successful if Inspectors are very careful in the first place to see that the Government is getting gilt-edged security for every dollar expended. I feel quite safe in stating that no sentimental reasons can affect my judgement of a parcel of land or influence any recommendations that I may make." In 1931, having risen through the administrative ranks of soldier settlement, Murchison went to work for the Canadian Farm Loan Board and remained with this agency until his appointment as director of soldier settlement (the Soldier Settlement Board had been abolished in 1930 in favour of administration headed by a director). In the course of a long and busy career that had carried him back and forth across the country, he had acquired an encyclopedic knowledge of Canadian land use and of farm and small business practice. He was an experienced and tough-minded public servant with a big appetite for work and a reputation for having a "rather uncompromising mentality."[7]

One plan considered but quickly dismissed by the land settlement subcommittee of the GACDR came from its chairman, Colonel A Fortescue Duguid of the army's historical section. (In 1938 he had published the first volume of a projected history of the CEF.) Duguid proposed the setting up of a thousand or more "voluntary community settlements or villages" across the country, each of which would be home to 100 to 200 families, have 500 to 3,000 acres of land, and be operated "on a co-operative communal basis (not Communistic)."⁸ This proposal, a working group of the subcommittee reported, was "basically unsound." When it came to running farms or smallholdings, "the average Canadian" was "essentially an individualist."⁹ The typical Canadian of British stock, the Toronto district superintendent of soldier settlement told Murchison, was "too much of an individualist to willingly submit to sharing his labour; his possessions; his leisure and his home life on a wholesale basis."¹⁰ To make communal living work, those involved had to be either "deeply religious" and with "unquestioning faith in their leaders" or else "zealous fanatics of some Ism." Canadians were neither, and Duguid's plan was clearly impractical.

As might be expected, the experienced Murchison, a plain man of business well placed to shape events, needed no convincing about any of this. His own ideas about what a new land settlement scheme should look like were set out in a letter to Woods on 13 May 1940.¹¹ It would be "economically unsound," he wrote, to require a settler to pay interest on a debt equal to or greater than the value of his land. From "a national standpoint," it would be better to have a plan that stressed "the home factor in relation to land utilization" over commercial farming. Ideally, a new settlement scheme should meet the requirements of full-time farmers, the many smallholders in the country who combined farming with other employment, and tenant farmers. In a twenty-three page double-spaced memorandum, dated 6 July 1940 and entitled "Land Settlement in Relation to Problems of Demobilization and Rehabilitation,"¹² Murchison argued that the soldier settlement scheme had from the outset failed to acknowledge financial reality by allowing land to be capitalized at up to 150 per ent of its value, with farmers indebted accordingly. For a land scheme to work, individual debt would have to be kept within "the sound range proven over and over again in land credit operations." Likewise, account would have to be taken of the many variations in Canada of "how a home on the land" related to the "general scheme of life."

To illustrate possibilities, Murchison provided details of six plans that would meet his criteria while accommodating 25,000 settlers at one-third of the capital cost of soldier settlement. In each case, strict purchase, payment, and subsidy limits would be set and priority given to "a conception of land settlement" that emphasized "home use and family job factors." Land settlement would reverse the disturbing trend of rural depopulation and would allow some of the funds being spent on urban relief to be put to more productive use. This would be "good public business" for the country. "It is not ... a matter of argument," he stated, "as to whether

Canada can afford land settlement but ... whether Canada can afford to neglect land settlement." A well-conceived and well-administered program of land settlement held the promise of "a healthy way for people to live, to feel secure against want, to raise families of healthy children, and by thrift, honesty and hard work earn the respect and confidence of fellow citizens." Canada had "a large number of land-hungry people," and Canadians lived in a "land-hungry world."

On 3 April 1941 the Sub-Committee on Land Settlement considered a memorandum from Murchison, and on 30 May and again on 4 June he appeared before the House of Commons Special Committee on the Pension Act and the War Veterans' Allowance Act.[13] When the subcommittee eventually reported, it was his thinking (and language) that dominated.[14] The subcommittee found that there was "a definite place" for land settlement in Canada's rehabilitation program, that state assistance would be required to make this work, and that the key to success was to keep "the cost per unit of settlement ... within reasonable limits." It would be "unsound" to make "large state loans to establish untried or partially experienced settlers on fully equipped commercial farms." Instead, the "home factor" should be given priority. This meant a concentration on properties on which families would be self-supporting and on smallholdings, where farming could be combined with external employment. The subcommittee likewise advanced some working principles, all of them in keeping with the ideas put forward by Murchison. These called for low unit costs, sound debt arrangements, stress on the "home factor" rather than on "'going concern' farming," a combination of subsidies and loans, and flexibility in relation to choice of settlers, acquisition of properties, and financial arrangements.

On 3 October 1941, Mackenzie requested that a bill be drafted on the basis of the subcommittee's report, and on 22 December Murchison sent the proposed legislation to Mines and Resources Minister T.A. Crerar.[15] In doing so, he told the minister that a survey done in cooperation with the Bureau of Statistics showed a total of about 70,000 farms in Canada where the owner was over age sixty and on which no male relatives over fourteen were living. This pointed to the ready availability of properties for settlement within the cost limits envisaged in the draft legislation. The next step came on 20 April 1942, when Mackenzie moved a resolution preliminary to the introduction of the bill.[16] Having surveyed the history of soldier settlement, he highlighted "three vital differences" in the scheme embodied in the bill about to be introduced.[17] Whereas soldier settlement had favoured full-time farming, the new legislation would "assist men in taking up smallholdings where the veteran will make his

PROGRAM DEVELOPMENT   93

home and derive a substantial portion of his income from employment apart from his cultivation of the land." Again, whereas the soldier settlement scheme had covered veterans who had served in allied forces, the benefit now proposed would be confined to individuals domiciled in Canada at the time of enlistment. Third, and most important, no recipient of assistance would "be encouraged or permitted to assume an uneconomic and unbearable burden of debt." In the same spirit, the legislation also made provision for training in farm methods. Analysis of 200,000 occupational history forms incorporating data processed to 31 October 1941, the minister explained, showed that of 17,588 navy enlistees, 1,042, or 5.9 per cent, wanted to farm after their service. For the army, the equivalent figures were 136,913 and 29,067 (21.2%), and for the air force 46,225 and 3,343 (7.2%). Over the three forces the average was 16.7 per cent. The new program would have as its administrative head a director who would be authorized "to buy or acquire land and farm property" to be vested in him "as a corporation sole."[18]

The next day the bill, numbered 65, was introduced and given first reading.[19] Second reading followed on 23 April,[20] whereupon the legislation was referred to another special committee. It had fifteen members (Mackenzie was one of them), was chaired by Cyrus Macmillan, met from 30 April to 16 July, and produced five reports.[21] Its *Minutes of Proceedings and Evidence* were published in English (500 copies) and French (200 copies) in eleven instalments.[22] In its submission to the special committee, the Canadian Legion commended the government for its land settlement initiative but argued that it should commit in advance to come to the rescue of the project should adverse market conditions arise. "Never again," the Legion asserted, "must we allow veteran settlers to buy high and sell low without some adequate and swift means of adjustment, should debt again begin to pile up."[23] Unfortunately for the Great War soldier settlers, assistance had been slow in coming "and often as a result of political pressure."[24] This experience must not be repeated. The Legion also called for involvement by the dominion housing authorities and for the expansion of the envisaged scheme to include establishment in fishing operations (here its voice was heard). On 20 July, in committee of the whole, the Commons considered bill 65, as amended by the special committee, and third reading immediately followed. On 1 August, now incorporating amendments made during Senate consideration,[25] the bill was given assent.

Entitled "An Act to Assist War Veterans to Settle upon the Land," cited as "The Veterans' Land Act, 1942," and commonly referred to as the VLA, the statute had a lengthy preamble, thirty-eight sections, and a schedule that fixed the terms of the affidavit to be sworn by vendors of land.[26] On

25 November, Murchison added the title "VLA director" to his existing title, "director of soldier settlement." Like Woods, he had found a new mission in life that would occupy him well into the future. The VLA mixed loans and subsidies and was another discretionary benefit rather than an entitlement. Under its terms, a successful applicant for a property had to make a down payment of 10 per cent of the cost of "land and improvements and building materials" to a maximum value of $3,600. In addition, up to $1,200 could be lent to an individual to cover the cost of farm equipment and livestock. Interest on loans was set at 3.5 per cent, and principal and interest payments were to be made over twenty-five years. The debt incurred by an individual could not exceed two-thirds of the cost of the land acquired or, assuming maximum allowable costs ($4,800), 50 per cent of the entire enterprise. For its part, the government was committed to grants equal to one-third of the cost of the land acquired by an individual (minus the 10 per cent down payment) and the full cost of equipment and stock within the $1,200 limit. Section 34 of the act provided for the appointment of regional committees to advise on the acquisition of land by the VLA administration and the selection of veterans to be assisted. Under section 7, a veteran who wanted to re-establish as a fisherman could be assisted in the purchase of fishing equipment. This, Mackenzie explained in going over the amendments made by the special committee, did not contradict "the general policy of rural settlement and rural home ownership, envisaged by the Act"[27] To be eligible for the VLA benefit, a veteran who had served only in Canada would need to have been in uniform for a minimum of twelve months.

Title to a property acquired by a veteran under the VLA – here was a powerful work incentive – remained with the director and could not be transferred or conveyed during the first ten years of the agreement. This meant that the government's grant towards the purchase of land would be held back until a veteran had proved himself under contract. In the event that a veteran failed to live up to an agreement, provision was made for foreclosure. Veterans who already owned farms qualified for loans under the VLA, but again within tight limits. When the bill was being drafted, Murchison objected to justifying the grants to be made by the government on the grounds of "national gratitude to men who have risked their lives in the service of the State." This, he argued, was not measurable in terms of the bill but might lay the foundation "for a grant of some kind by all those who served."[28] Crucially, as its title clearly stated, the VLA was primarily a land rather than a housing act. The GACDR Sub-Committee on Land Settlement had been asked to consider the matter of urban housing policy for veterans, but had decided to leave this agenda item for the attention of the administrator of the 1938 National Housing Act. If PC7633 promised training rather than jobs, the VLA emphasized smallholding and farming over housing. Recognizing that the effect might be to create inequality between urban-dwelling veterans and VLA smallholders living nearby and looking forward to a government subsidy in return for good performance, England urged in April 1942 that steps be taken to explore the possibility of a veterans' urban-housing plan.[29] Woods backed this idea and wanted a GACDR subcommittee on urban housing appointed, but this did not happen, and it constituted a planning omission that would have big consequences later on.[30] The key architects of Canada's program for Second World War veterans recognized the importance of having a housing policy tailored specifically to ex-service needs, but except for the housing that came with land provided under the VLA, Ottawa did not at this stage act on this understanding. In the housing market, veterans would have to rely on the programs available to Canadians generally. If there was no guarantee of jobs for those serving, there was no guarantee of housing either.

On 8 December 1942, regulations for the making of loans were approved and the same month VLA *Handbook No. 1* was issued. This made known that settlement operations would be kept on a small scale while the war was in progress; there was now, it was explained, ready employment for those being discharged from the armed forces, while required building materials were needed for war use and the manufacture of farm machinery was restricted. This approach also acknowledged the importance of not putting those serving overseas "at a disadvantage in participating in the benefits of the Act."[31] In the first phase of VLA administration, a head office was opened in Ottawa, and seven district and thirty-two regional offices were established across the country. Each district office was headed by a district superintendent, and the regional offices were headed by regional supervisors, who worked with the advisory committees. The latter provided an outlet for public service in wartime while reassuring local elites about the effects of a government initiative with the potential for broad social change. A veteran applied to the program through the regional office and was interviewed there (along with his spouse, if married) by the advisory committee.

In January and February 1943, Murchison toured Great Britain to build a contact network within the forces for the program and to explain its terms at a series of informal meetings. He reported a high level of interest among the men on active service in what he had to say, a demand for easily understood information about the VLA, and support for the policy of "restricted settlement" until hostilities ended.[32] In practice, this policy limited settlement to disabled veterans and to those facing "exceptional circumstances."[33] For the moment, the main work of the VLA administration was banking land to be held in reserve for those serving overseas. To 31 March 1944, 51,372 acres had been acquired for agricultural settlement at an average cost of about $18 per acre.[34] To the same date, appraisal had been completed on 115 blocks or parcels of land suitable for smallholding settlement, 60 had been approved for purchase, and 28 actually acquired, at an average cost of $135 per acre. On 14 October 1943, with land values on the rise in the country, the VLA limit for the purchase of a property by a qualified veteran was increased, by PC 7990, from $3,600 to $4,800 (in May 1945 it was bumped up again, to $6,000). In the fall of 1943 also, having established a farm equipment division, the VLA administration made an agreement with manufacturers for delivery, in 1945, of enough agricultural machinery to establish 7,000 veterans. At the same time, yet another VLA division, this one devoted to building supplies and construction, was busy planning for the 1945 construction of 3,000 houses, mostly on smallholdings. Its work involved the making of surveys, the preparation of architectural plans, and the acquisition of construction materials.

To 31 March 1944, 736 ex-servicemen had sought support under the VLA, and 322 of their applications had been considered by advisory committees. Of the latter group, 151 were ruled qualified and 92 unqualified, with 79 cases still pending. Of the 151 applicants approved at the committee level, 4 were deemed qualified for full-time farming, 102 for smallholdings, and 3 for commercial fishing. Out of this group, 58 had actually applied for establishment on a property, and of these 34 had been approved and 15 declined, leaving 9 pending. To the same date in 1944, the cost of farming establishments had averaged $2,822 and that of smallholdings $2,433; both figures were well within VLA limits.

The land acquired by the VLA administration in the first phase of its operations included hundreds of properties in British Columbia owned by dispossessed Japanese Canadians. Following Japan's attack on Pearl Harbor on 7 December 1941, anti-Japanese sentiment (which had a long history in the Pacific province) intensified, and pressure on the dominion government to act grew to fever pitch. In response, in February 1942, Ottawa ordered the removal of all Japanese Canadians from a protected zone along the British Columbia coast. The leading cabinet spokesman for this action was Mackenzie, who now became the hammer of the Japanese Canadian minority in the province. A small number of Japanese Canadians were sent to internment camps, but the majority were assembled at Hastings Park in Vancouver and then dispersed by the British Columbia Security Commission, the administering agency, to various destinations in the interior of the province. They were said to have been "evacuated" in their own interest, but in January 1943, after appraisals had been completed, the sale of their vacated properties, which were being administered by the secretary of state in his capacity as custodian of enemy property, was authorized by order-in-council. Ostensibly, the properties were sold to bring them, in the absence of their owners, "under control of competent authority"[35] and to provide for the payment of local taxes, but behind this was the larger agenda – personified by Mackenzie – of dispossessing the Japanese Canadians once and for all and getting the country ready for postwar re-establishment. In the event, 7,086 parcels of real and personal property belonging to Japanese Canadians were sold by the Custodian of Enemy Property for $2,591,456, and included in this sale were more than 700 properties transferred for VLA use. Initially, the director of the VLA offered the custodian $750,000 for 768 Japanese Canadian properties valued at $867,021 by soldier settler appraisers. This price was refused, but in June 1943 agreement was reached on a price of $850,000. A second deal between the parties followed in November 1943, involving twelve parcels of land on the mainland and thirty-three on Vancouver Island and the Gulf Islands. Ultimately, though, because of difficulties with some titles, the actual number of properties acquired by the director of the VLA was 741 and the price paid to the custodian $792,265. Just as the advent of soldier settlement had cost First Nations dearly in terms of land, the advance of the VLA was linked to yet another exceptional transfer of assets from an embattled minority.

One of the properties acquired in British Columbia by the director of the VLA was the farm of soldier settler Zennosuke Inouye. In the dispersal of the Japanese Canadians, no exception was made for those who had served in the Great War, and one veteran caught up in the government sweep is said to have thrown his medals into the Skeena River in disgust. Inouye was part of a minority within a minority within a minority: Japanese Canadian, veteran, and soldier settler (four other Japanese Canadian soldier settlers in the province also saw their land pass into VLA hands). In 1941 he was running a going concern, was well known and respected in his neighbourhood, and had served for many years as president of the Surrey Berry Growers' Co-operative Association (producers of Sovereign Brand strawberries and jam berries). He was still paying off his loan from the government, but unlike many other soldier settlers, he had survived the Great Depression, was still on the land he had acquired in 1920, and was financially afloat. In 1938, in an unregistered transaction, he had sold approximately ten acres of his property to Kahichi Hori, another farmer, for $600. Then, on 9 May 1942, with relocation pending, he leased his own part of the original farm to Albert John Jones, Denzil Lester Jones, and Dennis Cecil Jones for one year, starting 9 May 1942, with an option to extend the lease for another year. For their part, the Jones brothers agreed to a yearly rental of $1,000. Of this amount, $750 would go to Inouye on the execution of the lease, and the remaining $250 would be used to cover municipal taxes owing during the lease and to make payment on Inouye's debt as a soldier settler.

Many Japanese Canadian owners made lease arrangements of this kind before their relocation, a process that took many months to complete. But their efforts to protect themselves were soon superseded by Ottawa's decision to sell their properties compulsorily. In Inouye's case, an appraisal of his property was completed in July 1942, and the property turned over to the director of the VLA effective 1 January 1943 for $3,908. When legal fees of $15, tax arrears of $180.19, a balance of $1,738.56 in soldier settlement debt, and a transfer of $730 to Kahichi Hori were deducted, Inouye was left with a credit of $1,244.25. His chattels were listed in an inventory he signed on 17 September 1942. These were disposed of variously by the custodian. Some were bought by Donald Bain, to whom the director of the VLA leased the land on 29 April 1943 after the lease to the Jones brothers expired. Others were sold at public auction in September 1944. Various chattels left with Frank Smith – "a very good and kind neighbor during all the time I have been living at Surrey" – were eventually forwarded to Inouye in exile.[36] On 27 September 1944, after the auction of his chattels, the custodian's office sent Inouye a list of personal effects that had been put in storage in New Westminster, where they would remain until claimed. When the proceeds of the sale of his chattels and other adjustments were taken into account, he was left with a balance with the custodian of $2,160.28 (as of 30 January 1946). For a man whose life since the end of the Great War had been that of an independent proprietor, he had fallen far and fallen fast and was now subject to tight control by the Canadian state. By an extraordinary turn of events, land sold by the Government of Canada to re-establish a veteran of one war had been seized from him in connection with efforts to accommodate the veterans of another war.

Before being scattered, the Inouyes had a photograph taken. It showed a family that exemplified everything that soldier settlement had hoped to achieve, but in the unforgiving circumstances of war their record of accomplishment was to no avail. From the assembly point at Hastings

The Inouye family in 1942. Back row (left to right): sons Arthur Rizo, Robert Zenso, and Tom Futari; front row (left to right): daughters Beverley (Kiyoko), parents Hatsuno and Zennosuke, and daughter Mary (Yasuko) (Courtesy of Beverley Inouye)

Park, Vancouver, Zennosuke (evacuee registration no. 03243), his wife Hatsuno, and their daughters Beverley (Kiyoko) and Mary (Yasuko) were sent to the small town of Kaslo, on the west side of Kootenay Lake, in the southeast interior of the province. The Inouye sons – Arthur, Robert, and Tom, who were twenty-one, nineteen, and seventeen, respectively, and already self-supporting – went to Vernon, where they worked on the fruit farm of R.H. Macdonald. In Kaslo, the Inouyes lived in one room, and Zennosuke worked as a caretaker for the British Columbia Security Commission, which favoured veterans for employment at resettlement locations. From this unexpected destination, always the fighter, he began a prolonged campaign to get his land back. In the spring of 1943, he was one of fifteen evacuees reported upon by Royal Canadian Mounted Police intelligence in connection with a survey, directed by Dr Kozo Shimotakahara, of Japanese Canadian property owners to determine whether they actually wanted to sell their properties. In July 1943, Inouye told the Vancouver office of the custodian that it was "absurd to sell the property of one returned soldier" to give to another returned soldier; the property of returned soldiers should be "excluded from the ordinary Japanese property."[37] In reply, F.G. Shears, director of the Vancouver office, wrote that while personally he could appreciate Inouye's "feelings in this matter," it was necessary "for the Custodian's policy to be administered in a uniform manner relating to all persons of the Japanese race, the situation in the present war not being analogous to that obtaining in the last."[38] He assured Inouye that the proceeds of his farm would be made available to him and noted that VLA officials "would be the proper body to which application might be made for consideration in regard to your retaining this property on the grounds which you mention in your letter"; the custodian's office wished "to administer all properties under our control in the best manner possible in conformity with the broad policy which must of necessity be adopted in the present circumstances." Inouye, it turned out, was not deterred.

While the energetic Murchison was pushing forward the administration of the VLA, Woods and his associates, operating out of the Daly Building in Ottawa, were busy expanding and refining policy under PC7633 and recruiting additional staff. For administrative convenience the benefits on offer were numbered 1 to 6, as follows: 1, the out-of-work payment; 2, the grant for vocational or technical training; 3, the awaiting-returns grant for those engaged in agriculture or other individual enterprise; 4, the grant to those temporarily incapacitated and therefore unable to work or take training; 5, the grant to those resuming interrupted education; and 6, the unemployment insurance contribution. Forms were quickly devised to cover the applications as required; the combined training and out-of-work application form, known as WD1, began a numerical sequence (WD2 being an information leaflet, WD3 the form used by district offices for recording an individual's rehabilitation benefits, etc.), thus facilitating orderly record keeping. Data accumulated in the region was sent to Ottawa and coded there on cards.[39] To qualify for the out-of-work benefit, an applicant had to be "capable of and available for work but unable to obtain suitable employment."[40] Applications were considered by district rehabilitation boards, each of which brought together the district administrator, the district welfare officer, a departmental medical officer (if needed in a particular case), and an "outside person with experience in vocational guidance and technical training."[41] The board could authorize payment of the out-of-work benefit for one to four weeks at a time and could order an applicant to take vocational training in order to qualify. Continuing payment was subject to further review by the board, and monthly progress reports were required for those in training. Moreover – and this provision left no doubt about the commanding role of officialdom – discretion rested with the minister of pensions and national health to "refrain from authorizing any payment, ... approve an application previously declined, or rescind or amend approval formerly made."[42] An individual's refusal to take training or his abandonment of a course in progress constituted "sufficient cause" for a board to decline the out-of-work benefit.[43] Boards were instructed to make training available through the War Emergency Training Programme or through private employers, as arranged. They were told to favour training likely to lead to permanent employment over training for jobs that would disappear with the war. In the case of a man engaged in agriculture who applied for the awaiting-returns grant, the board was to base its decision on individual need, "having regard to any other income and perquisites from the property," and be guided by an investigative report from a soldier settler supervisor.[44]

Given the pivotal role mapped out for the rehabilitation boards, Woods gave priority to making them operational. When he heard that the district administrator in Montreal was planning to send a representative to the district rehabilitation board (on the assumption that it was external to DPNH), he was quick to correct this misapprehension. "The Rehabilitation Board," he wrote, "is your Board, and as a District Administrator you are required to direct the activities of it."[45] In the same vein, having heard from the acting district administrator in Halifax that the board there was complete, Woods gave him this direction regarding the proper relationship between welfare officers and other district officials under the new dispensation: "It is not the intention to isolate this great problem of rehabilitation in a water-tight compartment under the Welfare Officer. He has neither the experience, the time, nor the staff to do this. It is essential that the District Administrator preside at the meetings and direct the policy under this new Order, and that the staff under him become familiar with the problem of rehabilitation, so that when the time of demobilization arrives they will be trained in the technique that is necessary and it will be merely a question of adding additional staff."[46]

On 24 January 1942, having toured the country with England to drum up support for the new program from provincial governments and other interested parties and to meet with welfare officers and other departmental staff, Woods issued a cautionary circular to district officials.[47] He began by stating frankly that in some districts he and England had found "a lack of clear appreciation of the intent" of PC 7633. As its name stated, it was "a re-establishment measure." Accordingly, money spent under its aegis should be directed to this purpose, that is to say, it should "represent a contribution towards the discharged man's rehabilitation." PC7633 had been designed to overcome the "economic handicaps" a discharged man suffered through "dislocation from private life" and to give him a skill if he needed one to get to work. The order was not intended to provide for the maintenance "by the Dominion Pension authorities" of a physically fit ex-serviceman unfit for work. PC7633 would not be administered "in a narrow or parsimonious way," but it was important to remember that if an individual was paid the out-of-work benefit "for any appreciable length of time," he would "be worse off as a result." The order must not therefore "be permitted to degenerate into a dole or relief measure." This meant that out-of-work benefits should be made available only "for a week or so" while a man was "awaiting a job or commencement of a course of training." It was not the government's intention "to subsidize idleness," and doing so would impede the war effort. "This is constructive legislation," Woods asserted, "designed to build up the individual and it must not be used to break down his morale which would be the case if veterans came to regard it as a dole or relief measure to take care of problem cases who feel they are unable to work. The Order is constructive because it enables the discharged man to acquire a skill, or if he has one to improve that skill by training. It enables him to complete his education and thus fit him for after work. It gives him social security in that it brings him within the pattern of Unemployment Insurance." Nobody "should be permitted to rest on out of work benefits for very long," and it was incumbent on welfare officers and other officials to keep reviewing the circumstances of individuals "with a view to moving them either into employment or into training." The longer men remained on out-of-work benefits, the harder it would be to deal with them, and "the test of the Welfare Officer" was his degree of success in keeping "cases moving and into employment." In the course of his travels with England, Woods noted, some cases had come to their attention in which an applicant had "disclosed that he had been a social problem prior to his enlistment, on relief for a number of years, and ... not able to compete in the labour market or to take training." The answer here was that those incapable of rehabilitation were not covered by PC7633 and were charges on the "local authorities from whence they came." Just because an applicant wore a uniform for a while "should not debar or disfranchise him from social benefits which he enjoyed prior to his enlistment."

On 19 February 1942 Woods forwarded to district administrators and welfare officers tables giving the monthly return of benefits paid under PC7633 for December 1941 and January 1942.[48] In December there were 311 recipients of the out-of-work benefit, the largest number (71) being in the Montreal District. In January the out-of-work benefit total rose to 445, the largest number (91) again being in Montreal. The cost to the government of benefits 1 to 5 in December was $15,937.99 and in January $24,573.56. Commenting on these statistics, Woods expressed deep concern that some recipients were receiving out-of-work benefits for up to sixteen weeks. "It is again emphasized," he wrote, "that the longer a man is receiving out-of-work benefits the more difficult his problem of rehabilitation is going to be." To get at the problem, he suggested that a list be complied in each district of those receiving the benefit for more than four weeks and that a special meeting of the district rehabilitation board, to be attended by the local superintendent of the Unemployment Insurance Commission, be held to consider what else could be done to move the recipients in question along. The cases of those benefiting for more than four weeks "should be closely examined and constantly scrutinized with a view to finding a solution," Woods stated. When "a determined drive" at the district level, combined with a buoyant labour market, brought the number of recipients of the out-of-work-benefit down to 87 at the end of July, he encouraged his regional officials in Montreal, Ottawa, Winnipeg, and Edmonton to consider why their numbers were comparatively larger than those reported by the other districts.[49] Ever vigilant and protective of the public purse, he now also called for attention to be given to the use being made of the temporarily incapacitated benefit. In Alberta, of 2,955 men discharged from the army to 1 July, 53 (1.8 per cent) were receiving benefit 4, whereas in the Ottawa military district only 6 of the 5,103 discharged qualified for it. "Presumably," he ventured, "Alberta men are no more incapacitated as a group than the men from any other Province." The answer in such instances was for each district rehabilitation board, using centrally provided data, to compare its performance with that of its counterparts across the country and take remedial action.

To publicize the new benefit package, DPNH produced, in addition to the information leaflet known as WD2, a "blue card" listing rehabilitation benefits and, eventually, a booklet entitled *What Will I Do When the War Is Won?*[50] Woods was also active on the public-speaking circuit, giving addresses in both Montreal and Toronto in the first months of 1942. In sending a copy of his Toronto speech, given to the Downtown Kiwanis Club, to Howard Green, he observed that of 45,000 men discharged from the wartime forces, only 1,081 were registered with the government on 1 February as unemployed. Getting the figure below 1,000 was probably unrealistic because of the number of "social problem cases" among those discharged; 4,600 had been returned to civilian life as "unlikely to become an efficient soldier" and about 1,000 had been let go because of bad conduct.⁵¹ On 18–19 November 1942, Woods chaired a conference in Ottawa for the four personal service welfare officers based in Montreal, Toronto, Winnipeg, and Vancouver (an associate officer from Montreal was also present). These officials dealt with seriously disabled men, and Woods told them that they "were pioneers in a new field" and that, in connection with their work, tests were being devised "to steer discharged men towards the course for which they were best fitted."⁵² Those presenting at the meeting included McDonald, England, Murchison, Millar, R.S. Thompson, director of the War Emergency Training Programme, and two key officials in the evolving administrative structure under PC7633: director of rehabilitation A.M. Wright and chief welfare officer O.C. Elliott.

On 20 April 1943, following a barrage of complaints from departmental welfare officers, newspapers, Legion branches, and other concerned organizations, payment rates under PC7633 were increased effective 1 May.⁵³ The benefit rate was raised from $9.00 to $10.20 weekly for a single recipient and from $13.00 to $14.40 for a married person. In addition, payments, equivalent to those made by the Dependents' Allowance Board (DND) in the case of active service personnel were authorized for dependent children, as was an allowance for a dependent parent, the latter benefit not to exceed $15.00 monthly (a figure determined by the maximum allowable equivalent payment under the Pension Act and DPNH treatment regulations). Under the revised payment schedule, a married man with four children would receive $104.40 per month while he was on the out-of-work benefit or in receipt of a training grant, and a married man with six children would receive $120.40.⁵⁴ To further encourage training, various financial incentives were now also offered to pensioners, and special grants and travel and commuting allowances were made available to those studying away from home.⁵⁵ Simultaneously, the already available medical benefit of free treatment for twelve months following discharge was revised to include the allowances made available under the amended PC7633.

Woods justified these changes variously. The adjustment made in payment rates would increase expenditure by just over 10 per cent, but fell within acceptable limits vis-à-vis other payments made to veterans as well as unemployment insurance payouts and, crucially, maintained the incentive to work by ensuring that a man would not receive more while in training than he could expect to earn once his training was complete.⁵⁶ Failure to provide allowances for children would strengthen the hand of those – the Canadian Legion, the Canadian Corps Association, and various municipal bodies – who argued that the enlisted should be kept in uniform or on service pay and allowances pending rehabilitation. Nor was there reason to worry that augmenting allowances would discourage work. As employment opportunities had become available in the country during the war, the number of pensioners receiving DPNH relief had fallen from more than 10,000 to about 200, and more than 4,000 War Veterans' Allowance recipients had forgone their monthly government support in favour of jobs. "I am satisfied," Woods observed – his words went to the core of his philosophy of veterans' benefits – "that over 90% of the men would much rather work than drag out their period of training, or draw out-of-work benefits."[57] Under the new rates there would be a smooth transition from family income while in uniform to family income while in training, and the number of trainees with large families would be "comparatively small" (of 42,000 trained after the Great War, 29,000 had no children and only 2,400 had more than three). Although the full cost of the training program now embarked upon could not yet be foreseen, the result of an analysis of 350,000 occupational histories suggested a figure of $180 million. This total assumed armed forces of 600,000 and was to be understood in the context of the $165 million in gratuities paid out indiscriminately after the Great War. Of the 350,000 reported on by Woods, 33 per cent were said to have jobs waiting for them, 30 per cent would need training, 17 per cent would already be trained but have to find work, 15 per cent would want to settle on the land, and 5 per cent would want to attend university.

In July 1943 Woods put the case to Mackenzie that arrangements should be made, in consultation with the services, whereby rehabilitation training could begin overseas while general demobilization was in progress.[58] This would include vocational and trade training, pre-matriculation courses that might lead to university entrance, and university-level courses. To build cooperation with the armed forces and to overcome high-level overseas military resistance to the distribution of information about postwar plans, Woods went to the United Kingdom in August. The perspective of the brass who stood in the way of DPNH's publicity efforts, he later explained, was that "they did not want our boys to go into action looking backwards over their shoulders, as it were."[59] Woods travelled overseas on a mattress "in the belly of a bomber," wearing "a parachute, a Mae West lifebelt and a respirator."[60] He landed at Prestwick, Scotland, and went on to London by train. Meetings followed with High Commissioner Vincent Massey and General A.G. L. McNaughton, the commanding officer of the First Canadian Army. His visit was productive, and following his return to Ottawa he reported that the three overseas heads of the services were now committed to assisting DPNH "to the fullest" in spreading information about the evolving rehabilitation program.[61] From one senior officer he had heard that "whether one likes it or not, the conversation of the boys during their leisure hours inevitably turns to a discussion of what they are going to do when the war is over." With respect to rehabilitation training while troops were awaiting repatriation to Canada, Woods now advised that this should be done by the services themselves, which is what they wanted.

To facilitate matters, he recommended that a coordinating committee be set up in London (to be chaired by the high commissioner and to include a representative of Canadian Legion Educational Services). The purpose of this committee would be to "act as an intermediary between the Services engaged in training men who are awaiting repatriation to civil life, and the Minister of Pensions, who is responsible for their rehabilitation when discharged." After the Great War, Woods reminded the minister, "practically nothing" had been done by way of occupational training overseas for men waiting to come home, and "idle hands" had made mischief," resulting in "much discontent and some rioting, mainly on the question of priority in repatriation." Now was the time to head off this sort of trouble. In September, Woods told *Legionary* editor John Hundevad that his conversations overseas had shown "clearly and unmistakably" that what "the average serving man" wanted when he came home was a job.[62] There was "no tendency" on the part of those serving overseas "to expect to find a Utopia when they return." "They are not," he continued, "asking for anything soft, or to be pampered. Social security they regard as necessary insurance and protection against failure and misfortune, but the primary thing with them is an opportunity to earn a living under decent conditions, at wages adequate to provide for their needs and those of their dependents. They expect us to so order things that they can be assured of this. This is the nub of the situation; this is the hard core of rehabilitation. They believe that we in this country possess the resources and the genius to ensure this." The same month, McNaughton told Woods that he welcomed the proposal of DPNH to station a rehabilitation officer in London and that DPNH could "count on every assistance" from his command.[63]

From December 1943 onwards, understanding of the career choices likely to be made by veterans at the end of the war was informed by a substantial research study prepared by former British Columbia cabinet minister George Moir Weir. Born in Miami, Manitoba, in 1885, Weir was a graduate of McGill University and had a doctorate in education.[64] He had been a normal school principal and inspector of schools in Saskatchewan and head of the Department of Education at the University of British Columbia. In 1924, while teaching at the latter institution, he and Ottawa

George Moir Weir, author of the influential 1943 "Survey of Rehabilitation (Interim Report)" (UBC Archives, *Totem*, 1945, 37)

school inspector J.H. Putnam were appointed to co-chair a royal commission on public education in the province. In the British Columbia election of 1933, Weir carried Vancouver-Point Grey for the Liberals and was named provincial secretary and minister of education in the cabinet that T. Dufferin Patullo formed after the vote. As a member of the reformist Patullo administration, he played a prominent role in the effort to have public health insurance established in the province. Following his defeat in the provincial election of 1941, he was named acting director general of vocational education at DPNH, but before taking up his new duties he served as the first chairman of the Dependents' Board of Trustees (DND), which administered a supplementary allowance scheme. He was a thinker with excellent research skills and broad administrative experience, and he brought the perspective of academic social science to the administrative structure that was being elaborated by Woods.

Weir's report, entitled "Survey of Rehabilitation (Interim Report)" – "interim" was dictated by the fact that the results of many investigations in progress in the country were not yet available and finality was therefore impossible – was divided into twelve chapters and ran to 353 typed pages, double-spaced.[65] According to Weir's preface, his instructions from the minister in undertaking the study were to make his "investigation as objective as possible" and to "present a sound educational and social philosophy as a rational background for practice in the solution of our rehabilitation problems." After an introduction devoted to the general issue of rehabilitation and the scope and purpose of his inquiry, Weir addressed a broad range of rehabilitation-related topics: PC 7633 and its implications, the issue of full employment, the training capacities of the provincial and federal governments, postwar professional and employment opportunities both in industry and government (federal, provincial, and local), training needs, and vocational counselling. His penultimate chapter dealt with "unfinished business," and his last chapter philosophized about the future of social policy in Canada. His findings were based on visits he made to all the provinces, more than two thousand interviews and meetings, statistical data from forty-eight training centres, and questionnaires distributed to selected members of the army, navy, and air force. Weir praised PC 7633 as the veterans' "Charter of Educational Opportunity" and "the Bill of Rights for the provision of appropriate adult education" – a far-seeing measure whose "general principles" would probably soon receive wide application. PC 7633 encouraged enterprise by providing opportunity for "self-betterment" and worked to the mutual advantage of the individual and the government. This was in keeping with the mood of the times. Weir commended the chairman of the Canadian Chamber of Commerce's Post-War Planning Committee for observing that "our post-war world is not going to be a pre-war world" and that if business failed to plan, others would plan for it.

In a section on "The Attitude of Youth," he reported that young Canadians in uniform were asking whether the freedom from want promised in the Atlantic Charter (one of the four freedoms promulgated by US President Franklin Roosevelt and British Prime Minister Winston Churchill at their celebrated 1941 meeting in Placentia Bay, Newfoundland) would "mean opportunity to work at a decent job with a decent wage for everyone." Without this, the charter would be "just a cruel hoax rather than a reliant and realizable pledge." For the average Canadian, freedom from want began with a job and full employment, and meant eliminating "chronic unemployment" and the "depression unemployment" of the 1930s. Canada's young were not fighting on behalf of an "old economic order with its shibboleths, injustices, industrial feuds, and class bitterness" that was "not worth defending." Rather, they served in the hope of a world in which labour would not be treated as a commodity, human life would not be "exploited by irresponsible power or special privilege," private property rights would be constrained, and individual enterprise would be made compatible with "social good." PC 7633 was "a concrete step" in the direction they favoured for the country. The solidarity fostered by war was making Canadians – even extreme advocates of private enterprise – think collectively, and they were responding to the "socializing tendencies of the age." Canadians were "becoming more community-minded without becoming communists," and their social philosophy was now "Progress without Revolution; Stability without Reaction." PC 7633 exemplified this change in direction and pointed the way to a future in which there would be social security for all. When Canadians were asked where the money would come from to pay for all this, Weir reported, they responded by asking where the money came from "to fight the Hun."

Behind this optimism, however, was the reality of means testing; it was arguably the defining and limiting feature of past Canadian social welfare practice and was applied under the terms of PC 7633 to all but the out-of-work benefit. Thus, under section 6(2), the minister had discretion to reduce allowances payable to take account of "pension, wages, salary, or other income." In February 1943, arguing that it was "an anomaly to apply a means test to those endeavouring to improve themselves by vocational or university training and have no means test on out of work benefits," Woods made the case to the minister that this provision should be dropped, but the change he proposed was not made in the revised order that took effect on 1 May.[66] Means-testing rules continued to apply and were justified by Weir in his report as being necessary "to safeguard the financial interests of the taxpayer."[67] "A wealthy man's son," he wrote of the existing PC 7633 allowance for a single man, "for whom $10.20 a week would scarcely provide out-of-pocket expenses, would scarcely be prejudiced by not receiving this comparatively small amount. To the wealthy recipient such a sum would be a mere pittance. To the penurious person $10.20 a week might mean the difference between success and failure in his rehabilitation activities."[68] Assistance, therefore, "should be given on the basis of need as well as of merit."[69] Although Weir would later revise his thinking on this fundamental matter, the policy course the government set in October 1941 continued into 1944.

Another topic debated within the government in this period concerned the extent of the preference that Second World War veterans should enjoy in the general labour market (the existing veterans' preference in relation to civil service positions had already been extended to them, as had a preference for work under government contracts). At its 1942 biennial convention, held 24–27 May in Winnipeg, the Legion demanded "an all over preference in the matter of employment for all honourably discharged ex-service men and women, provided always that the individual is qualified to fill the position."[70] Since the 1941 special committee of the House of Commons had also recommended such a preference and the government had accepted it, attention next focused on how the preference should be applied. The matter came to a head at a meeting of the GACDR Sub-Committee on Employment on 9 April 1943.[71] This gathering heard from R.G. Barclay of the Employment Service Branch, Department of Labour, who had previously circulated a memorandum arguing the case for "a statutory preference ... created by law" that would make it compulsory for employers "to have on their staffs a certain minimum proportion of ex-service men where practicable and where not inconsistent with wage agreements." This was justified because those returning from overseas at the end of the war could find themselves at a "considerable disadvantage" owing to delay in repatriation and "lack of recent employment experience." Having listened to Barclay, the meeting next heard from Woods, who read a prepared statement calling for a continuation of the conciliatory approach being followed by DPNH in finding work for veterans. This approach was "based on goodwill" and community involvement, and had already led to the formation of more than one hundred businessmen's committees across the country in support of the cause. If the Employment Service would join in the good work being done by the businessmen's committees and the Civil Service Commission, and give priority to duly qualified veterans in job placement (this was not currently being done), all would be well and no legislation would be needed.

At the end of a pivotal discussion, the subcommittee formulated these choices: "1. Statutory obligation on employers to employ a quota of ex-service men where practicable and when not in conflict with wage agreements. OR 2. A campaign to encourage employers voluntarily and as a subsidiary part of this campaign the Employment Service of Canada to encourage employer demand for ex-service men by cultivation of a favourable attitude towards service experience, adequate assessment of veteran skills and adaptability for civil employment and offering of veterans to employers for vacancies." In a notable victory for Woods, the committee decided in favour of "the voluntary method," which would require salesmanship, community involvement across a broad front, and the moulding of public opinion. In a letter to Legion president Walker a few days later, Woods again made plain that he entirely disagreed with the notion of "a preference ... established by law."[72] Over time, "compelling employers to engage a percentage of discharged men" would only work to the disadvantage of veterans; the goal of a preference could be "accomplished by paving the way through Business Men's Committees and Service Organizations, and ... by the Employment Service observing a preference when they refer men to jobs." Walker, unlike George Herwig (who had become general secretary of the organization following Reg Bowler's tragic death by suicide) was instinctively drawn to the case for compulsion, and in his reply to Woods he highlighted the shortcomings of Canadian employers, many of whom, in his long experience working on behalf of veterans, had preferred "the services of the alien to that of the men who served their country nobly and well."[73] Walker looked forward to more discussion, but Woods had manifestly carried the day on yet another key issue. On 13 July 1943, in a masterful address to Kiwanians in Toronto, he defined the choices facing the country with respect to rehabilitation, as follows:

> To sum up the situation, I would say there are two ways in which the rehabilitation of discharged persons can be achieved. One is the compulsory way, requiring all employers to take a certain quota. This, whilst it may have one outstanding advantage, has many disadvantages which are apparent to you all, and should only be resorted to if the voluntary way fails.
>
> The voluntary way comprises equipping everyone with a skill or profession through which they can earn their living and then, through the medium of the Employment Service (in which in my opinion there should be preference in referring discharged men to jobs) and with the assistance of business men's committees which have been established in a hundred centres throughout the Dominion, endeavour to get employers to recognize their obligation to those young people who have served the State so nobly.
>
> With respect to the disabled it requires something further than that – personal interest on and study of each individual case – and Kiwanis can furnish this.
>
> There are limitations to what a Government can do and there are also responsibilities in the community as to what they should do. The two developed to the utmost can achieve successful rehabilitation.[74]

In short, as he had told a gathering of Kiwanians in London, Ontario, the previous month, "the democratic way" could "be achieved by the community," but "the compulsory way would have to be performed by the State."[75] In Woods's view there was no question of which was preferable.

Although Woods, a son of his times, often used the terms "discharged man" and "discharged men" in reference to those who had left uniform, he was nevertheless a staunch advocate of the view that the benefit package being developed in the country applied to women as well as men.[76] When women began enlisting, beginning with the Women's Auxiliary Air Force, the Pension Act had no provision for covering them, but on 1 October 1941 the government acted to remedy this situation. By PC4/7635 members of the women's forces became eligible for pensions for disabilities incurred while in the services.[77] These were payable according to percentage disability and at rates that were roughly two-thirds of those payable to men. However, no pension was payable to a dependant because of the disablement or death while in service of a member of the women's forces. The two-thirds pension scale was justified on the grounds that it accorded with the existing pay difference between men and women.[78] Subsequently, other post-discharge benefits made available to men were also extended to women[79] but the eligibility of members of the Canadian Women's Army Corps (CWAC) for the benefits of PC 7633 ran into a snag. The difficulty lay in the terms of their enlistment. Whereas members of the Auxiliary Air Force were being enlisted "on the same basis as airmen," members of the CWAC were not being signed up on the same basis as soldiers.[80] While it was true that the CWAC was organized on "a military basis" and was "under military control and supervision," it specifically did not "form part of the Military Forces of Canada."[81] Accordingly, a discharged member of the corps did not qualify as a "discharged person" under PC 7633 and was therefore ineligible for the benefits authorized by that order.[82]

On the initiative of the Department of National Defence, a subcommittee of the GACDR was formed to consider how to proceed, given this difference between the conditions of service of the two women's units formed to date.[83] It recommended that for benefit purposes, members of the CWAC should be treated as members of the armed forces, even though, legally, they were not. This would ensure that "there would be no question in the public mind as to any implied discrimination."[84] To put its recommendation into effect, the subcommittee proposed a list of executive actions, one of which was to amend the definition of "discharged person" in PC 7633 so as to make specific reference to members of the CWAC and the Auxiliary Air Force. PC 7633 would also have to be amended so as to set the out-of-work benefit for women at two-thirds the amount payable to men and to exempt "a married woman wholly or mainly dependent upon her husband."[85]

Ever conscious of the need to maintain a strict boundary between veterans and civilians (and thereby protect the status group rights of the former), Woods opposed the recommendation of the subcommittee on the grounds that admitting persons who did not belong to the armed forces to the benefits of PC 7633 – the CWAC uniform notwithstanding, might lead to claims from "many other uniformed bodies," which might then be "hard to resist."[86] To proceed as the subcommittee recommended would set an awkward precedent and might require more general changes to be made in veterans' legislation. In the end, Woods's cautionary advice to limit the meaning of "discharged person" to former members of the armed forces was heeded. On 1 April 1942, PC 7633 was amended as the subcommittee had advised, but before this was done another order (PC 1965), issued on 13 March, constituted the CWAC "as a Corps of the Active Militia on Active Service."[87] The procedure followed put the two women's auxiliary units on the same footing of service while maintaining a strict definition of exactly who was eligible for veterans' benefits. All ex-service women qualified as veterans, but Woods won on the point of principle – he kept the definition of "veteran" within established limits. In accordance with all this, when the formation of the Women's Royal Canadian Naval Service (WRCNS) was authorized in July 1942, it also was designated as being on "active service."[88] Jill Canuck was in, but Rosie the Riveter was out.

In October 1943, following these developments, Woods was asked by the national secretary of the Imperial Order Daughters of the Empire for an explanation of the post-discharge benefits available to servicewomen. He replied that women were "discharged from the Service under the same conditions as men."[89] They were equally eligible with men for the benefits of the Pension Act and for medical care under the treatment regulations of DPNH. Women were, however, paid "special rates of pension" and "special rates of hospital allowances." In both instances, the rates paid were lower than those paid to men because women were paid less than men while serving in the forces. Woods also noted that the out-of-work benefit payable under PC 7633 to a woman could "not exceed the rate of pay of the discharged person at the date of discharge." But all other benefits of this order were available to women "on exactly the same basis as that applying to men." Woods did not mention in his letter that since 1 July 1943, women in the armed forces were being paid at a basic rate that was four-fifths of the amount paid to men of the same rank, instead of the previous two-thirds.[90] At the same time that this change had been made, it was announced that women would now be given the same trades and professional pay as men and that the allowance paid to the dependants of women in the services (husbands and children excepted) would henceforth be the same as those paid to the dependants of men. A servicewoman married to a serviceman would in future be able to receive a dependant's allowance from her husband to a maximum income of $2,100.

In their consideration of the current and future needs of Canada's women veterans, the country's rehabilitation planners were assisted by the work of the GACDR Sub-Committee on the Special Problems of Discharged Women, the formation of which was recommended by Woods in January 1942.[91] A follow-up recommendation next flowed from the relevant GACDR subcommittee and was put into effect.[92] The job of the new subcommittee was "to consider and report to the General Advisory Committee on the special problems of civil re-establishment of women, as such, discharged from the Canadian armed forces."[93] The first meeting of the subcommittee was held in the Daly Building in Ottawa on 19 June 1942. Present were representatives of the women's branches of the armed forces and the nursing service, along with two civilian appointees: nursing policy adviser Laura Holland and Tory social activist Charlotte Whitton. On 23 June the subcommittee approved an interim report that listed the major problems it had identified in its initial *tour d'horizon*.[94] The first of these concerned "Problems of social care arising from or related to discharge for reasons of conduct." Under this heading, the subcommittee addressed the care that would be required at discharge for venereal disease, pregnancy, or alcohol or drug addiction. Women who contracted tuberculosis while in the forces might likewise have exceptional care requirements, as would any "special casualties" – that is to say, women who suffered amputations or who were made blind or deaf. The second major category of concern for the subcommittee was employment. How would women fare in vocational training, professional education, and establishment in individual enterprises and agriculture? And how would the demand for women workers in Canada be coordinated with post-discharge benefit opportunities and with the training available to and the work being done by servicewomen while in the forces? The subcommittee saw a need to concern itself also with pension provisions for women; the impact of their rates of pay and lack of dependants' allowances (these had not yet been granted) on their ability to save for their re-establishment; and the responsibilities for them of the rehabilitation branch of DPNH.

As only 239 members of the CWAC had been discharged by 31 May 1942 and only 61 members of the RCAF(WD) – the Royal Canadian Air Force Women's Division – by June 1942, the subcommittee understandably gave priority to the problems of care it had identified. It took the position with respect to venereal disease that the determination of claims for treatment and pension benefits after individuals left the service required that a number of steps be taken in advance. Women recruits should be routinely tested for infection, and no infected person should be accepted. Its attitude towards members of the armed forces who became pregnant was likewise categorical: it was "unanimously agreed" that it was in the best interest of all concerned that a woman certified by a medical officer as being pregnant should "be discharged as soon as possible and feasible, consistent with adequate adjustment to civilian life through collaboration with the Active Services and Social Services in the community." It was "undesirable" that pregnant women be employed in the forces, whether in subordinate or command positions. Retaining a pregnant individual in the women's forces would "injure" their "public prestige, public approval and moral tone." It would also "lead to considerable embarrassment" for the women concerned. In keeping with this approach, the government issued PC818 on 5 February 1943.[95] This authorized the minister of pensions and national health "to grant and provide aid in the form of special medical treatment, hospitalization and care in the case of female ex-members of the naval, military and air forces of Canada who have been discharged therefrom by reason of having become temporarily unfit for service according to prevailing medical standards." Regulations under this order were then issued on 4 March 1943.[96] Under these regulations, a woman who became pregnant while in the armed forces and did not qualify under any other arrangement of the dominion government could be provided with domiciliary care in Canada. This included pre- and post-natal care, and covered accommodation as required to ensure proper care in a hospital, hostel, or "private or other home." Time spent in domiciliary care would not detract from eligibility for out-of-work benefits under PC7633.

In its consideration of the employment issue, the Sub-Committee on the Special Problems of Discharged Women emphasized the collection of data under three headings: the occupational histories of women in the forces, their future training needs, and their likely job prospects once the war was over. The subcommittee assumed throughout that many women in the armed forces would not need any retraining or employment assistance because they would get married and become homemakers. The most detailed attempt to predict what was in store for ex-service women in the postwar world was made in Weir's 1943 report.[97] Based on survey research, he predicted that after the war, women workers would be most in demand in services, a category that included nurses, teachers, dentists, doctors, and other professionals. The next highest general categories of projected demand were "Vocational," which included more than a dozen sub-classes, and "Clerical." The category "Labourers," which included charwomen, cleaners, and other unskilled workers, was rated eighth of nine.[98] Weir also reported on a survey he had done in October 1943 on the educational and occupational preferences of women in the armed forces.[99] In all three services, the leading occupational choice turned out to be stenography. In the case of the army and air force, this was followed by "Home-maker" and "Nurse" and, in the case of the navy, by "Teacher" and "Clerk." Weir found the number opting for stenography to be "disconcerting" and urged that women be encouraged to study nursing, social work, household economics, and other subjects for which there promised to be a big demand in the postwar world.[100]

Just as PC7633 broke new ground in social policy towards women in Canada, it also triggered a wave of change in the country's universities.[101] In the autumn of 1942, the executive committee of the National Conference of Canadian Universities (NCCU) appointed a committee to look into the situation that universities were likely to face in the postwar period.[102] Chaired by President N.A.M. Mackenzie of the University of British Columbia, the committee included senior university officials from across the country. The secretary of the group was NCCU secretary and University of Toronto registrar A.B. Fennell. Responding to an urgent call to national service, the committee presented an interim report in January 1943 and met again at Ottawa on 31 August 1943 to continue work leading to a final document.[103] Its initiative opened a new phase in relations between government and universities in Canada and was indicative of the increasingly long reach of Ottawa's evolving rehabilitation program. For Canadians serving on land, sea, and in the air in 1943, the shape of the postwar future their government imagined for them was coming into sharp focus. In the main, this was a future of limited assistance combined with training and education on the way to work and independence of government. In 1944 and 1945, the program that sought to achieve these goals would be rounded out and given an all-inclusive name that caught the spirit of the times.

5 Ready for Release

In the rhetoric of Second World War Ottawa, "rehabilitation," "reconstruction," and "re-establishment" were closely linked concepts, and at DPNH it was understood that they required coordinated action across a broad social and economic front. Getting people ready for work – rehabilitation – assumed a simultaneous effort – reconstruction – to ensure that jobs would be available for those who completed training courses. And only if these two pieces fitted together could the smooth outcome everyone hoped for – re-establishment – be realized. In 1941 Woods had played an important role in launching the government's Committee on Reconstruction, headed by Principal F. Cyril James of McGill University, which functioned until 1943.[1] This committee began its work with high hopes but eventually faced considerable bureaucratic resistance and had limited effect. In 1942, while James and his colleagues were going about their business, the House of Commons formed its own special committee on reconstruction and re-establishment. The all-party committee (Mackenzie was one of its members) was chaired by BC Liberal MP J.G. Turgeon and delivered four reports in 1942, four more in 1943, and two in 1944.[2] On 23 February 1944, Weir appeared before the committee.[3] He was introduced by Mackenzie, who summarized and tabled his 1943 rehabilitation survey. Mackenzie stated on this occasion that what rehabilitation required was "jobs for the fit – and fitting the unfit for jobs." When his turn came, Weir told committee members that there was "very little sense" in training someone for a job that was unlikely to be available. "What we wish to do," he asserted, "is to train lads for jobs that will be there when their training is completed." This would require "continuous industrial surveys," but there was good reason to be optimistic. Indeed, some of the best-informed observers believed that the return of factories to peacetime production would produce a shortage of trained workers soon after the war ended. In response to a question from Saskatchewan MP Dorise Nielsen, Weir offered the assurance that ex-service women faced "absolutely no discrimination" in relation to vocational training and received the same training allowances as men. (In another sign of the times, pension rates for women were ultimately increased to four-fifths of the male rate and then to parity.)

If this exchange was hopeful, so too were the proceedings of the biennial convention of the Canadian Legion, held in Vancouver from 4 to 7 June 1944. Legion membership grew rapidly during the war, and the Vancouver gathering heard a glowing report about the organization's structure (45 branches, 34 ladies' auxiliaries, and 2 junior auxiliaries had been chartered since 31 March 1942) and about its finances and its good works at home and overseas.[4] In his report to his comrades, Walker gave high praise to the Legion's legislative accomplishments while acknowledging the beneficial role of public opinion and "of many a government official."[5] In its dealings with government, the Legion had found that the best results came not through "coercive tactics" but through "painstaking work" by first building a case and then advancing it "by friendly discussion with the appropriate authorities." The "close contact" between the organization and officials in the development of the government's rehabilitation policy had produced "excellent results," and while many improvements were called for, there was reason to be pleased with what had been achieved to date. The country still had "a long way to go" in veterans' affairs – the Legion, for example, still wanted the introduction of the "due to service" principle reversed – but progress had undoubtedly been made. "Although we shall continue the good fight with undiminished vigour," Walker promised, "blood-and-thunder oratory, half-baked proposals and rabble-rousing gestures will never be practised by us. A just cause, fully and correctly and vigorously pressed, is what gains results, as we have proved on many occasions." It was this constructive approach that had now led the government to accept the Legion's proposal for the creation of a department of veterans' affairs – a "most gratifying" development. Mackenzie, however, traced the same initiative to remarks he had made on 30 June 1942 to the special committee on land settlement, which had then been endorsed by the country's veterans' organizations and all political parties represented in the Commons.[6]

The legislative process leading to the creation of the new department began on 20 March when Prime Minister King introduced a resolution in favour of the action contemplated (he simultaneously introduced resolutions calling for the creation of departments of reconstruction and social welfare, the latter eventually known as National Health and Welfare).[7] As proposed, the veterans' affairs department would "replace in part the Department of Pensions and National Health ... and assume the management and control of ... all matters not by law assigned to any other department relating to the care, treatment, training or reestablishment of members and former members of the armed forces and other persons" and all other matters as might subsequently be assigned to it.[8] The words "other persons" here ensured the continuation of selected veterans' benefits to individuals – "merchant marine, salt-water fishermen, fire-fighters, A.R.P. [Air Raid Precautions] workers and many other groups" – who, though not enlisted, worked closely with those in uniform and were crucial to the country's military effort.[9] Debate on the resolution followed on 17 April, and after the resolution was agreed to that day, the requisite Bill 83 was introduced and given first reading.[10] Second reading followed on 16 June, and the committee stage was completed three days later.[11] Third reading was then given on 20 June, whereupon, after the House had agreed to a minor amendment made in the Senate, the bill received assent on 30 June.[12]

Although debate ranged widely as the legislation moved through the Commons (some MPs liked to go over the business of aggrieved constituents on such occasions), there was general agreement among the parties that the government was taking an essential step. The nationalist Quebec MP Liguori Lacombe claimed that the bill infringed provincial rights and was therefore unconstitutional, but the matter of dominion responsibility for veterans' affairs had long since been settled in Canada, and his intervention went nowhere.[13] More typical of the views expressed was the speech made by Winnipeg MP Stanley Knowles of the CCF. Having noted that there were eight ex-servicemen of the current war on relief in his home city, Knowles went on to make the case that if men came back from overseas and were discouraged and disillusioned by "ingratitude or lack of appreciation" for what they had done, the country as a whole would suffer.[14] Just as the country was being required to spend "millions and billions" to fight the war, it must be ready to spend similar amounts to ensure the physical, psychological, and economic rehabilitation of those who served. There must be no "soured generation" after the war. As always when it came to veterans' benefits, the debate among Canada's political parties was not whether there should be such benefits but whether the government was doing enough. Believing that the principle of the bill was self-evident, Mackenzie did not enter the debate on second reading, but after this had been achieved he defended his department against the charge that its veterans' affairs wing had "too many brass hats."[15] In fact, he asserted, 80 to 90 per cent of the public servants in question had passed through the ranks in the Great War. But Mackenzie also praised his fellow MPs for their action on second reading: they had lived up to the country's "old tradition of a splendid unity of thought, and

... unity of action, in regard to the problems of ... returning ex-service men." The veterans' affairs legislation of the previous quarter century, he said, had not been "the effort of any one party" but was "the result of the conjoint sympathies and work and efforts of every single party in the dominion." It was this spirit that had animated the debate just finished, and the minister thanked the members for their "kindly references" to his own role and their "sympathetic attitude" towards his department. "All of us," he said, looking forward to committee review, "have the same idea in our minds, which is to produce a piece of legislation here that will stand the test of time, improved as it must be from year to year when new activities show that these improvements are advisable. This will be done, of course, to serve the purpose we all have very close to our hearts, namely, to establish an administration for the boys who are overseas to-night, and also those who have been discharged already, 136,000 of them, and who are now back in Canada, those who shall have saved Canada by their heroic fortitude and their wonderful example."[16]

An Act to Establish a Department of Veterans Affairs (the short title was the Department of Veterans Affairs Act) had twelve sections and specified that the new minister's "duties, powers and functions" extended (unless by law otherwise assigned) to the administration of all statutes and orders "relating to the care, treatment, training, or re-establishment in civil life, of any person who served in the naval, military or air forces of His Majesty, any person who has otherwise engaged in pursuits relating to war, and of any other person designated by the Governor in Council, and to the care of the dependents of such person" and "all such other matters and such boards and other public bodies, subjects, services and properties of the Crown" as might be "designated, or assigned to the Minister by the Governor in Council."[17] Subject to the approval of the latter, the minister was authorized, *inter alia*, to make regulations deemed "necessary and advisable" relating to hospitals, workshops, and other institutions, treatment and training, artificial limbs and appliances, the administration of properties of persons in care, guardianship of the insane, payments of grants and allowances, reciprocal arrangements with other governments, sheltered employment, transportation expenses for totally blinded pensioners, burial expenses for destitute veterans, treatment of incurable and chronically ill veterans, unemployment relief, compensation for industrial accidents, and the administration and use of canteen funds. By section 8, the references to DPNH, its minister, and deputy minister in the Pension Act, the War Veterans' Allowance Act, the Veterans' Assistance Commission Act, 1936, and orders and regulations issued under those acts were changed to take account of the new reality. By the same token, responsibility for the administration of soldier settlement and the Veterans' Land Act, 1942, was transferred from the minister of mines and resources to the minister of veterans affairs, and the relevant legislation and orders were changed accordingly (in the case of the Soldier Settlement Act, this also involved changes in references to the former Department of the Interior and its minister and deputy minister). References in statutes, orders, and regulations to the Department of Soldiers' Civil Re-establishment and its minister and deputy minister were likewise brought up to date. Under section 12, the Department of Veterans Affairs Act was to come into force on a date fixed by vice-regal proclamation. In the event, the required document was approved on 13 October and the legislation came into force on publication in the *Canada Gazette* of 21 October 1944.[18]

On 13 July, while the changeover from the Department of Pensions and National Health to the Department of Veterans Affairs was pending, PC7633 was amended and reissued as PC5210.[19] The purpose of this action, Woods explained to Treasury Board secretary W.C. Ronson, was to consolidate all the changes that had been made since 1941 and, in the interest of easy reading, to simplify the document that was the "cornerstone of our whole rehabilitation programme."[20] Like PC7633, following the introductory matter, the new order was in two parts. The first itemized the rules and regulations for the rehabilitation benefits being made available, now categorized as follows: "Benefit Number One – Out-Of-Work Benefit"; "Benefit Number Two – Vocational and Technical Training"; "Benefits Number Three and Number Four – Awaiting Returns from Enterprise; Temporary Incapacity"; and "Benefit Number Five – University Education (Undergraduate)" and "University Education (Post-Graduate)." Except for the out-of-work benefit, these were now made retroactive to the beginning of the war. According to Woods, although this change might involve extra expense, the sum would be "inconsiderable," because those discharged before July 1941 were already rehabilitated and had "now forgotten any effects of their military service."[21] Part two of the new order dealt with unemployment insurance arrangements.

PC5210 not only retained the means-test provisions of the previous order but extended them to the out-of-work benefit – a change, Woods asserted, that would produce savings. On 25 July, Woods responded to a memorandum by Weir entitled "Should the So-called Means Test be Abolished?"[22] Tracing the means test back to the Elizabethan Poor Laws, Weir quoted approvingly a source that described it as "a running sore on the social life of the nation." "Whether or not a Means Test," he ventured, "is a measure of financial probity, as asserted by the rightists, or of social oppression, as maintained by the leftists, is an open question. Perhaps the votaries of so-called thrift and individual enterprise tend to err on the side of severity; while the social enterprisers may equally err on the side of indulgence or so-called state paternalism." Weir's own view was categorical: the time had come to consign a time-worn legacy of "chill penury" to "the limbo of forgotten things – along with the religious Test Acts of the Stuart Period, the dinosaur, the dodo and other monstrosities." "Most serious-minded people," he continued, "even if hard pressed taxpayers, will wish to see it interred quite deep, – so deep indeed that no reactionary government or economic Bourbons will ever attempt its exhumation." In reply, Woods said that he had read what Weir had to say with interest and would keep it on hand for future consideration as required (he ordered that a "means test" file be created).[23]

Woods also heard on the same subject in July from Colonel G.G.D. Kilpatrick, army director of education, who cautioned that if "the sons of the well-to-do" were denied benefits, they would feel that they were being denied something that was their right through service.[24] Although the government might not intend a particular benefit as a reward or right, once it was made known it would be interpreted as being available to all, irrespective of individual means. "A 'means test,' rigidly applied," Kilpatrick cautioned, "would create resentment and it would have the further unfortunate result of keeping many from University training – for the lad who entered service as a boy, leaves it a man and he does not propose to put further burden on his parents who have been straitened by taxation. If his parents have to bear the cost of his education he will not go to the University but into business. This is not conjecture, but the expressed opinion of many." In response, Woods noted that the government did not refuse assistance to attend university because of parental financial status. "It is not intended," he wrote, "to apply any rigid means test. Now that our income tax has the effect of levelling all incomes, the means test is not very important. A very small percentage is affected by it, and it most certainly will not be 'rigidly applied.'"[25]

In August 1944, to the great satisfaction of the Canadian Legion and in a striking policy shift, the evolving program for veterans was further advanced by the addition of gratuity and re-establishment credit schemes applicable to all in uniform save National Resources Mobilization Act conscripts who had done Canadian service only. In September 1943, before leaving his post as executive secretary of the GACDR, England wrote a long memorandum on the possibility of paying a gratuity now that a set of rehabilitation and land settlement benefits was in place.[26] He urged caution, noting many possible pitfalls, including the stirring-up of trouble between ex-service personnel and civilians. Women in uniform, for example, were being "fairly adequately" compensated compared with their civil service counterparts and did not pay income tax. Moreover, unlike the latter (some of whom had been refused permission to enlist), ex-service women qualified for all the re-establishment benefits now on offer and for preference for public service employment. Justifying the payment of a gratuity to women veterans thus advantaged might "prove difficult ... at least to the female civil servant, who worked without the glamour of uniform and received no opportunities for advancement or retraining or sickness benefit, medical and dental attention or out-of-work protection." In general, England feared that the payment of gratuities "with no identifiable social need or purpose" to "limited favoured groups" might stir the pot in the country. The payment of a gratuity might also negatively affect the rehabilitation program by encouraging individuals to postpone going to work or taking training and by encouraging spending and therefore inflation, which in turn would trigger a need for cost-of-living bonuses for benefit allowances. Cash payments to men who were "temporarily idle" were "bound to cause difficulty." If, England concluded, "a general attack" on idleness was to be made, perhaps the best approach would be to limit the gratuity to those who had served in a theatre of actual war and make payment to an individual, less costs incurred on his behalf under the Post-Discharge Re-establishment Order, in the form of a "savings bond" eighteen months after discharge. This approach, he wrote, "would have the effect of encouraging a man to accept employment and look after his own re-establishment under his own steam so that he would be able to qualify for the total amount of the savings grant and might discourage many from seeking to make use of re-establishment benefits simply as a means of livelihood, and because they want to get, as they would say, all that is coming to them or what they are entitled to in their view."

On 27 January 1944, in the Speech from the Throne read at the opening of the fifth session of the nineteenth Parliament, elected in 1940, the government grasped the nettle by promising "a measure to provide war service gratuities for all who have served in the armed forces," along with "measures to supplement the existing rehabilitation programme."[27] Because a gratuity would be payment for military service, the prime mover in what followed was the Department of National Defence, but by definition, the Department of Pensions and National Health was also involved.

In February, having reviewed a proposal for a gratuity set at $10 per month of home service and $20 per month of service abroad, applicable to all ranks and single and married persons, Woods observed that "its levelling of all ranks would undoubtedly commend it to the majority of the public."[28] Unfortunately, the numbers worked out in such a way that half of the men who served overseas for less than three years would receive less under this plan than their Great War counterparts received, while those who served overseas for more than three years would receive more than their 1914–18 equivalents. In sum, "half of those who served overseas would be treated less generously than last time." The solution, Woods suggested, was to provide "a basic gratuity for overseas men of $240 plus $15 per month for length of service." In March, his advice not having been followed in a revised scale that was otherwise equitable, he cautioned the minister against putting "ourselves in the position of paying any less than we did the last time."[29]

A voice from the ranks heard in this pivotal discussion was that of Sergeant K.G. Glass, who in January 1944 wrote to the veterans' welfare officer in London, Ontario, on behalf of eighty-five airmen stationed at nearby Aylmer. The men, he reported, felt "very strongly" that there "should be a decidedly larger grant upon discharge than one month's pay."[30] They were also of the view that paying out a larger grant "in several installments" would "prevent any tendency on the part of the spendthrift" to blow the award. "We believe," Glass pointedly wrote, "that it will take a lot more than a month's pay – say $45 for a private or LAC [leading aircraftman] – to enable him to tide over the time from discharge to beginning of pay cheques." By the same token, the clothing allowance now available needed to be increased and recognition given to the housing needs of urban dwellers:

> The city men feel very strongly – and the former rural citizens support them – that as at least 50% if not more of the men in the Service were city (*not* suburban) dwellers before the war, and knew nothing of farming, that they will be returning to the city to live on discharge from the Service – yet no provision at all is made under the Veterans' Land Act to help them build a city home. Many might come under the "smallholdings near urban centre" clause, yet many cannot afford transportation to or from their work from outside the city, or wish to live in the city. A large percentage would not be allowed to live *outside* and yet hold jobs *inside* the city – municipal employees, teachers (like myself – specifically prohibited from being outside the city). We quite see … that at present no urban

scheme similar to the rural and suburban scheme can be put into effect because of shortage of materials, etc., yet we feel that provision for an urban scheme can be *now* made and proclaimed later. We suggest a scheme based on the National Housing Act, with the Govt. paying about the same percentage of the cost as for rural and suburban dwellers.

As 1944 advanced, the matter raised in this penetrating letter of providing additional cash following discharge was high on the agendas of both senior military officials and the Department of Finance. The service chiefs advanced their ideas in a January 1944 memorandum, and a complex back and forth followed with Finance (its sherpas on the file were E.B. Armstrong and the young Mitchell Sharp).[31] Debate was ultimately resolved according to a plan advanced in an unsigned 17 July Finance memorandum (probably written by W.A. Mackintosh, a Queen's University professor who worked in Ottawa during the war).[32] This formative document made the case that while Canada had devised "about the best program in the world for the rehabilitation of veterans," its effort had failed "to get full credit ... either from the veterans themselves or from the general public." What was needed was to treat the benefits on offer as a whole and roll them into one overarching package – a *"veterans' charter"* (my italics) – along the lines of the bold legislation recently enacted in the United States and popularly known as the G.I. Bill of Rights. At the same time, the fact that the existing benefit package promised "little or nothing" to those veterans who might be expected to re-establish themselves easily must be addressed. As things stood, the government's program did not take sufficient account of "the limitations of human nature" and of the demand that could be expected "for some kind of reasonable equality of treatment for all types of veterans."

The answer was "to recognize at once that the over-all program should consist of two major elements, namely, War Service Gratutities and Rehabilitation Grants, and should be based on the two major principles of (1) a grateful country giving some gratuitous reward for the faithful service rendered and for the risks taken; and (2) a far-sighted country willing to do a lot of hard thinking and incur financial expenditures in order to ensure that the veteran will re-establish himself into civil life and become an efficient and effective unit in a sound economy." The gratuity should be treated as a "gift made absolutely without strings of any kind ... to be used by the veteran for whatever purpose he pleases, whether for productive purposes or for providing an opportunity to look around for a time and seek the best future for his civilian endeavours, or for a holiday, or for merely 'a bust.'" It should not be related to rank or marital status but should acknowledge duration and location of service and "take proper account of the degree of risk run by men who were actually on the firing line," with "a flat additional payment or bonus" given "for actual combat service." On the rehabilitation side of the equation, the amount of the gratuity should be used to set the minimum level of assistance to be made available to an individual veteran. Giving everybody something under the heading of rehabilitation would undoubtedly be more expensive than having a stand-alone gratuity scheme, but the dual approach would have the advantage of heading off claims of discrimination and of allowing the larger program to proceed without disruption. If "all returned men" were provided with a minimum rehabilitation grant, more costly payments to some of them – land settlers, university students, and vocational trainees – could be justified on the grounds of the conditions attached to them. This whole approach, the memorandum concluded, would also be sound economic policy:

> The danger of a very generous gratuities program, not integrated fully into a rehabilitation program, is that in a good many cases the money would be rapidly expended at a time when goods are still scarce, thus giving little value for the money and aggravating the inflationary dangers which still exist, and that in spite of the heavy Government expenditure the problem of the re-establishment of many veterans into civil life will still remain. In view of this, it seems sounder to shift some of the money that would otherwise be expended in gratuities over into the rehabilitation program and thus provide for a combined gratuities and rehabilitation program which, while undoubtedly costing a good deal more than the gratuities program recommended by the Service Departments, will nevertheless stand a much better chance of accomplishing a real job of re-establishment and of persisting against continuing pressures from this or that special group.

Accordingly, the rehabilitation grants now proposed would only be available for specified purposes. The gratuity would be free money, but the rehabilitation grant would be tied money.

Woods was handed the Finance memo by Mackenzie at a meeting on the evening of 25 July in Defence Minister Ralston's office. He reacted coolly to what he read, noting to his own minister the next day that there were more disadvantages than advantages in what was being contemplated.[33] The envisaged scheme would be "unnecessarily expensive" and

– using the example of a single man with three years' service, some of it overseas – went beyond what the Canadian Legion and the combined services had called for by way of gratuity payment. The proposed rehabilitation grant also ignored the reality that "a heavy percentage of those discharged will look to the Government for nothing beyond the clothing allowance and whatever cash gratuity is paid." After the Great War, only 8 per cent of veterans had taken vocational training, and only 4 per cent had become land settlers, while fully 88 per cent had "re-established themselves with their gratuity and asked for nothing" more. "If you tell this great body of men who will look after themselves," Woods cautioned, "that a deferred rehabilitation grant can be provided from which they can pay for furniture, or make a payment on a home, or go into business, or perhaps ultimately receive cash, OF COURSE EVERY SINGLE MAN AND WOMAN IN THE SERVICE WOULD TAKE ADVANTAGE OF IT." Carrying out such a scheme would "require tremendous administrative machinery" and would necessitate "a ledger and control account for every person who served." Again, the proposed rehabilitation grant would have the effect of promoting inequality in rehabilitation expenditure outcomes and was unlikely to satisfy the veterans themselves. One man might see his rehabilitation grant eaten up by his out-of-work benefit, while a man who left uniform and went to work would qualify for a payment he might not need. In sum, this was a case of good intentions gone astray:

> The proposal is based on the desire to direct part of the gratuity into avenues which will produce work, and a very laudable desire at that. I am inclined to think, however, that the great majority of discharged men will expend their gratuity in this direction, if provision is made for an adequate housing programme and assistance to those who wish to go into business on their own account. I think it is a wrong hypothesis to suppose that any large number of the men will dissipate their gratuity. The type of discharged man that does that will not get much benefit in any event out of the proposed deferred gratuity plan. I know it is a popular theory that discharged men do not get the best out of their war service gratuity, but it is the writer's experience after twenty-five years in rehabilitation work, that this applies to the exceptional rather than the average case.

The country's existing rehabilitation program addressed individual needs rather than giving "similar benefits to all," Woods continued, and if this program were "rounded out to cover those who want to purchase a home or go into business," it would meet the needs of almost everyone in uniform. The addition of a housing program would be especially attractive, in that it would create employment. With the addition of loans for tools, arrangements whereby those in need of credit to go into business could get it from banks, and a housing scheme for veterans, Canada's rehabilitation program "would be second to none in the world" – provided that the proposed war service gratuity was kept on the "modest lines" favoured by the services themselves.

Woods's fears were soon overcome by the insertion in the draft bill, at the suggestion of Finance Minister Ilsley, of a provision whereby a veteran who benefited from the VLA or was supported to take vocational training or go to university would be ineligible for the re-establishment credit (to the extent that this was used up thereby) and vice versa. Then, on 10 August 1944, Prime Minister King moved a resolution in the Commons in favour of the introduction of a measure (he had insisted on proceeding in this instance by legislation rather than order-in-council)[34] that would provide a war service gratuity to those who volunteered for general service and also to conscripted men who were "at any time obligated to serve without territorial limitation" or who had served in the Aleutian Islands.[35] By this definition, most conscripted men would be excluded, a fact that would help keep peace with the veterans' organizations (the Canadian Corps Association also pushed to have conscripts excluded from VLA benefits, but this effort ran up against legal complications and departmental resistance and did not succeed).[36] The amount of the gratuity would be a flat $7.50 for every thirty days served in the Western Hemisphere (excluding the Aleutians) and $15 for every thirty days served overseas or in the Aleutians, regardless of rank. A supplementary gratuity, which acknowledged rank, provided for seven days' pay and allowances for each six-month period of overseas service. Those eligible for the gratuity would also be eligible for a re-establishment credit (bills for approved expenditures would have to be submitted to claim this) of the same amount. Although King did not specifically say so, these payments (unlike the Post-Discharge Re-establishment Order rehabilitation benefits) would be entitlements and not subject to means testing. Gratuities, King explained, were given as a token of the country's gratitude for service, on which no price could be set and should not "be confused with rehabilitation and reestablishment." Together, the gratuity and re-establishment credit would give every veteran money to spend "without official restraint" and "an equal amount to be used directly in rehabilitation." Assuming service by the existing armed forces to 31 March 1945, King estimated the cost of the gratuities at $400 million. Because of the offsets in the case of those who took vocational training or university education or who qualified under the VLA, his estimate of the cost of the re-establishment credit scheme was $350 million.

Following the approval of his resolution, Bill 184, "An Act to Provide for the Payment of War Service Gratuities and for the Grant of Re-establishment Credits to Members of His Majesty's Forces in Respect of Service during the Present War," was given first reading.[37] Under the terms of the bill, veterans would be able to use their re-establishment credits to acquire or modernize a home, purchase furniture and household equipment, get started in a business or profession, buy an existing enterprise, purchase tools, instruments, or equipment, pay premiums on government insurance, purchase special equipment needed for educational purposes, or – here was language beloved of the bureaucracy – for "any other purpose authorized by the Governor in Council."[38] The next day, 11 August, it passed second reading (without a recorded division), was then scrutinized in committee, and after that immediately received third reading.[39] It then moved on to the Senate. Finally, on 15 August, legislation that would affect hundreds of thousands of Canadians, and had moved through the House of Commons in less than twenty-four hours, received assent.[40]

Since the gratuity would be administered by the Department of National Defence and the re-establishment credit by the Department of Veterans Affairs, both Ralston and Mackenzie were active in guiding the legislation through the Commons. One criticism heard in debate came from Karl Homuth, the Progressive Conservative MP for Waterloo South, Ontario, who complained about the constraints that veterans would face in spending their re-establishment credits: "The man may want to go into business, buy a small gas station on the corner. But the government says to him: We must first of all look into this and check up. Here we are by this bill saying to the returned men: Here is something of value to you, but we are going to see how you spend the money. I think it is ridiculous, nonsensical for us to say to the men: We are willing to trust you to go overseas and fight the battles of the country, to risk your life in preserving democracy, but when you come back we cannot trust you with this credit. There will be so much red tape, so much checking before the soldier can spend the money, that it is practically saying to the soldier: We cannot trust you to spend the money yourself. If this is a gratuity let us give it to the soldier."[41] By contrast, based on his own experience, Toronto Liberal MP J.R. Nichol saw wisdom in the government's balanced approach: "Much has been said as to whether these heroes and heroines, when they come back, should be given all these benefits outright ... that everything should be given to them at once and that they should do what they liked with it. I remember, following the last war, calling one day at a home where the young man had come back from overseas. He had been over there four years, and knew little more about what to do with money than a child would know. If my memory is correct he received something over $600. While I was talking to his mother he drove up the door on a motorcycle with a sidecar. The mother said, 'Where did you get that?' 'Oh,' he said, 'I bought that to take you out.' He had paid nearly six hundred dollars for that motorcycle. It was his right; he could do what he liked with the money, but the family were in humble circumstances and had a heavy mortgage on their home, and I have often wondered whether it was just right to distribute money in a lump sum or whether it would have been better for the government to try to protect such men against themselves."[42] For his part, Mackenzie emphasized that the gratuity/re-establishment credit scheme would provide both cash and credit and would safeguard both the "national interest" and "the man's own interest." Individuals would get to make choices with their own money, but the government's purpose of systematic re-establishment would also be advanced.[43] The government was not out "to regiment anyone," and the purpose of its expanding counselling effort on behalf of veterans was to offer them "cooperation and assistance."[44] Mackenzie was manifestly on firm ground in all this, and following passage of the legislation, Herwig congratulated the government for action on gratuities that commanded "general commendation."[45] Words of praise were likewise eventually heard from the Ontario wing of the Canadian Corps Association.[46]

The prime minister hailed the legislation as "a truly wonderful achievement," involving as it did the expenditure of about $750 million.[47] "I never dreamt," he mused in his diary "that at any time in my life, I would be bringing into Parliament a Bill that involved expenditures beyond a few million dollars for one purpose. This is ¾ of a billion dollars for one purpose. At the same time, it gave me great satisfaction to be the one to bring in the resolution and the Bill for gratuities for those who have served voluntarily in this war. I took the position very strongly yesterday at Cabinet Council that our service was volunteer overseas service, and that nothing was too good for those who were ready to risk their lives voluntarily in this war. I have supported everything that has been proposed and has been at all reasonable by way of gratuities, rehabilitation, outlays, etc. It was left to me to make the decision between having all the money given in gratuities in cash or part cash and part re-habilitation. I decided for the latter. The Defence Ministers were for the former for the most part but the Cabinet generally were for the latter."[48]

On 1 October 1944, with the building block of the War Service Grants Act, 1944 (the official short title of the August act) firmly in place, Mackenzie became Canada's first minister of veterans affairs and Woods its first deputy minister. As initially organized, the Department of Veterans Affairs (DVA) had administrative, rehabilitation, treatment, prosthetic services, veterans' insurance, and public relations divisions, as well as the existing Veterans' Bureau (which provided pension applicants with the services of advocates) and the Soldier Settlement and VLA administration.[49] Although governed by their own statutes, the Canadian Pension Commission (now chaired by J.L. Melville) and the War Veterans' Allowance Board (chaired from 27 October 1944 by Dougall Carmichael) were also attached to the department, which supplied them with staff and covered their administrative expenses. The assistant deputy minister was A.J. Dixon, the departmental secretary (acting in the first instance) F.L. Barrow, and the departmental counsel W.G. Gunn. The director general of rehabilitation was Sperrin N.F. Chant, a former University of Toronto psychology professor. He had enlisted in the RCAF in November 1940 and had brought to bear on its affairs his considerable expertise in counselling and testing, serving as director of personnel selection and manning from 1 July 1944. He was seconded to the Department of Pensions and National Health in October 1944, returned to the RCAF in March 1945, and left uniform in May 1945 with the rank of group captain. His principal colleagues in the Rehabilitation Services branch were director of rehabilitation A.M. Wright, whose public service career in veterans' affairs went back to 1919, and J.H. Hogan, assistant director, War Services Grants Act.

The upper ranks of the department consisted entirely of men who had military experience, and the belief was deeply ingrained that veterans could best administer veterans' benefits. Veterans were appointed to the jobs that opened up at DVA, and as a matter of policy the department held back on senior appointments while the war was in progress in order to give those serving overseas who were duly qualified an opportunity to compete for the positions once the fighting stopped.[50] The department had eleven district offices spread across the country, from Halifax to Victoria, each identified by a letter of the alphabet from A to L and headed by a district administrator. There was also an overseas office, located in the United Kingdom at 50 Pall Mall, London. The district administrators were now, in the words of Robert England, the focus of a "complex machinery of hospitals, medical treatment, reconditioning centers, vocational guidance, educational and training facilities, pensions, land settlement, Re-establishment Credits, welfare, employment, infirmaries and

DVA's first director general of rehabilitation, Sperrin Noah Fulton Chant, in his RCAF uniform. He was seconded from the RCAF in 1944. (Courtesy of John Chant)

even burial arrangements."[51] In 1944 the department ran twenty hospitals, situated in seven of the nine provinces (Prince Edward Island and Saskatchewan were served from neighbouring jurisdictions).

An urgent item of business for the new department was to make arrangements for the administration of the re-establishment credits for which veterans now qualified (though not, it was soon decided, veterans who chose to live outside Canada). The lead in this work was taken by England, who joined DVA as a special executive assistant. By 8 February 1945, he was able to report to Woods that the required regulations, procedures, and application forms were ready, that sufficient staff was available in district offices to meet expected demand once newspaper advertising began, and that re-establishment credit advisory committees had been formed in all the districts.[52] The members of those committees – yet another instrument for building support among local elites for a big program of national spending with the potential to shake up regional social hierarchies – had been endorsed by local boards of trade, Canadian Legion representatives, rehabilitation committees, and district administrators. Their existence was indicative of "the sense of responsibility of the business community in respect of the returned veterans."

DVA officials were also kept busy in the first phase of the department's existence with spreading the good news to those in uniform of the benefit package that awaited them. The leading official in this work was Emerson Baker Reid, who brought his considerable expertise in public relations to the department in December 1944.[53] A journalist, Reid (known as Tim) was born in Toronto in 1901 and attended Parkdale Collegiate Institute, 1913–17, and the University of Toronto (general arts), 1919–20. He was a general reporter for the *Windsor Daily Star*, 1922–23, and *Hamilton Herald*, 1923–25, editor of the *North Bay Nugget*, 1925–27, and city editor of the *Toronto Daily Star*, 1927–34. He next worked as an account executive with the McConnell, Baxter and Eastman advertising agency, briefly moved on from there to be advertising manager for H.R. Bain and Co., but then returned to McConnell, Baxter and Eastman. In 1938 he became executive editor of the *Sudbury Daily Star* and the *North Bay Nugget*. He enlisted in the RCAF at North Bay in November 1940 and was eventually posted to London, England, where he did outstanding public relations work.

In 1943, having encountered personal headwinds, Reid returned to Canada and left uniform but soon found his way into the evolving DVA operation. His new unit there placed advertisements in newspapers and magazines, cultivated good relations with the press, sponsored radio programs, promoted the work of the citizens' rehabilitation committees that had been formed across the country, cooperated with the National Film Board on the production of films, and answered numerous inquiries.[54] The radio programs were built around veteran case histories and included a follow-up "question box" interlude, during which many commonly asked questions were answered. At the top of the public relations list, however, was the booklet *Back to Civil Life* (Woods suggested the title), which was eventually distributed to every man and woman in uniform and, through the Dependents' Allowance Board, to their families. The first edition of this tightly written, pocket-sized, and attractively designed publication was issued on 1 June 1944. A second edition, revised to 25 August 1944, was quickly prepared after the passing of the War Service Grants Act, and a million copies were printed and distributed at home and abroad.[55] Thereafter, this official publication, with an exceptional circulation and utility and published in English and French, was revised and reissued as required. The text had a foreword by Mackenzie, followed by consecutively numbered sections (127 in the second edition) organized under general headings. It set a high standard for clarity and comprehensiveness and served the government's purpose admirably.

In the foreword (what follows draws on the language of the second edition), Mackenzie explained that the purpose of the booklet was to inform those in uniform, their prospective employers, and the general public of

DVA's public relations director, Emerson Baker (Tim) Reid, in his RCAF uniform (LAC, Military Service file)

Below:
Pensions and National Health advertisement on the progress of postwar planning (DVA, 32-3, vol. 4)

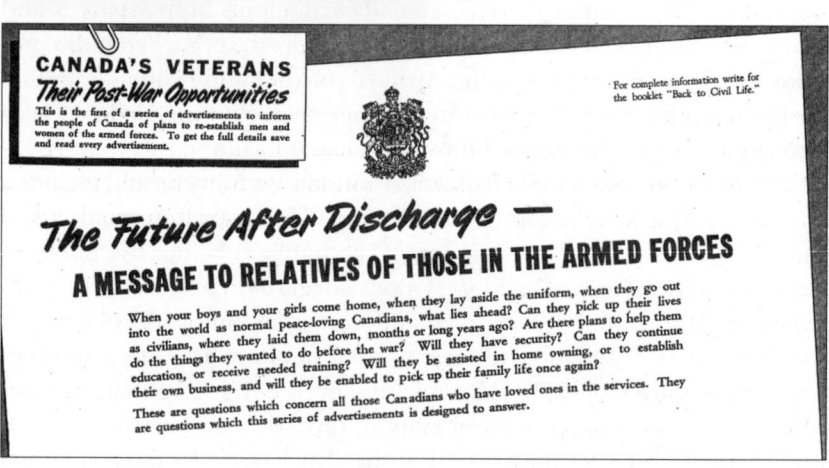

Canada's plan for civil re-establishment. "Canada's rehabilitation belief," he wrote, "is that the answer to civil-re-establishment is a job, and the answer to a job is fitness and training for that job. Our ambition is that these men and women who have taken up arms in defence of their country and their ideals of freedom shall not be penalized for the time they have spent in the services and our desire is that they shall be fitted in every way possible to take their place in Canada's civil and economic life. We believe this ambition and this desire can be achieved. Results up until the present indicate this belief is well founded." The first sentence under the

> **BACK TO CIVIL LIFE**
>
> PREPARED TO INFORM MEMBERS OF THE ARMED FORCES AND CANADIANS GENERALLY OF STEPS TAKEN FOR CIVILIAN REHABILITATION OF THOSE IN UNIFORM
>
> *Issued under the authority of*
> **HON. IAN A. MACKENZIE**
> MINISTER OF PENSIONS AND NATIONAL HEALTH
> JUNE 1st, 1941.

The first edition of the pocket-sized booklet that explained the program known eventually as the Veterans Charter (LAC, Amicus no. 6716389)

first heading – "Objective of the Program" – reinforced Mackenzie's message: "The objective of Canada's plan for the rehabilitation of her armed forces is that every man or woman discharged from the forces shall be in a position to earn a living." Realizing this goal would require that veterans "help themselves" and that employers create opportunities for them; the government's role was to assist those who had served to get started again: "When John Brown ex-sailor, soldier or airman, or Mary Smith, ex-member of the women's services, is ready for civilian occupation again, many courses are open. They may want to return to their old jobs, they may want to learn a new trade, they may want to complete their education or need some assistance after starting business for themselves. The desire may be to have a part in Canada's great agricultural industry or to own a home with three or four acres of land on the outskirts of the community where they are regularly employed. All these things are available and towards them all ex-members of the services are eligible for Departmental, and if necessary, financial assistance." Those who served had not counted the cost when they had enlisted, and the plans of the country to provide them with "opportunities for training and completion of education" would not stint either.

In summary, the benefit package on offer by the time of publication of the greatly expanded third edition of *Back to Civil Life*,[56] revised to 1 April 1946, had evolved to include a $100 clothing allowance that was not subject to income tax (those discharged could also keep their uniforms); the rehabilitation grant (dating from December 1940), also income-tax free, of 30 days' pay and one month's dependants' allowance ("to provide the serviceman and his dependents with some ready money while getting started in civilian life"); free transportation and travelling expenses home or to another destination in Canada up to the equivalent cost; repatriation to the home country of an individual who had come to Canada to enlist; arrangements for the return of dependants from overseas; access to "special facilities" in the national, regional, and local offices of the National Employment Service, and "preferred attention" in the local offices of the Unemployment Insurance Commission; the work guarantee that was provided in the Reinstatement in Civil Employment Act; the gratuity and re-establishment credit benefits provided in the War Service Grants Act; the means-tested and mainly discretionary out-of-work, awaiting-returns, and training and education benefits that were first made available under PC 7633; the opportunity to apply to qualify for a farm, smallholding with "main income ... derived from some source other than the operation of the holding," or a smallholding "coupled with commercial fishing as the chief occupation," under the Veterans' Land Act; preference in civil service employment; the advantages of a revised veterans' insurance act (also passed in 1944);[57] medical treatment (organized in twelve classes, and providing, as class 3, universal and unconditional coverage for one year from discharge); and the continuing discretionary benefits provided under the Pension Act and the War Veterans' Allowance Act. In the case of the Pension Act, the distinction made through the insurance principle in 1940 between disability or death incurred in service abroad compared with service in Canada still applied, though in 1941, under Legion pressure, the government had relented to the extent of authorizing the Canadian Pension Commission to make an award otherwise outside the limit for service in Canada only, provided there were "necessitous circumstances." In 1943, thanks to effective lobbying by the Canadian Soldiers Non-Pensioned Widows' Association, eligibility for the War Veterans' Allowance had been extended to selected widows of Great War veterans according to existing service and income criteria.[58] In 1944 the benefits of the act were also applied to veterans of the Second World War.[59]

To get ready to carry out its medical obligations to disabled pensioners and to honour the commitment to provide general medical service to all veterans for one year from discharge, DVA made sweeping changes in the hospital and health-care system it had inherited from DPNH (where there had been a failed attempt to maintain existing and separate control). Effective 12 June 1944, treatment regulations, which had become "somewhat cumbersome and unwieldy," were consolidated and simplified by PC 4465 following a review undertaken by a special committee chaired by the former Legion president Alex Ross, which had Woods and T.D. Bain, a medical doctor, as its other members.[60] It was this order that formed the legal basis of the one-year general health-care benefit spelled out in *Back to Civil Life*. In 1943–44, DPNH had started an expansion of hospital facilities, and after the formation of DVA this effort was stepped up. Construction of new buildings was undertaken in Halifax, Montreal, London, Hamilton, North Bay, Toronto, Winnipeg, Vancouver, and Victoria; wings were added to existing hospitals in Regina and Edmonton, and grants for service were made to hospitals in Kingston and Port Arthur. The new Toronto hospital – Sunnybrook – was built to accommodate 1,450 beds.[61] The arrangements made for the seriously wounded built on the work of the GACDR Sub-Committee on the Retraining of Special Casualties and were shaped by complaints of war wounded about shabby experiences in existing DPNH hospitals. Paraplegic Jack Higman, the victim of a motorcycle accident in England, was shocked by what he found at Christie Street Hospital in Toronto: "They fed us, they changed the bed, they gave us enemas. That was about our life."[62] John Gartshore, who had been wounded in the Dieppe raid of August 1942, was likewise scathing about this old facility: "It was a factory. There were twenty-five of us on the ward ... I was there from January to April 1943 ... with a bunch of old World War I guys, who had been there since 1918. It was pretty awful."[63] When John Gibbons Counsell, another Dieppe casualty who had been rendered paraplegic, tried to get the Toronto hospital to purchase Everest & Jennings's self-propelled wheelchairs – he was using one himself – his request was refused by the superintendent of the Toronto Orthopaedic Division of DPNH. As late as April 1943, Mackenzie defended Christie Street Hospital as having "the finest and latest of surgical equipment and appliances ... attended by the cream of the medical profession of this great city."[64] But this optimism eventually proved unsustainable, a development that set the stage for radical postwar change.

In the latter part of the war, further refinements were made to the now well-functioning rehabilitation machinery. Working with the armed forces and other government units, veterans' officials established a training school for rehabilitation counsellors. During the fiscal year 1944–45 this had an enrolment of 299, which, in addition to DVA staff, included military officers, other public servants, and industry personnel managers.[65] Counselling as a profession took off in Canada with the Second World War, and DVA quickly established itself as a leader in the field. To facilitate the transition to work, the department worked in tandem with the Department of Labour, which agreed to place veterans' employment advisers in DVA rehabilitation centres and have veterans' officers in its Employment and National Selective Service (responsible for wartime labour allocation) offices across the country. In its first annual report, DVA broke down the 11,407 grants and benefits approved in 1944–45 under the Post-Discharge Re-establishment Order as follows: out-of-work benefit, 3,542; vocational training, 5,381; university training 1,094; awaiting returns (from farm or business) benefit, 802; temporarily incapacitated benefit, 588.[66] Not surprisingly, activity had picked up sharply towards the end of the year. As the war began to wind down, a confident, organized, and experienced DVA believed it was ready for the big wave of releases soon to come.

In January 1945 a new chapter in the government's program for ex-service women opened when DVA appointed a female executive assistant to Director General Chant.[67] The proposal for some such appointment had come from the GACDR Sub-committee on the Special Problems of Discharged Women, and Woods was sympathetic to the view that the women's side of the rehabilitation program should be presided over by women and that female veterans should be advised by female counsellors.[68] The person chosen for the executive assistant position was Olive Ruth Russell, who thereafter played a pivotal role in the affairs of Canada's women veterans. In *Back to Civil Life*, a subheading under "Object of the Program," printed in bold, left no doubt about the status of ex-service women in Canada's rehabilitation program: "Women are fully eligible." It was Russell's job to see that this objective was realized.

Born in Delta (Leeds County), Ontario, in 1897, she was originally a teacher by profession and served as principal of the continuation school in her native town.[69] In 1928 she left this position and enrolled at the University of Toronto, where in 1931 she obtained an honours BA in psychology. In 1935 she completed a doctorate in psychology at the University of Edinburgh. Her education included summer courses in educational and vocational guidance in Vienna and in counselling and personnel work at Columbia University in New York. But even with all these qualifications, she found herself earning less than she had before she had gone to university. She later attributed this in part to the effect of the Great Depression, but also considered herself a victim "of the fact that Canada lagged so far behind in developing Psychology and Guidance."[70] For some time after completing her graduate studies, Russell was a research assistant at the Ontario College of Education. Her next job was at Moulton College, Toronto, where she was head of mathematics and director of educational and vocational guidance. She enlisted in the

Olive Ruth Russell in her CWAC uniform. As executive assistant to the director general of rehabilitation, she led DVA's program for women veterans. (Susan Ruth Swallow, MA thesis, 153)

CWAC in May 1942 and, following basic training, was selected for the officers training course. She was thereafter one of the first two women appointed to the personnel selection branch, where she worked as a counsellor. Commenting on a draft article about her career and work, she told the women's editor of *Saturday Night* in July 1945 that she did not want to leave the impression with the magazine's readers that she was a "feminist." "It is true," she wrote, "I try to be very on my toes all the time to protect and advance women's right to freedom of choice as an adult citizen in a democracy, and do all I can to see that the equality of opportunity and benefits provided by the legislation for ex-service women may become a reality in practice, but I do try to be gracious about it all and try to avoid the antagonisms that so easily arise, especially in regard to the question of the married woman working."[71] This was revealing, but there can be no doubt about the strength of Russell's convictions as an advocate of equal rights for women in Canadian society.

On 15 March 1944 she explained her views on the impact the war was having on Canadian women in an address to the University Women's Club of Dalhousie University.[72] Women, she observed, were "participating in the war effort to an extent that few would have dreamed possible even a decade ago." In Canada the number of women at work in industry had grown from 600,000 at the beginning of the war to 1,200,000 in 1944, of whom approximately 27 per cent were married women. At the end of the war, when military-related work was no longer available, employment would have to be found for about 500,000 women. This situation made imperative the undertaking of research to determine the future work intentions of married women. "I have come across ... married women," Russell commented, "who tell me they can scarcely remember what their husbands look like. They married in haste shortly before their husbands went overseas and they say they feel they do not know them and have little idea what their reaction will be if and when they meet again."

Another influence on the postwar work situation would be the fact that in every field of employment they had entered, women had proved their competence and adaptability. Service women were showing great versatility, as were their counterparts in industry, "Rosie the Riveter" and "Winnie the Welder," who had abandoned their "pretty frocks and bridge teas" for "overalls, lunch pails and production charts." The result of their efforts was a growing trend in Canadian society towards greater equality between men and women. Evidence of this was to be found in the increased pay of women in the forces; instead of receiving two-thirds to four-fifths of what men were paid for the same work, they were now being given the same trades pay as men, and although initially ineligible for dependants' allowances, they now qualified for them. Among civilian workers, pay differentials between men and women had likewise been eroded in many instances. Women had found a "financial freedom" in the war situation, which men would henceforth ignore at their peril. While it was true that many women would get married and leave the labour market at the end of the war, it was also the case that many who had taken jobs since 1939 would want to go on working. It was thus crucial, warned Russell, "to avoid having women looked upon as competing with men for jobs":

> Some people are already beginning to discuss the demobilization of women as though the object were to take women out of employment regardless of their need to earn their living. Since woman's full right to work has been taken for granted in the war emergency and she has been able to prove her efficiency, is it not natural to assume that in the employment market after the war her claim to the right of employment should be based on her merits rather than her sex?
>
> The war has broken down much of the traditional prejudice of employers against hiring women for many kinds of work and it

seems highly desirable that in future we prevent the return of such prejudices. This must not mean that women are to prevent men from overseas and others from obtaining suitable employment, and it is hoped moreover that women will not become unfair competitors for jobs through the return of lower wage rates for women. The best way to prevent pre-war barriers to women regarding employment is to keep the demand for labour high enough so that every worker's help is needed somewhere. This can be done; and many of our Nation's statesmen have assured us that it will be done.

The right of women to work should be based on "merit," asserted Russell, and there should be no "discrimination on sex grounds." But it would also have to be recognized that women were "vitally important as homemakers and rearers of the Nation's children" and that many workers would be needed for "household duties." Survey data showed that women who had left housework and farm work were reluctant to return to those jobs and that married women who had gone out to work exhibited a range of opinion about becoming full-time homemakers again. This situation posed "a special challenge," namely, to transform housework and related jobs into "attractive and desirable occupations." The key to doing this was to introduce training and apprenticeship, and enforce pay and hours-of-work standards.

Once established at DVA, Russell began to work out plans with the newly created Department of National Health and Welfare and the National Film Board for a film project on home and family life. The aim of the project was to educate ex-service men and women in successful homemaking.[73] Involving both men and women was appropriate because homemaking was "a partnership for which both husband and wife must be prepared to share responsibility." Films would be produced in English and French and a short course introduced for ex-service women who were about to become homemakers.

If education for home life was a pet project, of necessity Russell's main concern at DVA was how the counselling of women should proceed. She explained her position on this in a lengthy statement she prepared for a counsellors' training course held on 19 February 1945.[74] To the end of January 1945, she noted, more than 43,000 women had enlisted in the Canadian armed forces, of whom more than 3,000 were now serving overseas. Added to these were approximately 4,000 nurses and 58 women doctors, more than 2,000 of whom were serving overseas. Altogether, about 47,000 women had entered the forces, about 5,000 of whom were still overseas. About 10,000 had already been discharged, which left about

34,000 in the women's forces, plus the doctors and nurses. Of the 34,000, about 5,900 were in the navy, about 14,400 in the army, and about 13,700 in the air force. Women who had already left the forces had for the most part been well counselled at DVA by men. Looking to the future, however, although the department would not be setting up a separate women's division, it would be appointing women counsellors.

The single exception, Russell continued, to the equality of the benefits between male and female veterans promised in *Back to Civil Life* was the provision that a married woman could not draw out-of-work benefits if her husband could support her and was legally obligated to do so. In practice, however, it was "unlikely" that women would pursue "some of the training open to men." On this critical point, Russell quoted approvingly from a report to the training branch of the Department of Labour by Laura (Taylor) Hardy, president of the Canadian National Council of Women.[75] "Open all courses equally to men and women and you will find only very few women will enter what might be classed as courses typical for men." While behind the scenes she was still working out her proposal for films and a course on homemaking, Russell told the counsellors that training for domestic life was also being considered. It was not possible to predict accurately how many ex-service women would want to undertake training courses, but the experience of the armed forces and the war industry suggested that demand would be substantial. DVA had to be ready for all eventualities, and it had to be acknowledged that counselling was both an "art and a science" and required both "objective measures" and "subjective appraisals."

From the requirements of counselling, Russell moved on to employment prospects for women, reiterating much of what she had said in her 1944 Halifax speech but adding a few refinements. Women's "special responsibility for family life" was undeniable, she observed, but the "hard fact" was that for many this way of life would no longer be possible. Before the war women had outnumbered men in the Canadian population, and after the war there would "be a much higher proportion of unmarried women." In truth, "thousands of Canadian women" would have to "accept the permanent function of breadwinner because of the loss of husbands and prospective husbands in the war." Added to these were the many other women who would not want to give up a "hard-won economic independence" and many married women who would now want to combine wage work with home management. Unfortunately, "some people" were "already beginning to discuss the demobilization of women as though the object were to take women out of employment regardless of their skills and their need to earn a living." Katherine Kent had summed this up in *Maclean's*, where she had written that it was beginning to look as if "the old game of employment by sex, rather than by merit" was "on the books" again.[76] This attitude had to be fought at every turn, and DVA could lead by example, Russell told the counsellors:

> I trust you will not think I am a feminist thinking only of advantages for women if I discuss further the matter of sex discrimination in employment. I am assuming that I am speaking to friends who share the generous and fair attitudes towards women characteristic of the Department, and also that you, as veterans, are eager to see that ex-service women, as well as men from the services will have just treatment after their war service is over ...
>
> The war has broken down much of the traditional prejudices of employers against hiring women, but there is danger of it returning ...
>
> After the war is over, can we justify saying to ex-service women (or to those civilian women who have worked so faithfully and efficiently and who wish, or need, to go on working) that we can no longer use their services? Can we look on them merely as competitors for jobs and accept policies and practices which would drive them out of employment after having worked so well in wartime? Most would agree that this is wrong; nevertheless, there is danger of it happening unless the matter is faced squarely now and employers count women in on their post-war employment plans.
>
> It does seem as though the position of women in regard to employment may need all possible support after the war. Is it not our responsibility to help create public opinion and machinery that will make it possible to put into effect the principle adopted by the Department of granting to women opportunities and pay according to abilities and services, regardless of sex?

"Fair play" required that women be treated equally. So too did the common good; women had skills that should and must be used in the national interest. No woman wanted to feel that because she had a job a man was denied work, and this need not be the case. The answer was to provide "suitable employment opportunities for all," and with the same determination that characterized the war effort this could be done. With this objective in view, Russell appended to her printed remarks wide-ranging lists of vocations for women and a bibliography of books and pamphlets

Harold Williams Jamieson, DVA's superintendent of education and former school principal (*Montreal Star*, 9 February 1954)

relating to the rehabilitation of women. Her initiative was indicative of the formative role that DVA was now playing in relation to yet another sea change in Canadian life brought on by the war.

The pace of change likewise quickened for Canadian universities in 1944–45.[77] At a meeting of the National Conference of Canadian Universities (NCCU) in Kingston in January 1944, registrar Thomas H. Matthews of McGill agreed, assisted by N.A.M. MacKenzie of the University of British Columbia and A.B. Fennell of the University of Toronto, to draw up the final report of the committee which the NCCU had launched in 1942 to consider the postwar reality that Canadian universities were likely to face.[78] This document, which was eventually printed by the University of Toronto Press and translated into French, was presented by MacKenzie to a full NCCU gathering at McMaster University in Hamilton on 12 June.[79] Harold Williams Jamieson, superintendent of educational training at DPNH and a product of the First World War's Khaki University, was also present at this meeting. Adopted the next day, the *Report of the National Conference of Canadian Universities on Post-War Problems* thereafter guided the universities' approach towards veterans.[80] As printed, the report had a one-page introduction, sections dealing with "Problems Arising from P.C. 7633" and "Other Post-War Problems," and nine appendices. The appendices covered a wide range of topics and were, in effect, research reports by some of the leading scholars and university administrators in the country. Thirteen recommendations were made in the report.

The introduction concisely spelled out the challenge that now faced the member institutions of the NCCU. Universities would soon have "heavy burdens laid upon them," but they would also now have an "unprecedented opportunity to render an essential service to the nation." In "an age of reconstruction," they would have to "reconstruct themselves."[81] The specific problems arising out of the Post-Discharge Re-establishment Order were to determine the number and distribution of ex-service students, pay for the new staff, buildings, and equipment that a surge in enrolment would require, and deal with the curriculum, scheduling, guidance, and other requirements of a unique student cohort. The recommendations made by the NCCU included the call for additional career survey research in the armed forces, the introduction of a procedure whereby universities could secure the early release "from industry, government services, or the Armed Forces" of individuals needed for teaching,[82] the establishment of a joint consultative committee to bring together university, military, government, and Canadian Legion Educational Services representatives, and the inclusion by federal, provincial, and municipal governments of university buildings in construction plans "to augment the available employment opportunities and prevent the onset of economic depression."[83]

Not surprisingly, the key recommendation, number six in the list of thirteen, concerned money. Noting that the current fees of students "did not meet more than one-half of the cost of their college education" and that the costs to be incurred on behalf of veterans would not be covered by their tuition payments, the NCCU made the case that further public financial help would be needed to enable the universities to deliver "the full benefits intended by the generous policy of the Dominion Government."[84] Backing up this recommendation was a thorough comparative study by Vice-Principal W.E. McNeill of Queen's University of the support afforded education nationally in Great Britain, Canada, and the United States. Although section 93 of the British North America Act, 1867, had made education (except for the protection of denominational school rights) a matter of exclusive provincial jurisdiction, Ottawa had been drawn into the field by "the close relation of Education to national welfare."[85] Over the years, Ottawa had educated Aboriginal Canadians, run military and naval colleges, offered military training in universities and schools, granted educational charters (to Queen's University and Frontier College), provided for technical and vocational education, trained pilots for civil aviation, maintained schools of navigation, given grants-in-aid to individual students, and financed youth-training plans and much more. The message in all this, though not directly stated, was perfectly clear: Ottawa had a national responsibility in relation to veterans, and there was no constitutional barrier to national public spending in the field of education to meet that obligation. Indeed, the dominion government could keep its promises to the veterans only by investing in universities on a countrywide basis. Simply put, a national duty required a national response. Nothing else would do.

The government gave its answer in a letter that Mackenzie wrote to the sitting NCCU president, James S. Thomson (president of the University of Saskatchewan), on 19 March 1945.[86] Since Canadian universities were diverse, it would be necessary to devise a formula for the payment of grants that would "ensure uniformity regarding the services to be rendered by the universities." Before a submission could be made to the Treasury Board, therefore, the universities would have to confirm their willingness to meet nine conditions. These Mackenzie spelled out as follows:

1 So arrange admission dates that fully qualified veterans can enter a university within three months of their acceptance for a course and without disadvantage to themselves.
2 Provide a counselling and advisory service for veterans which will cooperate with the Department of Veterans Affairs regarding the suitability of veterans for university education, as well as advise veterans on courses of study and aid their adjustment to their studies.
3 Provide summer sessions in order to accommodate veterans.
4 Avoid excessively large classes which would impair the effectiveness of instruction.
5 Insure adequate residence accommodation, and provide a housing service to aid veterans in procuring accommodation.
6 Engage additional, qualified instructors for veterans' classes when necessary.
7 Establish loan funds or other assistance for veterans to finance their courses beyond the period of eligibility for benefits under the Post-Discharge Re-establishment Order.
8 Control incoming numbers of civilian students so that veterans may have the fullest opportunity to make use of university facilities.
9 Re-adapt courses to the special needs of adult veterans seeking to enter professions.

DVA, the minister continued, regarded university education "as an exceedingly important part of the rehabilitation programme," not only because of the advantages it would give to individual veterans but because of its "broad implications" for the future development of Canada. The government was anxious to assist the universities but could not recommend that veterans be charged higher fees than those that other students paid; hence, the need for a formula that would "indicate the additional services to be provided for veterans." In conclusion, Mackenzie asked Thomson whether he would consider it advisable to appoint a commission to supervise the payment of grants should they be made available.

Thomson's reply, dated 2 April 1945, assured the minister that the universities were not out "to 'cash in' on any scheme of education for demobilised men and women." At the same time, they would be "gravely handicapped" unless assisted.[87] To ensure that money was spent for the purpose intended by the government, either a commission could be set up to supervise expenditure or the universities could submit signed statements, with requisite accounting, specifying that the funds received had been used to educate veterans. After meeting with Woods in Ottawa, Thomson reported to the executive committee of the NCCU in Toronto on 30 April 1945 on the proposed establishment by DVA of an advisory committee on university education.[88] This idea was endorsed by the executive, and the Advisory Committee on University Training for Veterans was then established by PC 3206 of 3 May 1945.[89] The purpose of the committee was to advise the minister of veterans affairs "on matters relating to the university training provided under The Post-Discharge Re-Establishment Order."[90] Woods was named chairman and Jamieson secretary, their colleagues including presidents of four universities (New Brunswick, Toronto, Saskatchewan, and British Columbia) and one college (Carleton), two principals (McGill and Queen's), and two rectors (Laval and Université de Montréal).[91] Under its terms of reference, the committee was to advise on policy that concerned : "(a) ... contributing to the additional counselling, instructional and administrative costs incurred by Canadian Universities in their service to discharged personnel. (b) ... undergraduate and post-graduate training outside of Canada. (c) ... ensuring that suitable Canadian University facilities are used to the fullest extent. [and] (d) Other problems which may arise as demobilization proceeds."[92] Members would be reimbursed for "actual and necessary expenses" when away from home on committee work.[93] At the first meeting of the group, President Thomson pronounced that the policy of the government with respect to university education for veterans was "more enlightened" than that of any other country he knew about.[94]

With the Advisory Committee in place, Woods recommended favourably to the deputy minister of finance the request of the executive committee of the NCCU for the payment by the government of a grant of $150 per year above and beyond tuition fees on behalf of each student veteran.[95] Action was then taken by PC215/4940 of 13 July 1945, which applied to the period 1 July 1945 to 30 June 1946, authorized the $150 per student payment (officially called a "supplementary grant"), and set a cap of $500 on the tuition fees, student fees, athletic fees, and subsidy that the government could pay on behalf of a discharged person. To qualify, a veteran was required to commence or resume university work within fifteen months of discharge, unless exempted from this regulation by the minister. In short order, Canadian universities had enthusiastically entered the age of formula financing, student loans, professional counselling, and, more generally, big government.

During 1944 and into 1945, the Veterans' Land Act (VLA) administration continued to acquire properties in preparation for the general demobilization to come.[96] By the end of the fiscal year 1944–45 (31 March 1945), 5,511 properties had been considered for farm use and 2,631 approved for purchase. Of the latter, 1,467 – encompassing 309,423 acres – had actually been bought (at an average price of $21.58 per acre) and the purchase of the remaining 1,164 was pending. To the same date, 1,757 blocks or parcels of land had been considered for smallholding use and 1,149 approved for purchase. Of the latter number, title had been secured to 977, encompassing 15,448 acres and bought at an average cost (including improvements) of $148.58 per acre. The purchase of the remaining 172 properties identified as suitable for smallholding settlement was pending. Of the parcels of land in British Columbia that had belonged to Japanese Canadians and had been bought from the Custodian of Enemy Property, 175 were classified as suitable for farm use and 524 for smallholding. Taking account of property leased before distribution to ex-service applicants, as of 31 March 1945, the VLA administration had on hand 292,109 acres of farmland and 13,773 acres suitable for smallholdings. To 31 March 1945, 4,097 applications had been made under the act and 1,161 applicants deemed qualified – 355 for farming, 794 for smallholding, and 12 for commercial fishing; 382 applicants had been turned down and 318 decisions were pending. Capital costs to the same date averaged $4,349 for farming (including an average of $1,002 for chattels), $3,319 for smallholdings (including an average of $257 for chattels), and $2,245 for commercial fishing (including an average of $1,560 for land and improvements and $865 for equipment). A second and revised edition of *Handbook No. 1* was published in July 1944, and progress was made during the year in opening up provincial Crown lands for settlement use. In December 1944 the superintendents of the regional offices met with the director in Ottawa (the third such meeting) and discussed the last details of organization and ways and means of advancing settlement operations. On this occasion, Murchison mused that while the last two years had been strenuous, they had also been productive. "It is the busy people of this world," he said, "who get things done because there is not time to leave them undone."[97] While it was true that VLA senior staff were approaching retirement age and therefore "looking for the shade of a friendly tree" under which to spend their remaining days, "philosophizing on the iniquities of the world in general," they brought to the big job at hand "the calmness of judgment' that came from "mature experience." Woods, who was present at the meeting, was described by Murchison as "an old associate in Soldier Settlement and sundry other activities."

In a policy statement sent to officials at the beginning of 1945, Murchison authorized the immediate settlement of veterans who qualified under the act.[98] The policy of holding back, for those serving overseas, the land that had already been acquired would be continued, but 3,000 smallholdings would be subtracted from this total and houses built on these properties in 1945. To meet "exceptional needs," a small number of the farms already banked would also now be made available. Qualified applicants for farms, Murchison explained, should locate properties that suited their needs and then seek VLA approval and purchase (all VLA-supported properties were registered in the name of the director). A duly qualified veteran wanting to establish on a smallholding or in commercial fishing could either opt for one of the smallholdings across the country on which houses would now be built, or locate a suitable property and then seek VLA approval and purchase of it. Within the body of qualified applicants, priority was to be given to those who had served overseas ("outside the Western Hemisphere, but including service anywhere in a sea-going ship of war, service in an air crew on coastal patrol operations and service in Greenland, Iceland and the Aleutian Islands"), and to those receiving disability pensions or "confronted with exceptional circumstances." Within the priority groups, priority would be given to those who wanted to establish themselves in the provinces in which they had lived before enlistment. In a letter that accompanied this directive, Murchison reminded his officials that the act itself, the regulations issued under it, and a flexible administrative policy gave them "ample scope to exercise sound judgment" in dealing with applicants, who should be given "the benefit of the doubt."[99] "No member of the staff," he wrote, "appreciates more than the Director the difficulties confronting responsible officers in evaluating the human equation but we must keep in mind that the long range welfare of the veteran and his family are a responsibility we must discharge to the best of our ability. If for good and sufficient reason we cannot help a veteran under the terms of this Act, let our decisions be temperate and our contacts conducted along lines which give the minimum cause for ill feeling."

Earlier, Roman Catholic naval chaplain Father Andrew MacDonell had suggested to Mackenzie that "specially selected chaplains" should be designated to proselytize among those in uniform the virtues of land ownership and to "act as liaison officers between their respective Churches and the Director of the V.L.A."[100] In a spirited testament on behalf of small proprietors, MacDonell argued that what was at stake in the government's land act was of fundamental importance to society: "Land ownership is democracy's best defence because it safeguards democracy's heritage of freedom and security. The family farm is the classic form of true private property, the right to which must be defended at all costs. In a similar category are the artisan's tools, a fisherman's boat, a widow's competence. Every means should be taken, therefore, to get as many ex-servicemen as possible on the land, thus building not only for the soldier but building for the future of his family, for the country, and for Church and Religion ... He who owns land breathes the air of a free man. He who owns the land he tills is armoured with security. In hard times he need not stand in a bread line." In response, Mackenzie told the priest that he had not before heard the "objective policy" behind the VLA "stated completely in so few words."[101] At the same time, the "additional services" proposed by Father MacDonell were superfluous in present circumstances. Indeed, so great was the interest in land settlement in the armed forces that the director of the VLA was concerned about the ability of his organization to cope with the demand for its services.

In November 1944 a thorny issue relating to the administration of the VLA arose as a result of an exchange between Murchison and A.R. Harvey, president of the Vancouver Real Estate Exchange.[102] When Harvey requested an explanation of section 33 of the act, which forbade the paying of fees and commissions in the transfer of property to the director,[103] Murchison gave a blunt reply: The section in question had been inserted to prevent "the operations of unscrupulous agents" and to protect officials from any suspicion that they had "a personal interest in land transactions passing through their hands."[104] In response, at its 20–21 November convention in Toronto, the Ontario Association of Real Estate Boards ("composed in the main of fathers of returned Soldiers and of Soldiers themselves") passed a resolution objecting to Murchison's "insulting statements" and calling for the removal of section 33.[105] Mackenzie answered for the government, expressing regret that Murchison's remarks had caused offence but stating firmly that section 33 would stand.[106] It had been given full consideration, he maintained, and was in keeping with the intention of the act: "The agent has a legitimate function to perform where a would-be vendor has to search for a buyer. Under the Veterans' Land Act there is only one buyer, the Dominion Government. No vendor needs an agent to find that buyer. On the other hand the Government has established an organization of trained and experienced personnel to do its buying. In the circumstances we cannot find that there is any useful function for a vendor's agent to perform or that his activities would contribute to the successful administration of the Act, which has one single purpose, that of enabling ex-service personnel with the requisite inclination, experience and background to establish themselves in farming with reasonable prospects of success."

Subsequently, arguing that many veterans interested in land settlement were dissatisfied with the service they were receiving and that brokers all over the country were being approached for assistance regarding the purchase of suburban property, the Canadian Association of Real Estate Boards tried again. Specifically, it sought the introduction of a procedure whereby realtors could list farms with local VLA officials, whereupon veterans looking for property would be referred to them for help, with "any commission involved" being "well earned."[107] But this proposal also met a frosty reception in Ottawa and went nowhere. As Murchison explained to Mackenzie, to have 5,000 real estate agents in Canada positioned to collect commissions would create endless difficulty.[108] Agents whose deals fell through would blame VLA administrators, while the same officials might be criticized by veterans for putting the interest of agents first, the result being that "the Minister would be submerged with complaints and criticisms of all sorts, however ill-founded." "Personally," Murchison ventured, "I prefer the wrath of my many friends who are in the real estate business here and there across the Dominion to the wrath of a numerically larger part of the population." Toronto Liberal MP A.W. Roebuck lobbied DVA on behalf of the aggrieved realtors, but the department heard supporting words from the Canadian Corps Association and the United Farmers of Alberta and refused to budge.[109]

The decision of the VLA administration to build houses on smallholdings reflected growing concern in the country as the war progressed that demobilization would bring a major housing crisis. According to one estimate, 50,000 to 100,000 housing units would have to be built in the first year after the war ended and 700,000 in the first postwar decade.[110] Speaking in May 1944, J.L. Price, president of the National House Builders Association, said that there were two schools of thought about the housing future of Canada – one "defeatist" and the other, to which he belonged, "moderate."[111] The defeatist perspective was that employment and wages following the war would be such that only about 40 per cent of families would be able to afford their own housing, the remaining 60 per cent depending on the government "to keep a roof over their heads." This, he urged, was "a most demoralizing doctrine" that should be "vigorously stamped out." By contrast, moderate thinkers believed that postwar economic conditions would be such that most people would be able to afford their own housing (which at the time meant single-family detached dwellings), with only a small minority requiring government help; those now in uniform should be assured that suitable and fairly priced houses would be available to them following demobilization.

Woods was of like mind, and in March 1944 the distribution of the report of the reconstruction committee's subcommittee on housing triggered the appointment of a GACDR subcommittee "to study the general question of urban housing facilities for discharged men, having regard to the provisions made for rural housing under the Veterans' Land Act."[112] K.M. Cameron, chief engineer in the Public Works Department, was named chairman, the other members being W.A. Mackintosh, Murchison, Price, F.W. Nicholls (director of housing, Department of Finance), and A.W. Mathers of Toronto. C.N. Senior, a former newspaperman who was Mackenzie's secretary and now GACDR executive director, acted as secretary.[113] At the 18 April 1944 meeting of the subcommittee, Murchison submitted a memorandum that argued the case for financial aid to veterans to buy houses in urban areas.[114] The assistance he envisaged would be administered by a new government agency and would cover the needs of about 100,000 veterans. Subsequently, a new national housing bill was prepared for submission to Parliament, a resolution preliminary to this bill being introduced in the Commons on 31 July, followed by the introduction and first reading of legislation on 5 August.[115] Woods pushed for the inclusion of a clause, which he understood was being contemplated, specifying that the cost of any benefit conferred on veterans be charged to a department other than DPNH.[116] This would safeguard the interest of veterans "until the most suitable formula of benefit" for them could be settled. "Such a clause," he wrote "will be of assurance to members of the forces that their problem is under consideration; it will be a pledge to some form of action; and it will involve no hardship because, until the wartime demand upon labour and materials has diminished, there can be no large scale building of houses even by those who have already been discharged."

The benefit for the veterans now favoured by the GACDR subcommittee on housing was that, in agreements made under the proposed new national housing act, they should be entitled to a rebate "of half of one month's interest for each month of ... military service."[117] But this recommendation ran into criticism in the GACDR itself on several grounds – that it would be dangerous to tamper with interest arrangements under the housing act; that the likelihood of veterans comparing the proposed housing benefit with the benefit available under the VLA pointed to the need for "a substantial capital grant" (as Murchison had recommended); and that any benefit given to veterans for new home construction would have to be extended to veterans who had already had houses but were still paying them off.[118] An argument heard in GACDR deliberations against the introduction of the proposed capital grants for urban housing held that establishing a farm or a smallholding was by definition different from buying a house in a town or city in that the properties covered by the VLA were directly related to making a living and "had definite rehabilitative value not associated with an urban home." It was this difference that justified government financial support in one instance but not the other. It was also the case that nobody could succeed in farming "if saddled with a debt representing close to 100 % of the value of his property."[119] Accordingly, without the VLA provision for "a free grant," veterans would eschew land settlement as a re-establishment option. Again, if the comparable support was given to veterans to buy urban houses rather than locating on smallholdings in "semi-rural surroundings," the advantages of urban life would mean that there would be few takers for smallholdings.[120]

Ultimately, the proponents of interest rate support prevailed, and on 2 August Woods made a specific proposal to Mackenzie in this regard.[121] It called for a special section of the housing act whereby veterans approved by the minister of pensions and national health would qualify for interest relief on properties acquired to a maximum value of $4,800, depending on the duration of their service. Under this arrangement, assuming an interest rate of 2.25 per cent, a man who had served overseas for four years, bought a house for $4,800, and made a down payment of $480 would qualify for $388.80 in interest relief, to be paid out monthly for four years. This scheme would also apply to veterans who already held mortgages, and an equivalent financial advantage would be extended to those who opted for home improvement or extension loans. Woods now further recommended – the Legion was pushing hard for this – that the government guarantee chartered bank loans to veterans requiring cash to establish or re-establish themselves in professions or businesses. The guarantee would apply to loans of up to $2,500 ($1,000 for retail merchants and $250 for craftsmen seeking to acquire the tools of their trade), with one dollar lent for every three dollars invested by the veteran. To get all this started, an order-in-council was drafted adding a part three to the Post-Discharge Re-establishment Order (now consolidated in PC5210),[122] but this initiative was soon overtaken by the cabinet decision in favour of the gratuity/re-establishment credit package. The House of Commons Special Committee on Reconstruction and Re-establishment urged action through the housing legislation and through the programs and services of the Department of Reconstruction and DVA in order to give veterans "every opportunity to establish themselves adequately in decent home surroundings."[123] But no action was taken to introduce a separate urban housing program for ex-service personnel. Veterans enjoyed a preference in relation to a limited supply of houses constructed during the war by Wartime Housing Limited,[124] but no mention was made of them in the National Housing Act, 1944, which was given assent on 15 August and whose terms applied equally to all Canadians.[125] Veterans could use their gratuities and re-establishment credits under the War Service Grants Act to get into the housing market – either privately or through the new housing legislation – but beyond that, Ottawa would have no specific obligation to them. "From the standpoint of social stability," Senior told Woods on 25 July 1944, "I would think it of the highest importance to go to the limit to make it attractive to veterans to become home owners."[126] But what was actually decided upon in the summer of 1944 – concisely summarized in *Back to Civil Life* – manifestly fell well short of this mark, and this outcome was fraught with trouble for DVA in the postwar period. In a crucial round, Woods and his associates had not got their way.

In a radio broadcast on 30 December 1944 – one of a series in which he addressed in layman's terms the government's evolving plans for veterans – Woods explained the purpose of the War Service Grants Act and detailed how the legislation would be administered.[127] Re-establishment credits, he said, offered an alternative path to re-establishment for those who did "not need, or wish, to take training or settle on the land," and their administration would "not be surrounded by red-tape." They were not repayable, and in this instance "credit" meant "outright grant." Moreover, an eligible veteran could draw on his or her credits as required within ten years of discharge. This arrangement would facilitate "careful and long range planning." The re-establishment credit ("a duplicate of the gratuity") belonged to the individual veteran, and the government's only interest in regulating the use of the funds involved was to see that they were "wisely expended." Whereas the gratuity could be spent by the veteran "according to his conscience and his judgment, without control," the re-establishment credit was specifically directed at "certain constructive purposes." Eligibility for the re-establishment credit required that a veteran first apply for and be granted the gratuity. When the first gratuity payment was made (this award was paid out in monthly instalments until exhausted), a veteran who had not applied for training or land settlement could then apply for the re-establishment credit. Veterans had choices to make, and it was important that they prepare themselves to act by studying the overall rehabilitation program.

As plans for assisting Second World War veterans thus matured in 1944, the soldier settlement scheme was in a new, and final, phase. Starting 19 November 1942, based on a recommendation from the special parliamentary committee on land settlement of veterans, PC 10472 provided for a reduction in the debts of the remaining soldier settlers, as recommended by the director of the program (i.e., Murchison, who now wore two land settlement hats).[128] Applications for this relief had to be made by 31 December 1943, and 1,550 settlers, more than 80 per cent of them in Saskatchewan and Alberta, actually benefited. Dissatisfied with this action, a delegation of nine settlers presented a petition to a cabinet committee in May 1944. This called for the cancellation of all remaining soldier settler debt, the grant of clear title to settlers still on the land, and a cash payment to the settlers who had given up their land since the beginning of the war in 1939. These demands were refused by the government on three grounds: that fewer than 5 per cent of the settlers still on the books had signed the petition; that most soldier settlers still in debt were meeting their payments; and that it would be "a breach of faith with those who had repaid their loans and with those who had kept their agreements in good standing" to grant the request.[129] A 1944 DVA publication on soldier settlement noted that during the fiscal years 1939–40 to 1943–44, of the $5,230,642.31 owing by soldier settlers, $4,506,225.08 had actually been paid and, in addition, $1,293,235.90 had been made in advance payment. The reality was that, thanks to the good economic times that had come with the war, most of the remaining soldier settlers had been able to fulfill their contracts with the government. Most of them were now making "excellent progress" – 1,648 had paid off their loans and acquired title during the first five years of the war – and the benefit of the War Veterans'

Allowance Act was available to the "small number" who were still in financial trouble.[130] As of 19 August 1944, as the soldier settlement scheme headed for the history books, of the original 25,017 settlers, 5,358 had paid off their loans and 5,696 were still under contract. In a bitter 1948 submission to a House of Commons special committee on veterans affairs, having surveyed the troubled history of a flawed initiative, President H.C. Baker and Secretary Alfred J. Sibley of the Soldier Settlers' Association of Canada called for immediate action by the government to give "clear title to all lands held by soldier settlers of World War One, their widows and next-of-kin."[131] "The savage vindictiveness with which soldier settlers have been pursued," they maintained, "would give one the impression that they were Nazi enemies, instead of our own Canadian soldiers." The soldier settlement scheme finally ran its course in 1964, with the last settler still in arrears to Ottawa refusing to make a last payment of $10.[132] It was a fitting end to a troubled history.

Exiled in Kaslo in the British Columbia interior, Zennosuke Inouye was still campaigning in 1944 to recover his property in Surrey. In January, as part of an extensive and continuing correspondence with the Vancouver office of the Custodian of Enemy Property, having failed to get a satisfactory answer to matters he had raised in relation to the lease of his property, he issued this challenge to authority: "As an owner of property, though it may be small in size and value, I am always concerned how it is being handled by you, and I believe I am entitled to any information in connection with the matter. It is my desire that a little more sympathetic attitude should be extended to me whenever such enquiries are made to you, and I think you are duty bound to report to me."[133] On 4 October 1944, in a letter from Kaslo that fully orchestrated a case he made over and over in the months that followed, Inouye appealed directly to Prime Minister King:

> Your petitioner is an ex-service man of Japanese origin who served ... in the last Great War, and is a pensioner due to war disability.
> After returning from the overseas service in 1919, your petitioner acquired from the Soldier Settlement Board 80 acres of wild uncultivated land which is known and described as S¼ of NW¼ of Sec. 32 ... in the District of New Westminster in the Municipality of Surrey. By strenuous and faithful labour through 23 long years on the part of your petitioner, 32 acres of this land were cleared out of which 20 acres became valuable productive small fruit farmland;

two dwelling houses, two root houses, a barn and a woodshed were built there and your petitioner raised his family there all of his five children being born and brought up there.

Due to the present war, your petitioner with his family has been evacuated from the home, and has been residing in the present address.

Recently, your petitioner has been informed by the Custodian of the Department of the Secretary of State to the effect that the above property was sold and transferred to the Director of the Veterans' Land Act, for the purpose of rehabilitation of soldiers who are returning from the present war. This transaction has been made without any consultation to me and without my consent.

Your petitioner believes that his loyalty to Canada has been well tested in the great war, and that it does not seem fair for the government to take away from one ex-service man a property so dear to him in order that it may be given to a soldier returning from the present war.

Your petitioner pray[s], therefore, from the above circumstances, that special consideration will be given this matter that the traditional British fair play may be exercised even in this extraordinary period.[134]

This was not, of course, a case on behalf of dispossessed Japanese Canadians in general but an argument by Inouye on his own behalf and as a veteran. Nevertheless, his appeals to officialdom elicited only polite bureaucratic replies, though he did not have the door slammed completely on him. "The only reply I am prepared to make to the protest you now file," Murchison (a man of many files) told him on 7 October 1944 in response to yet another missive, "is that pending clarification of your position as a member of the Japanese race The Director, The Veterans' Land Act, still proposes to retain title to this land."[135] This was ambiguous regarding future intentions and was indicative of Murchison's hesitation on the matter. By the same token, F.G. Shears, director of the custodian's Vancouver office, writing on 18 October 1944 in answer to his latest letter from Inouye, reiterated that his office was "carrying out an overall policy applicable to all Japanese properties in this area." In response to Inouye's claim that his property was worth $14,000, Shears noted that the sale to the director of the VLA had been on the basis of "current independent appraised values." The best he could offer the aggrieved Inouye was that his letter had "been placed on our file" so that his comments would "remain on record" and his "protest noted."[136] A case that tested the limits of veteran status, ex-service solidarity, and individual rights lived on into 1945.

As that year approached there was growing confidence in Ottawa about the plans that had been made for facilitating the transition from war to peace. In October 1944, the *Canadian Veteran* published a biographical sketch of Woods, describing him as "one of those many 'Other Ranks' who, without pull and by sheer merit" had "risen to the top."[137] The new deputy minister, this account continued, was knowledgeable, experienced, and a man of broad "commonsense." He had an "outstanding" administrative record, was known for his "all embracing" humanity and was "in every sense a good citizen and a good comrade." That was very much how Woods saw himself and liked to be seen, and in this he exemplified the tradition of remembrance, comradeship, and mutual aid that defined the veteran ideal. A deep social conservative, he stood for limited collective action in the service of individual responsibility and the preservation of king-and-country values. On the evening of 5 September 1944, he tuned into the CBC and listened to an episode of the Johnson Wax program, an American show hosted by Clifton Fadiman. He didn't like what he heard and a few days later wrote a complaining note to his minister.[138] According to Woods, the program had been "designed to reflect a disgruntled, bellicose attitude on the part of the United States service man." The soldier was characterized as "a ruthless individual," whose intent was "to blast out of society" what he considered "to be his rights." No mention had been made of what his government had done for him. Rather, "the whole trend" had been to emphasize grievance and promote the idea that the soldier had "a chip on his shoulder" that he would do something about when he returned. From Woods's perspective, such broadcasts did "incalculable harm" by implanting "in the minds of serving soldiers" that they were "a terribly wronged group" and that they should take "the law into their own hands." The program was in "bad taste" and "tended to create uneasiness, suspicion and an anti-social attitude." It would be easy for Canadians listening to the broadcast to lose sight of the fact that Canada had already "the most comprehensive programme in the world for rehabilitation of her service men," and that they only wanted "one thing," namely, "a job and security." In 1945 the mettle of the program he and his associates had carefully constructed for Canada's Second World War veterans would be put to the hard test of demobilization.

6 Golden Future Time

News that the war in Europe was over reached Mackenzie King early in the morning on 7 May 1945 in San Francisco, where he was attending the conference that led to the founding of the United Nations.[1] The next day, known to posterity as VE-day (Victory in Europe day), he spoke over the radio to the Canadian people, and after his return home he resumed campaigning for a general election called in April for 11 June. The outcome of the election was a small majority for the governing Liberals, who won 125 seats in a House of Commons of 245. In Quebec, where the government's conscription policy had stirred such bitter wartime opposition, the Liberals nevertheless won 53 of 65 seats, a sweep that saved the day for King. (Because of their wartime records on conscription, the other national parties were anathema to the province, and the Quebec-based Bloc populaire canadien was held to only two seats.) In King's own riding of Prince Albert, Saskatchewan, when the military vote was eventually added to the election-night totals, the prime minister lost his seat, but he soon found his way back into Parliament, thanks to a by-election in the Ontario riding of Glengarry. The election had been a very close call for the government, but the narrow victory meant continuity of administration: the same government that had so methodically planned for demobilization would be the government that would put the country's plans into effect. Although Canada had committed to send ground forces to the Pacific to assist in the invasion of Japan, the war in Asia ended before the troops could actually be sent, though Canadian naval and air forces were already engaged in the Pacific.

By VJ-day (Victory over Japan day) on 15 August (when Japan ceased fighting), mass demobilization was in full swing in Canada. On 4 September 1945, two days after the Japanese formally surrendered, the diplomat Charles Ritchie noted in his diary that the windows of the train on which he had returned to Ottawa from Halifax had been crowded with returning soldiers "whistling at the girls on the station platforms" and "making unflattering jokes about Mackenzie King."[2] "Train after train," he wrote, "travels across Canada from east to west laden with them, dropping them off by threes and fours at small towns and in their hundreds in the big cities ... The stations are crowded with them striding about self-consciously – men of the world – having proved something about themselves that is plainly to be seen in their sun-paled divisional patches and the ribbons on their chests – the 1939–43 Star, the Africa Star, the France and Germany award, the Voluntary Service Ribbon." His entry caught the flavour of the times as tens of thousands of uniformed Canadians made their way back to Civvy Street – the service term for civilian life – by land, sea, and air.[3] In 1945, 395,013 were discharged and in 1946 another 381,031.[4]

In this author's experience, veterans vividly remembered where and when they left uniform, but not much detail of the extensive attendant paperwork that found its way into the files of DND and DVA, some of which is available through Library and Archives Canada, Ottawa. At the discharge depots set up across the country, an individual leaving the military went through the discharge procedure required by his or her own branch of the services.[5] Typically, this included a medical and dental examination, and attention to the details of clothing allowance, discharge certificate, back and deferred pay, rehabilitation grant, etc. The service counsellor dealing with a particular individual also completed a "service interview summary." Recorded on form WD 12, this document found its way into the DVA counselling system and thereafter informed decision making about rehabilitation benefits. In the words of *Back to Civil Life*, the crucial WD 12 form recorded "facts relating to the pre-enlistment and service experience of the service man and any other information pertinent to his re-establishment." The purpose of the summary it gave was to provide DVA "with a comprehensive picture of the civilian potentialities of the veteran together with the recommendation of the In-Service Counsellor as to how they may best be utilized for the veteran's civilian re-establishment." The "outline of the abilities and desires of the veteran" included in form WD 12 constituted the basis for action by DVA officials as each case required.

To handle the onrush of business, DVA expanded rapidly. In fairness to those serving abroad, Woods made a recruiting trip overseas in 1945.[6] (He well remembered the resentment of 1914–18 veterans about the best jobs in the country having been creamed off while they were away fighting and sacrificing.) He found thirty-four men for senior executive positions in the department, and they returned to Ottawa forthwith to begin their new jobs. By February 1947, at the height of rehabilitation activity, DVA staff numbered 22,000.[7] To deal with the many issues posed by mass re-establishment, new arrangements were now also made at the cabinet level. A committee on demobilization and re-establishment, chaired by Mackenzie, was formed, and at its first meeting, held on 24 October 1945 and attended by four other ministers, recommended the dissolution of the old GACDR by order-in-council.[8] In its place, the new cabinet body received advice from the Advisory Committee on Rehabilitation and Re-establishment, created by PC4383 of 20 June 1945. This successor advisory committee was chaired by MacNamara and had Woods as its vice-chairman; it was instructed by its terms of reference to "consider and report," either at cabinet direction or on its own initiative, "upon any problem of an interdepartmental nature involving policy in respect of the re-establishment or rehabilitation of service personnel or the employment of war workers in civilian industry."[9]

At its first meeting the new cabinet committee decided that it would also be the channel of communication for any matter that the new Advisory Committee on University Training for Veterans wanted put before cabinet. Woods and MacNamara were present for this first meeting, as was Saskatchewan Liberal MP Walter A. Tucker, parliamentary assistant to the minister of veterans affairs and chairman of a House of Commons special committee on veterans' affairs formed soon after the new Parliament met. Tucker belonged to a small group of Canadians known as "dual service" veterans who had served in both world wars. The committee he chaired had sixty members, six of them, including Mackenzie, cabinet ministers; two of its members – Liberal Hugues Lapointe and Progressive Conservative A.J. Brooks – would later serve as ministers of veterans affairs.[10] It was formed in accordance with the now well established Canadian parliamentary tradition whereby legislation relating to service pensions and rehabilitation moved forward on the basis of the "agreed opinion" of a committee "consisting of ex-service members from all parties"[11] (Mackenzie had long pledged that after the war there would be a parliamentary review of the government's actions on behalf of veterans.) The clerk of the 1945 committee was A.L. Burgess, and its *Minutes of Proceedings and Evidence* were published in thirty-four instalments. Tucker asked to be kept informed of the views of the cabinet committee and was given assurance on this matter; Mackenzie promised both to keep "in close touch" in order to anticipate items of business coming before the parliamentarians and to keep the chairman of the new advisory committee informed about the government's intentions.[12] The function of the cabinet committee now launched, Mackenzie explained, was "to make recommendations to the Cabinet on all major matters pertaining to demobilization and re-establishment policies."[13] Just as a clear chain of command had functioned in the building of the rehabilitation program, there was now a clear chain of command, adapted to postwar circumstances, for administering it. Mackenzie launched proceedings at the special committee with a comprehensive survey of the history of veterans' benefits in Canada and a year-by-year account of developments since 1939.[14]

In the Speech from the Throne opening the first session of the twentieth parliament, delivered by Governor General the Earl of Athlone on 6 September 1945, the government promised "the consolidation, as a veterans' charter, of the various orders in council relating to the care, rehabilitation and reestablishment of war veterans."[15] Thereafter, Canada's entire program for the veterans of the Second World War – a program embodied in numerous statutes, orders, and regulations – was known as the Veterans Charter (the apostrophe after the word "veterans" in the throne speech was soon dropped). The name originated, of course, in the pivotal July 1944 Finance memorandum, which had called for the various benefits on offer to be "fitted together into a carefully work out, well-rounded, comprehensive whole."[16] The word "charter" was well chosen because it resonated with two historic documents of the time – the Atlantic Charter of 1941 and the United Nations Charter of 1945. The contrast with United States nomenclature is striking. The "The G.I. Bill of Rights" (in shorter form, "The G.I. Bill") was embodied in the Servicemen's Readjustment Act of 1944.[17] Like the Veterans Charter, it spread benefits far and wide and shaped an entire generation, but the difference in usage says something about the evolving outlook of the two countries. The language in the citation applied to the US act speaks for itself, but the word "charter" was gender-neutral, and its adoption was no doubt influenced by the fact that, rhetorically at least, the Canadian program, sought to promote equality in benefit eligibility between the men and women who served. Although the G.I. bill covered women veterans, members of the US women's forces were disadvantaged by the fact that unlike their Canadian counterparts, not all of them had been enlisted on the same legal basis as men. Because of this, members of the Women's Army Auxiliary Corps, the predecessor organization to the Women's Army Corps, and the Women's Airforce Service Pilots did not qualify for veteran status in the United States.[18] Thanks to the adjustment made in 1942 to the terms of enlistment of members of the CWAC, no such problem existed in Canada.

On 23 December, in its seventh and final report, the special committee chaired by Tucker recommended that "the Post-Discharge Re-establishment Order and Supplementary Orders in Council relating to grants for vocational and educational training and other rehabilitation benefits" be embodied in legislation, and the committee submitted a draft bill for this purpose.[19] Following consideration and approval of a preliminary resolu-

Eedson Louis Millard (Tommy) Burns, DVA director general of rehabilitation, 1945–46, went on to be assistant deputy minister, 1946–50, and deputy minister, 1950–55 (*Veterans Affairs*, 15 November 1945)

The perspective of the Co-operative Commonwealth Federation (Thomas Fisher Rare Book Library, University of Toronto)

tion, the bill, An Act to provide Rehabilitation Allowances for Veterans,[20] was introduced in the House of Commons by Mackenzie on 11 December and, with the cooperation of the opposition parties, passed through all three readings the same day. Leading off debate on second reading, Mackenzie told the House that the Post-Discharge Re-establishment Order had been, and would continue to be, "the backbone of the whole rehabilitation programme."[21] All veterans might not "have occasion to claim assistance" under the legislation being proposed, but it would cover everyone. When PC 7633 had been introduced, it had "offered assistance far beyond anything ever attempted in the past, for the purpose of promoting the civil reestablishment of a country's demobilized forces."[22] Since then, other countries had emulated Canada's example, but the dominion remained the leader in the field, with its legislation "unsurpassed ... in breadth, scope and flexibility."[23] Speaking for the Progressive Conservative Opposition, Brooks observed that while the bill under consideration had commanded "general approval" at the drafting stage, this should not be misunderstood: the history of veterans' affairs in Canada over the previous quarter-century had been an experience of trial and error, and no doubt many changes would be needed over time in the bill now before the House and in other legislation affecting veterans.[24] Brooks commended Woods and director general of rehabilitation General E.L.M. (Tommy) Burns (Chant's successor) for their efforts. Woods, he said, had "earned the confidence of the veterans of this country from one end to the other by his fair administration of the Veterans Allowance Act," and Burns was "respected and honoured by the soldiers generally."[25] Brooks hoped that they would inspire in veterans the fairness they exemplified and thereby spare the country in the case of the rehabilitation act the criticism that had been levelled against other legislation on behalf of those who had served. Speaking for the CCF, Clarence (Clarie) Gillis said that he and his colleagues, having been "fairly well represented" on the special committee (he was a member), were willing to see the bill passed, but on the understanding that improvements would be made "in the administrative machinery" of rehabilitation "right along the line," that the salaries of those responsible for carrying out the act would be improved, and that the mistake of thinking of the legislation under consideration as "settling ... permanently" with veterans not be made.[26] (In June 1944 the CCF had published *Marching Home to What?*, which set out its plan for the rehabilitation of the country's fighting men and women and renewed the call – a lost cause – for everyone in uniform to be kept on military pay and allowances during the transition to work and training.) Finally, on 18 December, after the House of Commons had approved minor changes made by the Senate, the bill, to be cited as the Veterans Rehabilitation Act, received assent.[27]

In March 1946, during the second session of the twentieth Parliament, the House of Commons appointed another special committee on veterans' affairs, which had before it the report of an interdepartmental committee on veterans' affairs appointed by Mackenzie on 11 January at the request of the 1945 special committee.[28] That committee consisted of secretary F.L. Barrow of DVA (chair), Colonel A.L. Tosland of DND, and E.B. Armstrong of the Department of Finance. Its job was to study various submissions made to the 1945 committee and "as a fact-finding committee to report thereon." Sixty members (including Mackenzie) were named to serve on the 1946 special committee, and Tucker was again elected chairman.[29] The published minutes and proceedings of the committee's meetings were eventually collected into two substantial volumes and constitute an important source for understanding events in Canada immediately after the war. Mackenzie described the committee, which produced twenty-five reports, as a "devoted band of loyal gentlemen" who, despite "contentions," "controversies," and "occasional animadversions" had done "a grand job – a wonderful job.[30] If he were "in charge of decorations and awards," he said, he "would recommend them all for the Canada medal." In sum, the committee would have "the eternal gratitude" of the country's veterans for the work it had done.

On 30 July 1946, based on the committee's recommendations, the minister moved twelve resolutions preliminary to the introduction of a series of bills to round out the Veterans Charter.[31] Since the subject matter of these had been debated exhaustively in the special committee, they moved quickly through the House and the Senate and were given assent on 31 August. Substantial changes were made in the Pension Act, Reinstatement in Civil Employment Act, Veterans' Land Act, War Service Grants Act, and Veterans Rehabilitation Act.[32] The Veterans' Business and Professional Loans Act realized the plan that Woods had advanced in 1944 for backing bank loans to veterans seeking to establish businesses, and the War Veterans' Allowance Act, 1946, replaced earlier legislation relating to this continuing benefit.[33] In the case of the Pension Act, the insurance principle was finally restored to veterans who had served in Canada only – an amendment for which the Legion and other veterans' organizations had fought long and hard ("at last," injected Howard Green when Mackenzie addressed the matter in the Commons).[34] Coverage under the Veterans Charter was now also extended by statute, variously, to a number of subgroups whose needs had been recognized during the war by order-in-council: by the Allied Veterans Benefits Act to persons domiciled in Canada who served in Allied armed forces and returned home after the war; by the Fire Fighters War Service Benefits Act to firefighters who served in the United Kingdom in the Corps of (Civilian) Canadian Fire Fighters; by the Special Operators War Service Benefits Act to "persons domiciled in Canada who entered enemy occupied countries to assist and encourage the forces of resistance"; and by the Supervisors War Service Benefits Act to "those supervisors who served overseas with the armed forces of Canada as representatives of the Y.M.C.A., Knights of Columbus, Canada Legion War Services or Salvation Army."[35] Under the Civilian War Pensions and Allowances Act, which also put into statutory form and built upon action taken during the war by order-in-council, consideration under the Pension Act only was conferred on members of the Corps of (Civilian) Canadian Fire Fighters and on a number of other groups that had rendered "useful service in the war"; namely, merchant seamen, commercial fishermen, Auxiliary Service personnel, Canadian Overseas Fire Fighters, Royal Canadian Mounted Police (special constables), Air Raid Precautions workers, potential recruits who had sustained disability "while taking treatment to fit them for enlistment," members of the Voluntary Aid Detachments, overseas welfare workers (including those who served with the Canadian Red Cross and St John Ambulance Brigade), and Canadian civilian air crew of RAF Transport Command, which had run a big aircraft ferrying operation across the North Atlantic.[36] Merchant seamen were provided for in the Merchant Seamen Compensation Act, which likewise received assent on 31 August.[37] By an earlier act, given assent on 26 July, women who had served in the Women's Royal Naval Service and the South African Military Nursing Service had likewise been brought within the legislative framework of the Veterans Charter (they were eligible for the full benefit package).[38] In practice, the Veterans Charter was a multifaceted and flexible public program that could be deployed in whole or in part as circumstances required.

As the final elements of the program were being put into place, the publicity machine supporting it was running at full throttle. Published in both English and French, *Back to Civil Life* was revised twice in 1945–46. During the same fiscal year, DVA appointed regional public relations officers in Vancouver, Winnipeg, Toronto, and Montreal and, led by director of public relations Tim Reid, began publication of the relentlessly optimistic *Veterans Affairs*. Issued in newspaper format and with an initial circulation of 10,000, this tightly written and lively publication emphasized success, favoured "human interest" stories, and covered the administration of the Veterans Charter as the government wanted it known.[39] On 25 April 1945, DVA released a *Reference Manual on Rehabilitation*, a loose-leaf volume of 600 pages, and in 1947 followed up with *The Veterans Charter: Acts of the Canadian Parliament to Assist Canadian Veterans*. This publication brought together under one cover the relevant statutes and some of the most important regulations. Included in the volume was a succinct summary of the history of veterans' legislation in Canada and a comparison of the rehabilitation benefits being provided to veterans of the Second World War in Canada, the United Kingdom, Australia, New Zealand, the Union of South Africa, and the United States (Mackenzie and Woods had made a fact-finding visit to Washington in the autumn of 1943).[40] Not surprisingly, the benefit-by-benefit analysis positioned the Canadian program to advantage. Other reference publications issued to facilitate re-establishment were the 60-page *Handbook on Rehabilitation*, intended for use by counsellors, citizens' committees, etc.; *The Directory of Dominion and Provincial Agencies of Demobilization and Rehabilitation*, a listing of agencies involved in rehabilitation matters; and the *Reference Manual on Provincial Rehabilitation Measures.*[41]

Reid and his colleagues in the DVA Public Relations Division were also inventive in getting out the good news of the Veterans Charter through press releases, commercial advertising, popularly written pamphlets, films, film clips, newsreel items, radio broadcasts, collotypes, posters, displays, and speakers series. These efforts meshed with the work of an interdepartmental Demobilization and Rehabilitation Information Committee established by PC8096 on 17 October 1944.[42] The purpose of this committee was "to co-ordinate the information activities of government departments connected with demobilization, rehabilitation, readjustment to civil life and related matters among both members of the armed forces and the general public, and to institute information programmes on such matters where necessary." A. Davidson Dunton was appointed chairman but was eventually succeeded by G.C. Andrew of the Wartime Information Board, who initially served as secretary.[43] DVA was represented on the committee by Reid. Subcommittees were formed devoted to research, publications, radio, advertising, film, speakers, and news and pictures. Press surveys were prepared by the committee, while the research subcommittee – J.D. Ketchum of the Wartime Information Board was convenor and Chant represented DVA – undertook public opinion research and prepared extensive surveys of re-establishment trends (its Montreal-area survey ran to forty-five tightly packed pages). In a 1944 national poll, respondents were asked, "From what you have heard or read, do you think the government in this war is doing too much for returned men, or not doing enough for them?"[44] Four choices were offered, and the national responses were as follows: "Not Enough" (40 per cent), "About Right" (44 per cent), "Too Much" (2 per cent), and "Don't Know (14 per cent)." The results were also broken down by region, gender, income, education, occupation, and by whether or not respondents had relatives in the services.

Pamphlets and booklets issued by the government and the services to facilitate the return to civil life included *Future for Fighters* (written for the Wartime Information Board by Dr E.A. Corbett),[45] *What's Ahead, The Common-Sense of Re-establishment* (500,000 copies in English and 110,000 in French), *The Machinery of Re-establishment, The Role of Information, A Home on Civvy Street, Dismiss – But What of a Job?, Vocational Training on Civvy Street, Naval Rates – Their Meaning for Employers, Employers Guide – An Aid for Employing Former Members of the Royal Canadian Air Force, Your Own Business on Civvy Street, A Farm on R.R. No. 1,* and *It's Your Money.*[46] These were augmented with a variety of film resources, which drew on the expertise of the National Film Board. Films rushed into production

Clockwise: The Canadian Legion's Alberta Command asks the question of the hour. (Royal Canadian Legion, DVA, 14-4-3, vol. 2)

A cartoonist's summary of the postwar situation (*Veterans Affairs*, 15 December 1945)

A newspaper voice for Canadian veterans (DVA, 32-3, vol. 2)

The Toronto YMCA opens its doors (DVA, 32-3, vol. 3)

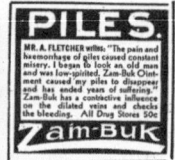

included *Demobilization Process, Road to Civvy Street, Home to the Land, Reestablishment on the Land, Return of the Veteran to Industry, Reorientation to Canada, Canada Plans for Her Veterans, Civilian Application of Service Trades,* and *New Faces Come Back* (about the wonders of plastic surgery for burn casualties). On the evening of Thursday, 19 April 1945, participants in Counsellors' Training Course no. 5 attended a session on "Audio-Visual Aids in Counselling Discharges" at the main auditorium of the National Research Council, Sussex Street, Ottawa.[47] To prepare for this event, which featured the film *Welcome Soldier*, they read the text of a talk by NFB film commissioner John Grierson.

The CBC was ultimately represented on the Demobilization and Rehabilitation Information Committee by Andrew G. Cowan, who was recalled from service overseas as a war correspondent for this purpose. In October 1945 he reported to the committee on the re-establishment-related programs which the CBC had broadcast during the previous year or was now planning to broadcast.[48] His list included *The Soldiers Return* ("forty-one talks by outstanding Canadian authorities on the problems of veterans' readjustment to civilian life and their return to the family, community and industry"); *Repat Reporter* (featuring Royd Beamish, who had served overseas as a public relations officer); *The Johnny Home Show* (launched on 13 July 1945 with script by Staff Sergeants Frank Shuster and Johnny Wayne of the *Army Show*, who had a big future before them in Canadian radio); *Ex-Service Show* (a variety program broadcast from L'Hermitage, Montreal, and directed by ex-RCAF servicemen Hugh Green and Robert Tufts); *Servicemen's Forum* (originating in "Army camps, Air Force Stations and Naval barracks," featuring discussion by service personnel of postwar problems, and prepared by naval officer Donald McDonald and army officer Robert Allen); *Citizen's Forum* (supplemented with "study bulletins and special pamphlets"); *Civvy Street Report* (devoted to the progress being made on a regional basis); and *The People Next Door* (written by Elsie Park Gowan with the assistance of Dr Kathleen Jackson, exploring "the theme of good family relations" in connection with "some of the problems of rehabilitation"). *The Johnny Home Show* had as its main characters "two returned men, Johnny Home and Sam Lightfoot, the Home family, and their neighbours in Beaversville." The action centred on "the efforts of Johnny and Sam and their comrades to become re-established in civilian life." The program was heard "at an excellent listening time" on twenty-nine stations in Canada and two in the United States.

On its French network, the CBC had adapted *Jacques Belhumeur en civil* from *The Johnny Home Show*, but this program had attracted criticism (unspecified in Cowan's account) and had been withdrawn. Rehabilita-

Left: C.N. Senior was a newspaperman who worked in Ian Mackenzie's office.

Below: The letterhead of one of the many citizens' committees formed across the country (DVA, 6885-50/V.1)

tion information was, however, being featured in the well-established and popular serial *La fiancée du commando,* heard three times a week. In its first phase, this program dealt with "the adventures of two French Canadian commandos who landed in France during the Dieppe raid and remained there to fight with the Maquis and to marry French girls." The main protagonists were now back in Canada, and the program had moved on "to dramatize the problems of their rehabilitation." Looking to the future, the French network of the CBC was preparing "a series of talks by outstanding speakers" along the lines of *The Soldiers Return.* Commercial publishers were also active in the rehabilitation field. In 1944 Wm. Collins

Sons & Co. Canada Ltd brought out *When the Boys Come Home: Their Post War Opportunities in Canada* by C.N. Senior, and in 1950 Robert England published *Twenty Million World War Veterans* with Oxford University Press. Norman Senior's book, dedicated to his son Bob, who was serving in the navy, had a foreword by CAAE president Wilfrid Bovey. Readers were informed on the title page that royalties from the publication would go to the Disablement Fund, which supported injured veterans.

Ensuring that its district administrators and counsellors were fully informed, and strengthening links with the citizens' committees that had been organized across the country at its behest, were other key priorities of DVA in this period. During 1945–46 twelve regional conferences were held for chairmen of the latter groups (by the spring of 1946 there were more than 700 of them), and from 22 to 25 January 1945 a national conference, called by the minister of national war services, was held at the Seigniory Club in Montebello, Quebec.[49] This gathering, attended by officials from a variety of government departments, brought together representatives of the citizens' war services co-ordinating committees and representatives of the citizens' rehabilitation committees that DVA was so assiduously promoting. The purpose of the conference was to devise ways and means of keeping up the level of local voluntary war services and supporting the rehabilitation committees "in canvassing the whole field of re-establishment services on a community basis."[50] Beginning in February 1945, Reid directed regular information bulletins on the progress of events to the chairmen of the citizens' committees and DVA district administrators, superintendents of rehabilitation, and veterans' welfare officers.[51] In the same year, the department published *The Community and Re-establishment: Suggestions for Activities of Citizens' Committees*.[52] This began with a preamble that made the case for community involvement in re-establishment through a fictional conversation among some uniformed men who were about to be discharged:

> A group of soldiers sat around an army discharge depot. They were men who, only a month before, had come back from overseas – from the fighting in France, Belgium, Holland and Italy, and from non-combatant but equally important posts at headquarters in England and in the field. They had had their thirty days leave in their home communities. Now they were back, awaiting discharge or other disposition.
> The talk turned naturally to home and what they had found there. They had found changes and, as soldiers always do, they were taking advantage of their right to grouch.

"It wasn't what I expected," said one. "My wife has changed. Everything has changed."

"Too true," said another. "People didn't recognize our ribbons or our divisional flashes. It was impossible to get a lift."

"I found my wife and youngsters living in two rooms," a third man said. "There just didn't seem any place for me."

Put yourself in the place of these men. They've been away, close to the war, three, four or five years. They've seen people die. They've seen homes blasted by bombs. They've experienced shortages, of necessities as well as luxuries, under a strict system of rationing.

They come home to a land of plenty. They come home to a wife who has changed over the years, because she has had to be independent and to make her own decisions. They come home to children who scarcely know them. They don't realize they have been away from the children during the formative years. They have kept a picture of Canada as it was, of their homes as they were. It is a shock to discover that things are not as they had been and during that period of readjustment a little understanding and help will be needed.

The men and women coming back have changed too. Possibly, this may cause concern to their relatives and friends, and this concern may lead to restraint after the first joy of meeting. The families will require guidance and understanding in order to re-adjust themselves to the sailors, soldiers and airmen they are greeting.

No government agency – no government legislation – can meet these problems.

The text that followed was divided into sections with self-explanatory headings: "It's a Community Problem" "There Will Be Just Complaints," "Mutual Confidence Is Essential," "The Veterans' Problems," "Know the Legislation," "Welcome Home," "What About the Churches?," "To Assess the Problem," "No Need to Wait Until Discharge," 'The Veteran's Wishes," "How About a Home," "Legal Aid," "Now for a Job," "Jobs for So-called Disabled," "If Training is Needed," "To Start a Business," and "Use Publicity Wisely" (there was also a conclusion). According to this account, one citizens' committee had organized 83 church subcommittees, representing "all creeds and all denominations." Though "welcome home" was commonly understood to mean "a brass band at the station – the mayor or reeve making a speech of welcome and a parade up Main Street," this was not enough, and the reality was that it would "be impossible to avoid a man coming home and finding no one to greet him except the station

The promise of a better tomorrow (DVA, 65-25-1, vol. 1)

taxi driver." A true welcome home, readers of this pamphlet were told in italics, "embraces much more than the station ceremony. It goes on, day after day, until a man is re-established. It goes on until he is again a citizen of his home town or city and until his adjustment into the home life and the economic life of his country is complete." This was the work for which the citizens' committees had been called into existence. The "state, community, and veteran" were interdependent, and each "must lean on the other ... bear a full share ... and be prepared to cooperate."

As a further boost to the work of the citizens' committees, the energetic DVA publicity department provided them with a model news items and an editorial, along with a radio speech and several possible spot announcements. "Here is an announcement," one of the latter ran, "on behalf of one of (name of town) own citizens. He is a young man many of you know. He was born here, went to school here, and enlisted early in the war so that we (name of town) could continue to live the way we always have. Now he is back, discharged, because he has done his share. He has a job but he needs a home, so that he and his wife can continue the happy, normal home life he gave up to enlist. He is just one of many such veterans in (name of town) looking for accommodation, from rooms to houses. Have you space which you can make available for a housekeeping flat[?] Have you an apartment or house which is becoming vacant[?] If you have living quarters you can make available it is urgently needed. Please phone the Veterans Housing Registry. The number is ..."[53] To get its own staff ready for what lay ahead, DVA held a series of national meetings for district administrators.

Above: DVA's purpose explained at the entrance to its London, Ontario, district office (*Veterans Affairs*, 1 October 1948)

Right: Leading Aircraftsman Joseph H. Bolduc (left) talks over his plans with DVA official Henri Frechette (centre) and Flight Lieutenant W.H. Waddell (right) at DVA's Montreal Rehabilitation Centre (*Veterans Affairs*, 15 October 1946)

On discharge from the forces, to facilitate contact, a veteran was given the name and address of the chairman and secretary of the citizens' committee in or near his or her community.54 To obtain Veterans Charter benefits, the discharged man or woman was directed by *Back to Civil Life* to one of the rehabilitation centres that DVA had established in major cities across the country or, in the case of those living outside urban areas, to one of the offices of the Employment Service of Canada, each of which, by arrangement with the Department of Labour, now had a veterans' officer on staff. The rehabilitation centres were "designed to avoid giving the veteran the 'runaround'" and offered all services under one roof, with provision made "for assistance in things such as counselling, for dealing with applications for pension, for applications for re-establishment credits, for authorizing training, and for certain of the treatment services." They were staffed by ex-service personnel who understood veterans' problems, had themselves experienced re-establishment, and were ready "to give sympathetic, speedy consideration to the needs of ex-service men."[55] To give "immediate assistance" to the veteran who only wanted to go to work, there were Department of Labour officials in each centre ready to help.[56] For the benefit of his colleagues at the Montreal rehabilitation centre on St James Street West, district superintendent Major H.M. Bell produced a detailed typewritten, single-spaced, nineteen-page "Officer's Hand-Book" that offered this general advice:

> Our relationship to ex-servicemen is that of the reception office of a great insurance company to its clients who enter to enquire as to the application of clauses in the policy they hold, to the circumstances of the day or year. It should be as efficient, friendly and concerned, as the best life insurance companies insist upon. After all, in our case, a man is cashing in on his life. We have maintained high standards, polished desks and equipment, schooled ourselves in our classrooms twice weekly and we have acquired somewhat of the attitude of mind we think is required. We will keep improving we hope. Our best reward will be when we see the amazed expression on some chaps' face who expected a "snoody" reception, and found a comrade still "carrying on."
>
> To do this job well means that the Montreal area will reflect in satisfaction, contentment and security much that the "old comrades" of the last war dreamed of and put into veteran legislation through the leadership of Walter S. Woods, Esq., the Deputy Minister of the Department of Veterans Affairs. To do it honestly, happily and with imperturbable good humour will mean that your comrades from the battle fronts will know that they are being cared for expertly and with undemonstrative efficiency ... This work demands intelligence and self-discipline. The plan we administer is the most clearly thought out rehabilitation measure brought down in the United Kingdom, the Dominions and the United States. Its skeleton of legislation and muscles of regulation, require the vitalizing effect of spirit and mind, heart and hand. It is our contribution to bring all we possess and can cultivate of the latter, spirit, mind and hand to the task.[57]

Writing in the same vein, Woods issued a circular to officials on 31 January 1945 reminding members of rehabilitation boards of the minister's statement that whenever a case was in doubt, they were to "lean backwards in favour of the man."[58] This was to be "the guiding principle" in the administration of training benefits. In all their dealings with veterans, DVA officials were to remember that they were "employed to serve our ex-service men and women." This in turn required an attitude "of helpful assistance rather than a tendency, consciously or unconsciously, to refuse benefits to ex-service personnel based on technicalities." When "a specific request" could not be met, an effort should be made to accommodate the veteran rather than "meet his or her particular application with a bare refusal." Not surprisingly, the rhetoric of the Veterans Charter emphasized service and respect on the part of those administering the program, and no doubt there was much in this that was sincere and deeply felt. But behind the language of care and gratitude was the underlying reality of direction and control. Veterans could propose, but counsellors could say yea or nay. Only the gratuity and the re-establishment credit were entitlements, and the use of the latter was closely monitored; every other benefit was discretionary. "Every now and then," one counsellor wrote to Olive Russell in April 1945, "a nice straightforward case comes in and it is so nice, no problem and therefore no apparent hedging on my part."[59] Nor did rehabilitation administration always meet the high standard imagined by Bell, even in his own city. On 31 January 1946, Burns told Woods that the lack of proper facilities in Montreal, Toronto, and Winnipeg had led to "hasty and inefficient counseling" and that veterans had encountered an "atmosphere ... of overcrowding, hurry and nervous tension."[60] In some cases veterans had to be told to return for counselling two or three weeks later, and though backlogs had now been overcome, the pressure on the system had undoubtedly led to individuals being given advice about training that might prove unproductive. By Burns's estimate, insufficient office space had reduced the effectiveness of the Montreal rehabilitation operation "by at least one-third."

Despite such glitches, and to the great relief of many, the aftermath of the Second World War did not see a repeat in Canada of the toils and troubles that had overtaken the country in the years immediately following the armistice of 1918. In April 1945, Wilfrid Bovey warned a gathering of Legion, business, and government officials at the Seigniory Club that Canada's free enterprise system now had its "last chance" to deliver full

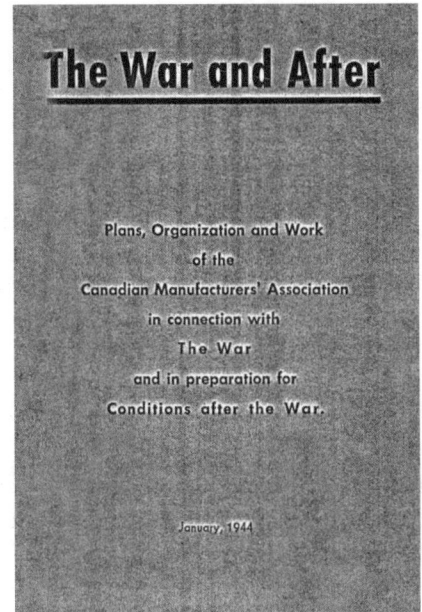
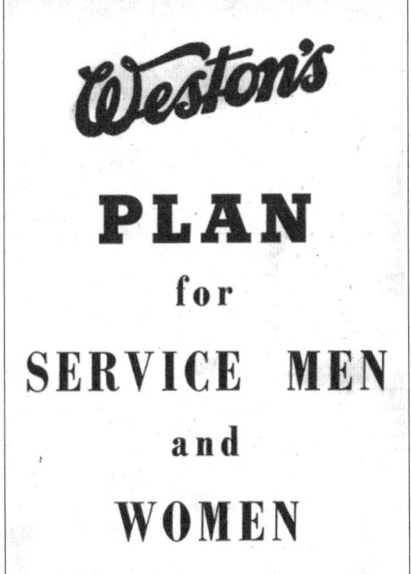
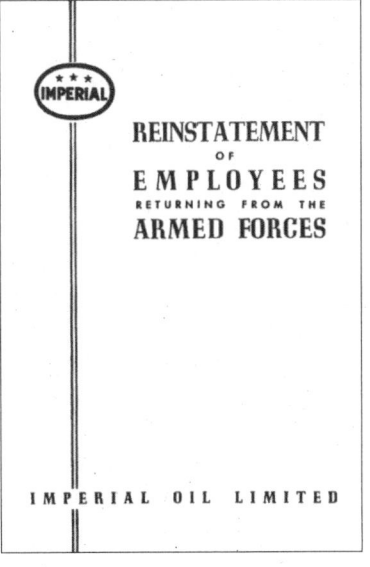

Canadian business welcomed the self-help and voluntary approach of the Veterans Charter and planned accordingly (DVA, 65-42, vols. 1 and 2)

employment and that the country could not go back to "pre-war economics" and "to pre-war care for the less privileged."[61] In the same vein, Department of Labour official Byron F. Wood sounded the alarm about the possibility of unemployed veterans turning inward and lining up against the rest of the population, with devastating results for all concerned. In reality, the worst did not happen. The transition to peacetime conditions that began in the spring of 1945 certainly had its ups and downs – housing, as will be seen, was the biggest source of postwar irritation and trouble – but employment conditions remained generally favourable, and the national economy remained robust. Many factors contributed to this very different outcome. Canada had matured industrially during the war and, given the destruction the conflict had entailed elsewhere, was well placed among the trading nations of the world. The government in Ottawa, moreover, now understood that it had to act to keep up the level of demand in the economy and had made plans accordingly, with the Veterans Charter prominent among them. Canada emerged from the war with a sophisticated national public service well versed in the requirements of rational planning and the techniques of Keynesian economics. As events unfolded, the country did not fall back into depression but moved from strength to strength. When the next national election was held, on 27 June 1949, the Liberals, now led by the Quebecer Louis St Laurent (King having left office on 15 November 1948), won an overwhelming victory, whereupon Canada entered the golden future time of the 1950s, a decade of truly remarkable economic growth and public policy achievement. Having been born in the first quarter of the twentieth century and then lived through the Great Depression of the 1930s, most of those who served in the Canadian armed forces during the Second World War lived on into prosperity and the building of the Canadian social safety net, parenting the postwar baby boom along the way. Like their American counterparts – to borrow Tom Brokaw's evocative phrase – they became in many respects their country's "greatest generation,"[62] leaving behind them a legacy of personal discipline and success, public service, and social solidarity (though, despite their number, no Second World War veteran ever became prime minister). Out of the collective action of war, came a more statist Canada and a new balance between individual and collective good.

Benefit statistics under the Veterans Charter well reflected the overall trend of postwar events. The monthly total of veterans registered as unemployed, never massive or unmanageable, showed a marked downward trend in 1947–48, though there was a return to higher numbers in 1948–49 and 1949–50 before the expansionary times of the 1950s began in 1950–51.[63] In May 1945, the month fighting ended in Europe, only 734 received the out-of-work benefit (available nine days after the period covered by the initial rehabilitation grant and payable for up to one year, depending on duration of service, in the eighteen months following discharge). By July this number had dropped to 599, but by December it had grown to 8,549.[64] The peak monthly recipient total was reached in April 1946 when 48,521 (including 417 women) received the benefit.[65] In November 1945 the minister of national defence reported having received representations from the Sir Arthur Currie branch of the Canadian Legion in Montreal and from the Toronto Veterans Rehabilitation Committee, calling on the government to slow down the rate of discharge from the armed forces because of the existing level of unemployment.[66] Nothing came of this initiative, but in May 1946 Woods recommended that the cabinet committee consider the possibility of extending the period during which the out-of-work benefit could be received beyond the existing twelve-month maximum. Unless there were more employment opportunities available in the winter of 1946–47 than there had been during the winter of 1945–46, he cautioned, the government would face pressure to make this change and should get ready for that eventuality.[67] In practice, the government was able to stay on course, and by November the monthly total of recipients of the out-of-work benefit had dropped to 16,112.[68] The number spiked again in the winter months of 1946–47 but fell back to 1,835 (a figure that included 47 women) by November 1947.[69] Beginning in February 1946 the payment of the out-of-work benefit was made through the Unemployment Insurance Commission, and in early 1950 eligibility ran out and payment ceased altogether.[70] To 31 March 1951, the out-of-work benefit had been paid to 162,872 veterans at a cost of $28,103,131. To the same date, 532,588 veterans had had unemployment insurance contributions of $51,309,662 made on their behalf – the peak years were 1947–48 and 1948–49, when 194,967 and 127,633 benefited, respectively.[71] In hindsight, Woods offered the following assessment, typical of his general outlook on the world, of how things had gone in relation to the out-of-work allowance: "There is no question but that the benefit was abused by some. There were veterans with real or imaginary ills who were difficult to deal with, and there was also the type who felt that because he had worn the uniform the country owed him a living. In the main, however, veterans had no desire to live on the allowances for any extended period, and got jobs as soon as they could. There was, however, a notable lengthening of periods of allowances while the War Service Gratuity was in payment during 1945 and later, as its receipt in no way affected the applicant's entitlement to out-of-work allowances, Gratuity

The Bank of Montreal on the *Veterans' Business and Professional Loans Act* (DVA, 6885-50/V.1)

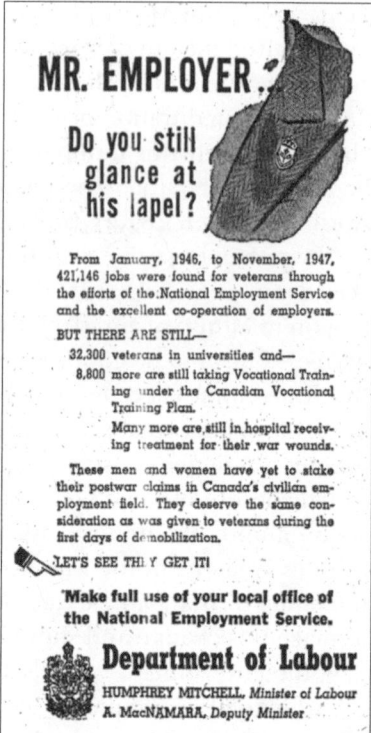

1948 Department of Labour reminder to business (*The Gazette*, a division of Postmedia Network Inc., Montreal, 5 March 1948)

and out-of-work allowances together enabled a few of the less provident and energetic to live without working, for a while."[72] Given a choice, Woods believed, veterans preferred work over dependence.

From the government's point of view, activity in relation to the awaiting-returns and temporary incapacity allowances also stayed within acceptable limits. The awaiting-returns allowance assisted veterans who went into business, farming, or commercial fishing, and its purpose was to tide the veteran over until an enterprise provided a living. If a female veteran was the owner of a farm and was approved for the allowance, she could receive a dependant's allowance for her husband (provided he was working full-time on the property) and children.[73] The allowance had a 13 December 1947 cut-off date. In September 1945, 1,200 veterans were receiving the awaiting-returns allowance, a figure that grew to 27,000 a year later.[74] To 31 March 1952, 50,792 veterans, including 276 women, had been approved for the benefit.[75] In 90 per cent of the cases the enterprise being supported produced a successful outcome, with payment being made for an average of thirty weeks at an average cost of $433.72.[76] In the remaining 10 per cent of the cases, support was stopped when it became clear that a successful outcome was not realizable. On average, in these cases, allowances were paid for nineteen weeks at an average cost of $280.19.[77] Overall, Woods judged this benefit as "one of most effective and least costly" parts of the entire rehabilitation package. As an admirer of self-help and "get up and go," he especially appreciated the fact that most of those assisted had "become employers of labour rather than seekers after jobs."[78] In practice, the temporary incapacity allowance had only a small number of beneficiaries – 4,754 to 31 March 1951 at a cost of only $450,809.[79] It was a short-term benefit and was usually given for two weeks or less, following which a veteran still in need would be referred for medical help. Its purpose was to meet a "veteran's sustenance needs during any short period he was laid up and did not need active treatment or had no entitlement to treatment under Departmental regulations."[80]

The outcome under the Veterans' Business and Professional Loans Act of 1946 was likewise relatively modest in scale, Under this legislation, a veteran who had volunteered for service and was not receiving a loan under the VLA could qualify for government backing for a loan from of chartered bank of up to $3,000 for a maximum of ten years at 5 per cent annual interest.[81] The loan could be used for a variety of business purposes, but could not exceed two-thirds of the proposed budget for a project or enterprise (at least one-third of total cost had to come from an applicant's own funds). To 31 March 1951, 6,092 loans, to a value of $11,230,736, were made under the act.[82] They were used for the purchase of interest in partnerships (1,638), purchase of businesses (1,501), purchase of tools, equipment, etc. (1,134), repair of the same (35), purchase of motorized units (1,133), and construction or repair of buildings (651).[83] The most active banks in the program were the Bank of Montreal and the Canadian Bank of Commerce, which made 1,694 and 1,293 loans, respectively.[84] By district office, the largest number of beneficiaries was recorded in Vancouver.[85]

Two thorny labour market matters adroitly managed by the government (mainly through inaction) in the intense 1945–47 demobilization and re-establishment period were the issues of preference and seniority for veterans. Government consideration of these matters went back to the work of the employment and demobilization subcommittees of the GACDR and thereafter to the deliberations of the Inter-departmental Co-ordinating Committee on Rehabilitation formed in February 1944 by DPNH and the Department of Labour.[86] Under the Reinstatement in Civil Employment Act, veterans had a legal claim on their old jobs, but in practice this legislation benefited fewer than 200,000 of those who served (to get a job back, one had to have had one before enlisting, and the job in question had to still exist).[87] In April 1944, Deputy Labour Minister MacNamara urged on the war cabinet blanket legislation to give all veterans with overseas service priority in hiring and seniority rights that recognized their military service. But this sweeping proposal was resisted in cabinet, with Munitions and Supply Minister C.D. Howe taking the position that industry would be jolted to be told at this juncture that there would no return to "a free market for labour" after the war.[88] Instead, on 27 June 1944, cabinet approved an arrangement whereby veterans with overseas service would be given priority in job referrals by the Employment Service of Canada.[89] This action was in line with Woods's view that it was better to proceed with employers by persuasion rather than compulsion. Following this development, on 5 August 1944, MacNamara established the Committee on Priority and Seniority Rights of Veterans, which was chaired by Department of Labour industrial relations officer M. M. Maclean, an official whose background was in the railway unions.[90]

Following the Legion's June 1944 Dominion Convention in Vancouver, general secretary Herwig was heard loud and clear on the business before this committee. The Legion had three goals: preference in employment for overseas veterans vis-à-vis employees taken on following the enlistment of the former; following a probationary period in employment, the counting of a veteran's period of military service in the calculation of seniority entitlement; and the carrying forward of these arrangements to a date in the postwar period to be fixed through negotiation.[91] The initial response of the country's national labour organizations – the Canadian Congress of Labour (CCL) and the Trades and Labor Congress (TLC) – was encouraging. In March 1944 CCL president A.R. Mosher told Herwig that his organization would gladly send a representative to a conference to discuss the issues at stake, and the same month TLC president Percy Bengough told the Legion official that there could be "no question" but that organized labour would "be sympathetic and friendly to the returning personnel of the Armed Forces."[92] "Labor could not be otherwise," he wrote, "as they in most instances are from the families and ranks of Labor. With the same aims and aspirations and with such common interests the natural result must be friendly cooperation. I don't believe that the seniority rules, as contained in some trade union agreements, present any impossible barriers. It is possible some isolated cases might arise in the future but none which cannot be adjusted if approached in the right spirit." This was promising, but when the full extent of the Legion's agenda became known, alarm bells sounded in the country's labour movement, with the United Steelworkers of America's national director, C.H. Millard, asserting that what was being proposed constituted a "subtle and sinister effort" to curb union power.[93] The backdrop to his comment was a sizable burst in union membership during the war years and a long struggle for legal recognition, a process that culminated in PC 1003 (17 February 1944), which introduced the principles of collective bargaining into relations between unionized workers and employers within the broad federal wartime jurisdiction. In what followed, the attitude of organized labour was that unions should not have to give up hard-won seniority rights in order to accommodate the legitimate aspirations of veterans to get back to work. It made no sense to take away one person's job to give it to another. Rather, the answer was a national policy of full employment and the avoidance of "a competitive struggle between veterans and displaced civilians for an inadequate number of jobs."[94] With work available for everyone, there would be no problem absorbing those who had gone into uniform. Veterans were Ottawa's responsibility, and it was for Ottawa to see that there was no "idle money, idle machines, or idle men" in Canada.[95]

In October 1944, Herwig spoke at the CCL annual convention, held that year in Quebec City.[96] The convention voted in favour of cooperation with the Legion, but the resolution it passed was not binding on member unions, and in December 1944 the CCL executive voted to leave the working-out of seniority arrangements for veterans to local affiliates, recommending that veterans hired within six months of discharge "be granted seniority on the same basis as if they had been employed in the industry at the time they entered the service."[97] At a 22 January meeting of the Committee on Seniority and Priority Rights of Veterans, attended by Herwig and CCL, TLC, and railway union representatives, there was a call for the holding of a national conference "at which all of the organizations actually holding agreements with employers would be represented.[98] This would be preceded by individual conferences with the main labour bodies to lay the groundwork for the larger gathering. Pat Conroy of the CCL told the meeting that his own organization was really only "an advisory body," and "any positive action required" must come from unions that were actually party to collective agreements. What the whole situation "really required," the CCL and TLC spokesmen urged, was "a full statement by the Government on its policy and plans in regard to full employment." There was no point in finding a job for a veteran only to have it quickly disappear. What veterans needed was "a complete guarantee of a permanent job or alternatively of a decent standard of living," and this was not a job for "either organized labour or the Legion but for the Government." The Legion pressed on this occasion for the adoption of a policy whereby "no contract between Labour and Management" could be construed so as to prevent an employer from employing a veteran in preference to someone hired since 1 September 1939. But such action, others in attendance countered, "would probably lead to a wide breach between veterans and organized labour." Hence the need for a conference and the working out of a solution "by mutual agreement."

Steps were subsequently taken on the government side to make this happen, but ultimately no such national conference was held, though the issue of seniority rights for veterans figured prominently in events leading to the 99-day strike at the Ford plant in Windsor, Ontario – a defining moment in postwar labour history – that began on 12 September 1945. With the company arguing that those returning from war were entitled to "more than just three cheers and a brass band to welcome them home," the United Auto Workers (UAW), which had already adopted a model contract clause covering veterans, saw Ford's real purpose as using veterans to undermine the interests of labour.[99] On 10 September, two days before industrial action began in Windsor, a subcommittee on seniority rights for veterans in employment, established by the new Advisory Committee on Rehabilitation and Re-establishment and chaired by Maclean, delivered its report.[100] According to this document, there were "wide differences of opinion" among the interested parties, ranging from the view that veterans should be able to bump out of jobs workers hired during the war to the view that no action whatever was necessary on the government's part in light of its commitment to full employment. The recommendation of the subcommittee was that the government be prepared to legislate to give precedence to veterans with overseas service vis-à-vis workers hired during the war who were laid off for more than 30 days but who had seniority rights in relation to rehiring. Three days later, acting Royal Canadian Navy director of rehabilitation A.M. Shoulds (a volunteer reserve lieutenant, who was a member of the Committee on Priority and Seniority Rights of Veterans) pressed the advisory committee to support the imposition of a quota system (Mosher had also spoken in favour of an arrangement whereby employers would have to hire veterans); but this proposal was a non-starter.[101] In October, MacNamara put forward a draft Overseas

Veterans' Employment Order that would require certain employers to list jobs with the National Employment Service and show that an overseas veteran was not available for a position thus listed before being allowed to hire anyone else. This draft – a far cry from what the Legion wanted and what Shoulds was advocating – was approved by the Cabinet Committee on Demobilization and Re-establishment but was then put in limbo by the full cabinet.[102] Also during the fall of 1945, Maclean held two meetings with national union officials to canvass their opinion on a resolution in line with the recommendation on precedence in hiring of the subcommittee he had chaired.[103] He encountered stiff resistance from the unions, leading him to recommend, on 27 December 1945, that the government take no legislative action on the resolution. In January 1946, MacNamara told Mackenzie that the Advisory Committee on Rehabilitation and Re-establishment had decided to postpone further discussion of the issue of seniority pending "further developments."[104]

The next of these came in the famous 29 January 1946 arbitration award of Justice Ivan Rand that ended the Windsor strike. Best known for the introduction of a formula whereby employees of a company who chose not to join a union would nevertheless have to pay union dues in return for enjoying the benefits of a collective agreement (known thereafter as the Rand Formula), this decision, which drew on the UAW's model clause, included a provision for granting seniority to veterans. Under Rand's wording, incorporated in clause 52 of the agreement signed between Ford and Local 200 of the UAW on 15 February 1946, a distinction was made between residents and non-residents of Essex County (where Windsor is located):

> A person who has been a member of the Armed Forces of Canada including the merchant marine at any time since September 1st, 1939, upon entering the service of the company and subject to the conditions of the probationary period, shall be given an immediate seniority equal to the length of time he served in the Forces and this constructive seniority shall be taken into account in his application for work; but this shall not entitle him on such entrance to displace a person then in the company's employ, except where the former was at the time of his becoming a member of the Forces a resident of Essex County, Ontario, and the latter was immediately before his employment by the company a non-resident of that county. To obtain the benefit of this clause, the person applying shall do so within one year from his discharge from the Forces

and shall at such time present his discharge papers. There shall be attached to such papers a certificate by the company showing the date when he was taken into the company's service.[105]

Speaking to the convention of the Canadian Manufacturers' Association held in Toronto in June 1946, E.L.M. Burns held up the arrangement devised by Rand as "a very fair solution."[106] "Seniority clauses," he said, "frequently operate to the disadvantage of the veteran who has not been previously employed in industry ... It is not an answer to say that the solution to this problem is that the Government should create full employment and then the veteran would be taken care of. The fact is that the industries and occupations where there are seniority agreements are among the best paid, and it is not fair that a veteran, who has served his country overseas in war, should be unable to get these lucrative employments because the jobs are held by those who started their employment and established their seniority while the veteran was absent fighting." If the principle advanced by Rand with respect to hiring veterans and the grant of seniority to them could be applied generally, the "source of injustice" would be removed. "Representatives of labor on the higher levels," Burns said, "recognize the justice of this contention, but the difficulty arises through the autonomy of local unions and the opposition ... [of] their recent members who would be adversely affected." In June 1946, with the Legion still pushing hard for comprehensive government action, the cabinet considered a proposal to extend the existing civil service preference to temporary and seasonal jobs but again decided to leave well enough alone.[107]

Ultimately, the issues of seniority and preference constituted a landmine that might have exploded on the government in the immediate postwar period but didn't. Nor, though this threatened to happen, did a war break out between organized veterans and organized labour. When all was said and done, veterans had their own stake in the integrity of collective bargaining arrangements, and many of them knew it. As one of Burns's correspondents, who had served in both wars and whose air force navigator son had been shot down over Belgium, wrote in August 1946, the issue of seniority cut two ways. "You are quite right," this veteran told the director general of rehabilitation, "in your assertion that seniority clauses frequently operate to the disadvantage of the veteran as I found out upon taking employment with the Canadian National Railways after the last war but I do think the disadvantages are far our-weighed by the advantages under the seniority clauses ... Now, like you, I sincerely think something should be done to improve the position of the veteran of this war but that improvement cannot come about by removing seniority clauses from working conditions ... Seniority clauses must never be abolished."[108]

The DVA-administered rehabilitation benefit received by far the largest number of veterans was the re-establishment credit provided for in the War Service Grants Act. Having had their way paid home, received their rehabilitation grants of 30 days' pay and allowances, claimed their gratuities (calculated individually according to location and duration of service, administered by DND, and paid out in monthly instalments), and used up their re-establishment credit entitlement (fixed individually at the amount of the gratuity), most Canadians who served in the Second World War, unless they had occasion to take advantage of the one year of free medical care on offer, went off the books of the Government of Canada. In effect, the gratuity/re-establishment credit package constituted the express lane back to Civvy Street and was used by the vast majority of those who served. Historians have rightly made much of the many who went to university – the educated are good at telling their own story – but in fact this group constituted only a small percentage of those who had gone into uniform. The much more common practice of Canadian Second World War veterans was to apply for and get the gratuity and re-establishment credit benefits and go back to work (with or without the help of the out-of-work benefit). In many cases this was accompanied by getting married, setting up house, and starting a family. Facilitating all this kept the administrative machine devised by DVA for handling re-establishment credit payments humming.

On 14 August 1944, the day before the War Service Grants Act received assent, a meeting, chaired by Woods, brought together a range of military and DPNH officials (DVA had not yet started up), along with the assistant comptroller of the Treasury, J.O. Hodgkin, to discuss administrative arrangements under the legislation.[109] Understandings were reached at this meeting about basic service and departmental responsibilities, and a follow-up meeting of the three services was held the next day.[110] On 16 August, at a meeting in Woods's office of key DPNH officials, it was decided that payment of re-establishment credits would be decentralized and made the responsibility of district offices.[111] In a circular dated 21 October, DVA acting secretary F.L. Barrow explained that veterans would be informed with their first gratuity cheques from DND of the amount of their re-establishment credits. A ledger sheet for each veteran covered would be established in Ottawa and a copy of this sent to the district office corresponding to the address given by an individual in applying for the gratuity. To make use of the re-establishment credit, a veteran would have first to apply and qualify for the gratuity. DVA could not act until this was done and the amount of re-establishment credit to which an individual was entitled determined thereby. By PC 8404 of 1 November 1944, the minister of veterans affairs was authorized "to appoint local, regional or provincial honorary advisory committees (and name a chairman for any such committee) to examine applicants and applications for re-establishment credits ... and to advise and report ... with respect to the qualifications of applicants ... in relation to the objects for which any re-establishment credit is proposed to be used and the soundness of the investment proposed by the applicant."[112]

Subsequently, these committees were established in district and sub-district offices, with regional advisory committees under the Veterans' Land Act empowered to act in the same capacity in rural areas. The committees were to consider applications referred to them by appropriate DVA officers, but any applicant could request committee advice. Applications were to be referred automatically to committees when a veteran was proposing to use "the whole or a large part of his credit for the purchase of a business" or when scrutiny of an application left "some doubt as to the bona-fides of the intention of the applicant to use the credit for his re-establishment."[113] Committees were authorized to check the veracity of statements made on an application and, in the case of proposals for the purchase of real property, to get "fuller information" from vendors.[114] In a circular dated 30 December, Woods spelled out the details of the administrative procedure to be followed.[115] "Whilst the Act requires that the expenditure of re-establishment credit shall be made to the satisfaction of the Minister," he cautioned, "staffs are reminded that this is the man's own money, is not a loan but a grant, and whilst it is incumbent upon the Department to exercise supervisions in order to ensure that the money is expended to the satisfaction of the Minister for one or more of the purposes named in the Act, we must avoid the attitude that this is the Government's money, and our investigation should not be pursued to the point of embarrassment of the veterans or the Government."

In the lengthy and detailed instructions that followed, Woods noted that no payment would be made until after 1 January 1945 (when the act came into force) and that an application form was now available.[116] This was to be used once the veteran had been informed of how much war service gratuity he or she was eligible to receive. Veterans were to be advised before making an application to be sure that they did not want "to make use of the Veterans' Land Act or the educational, vocational of technical training provisions of the Post-Discharge Re-Establishment

Top: The War Service Gratuity account of Winnipeg naval veteran Alan Keith Archer (Courtesy of Alan Keith Archer)

Bottom: DVA explains the re-establishment credit. (DVA, 32-6)

Order" (soon to be embodied in the Veterans Rehabilitation Act). On the application form, a veteran had to declare that he or she elected to forgo these benefits and that he or she would use "the proceeds of the grant made him from the credit for one or more of the purposes named in the Act." The form also made provision whereby an applicant could request that the cheque for the amount being claimed be issued "to a third party on his behalf, thus providing for transfer to Veterans' Insurance, Dominion Government Annuities, approved lending institution under the National Housing Act, or reliable vendor." Veterans had up to ten years from the date of their discharge to use up their credits and could make multiple claims over time until funds were exhausted. The application, Woods emphasized, was "not an application to have a credit established, but an application to make use of a credit which is already on the books." Accordingly, there was no need for a veteran "to hurry about the expenditure which he is going to make in respect of his re-establishment." Rather, he "should be asked to study carefully the purposes for which his credit is to be used and to choose the purpose or purposes best designed to aid him in his re-establishment." An individual might "choose one or more purposes" and "might call on his credit in whole or in part."

In the case of applications involving payment of $90 or less, payment could be made promptly unless there was "some suspicion" that the money requested was being directed to "wasteful expenditure." The onus was on an applicant to explain how the proposed use of a credit would assist in re-establishment, but officials were instructed to avoid "unreasonable requests for documentary evidence." In the case of applications involving payments of more than $90, a variety of rules applied, depending on the proposed purpose for using the money. A veteran wanting to use a credit in whole or in part to get a loan under the National Housing Act was required to produce a certificate from the lending institution and satisfy the requirement that the sum being requested in re-establishment credit was not more than two-thirds of the difference between the "lending value of the home" being purchased and the amount of the loan obtained to finance it. A veteran wanting to use his or her re-establishment credit for the purchase of a home not covered by the act had to supply, for scrutiny by the DVA legal department, "a reliable opinion as to the appraised value of the home or the purchase price, and details of the encumbrance or encumbrances." Again, strict limits applied on the contribution to a purchase that could come in the form of a re-establishment credit. For their part, DVA legal officers were instructed to "ensure that to the extent of Government payment," a veteran's interest in a housing transaction was protected. An applicant proposing to use his or her credits to repair or modernize a home had to produced evidence that he or she owned the property, along with "clear documentary evidence as to expenditure or proposed expenditure." In the case of an application involving the purchase of furniture – in practice a popular option – a veteran had to pay a minimum of one-third of the cost of the items purchased or to be purchased. Furniture acquired had to be "free of encumbrance" in order for re-establishment credit funds to be used for purchase, and instalment payments were not permitted. All of this highlighted the directive and supervisory approach of the Veterans Charter generally. According to DVA's "Routine Directions for Handling Re-establishment Credit Application," while direct payment to veterans was "in order," they were "to be encouraged to authorize payment directly on...[their] behalf to Dominion Government agencies, lending institutions, suppliers of materials and of equipment and vendors of physical assets subject to the provisions of the Act."[117] In the case of purchases of furniture and household equipment, "special scrutiny" was to be given to applications by single veterans, male and female, without dependants and to applications "for luxury furniture and non-essential goods." Indeed, as veterans went about their re-establishment using the benefits of the War Service Grants Act, they were never far from the eye of authority.

On 18 January 1945 the "Re-establishment Credit Regulations" were formalized in PC 165,[118] and in February, Robert England – who was now employed as a special executive assistant at DVA – reported to Woods on the state of preparedness of the department for receiving the flood of applications that could soon be expected.[119] Having toured the country, accompanied to Montreal, Toronto, Winnipeg, Halifax, and Saint John by J.H. Hogan, the assistant director of the War Services Grants Act, England listed the names of the chairmen of the re-establishment credit advisory committees that were now functioning in the districts. They were all male and were drawn mainly from the ranks of business. Many were Great War veterans, and all were prominent members of their communities, some with notable service club credentials. In "B" District (Halifax) the chairman was a 1914–18 veteran and General Trust & Executor Corp. manager, J.R. Machum, who had lost two sons on service in the RCAF. In "H" District (Regina), the chairman was H.E. Drope, a former president of the Board of Trade, who had been a prisoner of war in Germany during the First World War but had escaped through Russia. In "J" District (Vancouver), the chairman was the dual service veteran Brigadier Sherwood Lett, a lawyer and member of the board of governors of the University of British Columbia, who had participated in both the Dieppe raid and the Normandy invasion.[120] According to England, the district establishments available to administer a program that was about to move into high gear were "reasonably adequate," but he cautioned that supervisors would have to make staff adjustments as required "so as to avoid either surplus or deficiency in relation to the work developing." His advice in relation to the appointment of a director or acting director for the re-establishment credits division of the department was that this might profitably be delayed in the hope that a nominee with Second World War battle experience would become available for the position. In practice, Hogan, a Prince Edward Islander, moved from assistant director to acting director and, ultimately, director.

Having readied itself for action, DVA next launched a big publicity campaign to spread the good news of the re-establishment credit scheme.[121] Typical of this effort was a full-page advertisement in the 15 March 1945 issue of *Maclean's*. Headed "The Re-establishment Credit – An Explanation of the Grant," it informed the reader as follows:

> In planning the return to civilian life of men and women in the armed forces, Canada's parliament realized that assistance in re-establishment must cover a wide variety of fields. For many – particularly younger members of the forces – the best method of effecting permanent re-establishment will be through training or through an opportunity to continue an interrupted education. Others can be assisted through land settlement – either on full time farms or on smallholdings operated with some regular form of employment. In many cases a combination of these two things – training and land settlement – will be the solution. Legislation for this type of re-establishment was provided early in the war …
>
> There is, however, another very large group who do not need training and who are not suited for land settlement as provided under the Veterans' Land Act. After long months or years in uniform these veterans will need assistance also. There will be those who normally would have owned homes had it not been for their service. There will be those who own homes but who have been unable to carry out needed repairs and alterations. There will be veterans who sold businesses to enlist and who want to resume them, and others who are fitted for a business of their own but who need assistance in financing. The Re-establishment Credit is designed for this latter group, and primarily is an alternative to training and land settlement benefits …
>
> The Re-establishment credit is made available under the same Act of Parliament which provides War Service Gratutities. It is not a

loan but an outright grant, paid to an eligible veteran to aid in re-establishment if the veteran decides not to use land settlement or training benefits. It may be used in Canada only at any time in the ten years following discharge for certain specified purposes as outlined in this advertisement. The grant is called a "credit" because it is an amount carried on the ledger to the credit of the veteran for ten years until used by him for a re-establishment purpose.[122]

The remainder of the text explained "How to Apply for Re-establishment Credit," advised veterans to "Study all Measures before Applying," and listed the purposes for which the credit could be authorized. These were: "(a) To assist in home owning; (b) To assist in building a home; (c) To assist in home repair or modernization; (d) To buy household equipment and furniture; (e) To buy tools, instruments, etc., for trade, profession, or business; (f) To provide working capital for profession or business; (g) To buy a business; (h) To pay premiums on Dominion of Canada insurance; [and] (i) To buy special equipment required for educational or vocational training." Readers were encouraged to write the nearest DVA office for further information and to send the advertisement "to some man or woman overseas."

With so much money about to change hands, the appetites of Canadian retailers were inevitably whetted, and a fierce competition was soon in progress to attract customers who stood to benefit from the government's largesse. In a special bulletin issued on 16 June 1945, the Canadian Retail Federation called on retailers to refrain from "using advertising copy primarily designed to promote spending by veterans" and to cooperate with DVA's advisory committees.[123] In the same spirit, the Toronto Better Business Bureau issued a series of helpful publications, including *Rackets That Take Your Money*, a fact book for the protection of ex-service members.[124] This snappy booklet, which was also printed and distributed by the Winnipeg Better Business Bureau, warned against "Buying A Job," "Fake Veteran Organizations," "Excessive Cost of Mortgages," "The Picture Frame and Picture Enlargement Racket," and "Fake Used Car Salesmen." In general, veterans were advised to investigate before investing. To assist them in their decision making the Simpson's department store chain produced a large newspaper advertisement entitled "Primer on Re-Establishment Credits"; this told the re-establishment story through a series of optimistic illustrations with straightforward and concise accompanying text.[125] In sequence, the captions beneath the upbeat illustrations were "The Service Man Comes Home," "Receives His First Gratuity," "Applies for Re-Establishment Credit," "Buys or Builds a Home,"

The Simpson's department store chain on re-establishment credits
(*Halifax Mail*, 21 July 1945)

"Modernizes His Home," "Furnishes His Home," "Buys Tools or Instruments," "Goes Into Business," "Buys Insurance," "Buys Equipment," – "and lives a happy civilian life ever after." All the veterans shown in the illustrations are male, and gender roles are sharply defined. Simpson's advice to veterans was "to think long and carefully before spending."

 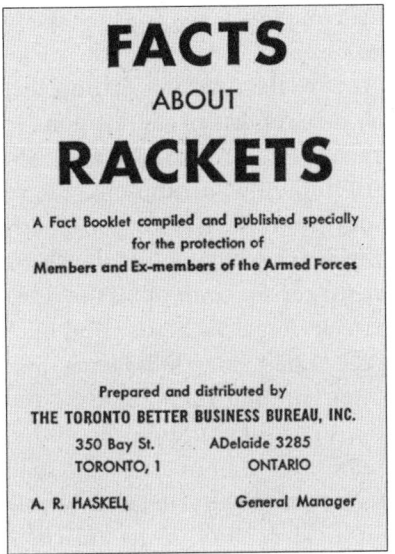

Cautionary words for veterans
(DVA, 32-6, and DVA, 65-42, vol. 2)

Despite the high-minded better business warnings, some veterans, with gratuity money in their pockets and credits with the Government of Canada, ran into trouble, either of their own or someone else's making. In March 1945 the Calgary superintendent of rehabilitation told Hogan that some single veterans who didn't need or want to use their re-establishment credits for any of the purposes specified in the act were scheming to get their hands on cash instead.[126] One of them had approached a local furniture dealer offering to buy furniture for $800 and then, without moving it from the store, sell it back for $600 and cut a deal on the difference. This dealer had refused to cooperate, but apparently another had gone along with the arrangement. In the circumstances, the Calgary official said that the "only recourse" was to make plain to dealers that "any evidence of skullduggery" would result in the business involved being cut off from consideration in any future applications for re-establishment credit. In April the *Winnipeg Tribune* reported that "high-pressure pirates" were at work in the city and regarded veterans "as fair game for their sucker schemes."[127] When the city's Better Business Bureau provided particulars of "attempted swindles," the paper advised veterans to seek advice from the business body or DVA before parting with their money.[128] Otherwise, the consequences might be "expensive stuff." In Toronto the manager of the Better Business Bureau cautioned against investment in a chinchilla company ("We produce the best fur in the world"), and from Edmonton came word of real estate racketeering.[129] "Each day," Captain Harper Prowse, MLA, wrote in the *Edmonton Bulletin* of 16 July 1945, "brings me new reports of servicemen, and the wives and widows of servicemen, being fleeced by racketeers. Most of these have to do with the purchase of homes or furniture, or the renting of houses. The most surprising thing about them is not the fact that there are racketeers at work, but that there are so many people who are willing to let themselves be landed for suckers in spite of all the warnings that have been issued."[130] The same week Gerald Richards published a three-part series in the *Calgary Herald* on the "financial pitfalls facing discharged servicemen contemplating investment of their re-establishment credits, gratuities, etc."[131]

In response to such abuses, the authorities did their best to counter the schemers' efforts. In August 1945 the Vancouver district superintendent of rehabilitation reported that his office enjoyed "excellent cooperation from local dealers" in its efforts to prevent deals involving cash refunds.[132] In September 1945, a discharged soldier, a furniture clerk, and an alleged accomplice were arraigned in police court in Montreal on charges of violating the Re-establishment Credit Regulations.[133] Another local sensation came along in June 1947, when the Halifax papers made much of the prosecution and conviction of a New Waterford merchant and a local veteran for yet another furniture kickback scheme – seemingly the great temptation from coast to coast.[134] But such events were infrequent and exceptional. Given the scope of the re-establishment credit administration, DVA accumulated relatively thin files relating to abuses and scams. Generally speaking, the government's plans for administering a complex benefit worked out efficiently and well. "There have been abuses," one Halifax DVA official commented at the time of the 1947 trial sensation, "but the thing could be easily exaggerated. We are continually investigating and occasionally questionable transactions are brought to light. But it is also true that very few servicemen are asking merchants for cash rather than credit."[135] The documentary record shows that overall this was indeed the case.

To 31 March 1951, 961,975 veterans had been paid gratuities at a cost of $469,065,790, the average payment per veteran being approximately $488.[136] Of the total expended, fully $212,438,577 was accounted for in 1945–46 and $221,727,743 in 1946–47, the peak years of activity.[137] To 31 March 1951 also, 961,975 re-establishment credit accounts had been established and 1,859,913 applications for payment received. Of the latter (multiple applications could be submitted until a credit was exhausted), 1,827,298 had been funded at a cost of $267,794,786, for an average cost of $146.55 per application.[138] By far the largest number of applications were for the purchase of furniture and equipment, with business and home ownership uses also being favoured but registering much lower totals. In terms of cost, the purchase of furniture and equipment soaked up $159,446,969 (59.5 per cent) of total expenditure. Next in line were home owning (not under the National Housing Act) at $30,131,523 (11.3 per cent), working capital for business at $23,167,053 (8.7 per cent), purchase of tools, etc., for business at $22,612,289 (8.4 per cent), and home repair and modernization at $14,691,751 (5.5 per cent). An added bonus was that as events unfolded, the rules were modified and a small number of veterans were able to take advantage of the opportunity to pay back their re-establishment credit and thereby qualify for training under the Veterans Rehabilitation Act or property under the Veterans' Land Act.[139] Added together, the gratuity and re-establishment credit expenditure totals for 1945–46 and 1946–47 constituted 4.1 per cent and 8.4 per cent, respectively, of total budgetary expenditure by the Government of Canada in those fiscal years.[140] The gratuity/re-establishment credit combination had a predictable cost and a limited lifespan and did much to keep up the level of demand in the country in the postwar period. Moreover, the emphasis in re-establishment credit spending on domesticity and, by extension, family formation also helped trigger the baby boom. Ottawa had good reason indeed to be pleased with an initiative that combined private satisfaction with public good.

Authorization of the allowances available for vocational and university training under the Veterans Rehabilitation Act required the completion of an extensive form, not by the veteran but by a DVA counsellor.[141] This gave particulars of educational and employment history and ended with the "Counsellor's Summary" and recommendation. The latter typically specified entitlement period, course of study to be followed, starting date, length of program, status of application for admission, fees to be paid by DVA, and maintenance grant required. To take effect, the recommendation of a counsellor needed district board approval and, if applicable, the signature of a medical officer. Obviously, authority loomed large in this procedure. Under the act, veterans were eligible for support for the period of their active service to a maximum of twelve months. In recommending grant support to assist with living expenses, counsellors took account of "Monthly Income, from other Sources, during Training" (this was authorized by section 13 of the Veterans Rehabilitation Act), but in practice the minister had discretion in the matter, and veterans and their spouses were encouraged to supplement their allowances with income from employment during the study period, provided this did not interfere with the successful and timely completion of training.[142] As of the issuance of PC5210 in July 1944, the basic monthly training allowance was $60 for a single veteran and $80 for a married veteran.[143] The married rate was supplemented with a monthly allowance of $12 each for first and second children, $10 for a third child, and $8 each for up to three more children. By the same token, a monthly allowance of $15 was paid on behalf of a dependent parent or parents and $18.20 per month "for a person acting in lieu of wife."[144] In 1948 the monthly allowance for a married veteran was increased to $90 per month and increases were also made for dependent children and parents.[145] Application for vocational training had to be made within twelve months of discharge or of the end of the war (eventually set at 31 December 1946 for this purpose), whichever came later.[146] University training had to be begun within fifteen months of discharge unless the minister agreed to a deferral.

Vocational training took many forms, but in the main it was the responsibility of the big training program the federal Department of Labour operated with the provinces to meet the needs of the wartime economy. From 21 March 1944, this program was known as Canadian Vocational Training (CVT), and beginning in 1945, its major responsibility was in relation to veterans.[147] At first, demobilization strained CVT, which scrambled to find the resources needed to meet the growing demand for its services, but eventually most of the problems were overcome.[148] On 31 March 1945, CVT had an enrolment of 3,607 veterans, a total that grew to 20,166 by 31 December and to 36,341 by 31 March 1946.[149] In January 1946 alone, 10,750 veterans entered the CVT system. Of the veterans who enrolled in CVT programs in 1945–46, 1.8 per cent took correspondence courses, 12.8 per cent attended private trade schools and business colleges, 38.1 per cent attended special CVT vocational schools, 27.1 per cent attended special CVT pre-matriculation schools, and 20.2 per cent took training on the job.[150] CVT was also active in directing veterans into apprenticeship training in trades governed by provincial apprenticeship acts. In the training of veterans in 1945–46, CVT made use of 106 private trade schools, 200 business colleges, 48 provincial or municipal schools, and 68 special training centres, which operated across the country from Halifax to Victoria and offered classes leading to a wide range of jobs.[151] Working with their DVA counterparts, CVT officials tried to steer veterans away from training for occupations that were threatened with "overcrowding" (such as electricians, plumbers, radio technicians, watch repairers, and, to a lesser extent, motor mechanics and machinists) and towards

Left: One of the many beneficiaries of Canadian Legion Educational Services (Royal Canadian Legion, *A Year of Service*, DVA, 1033-85/R5, vol. 7)

Below: Veterans in CVT commercial class, London, Ontario (*London Free Press,* 13 November 1945)

Bottom: Veterans in class, London, Ontario (*London Free Press,* 5 June 1946)

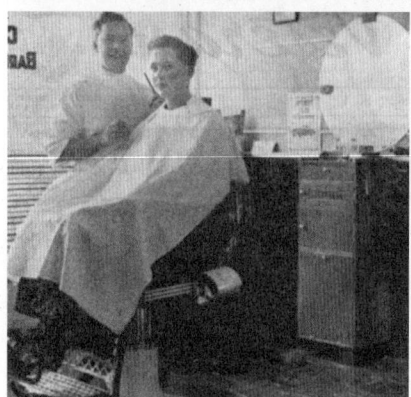
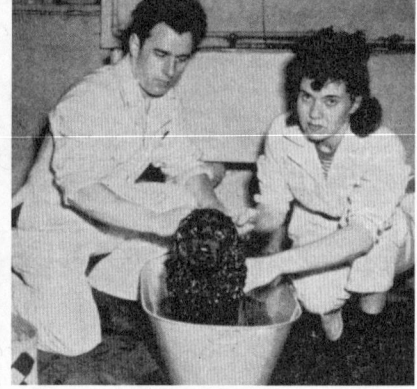

Clockwise: Instructor Gordon Duncan (far left) explains the use of the mitre box to veterans James Quait, Edward Lawrence, and John Creasey, London, Ontario (*London Free Press*, 10 January 1946)

Navy veterans Norman and Jacqueline Haddow of Vancouver opened a travelling day laundry for dogs. (*Veterans Affairs*, 15 February 1946)

A graduate of the CVT barbering school in Vancouver at work (*Veterans Affairs*, 15 March 1948)

Veterans Bill Vaughan (behind the camera), John Cleary (announcer), and Bob Alexander (piano) at the CVT School of Electronics, Toronto (*Veterans Affairs*, 15 October 1947)

Float of the Canning District Board of Trade, Apple Blossom Festival parade, Kentville, Nova Scotia, 1947 (DVA, 32-3, vol. 4, enclosure in Fenton to Burns, 13 June 1947)

occupations where employment prospects looked good (such as painting, decorating, and plastering).[152] To meet the needs of its ex-service students, CVT was also pressed into the business of finding and running accommodation facilities and managing cafeterias and canteens.[153] On 21 September 1948, Ontario launched the Ryerson Institute of Technology in Toronto to carry on the work of CVT at the former Training and Re-establishment Institute.[154] The new institute, now Ryerson University, remains a living memorial to a time of extraordinary transition and progress.

As its program for veterans proceeded, CVT was assisted in its efforts by the findings and more than eighty recommendations of the Royal Commission on Veterans' Qualifications. Established by PC 2486 of 10

April 1946 on the recommendation of the minister of labour, this commission was chaired by Wilfrid Bovey, who brought to the work his extensive experience at McGill University and with the Canadian Legion Educational Services.[155] His commission colleagues included Herwig, who worked in harness with D.S. Lyons, F.S. Smelts, Hector Dupuis, and F.S. Rutherford (when Rutherford resigned, he was replaced, under PC3342 of 8 May 1945 by Stewart R. Ross). The commission's purpose was to look into and report upon measures whereby veterans would be able to get credit in civilian life for skills and education they had acquired while in uniform. The commission opened an office in Montreal and eventually visited every province, hearing from a wide range of business, labour, technical, academic, and professional bodies. Its first and second interim reports, dated 22 June and 14 September 1945, respectively, were tabled by Labour Minister Humphrey Mitchell in the House of Commons on 29 October 1945.[156] A third and final report, dated 27 December 1945, was then tabled on 27 June 1946.[157] These documents were included in sessional papers but, probably because of the immediacy and practical nature of what was involved, were not worked up for publication by the King's Printer.

To 31 March 1951, 80,110 veterans received support for vocational training at a cost of $75,260,723.[158] Of this total, DVA spent $52,227,148 ($46,459,593 on allowances and $5,767,555 on fees), and the Department of Labour spent $23,033,575 on facilities. Though larger in number than the veterans who attended university at government expense, the ex-service men and women who were supported in taking vocational training cost the exchequer less, but in accounts of the period they have not been accorded the prominence they deserve. If the universities in short order produced a new generation of Canadian professionals, CVT just as quickly swelled the ranks of Canada's skilled workforce. Across Canada, CVT left behind it the framework for an improved and expanded vocational training system. Like much else about the Veterans Charter, the vocational training program had lasting consequences for Canadian society at large. Having helped win the war, Canadians built solidly for the peace.

In the autumn of 1945, as anticipated, veterans, both male and female, began to flood into the classrooms of Canadian universities by the thousand. Principal James, an economist by training, caught the flavour of the times when on 12 October he wrote to H.W. Jamieson, DVA superintendent of educational training, saying, "My own class has grown from about 52 last year to 295 and will be over the 300 mark next week, which gives you an idea of what has happened at McGill."[159] While principal of the university, James was now teaching three days a week. In 1946 about 35,000 were supported by the government to attend university. By comparison, the entire full-time undergraduate enrolment in Canadian universities and colleges in 1939 had been only 35,164.[160] The seven universities most favoured by the veterans – accounting for 75.5 per cent of such registrations in November 1946 – were, in order, Toronto, McGill, British Columbia, Saskatchewan, Alberta, Manitoba, and Queen's, with the Maritime and Quebec francophone universities lagging far behind.[161] In 1947–48 veterans accounted for 49 per cent of the student body of the University of Toronto, and in 1948–49 they accounted for 42 per cent.[162] As late as 1949–50, veterans still accounted for 21 per cent of all university students in the country.[163] Of the 33,828 studying in Canada as of 15 February 1947, 13,257 were registered in arts programs (including pre-professional). The next five largest groups of registrants were in engineering (8,093), commerce and finance (3,338), agriculture (1,477), medicine (1,186), and law (875).

In November 1945, to assist the universities with their teaching requirements, DVA made it possible for a supported postgraduate student to take a half-time university teaching post without loss of benefits. For a veteran who did this, "two months of half-time combined training and teaching" would "be regarded as the equivalent of one month in full-time training."[164] Study abroad was yet another option available to some veterans; the country most favoured was the United States (some US beneficiaries of the G.I. Bill likewise studied in Canada),[165] but veterans also attended institutions in the United Kingdom and other European countries. As of 31 December 1949, there were 630 veterans being supported in attending university in the United States and another 73 taking vocational training there.[166] By the same date, 1,713 of 1,892 Canadian veterans had completed their courses of study in that country.[167] Of these, 179 had not yet acted on their undertaking to return to Canada but were "being reminded regularly of the conditions under which assistance was granted."[168] By 15 January 1950, 1,710 student loans to the amount of $406,572.90 had been made to veterans. The average individual loan had been $238, and the average total amount per veteran had been $287.[169] To 21 December 1950, 377 recipients of these loans had commenced repayment, and $56,572.67 had been received back in principal and interest (payable at 5 per cent).[170]

An analysis of 9,119 veteran students in receipt of allowances at 30 November 1945 showed that 2,308 (25.3 per cent) were married and 6,811 (74.7 per cent) were single.[171] As time passed, however, and the

Veteran Peter Omond setting up tent accommodation, University of Western Ontario, London, Ontario (*London Free Press*, 14 May 1946)

baby boom got underway, the percentages tipped dramatically in favour of the married category. At its ninth meeting, on 20 November 1948, the Advisory Committee on University Training for Veterans (hereafter in this section the advisory committee) heard that the ratio of married to single veterans was continually increasing. Some 1,200 individuals had changed from single to married status between the final examinations in the spring and the beginning of the fall term, and 50 per cent of the supported veterans in university were now married.[172] By definition, the number of dependants the government was supporting was also increasing. At the University of Saskatchewan, the veterans were older than their civilian counterparts and in 1946–47 had an average age of 25.4 years.[173] According to a 1970 account, approximately 40 per cent of the veterans who attended this institution were married and "25 per cent had one or more children."[174] On 25 February 1946, President Thomson of the University of Saskatchewan told the advisory committee that the male veterans had developed in the services qualities that were not evident in the general undergraduate body: "This has come about by the discipline of having to live together. The services have done a remarkable job in developing a maturity of social outlook and a sense of responsibility which should be conserved and developed on the university campus."[175] This typified the situation across the country. Canadian universities had not only grown but had taken in students of very different outlook and expectations.

As the educational program of DVA moved into high gear, the advisory committee monitored events closely. At its third meeting, on 13 November 1945, it considered recommendation 41 of the Royal Commission on Veterans' Qualifications, which called for the establishment of an independent committee to deal with the postwar problems of universities. It was decided that it would not be "advisable to set up a separate organization independent of the Department of Veterans Affairs and unrelated to the Advisory Committee on University Training."[176] Instead, it was recommended that the minister of veterans affairs establish a board within DVA "to review and/or recommend financial or other assistance from the Dominion Government to colleges or universities for the training of veterans and, generally, to take appropriate action in respect to the needs of any or all of the colleges or universities referred to it by the Advisory Committee on University Training for Veterans or brought to its attention by the head of any college or university."[177] The recommendation was duly accepted, and on 4 December 1945 the Committee on University Requirements was authorized by PC7129.[178]

England was appointed for a ten-month term as chairman of the new committee, which had as its other members University of Ottawa rector the very Revd. Philippe Cornellier, Queen's University principal R.C. Wallace, and the Department of Finance and DVA officials R.B. Bryce and L.J. Mills.[179] Following a meeting on 25 February 1946, England submitted an interim report to the minister. This document ranged widely over the issues that had arisen in relation to the education of veterans and put forward a number of recommendations for the consideration of DVA and the advisory committee. The report noted that most universities had "abandoned the academic year and arranged to accept veterans twice or three times a year, concentrating courses within a shorter period."[180] By the same token, arrangements had been made at the bigger institutions "for all-year operation."[181] Universities were giving priority to veterans (as indeed they were required to do under the terms of the supplementary grant scheme), and it had been necessary for many of them to exclude some non-veterans. In the view of most of the universities, however, it was "not practicable to exclude completely all non-veteran freshman entrants."[182] The report concluded that the matter would "require tactful and firm handling by the universities" if veterans were to receive "priority in the very limited accommodation available."[183]

An appendix to the report gave a university-by-university survey of the situation with respect to the facilities available to meet the influx of veterans. At the University of Toronto, first-year science and engineering students were being taught in a surplus defence industry plant at Ajax, twenty-five miles from the city, where assembly-line huts had been made over into classrooms and laboratories.[184] At the University of British Columbia, where 3,200 veterans were already enrolled, 112 huts had been

Right: Former RCAF navigator Ross Bates studied pharmacy at the University of Saskatchewan. (*Veterans Affairs*, 1 July 1947)

Below: Army huts on West Mall, University of British Columbia, 1949 (UBC Archives, 1.1/688)

moved to the campus at a cost of $300,000, "half of them for general university purposes and half as residences for students."[185] At the same time, the university had a $5 million construction program in progress to provide a new physics building and new accommodation for pharmacy, home economics, and applied science, as well as an addition to the library. At McGill, where 3,076 were now enrolled, Sir William Dawson College had been established in the former RCAF No. 9 Observer Training School at St Johns, Quebec, and in February 1946, 400 single and married veterans were being housed and fed there.[186] McGill had plans for "an enlargement of [the] Redpath Library, new wings at Royal Victoria College and Douglas Hall, enlargement of Engineering building and Physics Building, with additional construction of Engineering, Physics and Chemistry group."[187] Like Canada itself, universities were having to adapt in myriad ways, but they were not only coping but prospering. A big short-term demand was allowing them to reinvent themselves and build for a brighter tomorrow. This was very much in keeping with the spirit of the times.

Not surprisingly, a continuing concern of the advisory committee was the academic performance of the veterans. On 4 December 1945, PC7224 had laid down that a grant could not "be continued to a discharged person who, having failed in one or more classes or subjects in any academic year, fails in more than one of the supplementary examinations next offered by the university in any such classes or subjects."[188] Thus, for the veteran, examination results were even more important than was normally the case. In practice, the veterans met a high level of achievement, though there were many casualties; in 1946–47, 77 per cent passed unconditionally, 10 per cent were able to continue with one condition, and 13 per cent failed to qualify for continued assistance.[189] At its 19 November 1947 meeting, the advisory committee heard that of 16,000 student veterans no longer in training, 4,000 had finished their programs, 3,000 had used up their entitlement, 4,000 had voluntarily withdrawn, and 5,000 had failed.[190] The number of withdrawals was said to be a reflection of the "good employment situation" in the country.[191] Of those who had not succeeded, 1,200 were repeating the failed year and paying for it themselves. In 1948, 81 per cent of the veterans passed without condition, 8 per cent passed with one condition, and 11 per cent failed.[192] In the view of Jamieson, the last-mentioned figure indicated "weaknesses in the universities' assessment of capacities during and at the end of the First Year."[193] Evidence of this was also to be found in "the large number who on repeating First Year did extremely well."[194] For veterans "of mature years and long service," failure was indeed "a serious problem."[195]

In November 1946 the advisory committee acted to assist deserving veterans who fell from grace and lost unexpired entitlement. The resolution in this regard recommended as follows: "A student-veteran whose assistance in university training has been discontinued because of failure to make the required academic standing, and who thereafter continues at university for one year at his own expense during which time he fulfils the academic requirements, and who is recommended by his faculty, may be reinstated not more than once during his university career."[196] This recommendation was given effect by a letter that Jamieson sent to all district administrators on 21 March 1947.[197] Of the 1,660 who failed in

1948–49, 817 repeated at their own expense. This was said to exemplify a small dropout rate and the "continued determination" of the veterans "to complete the course."[198] In November 1948, it was reported that DVA had a policy of following up dropouts and failures, who were said to constitute some 40 per cent of registrations.[199] On 6 February 1950, the advisory committee heard that 20 per cent of the ex-servicemen in the Toronto district were not receiving allowances and that of this group 20 per cent were repeating work.[200]

By contrast, thanks to PC4059 of 1 October 1946, veterans who succeeded in their studies could receive support beyond their service entitlement. The conditions for receiving additional help were straightforward: the veteran had to complete at least one year of study, pass all subjects, either achieve second-class honours standing or be in the top 25 per cent of his or her year, and be recommended for further support by the scholarship committee of the university attended.[201] In February 1951, Jamieson reported that 9,000 veterans had started university work without enough service credit to see them through to graduation. Fully 6,068 (67.4 per cent) of these had received extensions of benefits "on a 'scholarship' basis."[202] Indeed, second and third extensions had not been uncommon, and a few existing recipients were on their fifth and sixth extensions. During the academic year 1950–51, 28 per cent of the undergraduates and 40 per cent of the postgraduates receiving assistance were on extended benefits.[203]

To assist the veterans with their studies and fulfill one of the commitments made when the supplementary grant was given, the advisory committee promoted counselling services at the universities.[204] In August 1946, the Conference of University Veterans' Advisers was held at the University of British Columbia, and a committee was established to coordinate activities across the country.[205] The chairman of this committee was Sperrin Chant, now head of the Department of Philosophy and Psychology at British Columbia, and the vice-chairman was William Line of the University of Toronto (the two other members were from the Université de Montréal and the University of Alberta). In connection with the establishment of the committee, it was agreed that the Veterans' Advisory Service at the University of Toronto would act as a "central agency."[206] In March 1947 and again in January 1948, the advisory committee supported plans by the University Veterans' Advisory Service, of which Margery King was secretary, to hold national conferences.[207]

In November 1946, the advisory committee commissioned Chant to explore the possibility of making "a comprehensive objective study of the university training programme for veterans."[208] This was needed because the experience of the veterans could be expected to influence the work of universities generally. Chant's preliminary report, given in March 1947, recommended that the study to be undertaken "should be basically factual rather than a cumulation of opinion and impression; that it should be broad in scope; should extend over a period of years; and that interim reports on certain phases should be released from time to time."[209] On the strength of this advice, a subcommittee was appointed, consisting of Chant himself, principals James and Wallace, and University of Toronto president Sidney Smith to define the scope of the study and seek funds to support it.[210] Research was subsequently started with the objective of investigating "the unusual success of veterans in spite of the unfavourable educational arrangements that prevail at present."[211] In November 1948, when Chant reported again to the advisory committee on the progress of the study, it was noted that grant support from the Carnegie Corporation would be contingent on "an appropriate person" being named to lead the project and an outline being produced of the work to be done.[212] President MacKenzie of the University of British Columbia was assigned to review matters and to determine if England "might be persuaded to undertake the assignment."[213] When money was not forthcoming from either Carnegie or the Rockefeller Foundation, the hope was expressed that England would be able to complete the proposed study with the aid of a Guggenheim Foundation fellowship, but there is no evidence in the documentary record that this ever happened.[214]

Two groups of students of special concern to the advisory committee in 1946 and 1947 were those seeking admission to medical and dental faculties. In 1946, to facilitate applications from veterans, most medical and dental faculties deferred acceptances until September, with some even holding off until the fall term was almost ready to start.[215] By the spring of 1947, however, it was clear that there were more veterans who wanted to study medicine and dentistry than there would be places available for them. In the circumstance, the advisory committee was asked to consider establishing "a reasonable quota" for veterans in faculties of medicine and dentistry and ensure that qualified veterans would be notified of acceptance at an early date.[216] This would "permit candidates to proceed with the formulation of their housing and summer employment plans and would minimize the excessive 'shopping around' and hasty decisions with respect to second choices of occupation."[217] On the advice of MacKenzie, these delicate issues were referred to the executive of the NCCU for consideration.[218] On 19 November 1947, the advisory committee heard that while most faculties of medicine and dentistry were giving "priority to qualified veterans," there was "also a large backlog of highly qualified civilians applying for this limited accommodation."[219] To ease the situation, sixty Canadian veterans were now being assisted to study medicine and dentistry in the United States.[220] In February 1950, Jamieson reported to the advisory committee that there was "a backlog of 62 veterans academically qualified for admission to Medicine" and that 127 others were in premedical courses.[221] Many other veterans who had wanted to study medicine and were qualified to do so had moved on to faculties such as engineering and commerce, where admissions had been increased to meet the demand. In total, 1,672 veterans had been admitted to first-year medicine; of these, 22 were now being assisted to study in the United States and the United Kingdom.[222] The backlog for dentistry was 12 with another 33 in predental courses.[223] Some 759 veterans had been admitted to dental faculties, of whom 44 were now being assisted to study in the United States.[224]

An issue of a different sort arose in relation to law students studying at Osgoode Hall, Toronto. This was pressed on the advisory committee by the Canadian Legion and arose out of the fact that of 224 veterans registered in first year in 1947–48 (50 of whom were university graduates), only 126, or 56.3 per cent, had passed.[225] Among non-veterans, the passing percentage was 54 per cent. By comparison, in 1946–47, 72.1 per cent of the veterans in the first-year class had been successful. Of those who had failed in 1947-48, moreover, 39 were repeating at their own expense. The response of the advisory committee to this unfortunate situation was to recommend that the Canadian Legion, "with due deference to the autonomy in academic matters of the Osgoode Hall Law School," take the problem up with the Canadian Bar Association.[226] The committee also approved a delicately worded resolution requesting Jamieson to ask the dean of Osgoode Hall to provide "the facts relating to this matter if he cares to do so."[227]

Looking to the future, the advisory committee also concerned itself with the employment opportunities that would be available to veterans on graduation. On 12 November 1946, the committee heard a report from J.R. Dymond of the Wartime Bureau of Technical Personnel on the work of the Inter-departmental Advisory Committee on Professionally Trained Persons. The latter committee had been established at the urging of DVA and the NCCU, and was "surveying professional opportunities for young people in Canada."[228] The advisory committee endorsed the work of the interdepartmental group as "a major contribution to education in Canada."[229]

By March 1947, information had been submitted to DVA concerning medicine, dentistry, nursing, social service, veterinary science, forestry, osteopathy, petroleum engineering, and aeronautical engineering.[230] Simultaneously, a general report was being prepared for the inter-departmental advisory committee by F.E. Whitworth of the Dominion Bureau of Statistics. The aim of DVA in all this was that the research now in progress "should be perpetuated in such a way that continuous inventories might be established for each of the important professions in Canada for the particular use of universities, secondary school systems, and individual young Canadians making choice for their careers."[231] In November 1947 the advisory committee heard from Dr Orville Ault, director of personnel selection, Civil Service Commission, that the civil service, the country's "largest single employer," was "making every effort to secure a good proportion of outstanding university graduates" and would shortly be hiring 125 agricultural students for summer jobs.[232] In the same spirit, the National Employment Service was making officers available on campuses in the last month of each academic year.

The veterans sought to promote their own interest and welfare through local campus organizations (McGill was the hot spot in this regard) and through a National Conference of Student Veterans, which met for the first time in Montreal on 27 and 28 December 1945. In her letter inviting Mackenzie to attend, Barbara E. Jackson, secretary of the McGill Student Veterans' Society, wrote that while Canada's rehabilitation legislation was "probably the most generous in the world," there were improvements that could be made.[233] Four specific issues were identified by the New Brunswick Veterans' Club for consideration by the conference. These related to housing conditions, the need for a larger differential between the grants paid to married and single students, the need for "progressive increases" in allowances after the first year of the program, and inclusion of the cost of books in fee payments.[234] Mackenzie did not attend the conference, but Burns addressed the opening session, which drew about 175 persons.[235] Herwig attended the gathering on behalf of the Canadian Legion.

In his speech, Burns stressed that while DVA "wanted to see that veterans had every reasonable facility to complete their education without undue hardship or worry," those present should remember three things before making "any recommendation for increased allowances."[236] These were that the allowances were not "intended to cover the whole cost of subsistence and education"; that they could not be raised for university students without being raised for those on vocational training and those receiving out-of-work assistance (which in turn had to take account of wage rates); and that "university student veterans were already getting very much more in the way of benefits than those who took the Re-establishment Credit or vocational training." Subsequently, Burns reported to Woods that his speech had been "well received" and that the delegates had been "in the great majority, sound and reasonable."[237] "They appreciate," he continued, "the danger to their own cause of being singled out for more favourable treatment than they are already receiving. Toronto and Queen's Universities in particular seemed inclined to feel that the plan was essentially fair at the present time and that there was no great justification for asking for more."

Perhaps the most important outcome of the gathering in Montreal was the formation of the National Council of Student Veterans, which was headed by Len Starkey, the chair of the conference and the leader of the McGill society.[238] A brief submitted to the government following the conference incorporated all the resolutions that had been passed.[239] Its first section called on the federal government "to recognize full employment for all citizens as the cornerstone of its rehabilitation program." Specifically, the government was urged to "carry through a public works program, subsidize industries, and undertake any other measures ... necessary to maintain full employment." The rest of the brief was organized under three headings: housing, financial matters, and educational issues. Despite Burns's cautionary words, the section on finance included a resolution in favour of increasing the married allowance by $40 per month and the single allowance by $20 per month. The brief also made the point that twenty-nine educational institutions (twenty-six of them universities) had been represented at the conference by sixty-three delegates and that the gathering had therefore been "representative of the fifteen thousand veterans attending universities throughout Canada" and, because their problems were similar, "of the seventeen thousand veterans taking vocational training of all types."

In November 1946, a delegation from the McGill Student Veterans' Society (of which Frank B. Common was now president) went to Ottawa to press various claims, including the need for a commuters' allowance, but it did not have much success.[240] A second national conference was held at McGill on 27–29 December 1946. This time Jamieson attended and spoke on behalf of DVA. In his report on the proceedings, he observed that his "firm statement" to the opening session had been well received, especially by the representatives of the larger universities.[241] "It is evident," he continued, "that the great majority of student-veterans realize that their interests are not well served by continuous requests for unlimited assistance on the part of a minority which, for the past year, controlled the organization ... I am firmly convinced that existing provisions are meeting the essential needs of the persons for whom the legislation was designed and that a very small minority has dominated the representations made to this Department. The great majority appreciate the measure of assistance to those who are willing and able to help themselves." Jamieson also noted that the major universities outside Montreal "were not adequately represented" at the conference.

The big news at the 1946 gathering was Starkey's ouster as president. This happened in the second session, which was held in camera, and occurred after four members of the executive offered their resignations because of lack of confidence in the president. The issue at stake was his "political affiliation" and his "making use of his position as president, to further the ends of his own political party."[242] (Earlier in December, John Wallace and Jack Ord, two student veterans at the University of Toronto, had publicly charged that "ex-service students across Canada were protesting 'Communist domination'" of their national organization.)[243] Following a stormy debate, a non-confidence vote was carried by 43 votes to 14, whereupon Starkey resigned and John Schierbeck of Macdonald College, a thirty-three-year-old naval veteran of Danish extraction and a postgraduate student in horticulture, was elected chairman of the conference and then president of the council. After the uproar, the conference moved on to familiar business, but one report of the proceedings ended on this sobering note:

> It was felt that the Conference as a whole accomplished little that is likely to have very practical results. It was largely dominated by a "demanding" attitude on the part of certain delegates who seemed to feel that the function of such a Conference was to see "how much more could be obtained from the government." There was, however, very definite appreciation of what is already being done by D.V.A. and a growing feeling by many that it is time for the veterans to see what they can do for themselves rather than expecting the government to do more. One delegate who had attended both conferences summed up this growing sense of self-responsibility as being indicative of the fact that the veteran students are one year nearer to being civilians and one step further from being servicemen.[244]

Under Schierbeck's leadership, the National Council of Student Veterans kept up its lobbying campaign, though not with the previous intensity.[245] With Starkey's exit, DVA sailed into smoother waters in its relations with the organized veterans. In effect, its control over events, always firm, became even stronger. In the spring of 1947, veterans at the University of Toronto presented President Sidney Smith with an "Ex-Service Committee Brief."[246] This advanced four claims to "alleviate hardship conditions existing and affecting the student veteran on the Campus." The students wanted "tutorial assistance for all student veterans requiring it"; a cost-of-living bonus "to compensate for a general cost of living increase of $8.00 a month since August 1944"; a "Broadening of Veterans Life Insurance to permit insuring of Veterans' dependents"; and a "health insurance measure for a student veteran's dependents, similar to his own benefits ... to safeguard [the] health of the family and the financial stability of the veteran." Smith duly brought this forward to the advisory committee but without significant effect.[247] Tutorial assistance was left to the discretion of individual universities, and the proposed cost-of-living increase was refused because it would in effect be an increase in the living allowance, about which policy had already been established. Group medical insurance, the advisory committee heard, was already being studied by the Veterans' Advisory Service at a number of institutions.

Above all, the university presidents on the advisory committee were concerned about the continuation of the supplementary grant scheme. Since the initial allocation had been only for the period 1 July 1945 to 30 June 1946, this obviously created uncertainty. In 1946 the report of the Committee on University Requirements recommended that in future, while maintaining the limit of $150 per student, the supplementary grant should not be an across-the-board payment but should be "based upon the actual expenditures by universities in meeting the instructional needs of veterans."[248] This was because of "the wide variation in costs and fee scales, the difference in sources of other income and the wide variety of needs." The fixed grant system tended "to accentuate wide differentials in cost." When, by PC4060, the government renewed the program on 1 October for another year (1 July 1946 to 30 June 1947), it did so on the basis advocated by England and his colleagues.[249] On 12 November 1946, the advisory committee considered the grant issue again and unanimously agreed upon a resolution calling on the government to guarantee the payment of the supplementary grant for as long as veterans were attending universities under the terms of the Veterans Rehabilitation Act.[250] In fact, by PC3799 of 23 September 1947, the existing arrangement was extended for another year (1 July 1947 to 30 June 1948). In response to this, the advisory committee passed a lengthy resolution on 16 January 1948 requesting that the grants next be extended for the period 1 July 1947 to 30 June 1951.[251] On 20 January 1948, a delegation from the advisory committee met with Finance Minister Douglas Abbott, and on 6 March 1948, PC943 granted their request.[252] To 30 June 1950, $16,568,686 was paid in supplementary grants. By definition, the largest payments went to the seven universities that had attracted the bulk of the students, with Toronto taking 23.3 per cent of the funding. In rank order, the next five leading beneficiaries were British Columbia (15.2 per cent), McGill (11.6 per cent), Saskatchewan (7.2 per cent), Alberta (7.2 per cent), and Manitoba (6.0 per cent). By contrast, Laval ranked twenty-third in the list of universities receiving grants and the Université de Montréal twenty-fifth.

The legacy of the substantial public investment made in post-secondary education under the Veterans Rehabilitation Act was a fresh cohort of Canadian professionals and a university system that was more complex and capable than it had previously been. To 31 March 1951, 53,788 veterans were supported to undertake university training at a cost of $137,801,657 ($3,250,000 for matriculation courses provided through the Department of Labour, and $85,413,561 for allowances, $31,328,004 for fees, and $17,810,092 in supplementary grants, all paid by DVA).[253] One of the tens of thousands of beneficiaries was the future Liberal cabinet minister, Judy LaMarsh, who, following service in the CWAC, took advantage of the Veterans Rehabilitation Act to quickly complete an arts course and then study law at Osgoode Hall. In 1969 she remembered that the way forward for her after the war had been through "probably the best government program we ever had."[254] "I pay in income taxes in one year," she quipped, "whatever help I got from DVA." Her experience highlighted what, at its best, the Veterans Charter delivered for Canadians. Opportunity offered was opportunity grasped.

7 Building and Rebuilding

The progress that Judy LaMarsh achieved in life was exactly the sort of outcome that Olive Russell had in mind as she and her associates administered DVA's program for women veterans. Russell's "running mate" at DVA in 1945 was Mary Dinsmore Salter, another former CWAC officer and a psychology PHD (now best known for her later research, as Mary D. Salter Ainsworth, in the field of child psychology).[1] As part of the gearing up of the department, she was appointed superintendent of women's rehabilitation. As promised, DVA also recruited women staff members to act as counsellors, interviewers, and clerks in its rehabilitation centres across the country. In September 1945, the department issued a manual of instructions on women's rehabilitation, and in February and March 1946, with demobilization in full swing, it held training conferences on women's rehabilitation in Ottawa (18–21 February), Saskatoon (27 February – 1 March), and Vancouver (13–16 March).[2] A detailed record was kept of the proceedings of these conferences, and a summary of what was said at them was issued jointly by the superintendent of women's rehabilitation and the director of staff training. Discussion at the conferences centred on three matters: "(1) Liaison among those concerned with women's rehabilitation, (2) Occupational trends and training opportunities for women, and (3) Problems of adjustment and welfare of ex-service women."[3] The discussion on the second of these matters flowed along familiar lines, but the emphasis differed from that to be found in Russell's analyses. At the Ottawa conference, for example, Margaret Grier, associate director of National Selective Service, Department of Labour, pointed out that "the disorganization of women's normal occupations and pursuits during the war" had not been "as severe nor as wide-spread" as it superficially appeared.[4] The first wave of wartime women workers had been drawn from the ranks of the approximately "half a million girls and women" who normally lived at home, mainly in rural areas and small towns, because there were no jobs for them.[5] When this pool of labour had been exhausted, about 125,000 to 150,000 married women had been recruited. They had "come mainly from household service" or been drawn from the ranks of "young married women whose husbands were in the Services."[6] But married women had not been employed to the same extent in Canada as in other countries. The current expectation, Grier reported, was that "only 2 or 3 out of every 10" married women would want to remain in employment outside the home and that three-quarters of the single women who had gone to work during the war would eventually get married and "leave gainful employment."[7]

At the Saskatoon conference, Moira O'Neil, assistant to the supervisor of Placement Operations–Veterans, Unemployment Insurance Commission, argued that although the war had "opened employment opportunities for women ... [in] occupations previously considered male," the fact had to be faced that when men were "available as garage mechanics, truck drivers and such, most employers ... [would] prefer them."[8] Some ex-service women might "enter unusual occupations," but the majority could be expected to "go into the kind of work their sisters did before them."[9] Indeed, the experience of service life may have increased "the tendency to 'run with the pack.'"[10] It was true, O'Neil said, that "scientific changes" were creating new employment opportunities for women, but DVA counsellors would be "well advised to concentrate on the types of employment" in which women were "normally employed."[11]

The Vancouver conference heard a similar message from Fraudena Eaton, associate director of National Selective Service, Department of Labour. In her remarks she traced the history of the employment of women and noted that the entry of so many into the workforce during the war had from its inception produced the fear that there would not be enough jobs for all at the end of the conflict. This view in turn was feeding prejudice in relation to the employment of women.[12] But in fact the fear was unjustified because many of the married women who had gone to work had made "an easy transition back to their homes or to domestic employment at the lower wage level they had left."[13] Nevertheless, economic considerations would ensure that there would be more married women in the workforce after the war than there had been before. Given the prejudice against them, married women "would be well advised to consider opportunities for self-found employment, – in agriculture, owning small manufacturing establishments, crafts and trades ... or service occupations such as hairdressing." This would prevent them from being "at the mercy of the prejudice of an employer." Eaton also recommended caution in the counselling of ex-service women:

> She advised the counsellors to advise ex-service women generally to go into work accepted as women's work. She felt that although during the war many women performed jobs previously done by men

relatively few will remain in those jobs. She felt that many jobs fell naturally into a division of men's work and women's work in terms of physical strength, attitudes and aptitudes. She stated that the fields ordinarily accepted as women's fields offered interesting and satisfactory work and the reason that women have reached out to jobs usually done by men was not so much because of lack of satisfaction with women's work but because of the more favourable wage rate usually given to a man's job. She felt that if equitable wage rates could be arrived at there would still tend to be a natural division in the work most suitable to the two sexes, although there would obviously be considerable overlapping.

This was sobering, but as the DVA program unfolded, Russell was optimistic that the goals she had in mind were being realized and that the glad day of the postwar world she had envisaged was indeed dawning. In November 1945 she contributed an article entitled "Women Set High Standard of Service in War, Peace" to the first issue of *Veterans Affairs*, and throughout 1946 she maintained a busy travel and public-speaking schedule.[14] In a 25 March 1946 interview on the CBC in Vancouver, Russell was asked to react to the statement that because ex-service women did not "have to think quite as realistically as men in considering their re-establishment problems," some of them "were asking for unusual training courses – that is, courses a bit off the beaten track."[15] Russell shot back that she was glad to hear that this was happening. Those who thought that the only training available to ex-service women was for "hair-dressing and clerical work" were "entirely mistaken." All training opportunities applied equally to men and women. Any veteran wanting a particular course of training could have it, provided he or she met the requisite qualifying and eligibility criteria, applied within the entitlement time limit, and was setting out to do something appropriate to his or her rehabilitation. Women were already in training for over eighty-five occupations. These ranged "from the highly skilled and professional occupations" requiring several years of training, such as law, architecture, medicine, pharmacy, and social work, "to those occupations requiring shorter periods of training such as Book Binding, Linotype Operating, Photography, Egg Grading and even frog farming." This diversity was to be welcomed and did not conflict with the maintenance of good family life:

> Don't make the mistake of thinking that all unusual training requested by women is necessarily unrealistic. On the whole I think it very encouraging to find that so many women are showing initiative

in pursuing and preparing for occupations, which ... are a bit off the beaten track. For instance, some women are in training as Watch and Clock makers and one is in training for an Embalmer. Could you suggest any occupations that are less likely to go out of business than these, or any reason why they are not suitable occupations for women? Lest you think I am forgetting the importance of Homemaking as a career for women, I wish to state that in several centres in Canada a special course of training in Home-making and family living has been arranged for ex-service women. This course has been designed to meet the needs of those young women who will be establishing homes of their own and who recognize the importance of having training for that complex and important task. In this course, which is of at least four months duration, special emphasis is being put on both the practical household duties and general home management; budgeting, nutrition, child care and training, and the psychological aspects of family life. I am glad to be able to announce that in some centres evening classes in this subject are also being provided for those men who recognize that they too need training if they are to be successful partners in this responsible job of making happy homes.

Women had shown "their ability to perform all sorts of tasks hitherto not open to them," and "opportunities for them to use their talents to the full" should never be denied them again.

In July 1946 Russell told Betty Styran on radio station CKCO, Kitchener, Ontario, that when she had taken up her duties at DVA, she had thought her main job would be to select and train counsellors. In practice, she had had to spend much of her time reminding "employers, Citizens' Committees and all who were planning to welcome veterans and assist them with their re-establishment that there were ex-service women as well as ex-service men to be rehabilitated."[16] This effort had paid off, and the rehabilitation of women veterans was "proceeding much more smoothly that might have been anticipated." In the same vein, Russell wrote in the summer 1946 issue of *Echoes*, the magazine of the Imperial Order Daughters of the Empire, that whereas a year before there had been the "danger of employers forgetting that there would be women veterans as well as men," this problem had now been overcome.[17] Thanks to "the same adaptability, efficiency and dependability" that they had shown in uniform, ex-service women were now receiving high marks from employers.

Russell and her female colleagues in the rehabilitation branch of DVA could also take comfort in the department's attitude towards the employment of married women in the civil service. In 1944 the Civil Service Commission decided to drop five to seven thousand married women, many of whom had entered government service through wartime expansion.[18] Henceforth, moreover, the regulation would be strictly enforced that required a single woman civil servant to resign her position when she got married. In a 5 December 1945 memorandum to Woods, Director General of Rehabilitation Burns argued that instead of joining in the renewal of "policies of discrimination against married women," DVA should call for the end of such discrimination.[19] Canada had agreed, in the charter of the United Nations, to "the realization of human rights and fundamental freedoms for all without distinction as to race, sex, language or religion," and to bar married women from civil service employment would violate that pledge. In support of his case, Burns cited an April 1945 report of the Women's Advisory Committee of the United States War Manpower Commission. This report had concluded that discrimination against married women in employment was an injustice, an unwise limitation on the availability of workers with skills that were in demand, and a breeding ground for "practices of subterfuge and deception." The Government of Canada, Burns reminded Woods, was committed to full employment covering all who were "able and willing to work," and for the civil service to act otherwise would contradict that basic policy. It was also the case that married women who had served overseas were entitled to civil service preference as veterans. Furthermore, many male veterans with overseas service were counting on financial assistance from their wives while they were in rehabilitation training or re-establishing themselves in jobs and homes. If the civil service set a bad example in relation to married women, the government could scarcely blame other employers for following suit. To make "economic necessity" rather than "suitability for the job" the test of civil service hiring would be to promote "a dangerous practice" that, logically, "would involve men as well as women." The simple truth was that "the fact of marriage should not be the basis for denying a woman the freedom of choice granted to all other citizens in a democracy." The question of whether or not a woman should take a paying job was a private matter, to be decided by her and her husband, and there was no need for legislation on the subject.

The general reform advocated by Burns was not in fact introduced into the Canadian civil service until 1955, but married women veterans with husbands in training were apparently treated as single persons immediately after the war.[20] DVA, moreover, resisted the application of the civil service resignation rule to single female members of its own staff who got married.[21] In the same spirit, a $30 deduction formerly made from the

Mary Dinsmore Salter (later Ainsworth), DVA's first superintendent of women's rehabilitation (*Psychoanalytic Inquiry* 19 [1999]: 681)

allowance paid to married women veterans in training was cancelled on 1 January 1947.[22] Thereafter, married and single veterans were treated equally with respect to training allowances. In April 1947 Helen Hunt, Salter's successor as superintendent of women's rehabilitation, recommended that a deduction of the same amount being made from the awaiting returns allowances of married women veterans who had gone into farming or business should likewise be cancelled.[23]

The progress being made in the women's rehabilitation program was monitored at DVA headquarters in Ottawa by monthly reports from counsellors of women in the field. The operation and record of the program was also analyzed in two lengthy reports by the superintendent of women's rehabilitation. The first, submitted by Salter on 12 July 1946, covered the events of the previous year, and the second, submitted by Helen Hunt on 25 November 1947, covered developments from August 1946 to November 1947. Salter noted that women's rehabilitation was "proceeding most effectively" where it was "most separate."[24] The ideal arrangement kept the counselling of male and female veterans separate at the local level but within the same overall administrative framework. When she had come to DVA, Salter commented, no supervisor of women's training had yet been appointed at the Department of Labour, and not much had been done by Canadian Vocational Training to provide special training courses for women. Once Marion Graham had taken on this job, however, matters had speeded up and steps had been taken to offer training in practical nursing in all provinces but Saskatchewan. The courses in progress were almost all filled to capacity. But this was not true of homemaking courses, which had been established in Alberta, Saskatchewan, Ontario, and Quebec. These courses had been started too late, and plans to introduce them in British Columbia and the Maritimes had been dropped because there were too few applicants. The courses most in demand were for commercial training, hairdressing, and dressmaking. Ex-service women were doing well in finding jobs across the country, but there was "a growing discrimination on the part of employers against all married women."

In the report she submitted more than a year later, Hunt showed that the basic trends Salter had observed had continued through 1947.[25] Encouraging ex-service women to take training in practical nursing had been a priority in counselling, while demand for homemaking courses had remained low. Only in Saskatoon was there still such a course in operation. The training courses most favoured by ex-service women had continued to be "prematriculation, commercial, hairdressing and dressmaking." Hunt ascribed this "disappointing" result and the failure of many ex-service women to branch out "into new lines" to their prewar experience. Having lived through the Great Depression, ex-service women had given priority to "security," that is to say, to training for traditional women's occupations, when planning their future careers. The employment situation of ex-service women had also remained satisfactory, the greatest difficulty having been experienced in Nova Scotia and British Columbia. But the problems experienced in these provinces were minor blemishes on an otherwise rosy picture:

> Immediately following VJ day it was evident that employers, many of whom had also had service experience, were very ready to accept ex-servicewomen in their organization. This satisfactory condition has continued, even though at the present time the employer is requesting more often an employee with some experience following training. It has been very evident right across the country in conversations with representatives of the National Employment Service that placement of women veterans never became the problem that was anticipated. Nearly all state that they had expected some time would occur in which some of their offices would be flooded with ex-servicewomen seeking employment which was not readily available.

Happily, the expected crunch never came, and the transition to peacetime conditions was smooth.

Hunt included in her report detailed statistics on what had happened to ex-service women under the provisions of the Veterans Charter. To 30

Ex-service women delegates at the 1948 Canadian Legion convention, Saskatoon (Royal Canadian Legion, *Report of the 12th Dominion Convention*, 43)

September 1947, 11,507 women had taken training. Of these 9,083 had taken vocational training and 2,424 had gone to university. The 11,507 figure represented 23 per cent of the total enlistment and was higher than the equivalent figure for male veterans. To 31 October 1947, 264 ex-service women had received awaiting-returns allowances; and to the end of September, 200 had received temporary incapacity allowances. To 30 September also, 2,930 ex-service women had received out-of-work allowances. This was 5.8 per cent of the total enlistment and "considerably lower" than the equivalent percentage for male veterans. To 31 October, 131 women had received benefits under the Veteran's Land Act, of whom "87 were established on smallholdings and 44 in full-time farming." Also to October, ex-service women had received $3,804,489 in re-establishment credits. In order of expenditure, this money had been used for furniture and other household goods, home buying, working capital, premiums on dominion government insurance, and home repairs and modernization. This pattern of use was similar to that of male veterans.

A 1949 update of these figures showed that, from the inception of the rehabilitation program to 31 December 1948, 11,488 ex-service women had taken vocational courses and 3,320 had gone to university.[26] The vocational course trainees were subdivided into thirty specific and one "miscellaneous" occupational categories. The largest group, numbering 3,059, had trained themselves to be "Stenographers & Typists." After that came "Barbers and Beauticians," numbering 1,451; "Dressmakers and Tailors," numbering 1,021, and "Secretaries," numbering 964. Together, these four groups constituted 56.7 per cent of the total. Of the group that had gone to university, 915 were said to have done postgraduate studies, of whom the largest group, numbering 377, had studied nursing. Of the 2,405 who had registered for undergraduate courses, the largest group by far, some 1,179, had opted for "Arts and Science." Among undergraduates, the next five leading choices were "Health Nursing" (190), "Social Science" (130), "Education" (97), "Business Adm[inistration], Comm[erce] & Fin[ance]." (79), and "Physiotherapy" (68).

Despite the evident conservatism of the training choices actually being made by ex-service women, Russell was pleased with her accomplishment when she left DVA in August 1947, convinced of the success of the rehabilitation program. Her own re-establishment was as an assistant professor of psychology at Winthrop College ("The South Carolina College for Women") at Rock Hill, South Carolina. From there, she wrote to Woods on 6 November 1947 expressing her appreciation of his "attitude towards individual human welfare, and the national interest" and his "courteous, optimistic manner."[27] These qualities, she wrote, had been an inspiration to her. So, too, had been Woods's attitude towards Canadian womanhood: "I especially appreciate the fair mindedness you showed in matters pertaining to the status of women. Even though reactionary forces seem to be at work in many Government Departments and elsewhere, and many unjustifiable discriminations still exist, you set an example in regard to status generally that is bound in the long run to benefit Canadian women." These sentiments indicate an harmonious parting of the ways between these two makers of postwar Canada, but in truth, Russell's dealings with DVA and the dominion government generally were not always easy. In 1947 she was turned down by her superiors when she suggested visits first to Australia and then to England.[28] There is also evidence that Russell aspired to some other job with the Government of Canada which she did not get. Following a 23 July 1947 conversation with MacNamara, she wrote to him saying, "the amount I quoted as 'the price of a meal ticket' was considerably less than the salary I am justified in expecting."[29] "The kind of position in which I am really interested in the government," she continued, "is one in which I would have a voice in policy making, and such a position would naturally be at a salary at least equal to my present one, if not greater." Evidently, the job or the salary or both were not forthcoming; hence her decision to go to the United States. Russell and her female colleagues at DVA also failed in another regard. In report after report, she, Salter, and Hunt all recommended that a female voice should be maintained in the policy-making upper ranks of the department, as well as in its general administration, when DVA moved beyond the immediate postwar rehabilitation period and settled into its long-term role of caring for those who could not be expected to care for themselves.[30] This did not happen. When Russell left, she was not replaced, and when Hunt departed, the position of superintendent of women's rehabilitation was downgraded as part of a general scaling back of DVA activities. In the 1950s, with its glory days of demobilization behind it, DVA was a male veteran bastion, though, by definition, a portion of its clientele was female.

The entry of so many women into the labour force during the Second World War and the formation of the women's branches of the armed forces constitutes an extraordinary chapter in the social history of Canada in the twentieth century. An important part of that story of necessity concerns the rights of ex-service women under the Veterans Charter. Participation in war-related work and service in the armed forces gave women a claim that they had not had before. And given the wartime rhetoric of solidarity and sacrifice leading to a better tomorrow, this claim was hard to deny. Jill Canuck and her civilian sister Rosie the Riveter were new players on the Canadian political stage who could not be ignored. Understandably, Russell liked to play up her credentials as a veteran and play down the label of "feminist," but in reality the first role served the purposes of the second. Having advanced towards pay equity and made other gains while in the military, Canada's women veterans were equally eligible with men for almost all the benefits of the Veterans Charter, and DVA prided itself that this was so. There had never been such a social program in Canada before, and it produced impressive results.

It is easy, though, to exaggerate the gains made by women under the Veterans Charter and to confuse the equality of opportunity proclaimed in *Back to Civil Life* with what actually happened under the Charter's provisions. Servicewomen constituted only about 4.6 per cent of Canada's armed forces during the war, and the Veterans Charter was designed primarily with men – the other 95.4 per cent – in mind.[31] Women were equally eligible for benefits, but within the framework of a program that first and foremost sought to meet the needs of men. As volunteers, women were eligible for gratuities and, by extension, for re-establishment credits or training (including post-secondary education). But a much smaller proportion of women service personnel (one in seven) than men had gone overseas, and a correspondingly smaller proportion therefore qualified for the gratuity attached to overseas service. The veterans' preference in the civil service was likewise of limited advantage to women. It was given for service in a theatre of war, again a qualification that few women met. In 1945, to remedy this defect Salter called within DVA for a secondary preference. This was also being advocated publicly by the Canadian Legion. It would apply to all volunteers with a year or more of service and would therefore be applicable to most women who had served. Because of contemporary societal expectations and norms, another benefit under the Charter that held limited promise for women was the Veterans' Land Act. Woods understood this, and in fact few women qualified under the act. In June 1944 he told Colonel G.W. Beecroft, the overseas rehabilitation officer in London, England, that while under PC7633 it was literally true that men and women were "entitled to the same benefits," in practice the order would "be administered in a common sense way and in the case of a married woman, with entire regard to the rehabilitation of the family." Women, in other words, would not necessarily be considered for all benefits simply as individuals. Woods's comment said much about the underlying philosophy of the Veterans Charter, which emphasized eligibility criteria and equality of opportunity rather than equality of condition. If the Charter promoted greater equality between women and men, this would be incidental to its main business, which was to promote property owning and sturdy self-reliance.

The training program, too, had its limitations for ex-service women. Given a choice between training and re-establishment credits, most ex-service women, like most ex-service men, opted for the latter. Because of the emphasis in the re-establishment credit scheme on household formation, this facilitated a return to domesticity. In effect, the state provided tens of thousands of Canadians, men and women, with the means to settle down. Those who opted for training, of course, had to work within the confines of the available choices. Russell wanted women to go where their talents led them, but even she was concerned about preserving the role of women as homemakers – though, to be fair, this was in the context of a new cooperation and sharing of duties between spouses. In practice, DVA counsellors, who had the final say on who would be trained for what, stressed courses such as practical nursing, and only a minority of trainees found their way "off the beaten track" in the way favoured by Russell. She nevertheless left DVA convinced that the rehabilitation program for women had been a great success. Conversely, she and Salter and Hunt, for all their professionalism and hard work, failed to leave a strong female presence behind them at DVA.

Having said all this it must also be acknowledged that the Veterans Charter constituted an important step forward towards full legal, social, and economic equality for Canadian women. More than eleven thousand ex-service women took vocational training, and more than three thousand more went to university. These were substantial totals, and the subsequent

Wilfred Parsons Warner, director general of treatment services (Schull, *Veneration for Valour*, 44)

contributions of these women to Canadian life should not be underestimated. Social change often proceeds incrementally, and the generation of women who reaped the benefits of the Veterans Charter in all likelihood helped prepare the ground for the bigger gains women would make in the future. Within DVA, moreover, there was strong support for equality of opportunity in employment for married women. Thanks in part to DVA's efforts, ex-service women also did well in the job market immediately after the war. In 1946, 1947, and 1948, work, albeit gender-divided work, was seemingly available for almost all who wanted it. It was also widely recognized in government circles that the entry of women, both married and single, into the labour market was permanent and that there would be no return to prewar conditions. Finally, war and demobilization opened debates in Canada about pay equity and the appropriateness of employment by gender that would preoccupy the children and grandchildren of those who had answered their country's call to service between 1939 and 1945.

Mass demobilization also brought a revolution in DVA's hospital and medical administration. This was triggered on 30 January 1945 by a request from Mackenzie for the secondment from DND of the deputy director general of medical services, Brigadier Wilfred Parsons Warner. Warner's assignment at DVA was to "survey ... the entire hospital situation" and recommend "corrections" as required.[32] Born in St. Thomas, Ontario, in 1896, he had served in the Great War in the Royal Naval Volunteer

Reserve as a surgeon practitioner and been awarded the Distinguished Service Cross.[33] He graduated in medicine from the University of Toronto in 1920 and in 1927 became a fellow of the Royal College of Physicians of Canada. On 1 September 1939, while serving as a senior attending physician at the Toronto General Hospital, he was appointed to the Royal Canadian Army Medical Corps with the rank of captain and in October went overseas with No. 15 General Hospital. He was made deputy director general of medical services at DND on 1 July 1944, and from 3 November 1944 to 23 January 1945 was acting director general. A determined, energetic, and purposeful practitioner and medical administrator, he produced a scorching report for DVA that put Mackenzie's senior medical advisers on the defensive. One of them wrote the minister protesting that although Warner had "a low opinion" of the department's medical staff, the reality was that the staff received "high praise" for their treatment work, various complaints about other matters notwithstanding.[34] DVA's "real weakness" in relation to its medical effort, the writer argued, lay "in prestige, rather than in performance"; the department's medical officers seemingly did not "belong to the aristocracy of the medical profession," but they nonetheless "worked unselfishly" for their patients. The way forward was to capitalize on this asset rather than follow the advice of a report that had as a "significant feature" the opinion that the problems identified could be solved by bringing in "from the Department of National Defence some particular high ranking officer."

Mackenzie rejected this advice and instead listened to Warner (the high ranking officer in question), who was forthwith named to the newly created position of director general of treatment services at DVA. Sweeping reforms followed. Warner believed that the veterans' hospitals had not been well served by being staffed with medical officers who held civil service appointments. This system had made recruitment of good doctors difficult and had made it "almost impossible" to keep hospital staff "alive to medicine."[35] In place of the existing "Civil Service medical service," he favoured a more professional approach – building bridges to university faculties of medicine, turning the veterans' hospitals into teaching institutions, and relying on internes to do much of the work that had formerly been done by general duty medical officers with public service appointments and salaries. Through the summer of 1945 he worked out plans with university faculties of medicine whereby academic directors of services, consultants, and internes would work in DVA hospitals on its say-so rather than through the Civil Service Commission.[36] At the same time, he pushed forward a plan, urged by the veterans' organizations and announced by Woods on 4 June 1945 at the annual Ontario Legion convention, whereby veterans eligible for medical benefits but not living in a community with a DVA hospital would, in general, no longer have to see a doctor assigned by the department. Instead, they would be able to see doctors of their own choosing, who would be compensated by DVA.[37]

Both the reorganization of the hospitals mapped out by Warner and the good news of the "Doctor of Choice" program were explained by Mackenzie in a press release on 18 October 1945. The new arrangements for the hospitals, he said, "required extremely close liaison between the universities of Canada and the Department of Veteran Affairs," and they assured veterans of access to "the finest medical men in the country, and the most modern techniques of treatment."[38] The previous month, Mackenzie had rejected in no uncertain terms a proposal being floated (with the support of the Canadian Medical Association) for the transfer of the responsibility of providing medical care for veterans from DVA to the Department of National Health and Welfare. "It might as well be understood, for once and for all," he told Woods, "that as long as I am Minister of the Department, there will be no transfer of the treatment branch to the Department of National Health and Welfare. I know from personal experience that the C.M.A. has approached the Prime Minister on several occasions in regard to this ... but let it be understood, for once and for all, that we will brook no interference from the C.M.A. or any other medical association."[39] In a letter to Colin Gibson, the minister of national defence for air, in January 1946, Mackenzie, who had strong backing from the veterans' organizations on this issue, followed up by giving a firm no to the possibility of a general federal government medical service: "I have discussed this matter with appropriate officers of my Department and as Minister, charged with by far the major part of Government medical services, cannot see my way clear to give this proposal any support. It was after wide and extended experience in administering the Department of Health and the Department of Pensions as a joint Department that it was decided to place the handling of veterans from every standpoint – treatment, care, rehabilitation and training – under one Department specifically set up for the purpose. After having done that so recently, I could not now support any measure involving relinquishing any part or sharing in any way the responsibility for the medical treatment of veterans ... In view of the expression of opinions by national veterans' organizations and public opinion expressed that all veteran matters should be handled exclusively by one Department under one Minister, I think you will agree that my Department cannot divest itself of its responsibilities toward the veteran which have been placed upon it by Parliament so recently."[40]

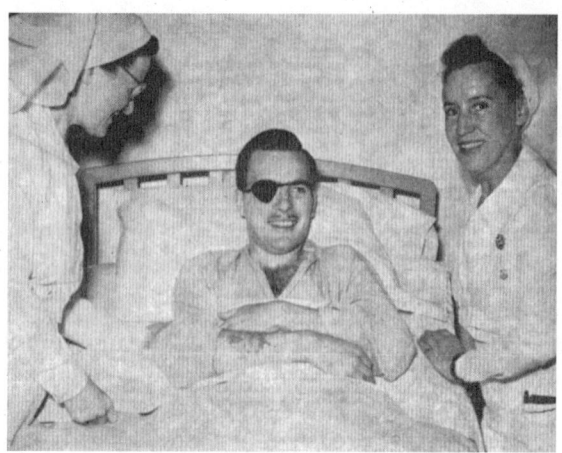

Dieppe veteran Ray F. Scott of Etobicoke, shown here with Matron Frances G. Charlton (left) and Assistant Matron Helen Sirrs (right), was the first patient at the new Sunnybrook Hospital, Toronto (*Veterans Affairs*, 1 November 1946)

In August 1946, Warner provided the secretary of the newly formed Interdepartmental Committee on Government Medical Services with a summary of the operations of DVA's Treatment Division.[41] This showed that accommodation in the department's hospitals had grown from 2,720 beds at the outbreak of war in 1939 to 6,767 on 1 April 1944, to 8,284 beds on 1 April 1945, and to 12,088 beds on 1 April 1946. With another 8,590 beds in the process of being added, the total number of beds available would soon exceed 20,000. Growth in hospital beds was mirrored in in-patient and out-patient statistics and by the number of professional and technical members on staff. In a section on "Veterans' Desires," having noted the attempts of the CMA to move the care of veterans to the Department of National Health and Welfare, Warner reported that all was now well and that existing arrangements were satisfactory to both the national medical body and the veterans' organizations. On 27 December 1946, by PC 5297, two navy, fourteen army, and four air force hospitals were transferred to DVA administration, thereby enlarging a system that was already substantial and multifaceted.[42] Ottawa was now a very a big player indeed in a field that, constitutionally, belonged to the provinces. As of 9 December 1946, there were 324 internes pursuing postgraduate medical studies at DVA hospitals across Canada, the largest such group in the country.[43] To further their work, Warner sought out opportunities for them in the United States and the United Kingdom and successfully urged the appointment by DVA of an adviser in medical education, a position to which Duncan Graham of the Faculty of Medicine at the University of Toronto was then named (he was called Adviser in Medical Education and Research).[44]

The Doctor of Choice program was originally intended to take effect on 1 October, but the difficulty in working out a national medical fee schedule with the CMA that met Treasury Board approval delayed proceedings.[45] In January 1946 the CMA agreed to the setting up of advisory committees on the new program in each of the DVA districts, and on 27 February Woods urged Treasury Board to act quickly to resolve its concerns about the proposed payment schedule.[46] The order-in-council authorizing the Doctor of Choice program – PC746 – was then issued on 2 March, and the scheme officially took effect on 21 March, but the difficulty with Treasury Board required another round of negotiations with the CMA and was not cleared up until August.[47] The department then issued in booklet form the fee schedule agreed upon, and in November this publication was circulated with a covering memorandum, signed by both Woods and Warner, to all licensed medical practitioners in Canada.[48] DVA's heath-care administration had been both improved and simplified.

As the energetic Warner pushed reform forward, he was also an active publicist for his own and the department's efforts. In an article entitled "Policy of Treatment Services, Department of Veterans' Affairs," which appeared in the June 1946 issue of the *Canadian Medical Association Journal*, he gave a full explanation of the principles behind DVA's change in direction. In the September-October 1946 issue of *Health*, the official publication of the Health League of Canada, he followed up with "Treatment Services for Canadian Veterans," and in 1949 published an account in the *Canadian Medical Association Journal* of the relationship between government services and the Canadian medical profession. In 1950 he published two articles in the *Legionnary* – "New D.V.A. Treatment Plan" (May) and "New Concept of Treatment Services" (July) – and in 1954 (August) published in this same journal an article with fellow physician C.C. Misener entitled "If Sickness Strikes ... The New D.V.A. Treatment Plan for Non-Pensioned Veterans." A decade after the end of the war, DVA was running a comprehensive health-care network that was well known for its progressive approach. A bed in a DVA hospital had become a first-class ticket and was well understood to be such. In making Warner director general of treatment services, Mackenzie had certainly acted boldly. As events unfolded, it turned out that he had also acted strategically.

In October 1945, Mackenzie told the special committee on veterans' affairs that his department was now "in effect giving a modified health insurance service to more than 650,000, or approximately one-third of Canada's male working population."[49] In effect, the entitlement which all Second World War veterans had to a year's free medical treatment following discharge was a prelude to medicare – and a benefit many wanted to see continued. As a result, DVA was soon hearing arguments from those temporarily advantaged in favour of making permanent the more liberal system of care. The existing treatment regulations encompassed thirteen classes, with eligibility criteria specified for each.[50] Under class five, some veterans of meritorious service could obtain treatment for non-pensioned conditions on a means-tested basis. On 25 March 1947, corresponding secretary W.R. Padwick of the Toronto & District Ex-Servicemen's Advisory Committee wrote to Mackenzie calling on behalf of his group for the elimination of the existing means test in the treatment regulations, describing it as a "penalty for thrift" that went against "the oft-repeated intentions of the people of Canada only the best for the boys and girls when they return from the War."[51]

Mackenzie responded that the regulations were being "administered fairly liberally" and that, while he appreciated the economic burden of ill health on average families, the broadening of service contemplated could only be accommodated within the framework of a national health insurance scheme, something that he and the government supported.[52] In a memo he sent to the minister in June, prompted by another such appeal, this time from the 18th Battalion Association, Woods observed that what was being sought was nothing short of the indefinite continuation of "the Rehabilitation program benefit of *one year's* free treatment."[53] But it was "very doubtful' that Canadians in general favoured this in relation to veterans with "adequate incomes, equal to or superior to the average of the population." Like the minister, Woods believed that the answer was beyond the scope of veterans' legislation and could be found only in the "general extension of public health services or health insurance measures." In yet another round of this debate, which highlighted the growing appetite in Canada for public medical coverage, Mackenzie heard in October 1947 from the secretary-treasurer of the Ontario Civil Servants War Veterans Association that the members of his organization were "unalterably opposed to this 'means test,' considering that in practice, it has the effect of penalizing the thrifty and bonusing the dishonest and the indigent."[54]

Working alongside Treatment Services, beginning in 1945, was the Casualty Section formed within the department's Rehabilitation Branch. The new unit was headed by Edward Arunah Dunlop.[55] Born in Pembroke, Ontario, in 1919, Dunlop came from a prominent business and Conservative political family (both his father and grandfather had served in the provincial legislature and the cabinet). Having attended Upper Canada

DVA's Casualty Rehabilitation Section was headed by blinded veteran Edward Arunah Dunlop (Canadian Paraplegic Association, Third Annual Report, 1948, 13)

College, Toronto, and Trinity College, University of Toronto (from which he graduated *in absentia*), he went overseas with the Queen's Own Rifles of Canada. He was wounded in the shoulder while serving in North Africa, and in 1943 was blinded and lost three fingers on his right hand during a training exercise he was directing in Scotland. This had happened when he attempted to dispose of a Mills bomb dropped by a fellow soldier. For his heroism he was awarded the George Medal. In 1944 he married Dorothy Joyce Tupper, daughter of Sir Charles Hibbert Tupper and Lady Tupper, and then studied political science at the University of Toronto (Dorothy helped him with notes) until called to Ottawa to work for DVA.

Dunlop had a clearly articulated philosophy of disability and rejected "obsolescent approaches to the employment problem" of disabled veterans.[56] These were the approach that sought "to schedule or reserve certain jobs for disabled persons" (elevator operator and night-watchmen were examples) and the approach that sought "to list jobs suitable for persons with a specific disability." Instead of training disabled veterans for job ghettos, Dunlop wanted to equip them to return to the general labour market and to jobs that were right for them but had hitherto

Left to right, at a reunion dinner of the Sir Arthur Pearson Association of War Blinded: Walter Woods, deputy minister of veterans affairs; Ian Mackenzie, minister of veterans affairs; Edwin Albert (Eddie) Baker, managing director and general secretary of the Canadian National Institute for the Blind; William Chester Dies, president of the Pearson Association; and James Learmouth Melville, chairman of the Canadian Pension Commission (*Veterans Affairs*, 15 August 1947)

seemed impossible. In Dunlop's program, there was no place for sheltered workshops, home industries, or colonies of the disabled. "The great responsibility of the Casualty Section," he said in a January 1945 speech, "is to insure, as far as is humanly possible, that no men get out and start in jobs at which they are less than 100 per cent efficient. It is easy for a handicapped man to get 'any job' – employers will take men on fairly freely. But after the war is over and memory has grown cold, the inefficient man will be the first man let out. The fact that the disabled soldier has a pension as compensation to him for the loss of some capacity, actually operates against him when times grow hard. There are three limitations which may be placed on a disabled man. First, the actual limitation placed on him, when, after medical science has reduced it to a minimum, a physical handicap still remains. This limitation is real and must be faced realistically. The second limitation is the limitation which the man may put on himself in his own mind. The third one is any limitation which the general public may put on him, owing to prejudice, ignorance or squeamishness. The measure of the success of the Casualty Section, and of the joint community efforts, will be found in the degree to which the latter two limitations have been removed."[57]

To achieve this objective, Dunlop favoured an individual case-work approach. In practice, this was carried out mainly by district casualty rehabilitation officers, who were quickly recruited and trained for the purpose, with extensive use made of the services of the Canadian National Institute for the Blind (CNIB), the War Amputations of Canada, and the National Society for the Deaf and Hard of Hearing. At the CNIB, Great War veteran Eddie Baker, who had been at the fore in 1922 in the formation of the Sir Arthur Pearson Club of War Blinded Soldiers and Sailors (from 1942 the Sir Arthur Pearson Association of War Blinded), remained an influential policy voice and a welcoming presence for another generation of veterans. As of 31 March 1947, 27,351 veterans were registered with the Casualty Section and were classified according to disability type and rehabilitation status, as shown in Tables 2 and 3.

TABLE 2

Distribution of disabled veterans according to primary disability

Description	Number	Percentage
Disabilities of the muscular, skeletal, and peripheral nervous systems	9,649	35.05
Amputations	1,895	6.88
Hearing disabilities	369	1.34
Seeing disabilities	969	3.52
Pulmonary tuberculosis and other respiratory disabilities	7,511	27.28
Cardiovascular disabilities	1,902	6.91
Organic neurological disabilities other than the peripheral nervous systems	845	3.07
Psychiatric disabilities	641	2.33
Miscellaneous disabilities	3,750	13.62
Totals	27,531	100.00

Source: Report of the Work of the Department of Veterans Affairs, 1947, 73

TABLE 3

Distribution of disabled veterans according to rehabilitation status

Description	Number	Percentage
Employed	11,665	42.37
In hospital	5,440	19.76
Under service but not ready for employment	4,795	17.42
Training	872	3.17

TABLE 3 (continued)
Distribution of disabled veterans according to rehabilitation status

Description	Number	Percentage
Ready for employment but still unemployed	1,886	6.85
Registered but not under service	2,612	9.49
Service contact lost	261	0.95
Totals	27,531	100.00

Source: *Report of the Work of the Department of Veterans Affairs*, 1947, 73

The employment numbers were indicative of "a continuous campaign of public and employer relations" being run by the Casualty Section.[58] During 1946–47 this featured contact with 571 service and foremen's clubs and personnel managers' associations (addresses were given, films shown, and exhibits displayed), as well as the distribution of information booklets and the making of various efforts through press and radio.

In October 1947 Dunlop produced a lengthy report, "The Rehabilitation Needs of the Crippled and Disabled in Canada," and thereafter pursued the goal of a national rehabilitation program.[59] In 1948 he moved on from DVA to become executive secretary of the newly formed Canadian Arthritis and Rheumatism Society. In this role, he was a leading participant in the 1951 national conference on the rehabilitation of the physically handicapped called by the ministers of Labour, National Health and Welfare, and Veterans Affairs, held in Toronto from 1 to 3 February.[60] Subsequently, he prepared a series of working papers for the National Advisory Committee on the Rehabilitation of Disabled Persons and in September 1958, following on from this work, produced a comprehensive work entitled *Rehabilitation for the Disabled in Canada: A Plan for National Action*."[61] "I believe," he wrote in the preface to this study, "that it is the duty of Canadian society to provide a proper range of rehabilitation services, readily accessible to all its disabled people, and so to marshal the efforts of its governments and voluntary associations. This is equally a matter of national self-interest, leading to enriched lives for tens of thousands of fellow citizens and their families; to a healthier community, nation and economy." In later life, Dunlop continued the family political tradition, sitting in the Ontario legislature from 1963 to 1971 as a Progressive Conservative member and serving briefly in cabinet as a minister without portfolio. When the *Toronto Sun* was launched in 1971, he became the first president of the company. Following his death on 6 January 1981, the Ontario government established a lecture series in honour of his remarkable career of public service in war and peace.

Albin Theophile Jousse (standing left) with Governor General Viscount Alexander of Tunis, Lyndhurst Lodge, Toronto (*Veterans Affairs*, July 1946)

Top left:
John Gibbons Counsell, president of the Canadian Paraplegic Association, discusses plans for Lyndhurst Lodge, Toronto, with Milton Gregg, minister of veterans affairs (far right), Toronto Maple Leafs notable Major Connie Smythe (second from right), and remedial physical instructor George White (far left), who had served in Smythe's battery overseas (*Veterans Affairs*, April 1950, 1)

Top right:
Neurosurgeon Harry Botterell in Basingstoke, England (Queen's University Archives, Harry Botterell fonds, 1001.50, box 6, folder 1)

DVA's publicity effort gave priority to finding employment for disabled veterans (DVA, 32-4-5)

Within the overall field of casualty rehabilitation an especially striking advance was made after the war in the care and re-establishment of veterans with spinal cord injuries. Following his negative experiences at Christie Street Hospital, John Gibbons Counsell, who was well connected in the business world (he was the brother-in-law of Bay Street notable Walter Gordon), took up the cause of reform with the support of the Toronto philanthropist and social activist Lewis Wood, who had been in on the founding of the CNIB in 1918.[62] While overseas, Counsell had been treated by the Vancouver-born neurosurgeon (Edmund) Harry Botterell, a University of Manitoba medical graduate, who broke new ground in the treatment of spinal cord injuries at No. 1 Canadian Neurosurgical Hospital in Basingstoke, England. In 1944 Counsell, Wood, and Botterell persuaded DVA to turn its home for disabled veterans at Lyndhurst Lodge, Toronto, into a rehabilitation centre devoted to a coordinated and innovative approach to the treatment of spinal cord injuries.[63] In the spring of 1945, Dr Albin T. Jousse, who had himself succeeded in the face of physical disability, became medical director at Lyndhurst and thereafter worked to great advantage with Botterell, who had returned to Canada in January 1945 and was now the director of the neurological service at Christie Street. Their efforts were coordinated with the work of the Canadian Paraplegic Association, which Counsell and six other similarly disabled veterans launched on 1 May 1945. In the words of the historian Mary Tremblay, it was "the first organization in the world founded and administered by individuals with spinal cord injury."[64] Through their constructive advocacy and planning, Counsell, Woods, Botterell, and Jousse – true Canadian heroes – brought about a revolution in Canadian medical and social practice.

1948 DVA pamphlet on behalf of tuberculous veterans (DVA, 32-3-1, vol. 2)

The 1948 Hamilton International Fair and Motor Show featured a pictorial exhibit on the capabilities of disabled veterans. Shown here discussing the exhibit are (left to right) DVA Hamilton district officials J. Hamilton and W.H. Northover, Queen of the Fair Margaret Stevens, and junior Chamber of Commerce members Bill Everett and Don Tiday (*Veterans Affairs*, 15 July 1948)

As of 31 March 1947, 1,322 amputees were "employed and performing successfully a complete range of jobs from farmer to fisherman, lawyer to log scaler, tailor to tinsmith, doctor to dock worker, accountant to artist."[65] To the end of January of the same year, of 477 paraplegics or near-paraplegics – veterans with legs paralyzed in whole or in part – 187 were working. "Paraplegia," DVA reported, "is one of the most serious of all disabilities. Until relatively recently paraplegics were considered to be permanent invalids, doomed to a bedfast existence. It must be emphasized that there is a great deal of work ahead in the rehabilitation of the

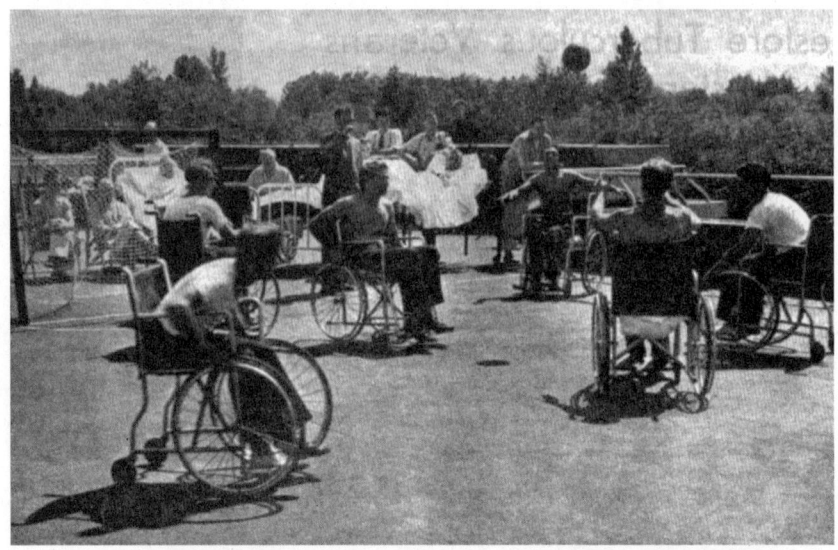

Paraplegic veterans on the roof of Shaughnessy Hospital, Vancouver, playing a football game they invented, which incorporated elements of basketball and hockey (*Veterans Affairs*, 1 September 1947)

Infantryman and amputee William Graham at work making artificial hands for DVA's Prosthetic Services (*Veterans Affairs*, 15 December 1946)

Olympic skating champion Barbara Ann Scott at Shaughnessy Hospital, Vancouver, signing the full-body cast of local son Bob Newlands, who had served with the Lord Strathcona Horse (*Veterans Affairs*, December 1949)

disabled, and that much has yet to be learned. Nevertheless, the strides which have been made in the rehabilitation of paraplegics, through the combined efforts of medical, vocational and social science, and the attitude of the disabled themselves, and of the community, provides a most hopeful and encouraging pattern for the future welfare of all the disabled."[66] Just as the First World War had brought significant advance in the understanding and attitude of Canadians towards disability, the Second World War ultimately also brought another wave of positive change, with DVA in the lead.

The Canadian Legion gave priority in the immediate postwar period to consolidating its position as the main organizational voice of Second World War veterans. In 1944, in preparation for the big demobilization to come, Herwig circularized branches about the need to accommodate the new generation of veterans, a task that would require openness to "new ideas" and tolerance of "the inexperience of younger men."[67] To establish "harmonious relationships," there would have to be "a great deal of tact, tolerance and understanding ... on all sides." The measure of success would be the ability "to assimilate young and old into the Organization" as circumstances required while still acting within the constitution. Success for an individual branch lay in anticipating "future developments' and adopting a "flexible policy" that took account of "local problems." In practice, although there were bumps along the way, the Legion largely achieved this overarching objective. As demobilized men and women swelled its ranks, the Legion saw its branches grow from 1,172 in 1944 to 1,507 in 1946 and to 1,987 in 1948.[68] In October 1945 the veterans' organization took another step forward when it moved into a new headquarters building at 75 Sparks Street in Ottawa.[69] Already a considerable institutional presence across the country, the Legion entered the postwar world with big plans, new members, and considerable resources.

Two national conventions were held during the re-establishment period, the first in Quebec City, from 19 to 23 May 1946, and the second in Saskatoon, from 23 to 27 May 1948. These were celebratory and mainly forward-looking occasions, but echoes of the bitter wartime fight over conscription were still heard. In 1946 there was a heated debate over a resolution to allow conscripts who had served overseas to become members.[70] In the event, the proposed change was rejected, and in 1948 another such resolution produced the same result.[71] Only in 1950 did the Legion finally agree to open its doors to this particular group of Canadians who had served abroad in uniform.[72] No doubt, this change was helped along by the passage of time, fading memories, and fresh leadership. In 1946 Walker, who had gone overseas immediately after VE-day to meet with Canadian forces and further the Legion's cause, was succeeded as dominion president by dual-service veteran Basil Price (now a major general), who had served on the 1930s Hyndman committee. He in turn was succeeded in 1948 by Winnipeg investment executive and Great War veteran Lieutenant-Colonel Lionel Baxter. When Baxter suffered a heart attacked soon after being elected, his duties as president were taken over by British Columbian Alf Watts.[73] Elected president in his own right in 1950, Watts was the first Legion national leader to have served exclusively in the Second World War. His accession to the office underlined the success of the Legion in making an organizational home for members of the 1939–45 ex-service cohort. At its 1950 Dominion Convention, the Legion adopted standard dress for members: blue beret, blue blazer, and grey pants for men; blue beret, blue blazer, and grey skirt for women. Working alongside the Legion now was the National Council of Veteran Associations in Canada; it had been founded in 1944 and brought together the Army, Navy, and Air Force Veterans in Canada, the Canadian Corps Association, the Canadian Paraplegic Association, the Canadian Pensioners' Association of the Great War, the Sir Arthur Pearson Association of War Blinded, and the War Amputations of Canada.[74] The Legion remained the largest and arguably the most influential of the bodies that sought to represent the interests of Canadian veterans, but it was not their only voice. This was an enduring Canadian reality that successive governments acknowledged in policy making.

After the war ended, Canadian Legion War Services was quickly wound down, and the work of Canadian Legion Educational Services was turned over to DVA to be blended into its training and rehabilitation effort. In the changed circumstances of the time, the Legion concentrated much of its fire on employment, preference, cost of living, and pension and other benefit issues. The Legion's position on the statutory civil service preference – it believed it had an understanding with the government on this – was that, with a few required exceptions, all public service appointments made during the war were temporary and would "be thrown open to competition after demobilization."[75] Detailed statistics were kept on what was actually happening with civil service jobs, and the government was held to account for its record as an employer. This was an old Legion cause, but also high on its list of priorities now was something urgent and new – the housing crisis that came with demobilization. Its effect, Walker explained in a 9 March 1946 address to the Legion's Ontario Provincial Command, was corrosive:

Everyone knows that the problem agitating both veteran and civilian alike throughout Canada is the lack of adequate living accommodation. Veterans returning from Overseas find they have to double up with their parents and relatives. Others are living in almost unbelievable conditions with no relief in sight. Provincial Commands and Branches throughout the Country have had this emergency housing problem on their doorstep and have been at their wits end to find shelter for those who seek their aid ... The effect of the housing situation on both the morale and the gratuity payments of our comrades almost makes one weep. The rosy pictures painted Overseas have become a veritable nightmare for these disappointed men.[76]

As events unfolded, this outcome soured relations between the government and many veterans, greatly complicated the administration of the Veterans' Land Act (VLA), and made Murchison's last years in the service of the Government of Canada a testing time. Veterans dreamed of life on Easy Street (a popular phrase of the time, and the name was actually given to a postwar London, Ontario, right of way). But for a good many veterans, the cold reality of Civvy Street was daunting.

In a February 1945 submission to Prime Minister King, the Legion repeated a request that an urban housing scheme be added to the existing provisions of the VLA.[77] The needs of veterans would not be met by the National Housing Act (NHA) because the "small wage earning class" would not be able to afford to buy houses under the terms of that legislation. Arguing that the acquisition of a home was the precondition of "permanent rehabilitation," the Legion urged the government to introduce a large-scale program through the VLA that would give veterans priority in the country's tight housing market. Murchsion responded sympathetically, telling Mackenzie that veterans with "limited funds" at their disposal would not be able to take advantage of the financial arrangements available under the NHA and that their re-establishment credits would not suffice to overcome this.[78] A veteran wanting to build a house costing $5,000 in present market conditions, but assigned a loan value under NHA rules of $3,500, would have to come up with $325 to qualify for the loan and find the other $1,500 elsewhere, possibly by taking on a second mortgage. By comparison, the first 51,000 accounts established under the War Services Grants Act, had produced on average "slightly less than $250.00" in re-establishment credits. The cautious NHA arrangements assumed "normal or slack" market conditions, but in reality the construction industry would not soon be restored to its prewar state. In the strained circumstances of the postwar world, "orthodox loaning practices" simply wouldn't work, said Murchison; what was needed in order for veterans to obtain houses in volume was the revision of loan amounts available to them under the NHA, so as to reflect actual construction costs, and the guarantee of a steady supply of construction materials to satisfy their building requirements. If average veterans could not get "a better deal" under the NHA, thousands of them wanting urban housing could be expected to look for smallholdings under the VLA to meet their needs, thereby defeating the purpose of that program and creating a demand that, given rising land prices in the country, could not be met. In May a worried Murchison was appointed to the new Interdepartmental Housing Committee, and at its first meeting he secured agreement for the immediate construction of the 3,000 houses (fewer were actually built) which the VLA administration had been planning to erect on smallholdings.[79] The same month he told J.R. Baldwin, the secretary of the cabinet committee on reconstruction, that many of the veterans now looking for smallholdings under the VLA were doing so "more in desperation about housing than from any desire to take up permanent residence on the outer perimeters of our cities as a way of life."[80] In all likelihood, they would move into cities at the first opportunity, thereby defeating "the basic purpose of establishment under the Veterans' Land Act."

In November, DVA followed up the VLA administration's house-building initiative with a comprehensive national publicity campaign on behalf of the government to encourage the public to free up whatever accommodation could be found to meet the emergency. This effort was organized by the well-connected and able Tim Reid, director of public relations, who mobilized the support of veterans' organizations, commercial advertisers, and DVA's network of citizens' committees, and arranged for Woods to give a fifteen-minute national radio talk on the evening of 23 November.[81] In the first of a series of advertisements carried in newspapers from coast to coast, the reading public was told that the appeal being made was "only a temporary expedient" until Canada got "into high gear on housing." Those with space available were only being asked to rent it for "a limited period" until "sufficient homes" were ready to be occupied.[82]

On 5 November, while this campaign was in the planning stages, Murchison advanced a sweeping new proposal to Woods for general consideration.[83] Providing housing for veterans, he wrote, was "the most serious rehabilitation problem confronting the nation" and was compounded by the general public demand for accommodation and by the scarcity of building materials. Monthly applications for qualification under the VLA had now reached 3,000, two-thirds of them being for establishment on

Cartoonist Jack Boothe on the postwar housing crisis (*Globe and Mail*, 6 November 1945)

Advertisement used in DVA's 1945 housing campaign (*Ottawa Journal*, 23 November 1945)

smallholdings. By contrast, to 30 September, only 126 veterans had used their re-establishment credits for house purchase under the relevant part of the NHA. The "net result" of this imbalance was a demand that was "utterly impossible to meet" under the VLA as it stood. Nor was this situation likely to be improved by the creation of the Central Mortgage and Housing Corporation (CMHC), for which legislation was now before Parliament. This was because although the new corporation would "doubtless service a wide area of public need," it would probably act "on an ultrasound loaning basis" and thereby keep the benefits of the NHA out of the reach of "substantial numbers of worthy veterans." The answer to all this, according to Murchison was to repeal the VLA and replace it with a veterans' land and housing act. This would be administered by a director with wide powers to purchase and build houses for veterans and facilitate the financing they needed to make home purchases. On 9 November 1945, Murchison's proposal was considered by the cabinet committee on demobilization and re-establishment.[84] No agreement was reached on this occasion but because of the "extreme urgency" of the problem presented by Murchison, another meeting on the subject was scheduled for 12 November. At this meeting Murchison's plan proved to be a non-starter when Finance Minister Ilsley made known that he was opposed in principle to changing "the original intent and purpose" of the VLA.[85]

Thereafter, the government dramatically changed direction in housing policy. On 28 December 1945, responsibility for the conversion of existing buildings into multiple housing units was transferred from Finance to the new CMHC, which was now also made responsible for the administration of the government's emergency shelter regulations (hitherto the responsibility of the Wartime Prices and Trade Board).[86] In February 1946, the month after homeless veterans had hit the headlines by occupying the vacant former Hotel Vancouver building,[87] Minister of Reconstruction and Supply C.D. Howe told a press conference that the government's plan to build 50,000 homes in 1946 would put $450–$500 million in circulation. On 16 April, by PC1513, housing authority was centralized in his hands.[88] In a wide-ranging speech in the House of Commons on 22 July during debate on amendments to the NHA, Howe surveyed the history of housing before and after the war, explained the government's plans, and predicted that there would be "a critical period" later in 1946 when accommodation suitable for summer use only would have to be vacated and the capacity of urban housing to meet existing demand would thereby be "taxed to the limit."[89] Long-term relief required the building of tens of thousands of new housing units, he said, and this was what the government was working to achieve – by establishing clear priorities, freeing up supplies, and mobilizing labour. As part of the fresh approach, he explained, he had made an arrangement with the minister of veterans affairs whereby the creation under the VLA of "new small holdings ... with any urban characteristics" had to be cleared with his department.[90] In effect, instead of the expansive vision promoted by Murchison that would have seen DVA become a big player in the housing field, the department had been ordered to keep its housing activities within strict limits and to confine itself as much as possible to the original stated purposes of the VLA. On 12 September 1946, to the consternation of veterans and their organizations, the VLA regulations were amended by PC3724 to bring activities under them fully into line with the new reality of the government's centralized housing policy.[91] Under a revised regulation 22A, financial assistance under the VLA was limited to the establishment of two-acre holdings where land and water supply cost more than $500 per acre and to three acres of land where the equivalent cost was $500 or less. Excluded from these requirements were commitments made by the director before 12 September 1946, applications by disabled veterans with disability pensions of 50 per cent or greater, and applications for commercial fishing establishments. In effect, PC3724 built a firewall between the VLA and urban housing.

Two days before PC3724 was issued and following the occupation of the vacated Kildare CWAC barracks in Ottawa by veterans desperate for accommodation, Herwig told the Legion's executive council and its provincial commands that, with summer premises now being vacated, emergency shelter officials across the country were "being confronted with ever increasing numbers of homeless people" and that there were "many signs of revolt among veterans and others living in deplorable conditions."[92] The "illegal seizure" that had occurred in Ottawa had not only challenged the authorities but created "a very difficult situation" for the Legion itself, which sought to deal with the housing situation "in an orderly manner." In keeping with this, the dominion president was sending a message to all commands and branches calling on them "to conduct all their efforts to solve their local emergency shelter difficulties on the side of law and order" and "to forestall ... any illegal action" of the sort that had occurred in the nation's capital. In a brief presented to Howe on 10 October, the Legion pressed for government buildings to be turned over as required for emergency shelter use, for emergency powers to be used to facilitate "temporary billeting" or the requisition of "vacant or partially vacant buildings in congested areas," and for the curtailment of building on half-acre lots under the VLA to be rescinded.[93] Given the action already taken under the VLA to establish "many projects with a one-half acre lot as the minimum," stated the Legion's brief, "the veteran had a right to assume that this policy would be developed further, thus providing a place and a home from which some income could be derived, in conjunction with low income employment in urban areas." The VLA was "the only legislation under which the majority of veterans could acquire, on reasonable terms, a home of their own," and the government's action in limiting activities under the legislation had stirred "much bitter feeling."

Reid's comment on the brief was that continuing pressure could be expected from the Legion along these lines. The "hottest" issue now facing DVA – well evident in a flood of protest letters now streaming in to the government – was growing resentment among veterans about the recent reining in of VLA activity; this was "beginning to bring a loss of confidence in the department" and a feeling that further adverse changes would soon follow in its overall program.[94] Citing figures from a recently completed DVA survey of the housing needs of veterans across the country, Reid added his voice to that of those calling for action to subsidize urban housing. This, he believed, could be done "at comparatively low cost" provided that the principle behind the VLA was followed and the proposed subsidy introduced as "an alternative to re-establishment credit." In practice, however, DVA mounted a spirited defence of regulation 22A and defended the change under the VLA. In a press release on 17 October, Mackenzie acknowledged that the department's own action of building houses on half-acre lots as an emergency measure might itself be responsible for the "misconception" in the public mind that the VLA was a "housing measure."[95] But this misunderstanding contradicted the "original concept of the Act," he explained, and the government's purpose in regulation 22A was to keep a land act focused on settlement. Veterans with "lengthy and eventful service overseas" had re-establishment credits of $800 to $1,100 available to them, which could be used for urban housing, and 27,000 such veterans had taken advantage of this opportunity. This level of financial support compared favourably with the grants that smallholders under the VLA would eventually be entitled to receive. Moreover, veterans benefiting under the VLA had to wait ten years to acquire title to property (in the meantime they were deemed to be tenants at will), whereas veterans using their re-establishment credits to buy urban properties acquired title at the time of purchase. In sum, he asserted, there was no "breach of faith" involved in what had been done, and no change in underlying government policy was contemplated.

Despite this and other efforts by DVA to put the matter to rest, the controversy over regulation 22A persisted, with MPs taking up the cause of the disgruntled veterans across party lines (H.W. Herridge, a CCF member from British Columbia, was an especially dogged protagonist on this issue). Simultaneously, DVA faced trouble finalizing sales agreements with the occupants of the houses it had built on an emergency basis in 1945. These houses were constructed in projects at eighty-two locations scattered across the country and had produced cost overruns and claims of shoddy workmanship. Sixty of the projects had four to twelve units, twenty-three had fifteen to thirty, and ten had seventy-five to one hundred.[96] In rank order, from highest to lowest, the regional distribution of houses was as follows: Ontario, 1,162; British Columbia, 576; Manitoba, 242; Quebec, 187; Maritimes, 146; and Saskatchewan, 80. In January and February 1947, Woods, Murchison, and DVA housing adviser Charles E. Parish visited every province involved to inspect the houses with a view to advising the minister on the fairness of the prices at which they should be sold to veterans. They visited fifty-five projects, from Sackville, New Brunswick, to Victoria and inspected about 250 houses (a separate study was made of the troubled Braefoot Estate near the Victoria) and concluded that most of the construction defects they saw could be corrected.[97] On the basis of their report, final sales prices were decided upon and a difficult file eventually closed. In August 1947 Murchison and Reid discussed

Thomas John Rutherford, Veterans' Land Act director, 1947–59 (*Veterans Affairs*, 1 November 1947)

possibilities for improving DVA-project relations and agreed that, psychologically, the time for such action was right. In a characteristically direct letter, Murchison gave one of his district superintendents this assessment of where matters now stood in relation to an initiative that had a decidedly rocky history: "Practically all of these smallholding projects have been going through what might be termed a 'shaking down' process. In this or that project some of the most vocal critics have decided to seek other forms of rehabilitation. In other cases the more stable and responsible elements on the project have exercised a notable influence on those members who have been unduly critical of minor details. But there seems to be gradually emerging in all these larger projects a realization that in spite of whatever construction defects there may have been, the veterans have obtained good value for their money and are today in a much more advantageous position than many thousands of veterans who have not been accommodated under the V.L.A. at all."[98]

In October 1947 the combative and indefatigable Murchison stepped down as director of the VLA to become superintendent of farm settlement, and from that position moved on to CMHC, where he served under director David Mansur as general supervisor of the real estate division. His successor as director of the VLA, appointed on 17 October, was Brigadier Thomas John Rutherford, a native of Owen Sound, Ontario, and a dual-service veteran who had been temporarily blinded in a gas attack during the Great War.[99] During the winter of 1949–50 the VLA administration launched a "Build Your Own Home" program to assist the many veterans who wanted to build their own houses. This initiative proved very popular and, in the wake of so much criticism, won kudos for DVA. Then, in 1950, an agreement was worked out whereby CMHC would finance veterans to build their own homes on lots of one-sixth of an acre each, to be made available by the VLA administration through the subdivision of land that it already owned.[100] The veterans thus assisted would not qualify for VLA financial support but would be given help with construction. In 1953 this arrangement was extended to building by veterans on land not owned by the VLA director. Finally, in 1954, the VLA was amended to include a Part II ("Home Construction Assistance"), which provided for loans (but not grants) for house construction on urban lots and facilitated the formation of veterans' cooperative housing associations.[101] Thereafter – the application deadline eventually having been extended to 1975 – Part II applications came to dominate.

Slowly, incrementally, the Legion and veterans in general had achieved a housing scheme along the lines they had long wanted and which, ironically, Murchison, the enforcer of the hated regulation 22A, had pushed hard for within the government. But this change happened long after the great wave of demobilization and re-establishment had taken place. Above all, those leaving uniform at war's end wanted jobs and places to live, but they were not guaranteed either. Just as the Veterans Charter offered training but not jobs, it offered money for down payments but not houses. Nevertheless, to 31 March 1960, 225,540 applications had been made under the VLA, and 158,999 applicants had been deemed qualified, 6,827 of them under Part II of the act.[102] In addition, 1,598 First Nations people had been settled on reserves. To this date also, 61,328 certificates of qualification had been cancelled. These were substantial numbers, and the ameliorative social and economic effect should not be underestimated. In a poignant 1974 letter, one Manitoba veteran told DVA that he had done his best for Canada while in uniform, beginning in 1943, and had hoped that one day the country would do its best for him. He had not been disappointed.[103] Thanks to the VLA, he was able to buy a farm after the war and, "blessed with a good wife," had raised seven sons and four daughters. "I credit ... my happiness and achievement," he wrote, "first to God then to the V.L.A. people who have given me the chance, by their plan, to live ... in peace, neighborly love and contentment." It was stories like this one that, in the fullness of time and despite its immediate postwar troubles, gave the VLA a golden reputation.

BUILDING AND REBUILDING

Former Hong Kong prisoner Ken Inkster with his wife Susan, a CWAC enlistee, on their five-acre VLA smallholding near Langley, British Columbia (*Veterans Affairs*, 1 June 1949)

RCAF veteran Walter Penrose and his British wife, WAAF veteran Molly, on their VLA dairy farm in the Watrous district of Saskatchewan (*Veterans Affairs*, December 1949)

While the postwar housing crisis was playing out and many veterans were struggling to find accommodation, Zennosuke Inouye continued his campaign to get his property back. In October 1945 he found himself embroiled with the Vancouver office of the Custodian of Enemy Property over a piano belonging to the Surrey Berry Growers' Co-operative Association. On 1 June 1942 the property of the cooperative was leased to C.C. Dan & Co. Ltd. and registered with the custodian.[104] This lease was then renewed by the custodian for the period 1 October 1942 to 30 September 1943. Then, from 1 October 1943 to 30 September 1945, the premises were used by the custodian for auctioning Japanese Canadian chattels belonging to property holders in the area. The chattels of the cooperative itself were duly listed in 1942, but this list did not include the piano in question, which Inouye had stored with H.C.W. (Colin) Robinson of 277 Sandell

Road.[105] On 1 October 1945, W.J. Iverson of the Protection Department in the custodian's Vancouver office wrote to Inouye asking whether he wanted to sell the piano to Robinson or have it sold by the government.[106] The purpose of this initiative, Iverson explained to Robinson, was to facilitate the custodian's effort "to complete liquidation of all Japanese effects at an early date."[107] Robinson refused to cooperate: "Regarding the conversation you had with my wife and your letter which arrived today," he shot back on 5 October, "I wish to state that I have received a letter from the owner of the piano, in which he states that he does not wish to sell the piano. I have consulted my lawyer and have been informed by him that if the present owner does not wish to sell it he is not obliged to do so by anyone, also that permission must be obtained from the owner before I can move it, or anyone else. Now the owner emphatically states that he does not wish to sell the piano, therefore the piano remains in my possession until I have other instructions from the owner. He also states he may wish to have it shipped to him at a later date."[108]

For his part, Inouye, now writing c/o R.H. Macdonald, Vernon, British Columbia, inquired whether, with the war over, it would "not be possible to leave same piano in care of Mr. Robinson."[109] The instrument, he explained, was owned by "a number of people who are at present resident in other provinces," and it would be "very difficult to get in contact" with them to decide what to do with it. In a subsequent letter he gave the names of eighteen persons, including himself, who had an interest in the piano, having contributed to its purchase.[110] For his pains, Robinson was told by Iverson in a stern letter dated 19 October 1945 that he was "bound, in accordance with the regulations provided, to declare any property owned by Japanese evacuees which had been left in ... [his] care" and that in the case of the piano he had failed to do this. "The disposition of this piano," Iverson cautioned, "is entirely in the hands of the Dominion Government, acting through the Department of the Secretary of State, represented by this office, and we would instruct you that no action may be taken by you relative to this article of furniture without the consent of the Custodian. Moreover, if you are holding any other goods formerly owned by Mr. Inouye or any other Japanese, please advise this office without delay."[111] Thus it was that the Government of Canada, even when the war was over, sought to regulate neighbourly relations in Surrey.

The documentary record does not reveal what actually happened to the piano, but the record is rich in information about Inouye's many other efforts immediately after the war to advance his cause. In November 1945 he appealed to the Vancouver branch of the Department of Labour for relief now that the conflict was over. As before, he made his case on the grounds that his circumstances merited special consideration: "I always had the understanding that my family and I were evacuated from the coast only for the duration of the War. As hostilities are now over, my family and I are praying that some day soon, we shall once again live among our good neighbours and friends we used to know ... I hear that Japanese who came to Vernon after December of 1941 must venture east early next year. I sincerely hope that special considerations could be done whereby we might be able to stay. I am doing my best by calling on proper authorities here. My family and I pray, therefore, from the above circumstances that special considerations will be given these matters."[112]

In May 1947 Inouye met his old 52nd Battalion commander (the former Canadian Legion president Billy Foster, who was now a major-general), at a convention of the veterans' organization in Vernon, and appealed for his assistance. "Could you help me sir," he subsequently wrote in a draft letter to Foster, "I would be very grateful if you could. I am getting old now and I only live for the day that Canada will some day be again the place I fought for in 1914–18."[113] Although he had been told that he "was free to go anywhere in Canada," Inouye noted, he had been advised that he needed a permit from the RCMP when he had gone to Vancouver the previous fall. On this visit, he told Foster on 5 June 1947, he had glimpsed his farm and had found it looking "terribly neglected."[114] "The Custodian informs me," Inouye now wrote, "that my property was merely transferred to the Veteran's Land Act. The Veteran's Land Act informs me that since I am a veteran, they cannot sell my land. I was greatly relieved by this information; but now I find myself more confused than ever. If the Veteran's Land Act cannot sell my land to anyone, I would like to return. I have put my life's work into my farmland and now I have lost over five years of crops." In an encouraging reply, Foster confirmed that the director of the VLA did not intend to dispose of Inouye's land and that the government was considering "the course to be followed in connection with the property of yourself and two other Japanese soldier settlers in the same position."[115] If a decision was made in favour of Inouye and the other Japanese Canadian soldier settlers, he wrote, "it would not be a difficult matter to retrace the steps by which the properties were acquired by the 'Veterans' Land Act.'" Foster reported further that he was following up with Ottawa on whether Inouye would again be able to occupy his property.

Help from the Canadian Legion duly followed. In 1926 a Japanese branch of the Legion (Branch 9) had been formed in Vancouver with fifteen charter members (not including Inouye), with premises at 195 Powell Street, in the heart of "Little Tokyo."[116] In 1942, however, the branch had decided (under pressure from fellow veterans) to surrender its charter.[117] As a result, the branch name was struck from the list of active branches. But after the war, the Legion, true to its inclusive philosophy, was active in representing the interests of Japanese Canadian veterans. So, too, was the Citizens' Rehabilitation Committee in Lethbridge, Alberta, which spoke out on behalf of two Japanese Canadian veterans of the Second World War: Yasue Oshiro, a native of Raymond, Alberta, and Harry Higa, who was also Canadian born. At a meeting on 7 March 1946, the Lethbridge organization unanimously passed a motion protesting "the unfair treatment being accorded Japanese Canadians who have served in Our Armed Forces."[118] Sapper Oshiro, it was subsequently reported to Ottawa, had served in Canada, England, and Germany but had found when he had tried to rent a farm that he needed "a permit from the Minister of Labour on account of the regulations regarding Japanese."[119] Moreover, he had to report to the RCMP and have his photo and fingerprints taken and had to report to the police before he could move from one part of the province to another. In sum, he was being treated like "one of the Japanese who ... [had] been evacuated from the coast," was being "denied the privileges of Canadian Citizenship," and was not being "treated as a Veteran at all."[120] Sergeant Higa had married overseas and was expecting his wife to arrive in Canada soon. He objected to "being treated as a Japanese alien" and felt that this was "an injustice to his wife." Higa had "a splendid record in the army" but was having trouble getting re-established. He felt he was being treated "not ... as a Veteran but a Jap."[121]

Complaints of this kind could not be ignored by the Legion. Nor, for that matter, in the altered circumstances of the postwar period, could the dilemma in which Inouye found himself. Thus, in July 1947, he heard from F.K. McIntosh, pension adjustment officer of the British Columbia Command, that in the view of Dominion Command "he should be treated as a veteran and not as a Japanese, so long as his character is good."[122] When T.D. Anderson, the assistant general secretary, Dominion Command, took the matter up with Murchison, he received a reassuring message: "Mr. Inouye has written me on a number of occasions protesting the taking over of his property by the Custodian and raising the possibility of being permitted to resume occupation and active operation of the land. My replies consistently have been to the effect that pending clarification of his position as a member of the Japanese race, no action of any kind would be taken by this Administration to sell or otherwise dispose of the land which he formerly held."[123] Earlier, Murchison had told Foster that while he could not "anticipate the final decisions which may be reached," the three affected soldier settlers in British Columbia could "rest assured that their former properties" were in "safe hands" and that there was "no intention on the part of the Director of the V.L.A. to dispose of them" until the matter of their status as Japanese Canadians had been cleared up.[124]

In 1947, writing from PO box 1836, Vernon, his latest address, Inouye also sought to enlist the help of Tom Reid, the Liberal Member for New Westminster and a strong supporter of the relocation of Japanese Canadians carried out during the war.[125] Inouye's farm was only seven miles from Reid's property, and in a letter dated 4 December 1947, which carefully avoided any general criticism of government policy towards Japanese Canadians, Inouye reminded the MP that "two of my boys were at one time class students to your son, Adam, and my youngest son was classmate to your younger daughter at the Queen Elizabeth High School."[126] "I believe," Inouye told Reid, "my loyalty to Canada has been well tested in the 1st Great War, and that it does not seem fair for the Government of Canada to take away from one ex-service man a property so dear to him in order that it may be given to another soldier returning from the recent struggle. Mr. Reid, that place back on Sandell Road means everything to me. Its like having my whole life's work and accomplishment taken away from me. I am fully aware that the past circumstances which lead up to this difficulty was quite unavoidable, but since everything is now returning to its normal state, I would appreciate it very much if you could help me ... I should like very much to return ... home." Reid sent Inouye "kind personal regards," said he trusted that "you and your family are keeping well," and promised to "have further interviews with the government" to get action "without further undue delay."[127] Reid also sought to reassure C.W. Morrow, the member of the British Columbia legislature for Vernon, who had written to him on Inouye's behalf.[128] Since Canada was still technically at war with Japan, matters relating to Japanese Canadians were being held in abeyance in Ottawa.

Inouye's cause also made headway within the government in the immediate postwar period, though Murchison and Mackenzie were at cross purposes on the issue. Mackenzie was the leading advocate in the government after the war for the policy of blocking the return of Japanese Canadians to British Columbia – this policy held sway until 31 March 1949 – and he made no distinction in this regard between veteran and non-veteran. Thus, in a blunt and strictly private and confidential memorandum, dated 20 May 1946, about the administration in the case of Japanese Canadians of the rehabilitation benefits of the Veterans Charter, he issued this stern instruction to his deputy minister: "Pending the determination of Government policy with respect to the status of Japanese residents of Canada, the Director of Rehabilitation should be advised that, in the event of an application being received from a veteran, who is of the Japanese race, for re-establishment credit or any other benefit, based upon the presumption of his re-establishment in the Province of British Columbia, such an application should be refused on the ground that it would not contribute to his successful re-establishment in civil life. The veteran should be encouraged to seek his re-establishment in some other part of Canada, where public opinion is less hostile to the Japanese. As any assistance given under the powers conferred upon this Department, with respect to rehabilitation, must be adjudged to be in the interests of the veteran's successful re-establishment, it follows that any project contemplated by a Japanese in British Columbia is of such dubious merit that it should be refused."[129] This analysis did not augur well for Inouye, though he was, of course, seeking the restoration of a Great War benefit rather than a rehabilitation benefit available under the Veterans Charter. Moreover, responsibility for the Inouye file lay, in the first instance at least, with Murchison,

On 23 May 1946, Murchison seized the nettle in a memorandum to the minister pointing out that under PC5973 of 14 September 1945 "a person of the Japanese race" was not deprived of holding "land acquired or held ... prior to February 24, 1942."[130] This had clear implications for the government's policy of declining to restore the lands of the three soldier settlers dispossessed in British Columbia until "their status as members of the Japanese race" was established. "I cannot very well maintain this position," Murchison argued, "if the settlers concerned invoke the rights which are theirs under the terms of this order, as it would seem to me that the terms of the order imply that the right of occupancy is recognized." Nonetheless, he continued, "I have noted your request that no action be taken upon any application for re-instatement of Japanese in B.C. without reference to you."

This submission went nowhere, but in June 1946 Murchison heard from MacNamara, who had now also heard from Inouye and had under consideration the issuing of a licence to him to return to his property.[131] Subsequently, MacNamara explained that the policy of his department "insofar as any Japanese who served in the Armed Forces of Canada is concerned is to issue a licence for this purpose upon the request of the veteran."[132] The case for the reinstatement of Inouye was "a very strong one," but the Department of Labour would take the advice of DVA in the matter. Armed with this analysis, Murchison tried again with Mackenzie but was rebuffed in no uncertain terms. "With reference to your memorandum of the 18th instant," he heard back from Mackenzie's private secretary on 25 June" ... together with copies of correspondence from the Deputy Minister of Labour, relating to reinstatement of Japanese soldier settlers in the Fraser Valley, the Minister's comment is – 'No. I.A.M.'"[133] In keeping with this, Murchison informed MacNamara on 30 July 1946 that Mackenzie was "opposed to re-consideration of the re-instatement of Japanese Soldier Settlers in the Fraser Valley."[134]

This looked final, but Mackenzie's veto – part of his larger agenda for the permanent dispersion of Japanese Canadians – was ultimately overtaken by events. In 1947 CCF members of parliament, who claimed there had been a fire sale of Japanese Canadian assets during the war, were able to pressure the government into referring the matter of the conduct of the Custodian of Enemy Property in this regard to the House of Commons Standing Committee on Public Accounts. Its investigations led to the recommendation that a royal commission be appointed. The government accepted this advice, and on 18 July 1947 a one-man royal commission was announced. The commissioner chosen for the delicate work at hand was Justice Henry Irvine Bird of the British Columbia Court of Appeal, an officer veteran of the Great War. The terms of reference given Bird were immediately disputed by Japanese Canadians. As a result, revised terms of reference were issued on 17 September 1947, with a further amendment made on 22 January 1948. The purpose of the royal commission was to inquire into the claims of Japanese Canadians that "real and personal property" belonging to them and vested in the custodian had been disposed of for "less than fair market price," and that "personal property" belonging to them and vested in the custodian had been lost, destroyed, or stolen while in the care of that official, with the consequent loss of fair market value.[135] The commissioner was to examine each claim "and make a report to the Governor in Council setting forth the claims, if any, which in the opinion of the Commissioner are well-founded and the amount which, in his opinion, would fairly and reasonably compensate the claimant for failure of the Custodian to exercise reasonable care." In practice, because of the number of claims, Justice Bird was assisted by seven other judges, who were authorized to hear evidence on his behalf.

While the royal commission was going about its business, Murchison left the position of VLA director. Then, on 18 January 1948, the recently married Mackenzie, whose heavy drinking had landed him in Mackenzie King's bad books, left the cabinet (he was moved to the Senate) and was succeeded as minister of veterans affairs by Milton F. Gregg, a New Brunswicker, who had won the Victoria Cross in the Great War and had served again in the 1939–45 conflict.¹³⁶ Ten days after Mackenzie's exit from cabinet, having filed a statement of claim, Inouye wrote to the secretary of the royal commission asking whether he could return to his property or not. "The reason I filed claim," he explained, "is that I cannot hang around waiting for developments and I cannot start any business without the cash. But if the Commission could give back my property, I would be grateful. I do not think this is asking too much for a veteran of the first World War."¹³⁷ Inouye got his chance to make his case directly to the commissioner when he appeared before Bird at Vernon on 16 and 20 February 1948.¹³⁸ At these hearings, Inouye, who was now described as "quite hard of hearing," was represented by R.J. McMaster, a lawyer who helped many Japanese Canadians, and the dominion government was represented by J.W.G. Hunter.¹³⁹ Bird listened to Inouye sympathetically and agreed that his claim was being heard without prejudice to his application for the return of his land. In July, Bird followed up with a letter to Gregg, asking whether the government would be giving "special consideration" to the claims of Japanese Canadian war veterans, Inouye in particular.¹⁴⁰

This triggered another review of Inouye's file in Ottawa, and following various consultations between officials there and in Vancouver, Bird recommended to the minister of veterans affairs that the Japanese Canadian veterans whose properties had been sold to the director of the VLA should have their properties restored to them.¹⁴¹ Of the four veterans involved, he noted, two – Seichi Kinoschita, who had fought in Great War, and Tom Imada, who had served in the Second World War – had already accepted payment for the sale of their land. This left only George Yasuzo Shoji (Great War veteran), whose claim was heard in Toronto, and Inouye, who was sent a permit on 20 December 1948 by the Japanese Division, Department of Labour, authorizing his return to coastal British Columbia.¹⁴² Gregg quickly accepted Bird's advice, and following due attention to accounting details between the Custodian and the VLA and soldier settlement administrations, Inouye was forthwith restored to his property and "to the position which he occupied as a former soldier settler ... at the date of the sale of the property to the Veterans' Land Act Administration."¹⁴³ Title was transferred back to the director of soldier settlement, and Inouye was positioned to resume payments. As of 1 October 1948, his debt as a soldier settler stood at $2,184.26.¹⁴⁴ Remarkably, he had survived the *grand dérangement* of 1942.

Unfortunately for him, his house on Sandell Road, rented at the time by the VLA administration, was destroyed by fire on 19 February 1949.¹⁴⁵ The building was insured for $300, but this must have been cold comfort to Inouye, now sixty-four years old and faced with the prospect of re-estab-

New Brunswicker Milton Fowler Gregg, VC, minister of veterans affairs, 1948–50 (Schull, *Veneration for Valour*, foldout)

lishing himself. Against this backdrop, the $23.05 – the difference between the $1,306 in rents collected and the $1,282.95 paid out in taxes and insurance – approved by the Treasury Board on 18 May 1949 for payment to him was of small consequence.[146] Eventually – but not until March 1951 – Inouye was also paid $1,665 by the Government of Canada to compensate him for above normal depreciation of his property while he was away from it.[147] The initiative for this payment came from Bird, and the amount was calculated based on advice received from Fred M. Clement, former dean of agriculture at the University of British Columbia, on behalf of Clement Consulting Services Ltd.[148] This was undoubtedly helpful, but what really saved the day for Inouye was a rising land market. Given his age and considering what he had been through, it is perhaps not surprising that he took quick advantage of this change of fortune to subdivide and sell some of the property he had fought so hard to get back. After so much adversity, the 1950s were, if land registry records are a good barometer, evidently a favourable time for him, just as they were for millions of other Canadians.[149] Happily, an investment he had made in 1919 finally paid off nicely for him and in a timely fashion.

Inouye died at Shaughnessy Hospital, Vancouver, now run by the Department of Veterans Affairs, on 5 June 1957, and was survived by his wife Hatsuno.[150] He had lived in British Columbia for many years and is buried in Valley View Memorial Gardens, Surrey. The record of his dealings with the Government of Canada in the 1940s may be but a footnote to the history in that period of the removal, dispossession, and dispersal of the Japanese Canadians of coastal British Columbia, but it is a footnote well worth remembering. The story of the little man or woman who confronts entrenched authority and wins is always worth telling in a democracy, but Inouye's experience also highlights the value and importance of veteran status. In the course of his long and fruitful life, he had many identities – son, brother, immigrant, soldier, settler, husband, parent, farmer, cooperative leader, neighbour, Japanese Canadian, evacuee registration number 03243, case number 142 (Bird Royal Commission), British Columbian, and Canadian – to name but some in a long list. But in the great upheaval that overtook him in the 1940s, it was his identity as a veteran who was a soldier settler that gave him the leverage required to get his land back.

In the end, the advantages he enjoyed in these capacities outweighed the disadvantages he faced as a Japanese Canadian in the turbulent situation of war and its aftermath. Although Mackenzie had also served overseas, made much of his war record, and was a constructive and relentless advocate for the Veterans Charter, he did not acknowledge an obligation to Inouye and other Japanese Canadian ex-servicemen as fellow veterans. This was because he gave priority to a root-and-branch campaign to solve once and for all what he saw as the problem of the Japanese Canadians. Mackenzie's policy, bluntly stated, was "no Japanese from the Rockies to the sea."[151] By contrast, the decidedly unsentimental Murchison, who conceded nothing to Japanese Canadians in general, saw Inouye's situation through the eyes of a veteran. Though he bought Inouye's land, he did not transfer it, thereby making its ultimate restoration possible. To their credit, Bird and Gregg, two more ex-servicemen, concluded that Inouye, who was always careful to conduct an individual fight (albeit with Legion help) and to represent himself as a veteran rather than as a Japanese Canadian, had been dealt with unfairly and must be treated separately and differently.

It was the opening provided by Murchison's *crise de conscience*, along with Inouye's astute and persistent campaigning and the fact that he had not accepted full payment from the custodian, that allowed to succeed in a difficult cause. He was not the only Japanese Canadian to seek recognition of his status as a veteran, but he alone succeeded. In June 1946, on behalf of thirty-four veterans remaining in Canada, the veterans at the Slocan City resettlement centre petitioned the government to restore their full citizenship rights, including the "right to permanent settlement" anywhere in Canada, and grant them "adequate material and financial aid" for re-establishment; but their appeal was not specific and went nowhere.[152] By contrast, Inouye wanted his property back. In practice, the policy shift that eventually favoured him (not explicitly acknowledged in the documents) made a distinction between Japanese Canadian veterans of the Great War whose properties the custodian had sold to the VLA and all other Japanese Canadian veterans of that conflict. The latter group included Masumi Matsui, winner of the Military Medal and president of Canadian Legion Branch 9 when Japanese Canadian veterans achieved the franchise in British Columbia in 1931.[153] In terms of the ideals of the veterans' movement, the unpublicized change made in favour of a subgroup of veterans was a small bureaucratic concession that showed the narrow limit of comradeship in relation to Japanese Canadians in this period.

Veteran status undoubtedly brought many benefits to a large subset of Canadians in the twentieth century and raised the bar on their obligations as citizens – at least, in relation to one another. But having this status was of little value to Japanese Canadian veterans of the Great War during and immediately after the Second World War. No exception was made for them in 1942, when fear was on horseback, and only one veteran – Inouye – got his property back from the government. Inouye was entitled to have his land back because he was a veteran *and* soldier settler, because his land had passed to the VLA, and – perhaps most of all – because he pursued his claim (though not through the courts). At the same time, other Japanese Canadians, including other veterans, could be dispossessed and dispersed because of their identity as Japanese Canadians. Such was the logic of Inouye's strange eventful history as a Canadian in the years 1942–49.

As Inouye pursued his cause to a successful conclusion in British Columbia, veterans in faraway Newfoundland, still a separate country, were contemplating their future, given the reality of pending constitutional change.[154] During the 1914–18 war, Newfoundland had sent a regiment overseas, along with a forestry corps (which also served in uniform) and a small number of nurses.[155] Newfoundlanders had also volunteered in substantial numbers for the Royal Navy, and indeed members of the Royal Naval Reserve were the first local men to go overseas. Having participated in the abortive Gallipoli campaign, Newfoundland's regiment suffered fearsome losses at Beaumont Hamel on 1 July 1916, the opening day of the battle of the Somme. The next year, in recognition of its valour and accomplishments, the unit was renamed the Royal Newfoundland Regiment. Following the war, Newfoundland veterans were assisted in their return to civilian life by the Civil Re-establishment Committee; a government scheme for disabled veterans not eligible for imperial benefits was administered by the Board of Pension Commissioners for Newfoundland.[156] The country's veterans asserted their interest through the Great War Veterans'

Association of Newfoundland (GWVA), which was launched at a meeting in St John's on 20 August 1918, and then adopted a constitution and by-laws.[157] In the interwar period, the GWVA was one of this small dominion's best-organized and most powerful lobbies. Like its Canadian namesake, it was a prop and stay to authority – but its brief, writ in blood, always had a special edge. Its approach was "to conduct negotiations with Government in a friendly atmosphere" and to present "the viewpoint of servicemen by reasoned discussion" but to do so "with the firm conviction of right and justice."[158] Newfoundland veterans had the reputation of being "a very conservative body of men who did not stint themselves in public services or in their desire to care for their less favoured comrades." The "taint of bolshevism," it was said "was not in their blood and their hearts were not hardened."[159]

Following the Wall Street crash of 1929, Newfoundland was quickly overwhelmed by a financial crisis, and by 1932–33, fully 63.2 per cent of a reduced government revenue was being eaten up by payments on debt, attributable in part to participation in the war.[160] To avoid default, Newfoundland resorted to various expedients and was helped along by the United Kingdom and, for a time, by Canada. In 1933 the hard-pressed government in St John's agreed to the appointment by the United Kingdom of a royal commission "to examine into the future of Newfoundland and in particular to report on the financial situation and prospects therein."[161] Based on the findings of this royal commission, chaired by the Scottish peer William Warrender Mackenzie, first Baron Amulree, Newfoundland agreed to the suspension of elected self-government. Beginning on 16 February 1934, the country was administered by a British-appointed Commission of Government, which had both executive and legislative power. Under this system there was a governor and six commissioners, three of them drawn from the United Kingdom and three from Newfoundland, but all named by London. The United Kingdom now backed Newfoundland's debt and sent the new government in St John's annual grants-in-aid to balance its books. The understanding on which the Commission of Government was introduced was that Newfoundland would get self-government back when it was self-supporting again and on a request from its people, but no definition of "self-supporting" was given, and no mechanism was spelled out for reasserting self-government. For its part, the GWVA supported the changeover to Commission of Government, a reversal without precedent in the history of the British Empire.[162]

In its first years in office the Commission of Government attempted a number of reforms but was unable to revive the economy, which remained depressed because of continuing problems in international markets. When the United Kingdom went to war on 3 September 1939, Newfoundland was automatically in the fight because of its constitutional position, and it was therefore a combatant in the Second World War for a week longer than Canada. The policy decided upon by the Commission of Government early in the conflict deviated sharply from what the country had done in 1914–18.[163] No units were raised for overseas service, and conscription, which had caused deep division when introduced in 1917, was eschewed. Instead, Newfoundlanders were encouraged to enlist in the British forces, and the Royal Navy, Royal Artillery, and Royal Air Force all recruited in the country. In October 1939 the Commission created a militia, known from March 1940 as the Newfoundland Regiment, for home defence. In May 1941 the Commission gave the RCAF permission to recruit in Newfoundland for its women's division, and thereafter other branches of the Canadian forces were also allowed to recruit in the country.[164] Newfoundland was said to be the only country from which Canada thus directly recruited during the war.[165] Many Newfoundlanders also volunteered to serve as merchant seamen, while others were recruited by the Department of Defence of the Commission of Government to go overseas to work on rescue tugs. Finally, a large contingent of Newfoundland men went to the United Kingdom as members of the Newfoundland Forestry Unit.[166] This unit was formed by the Commission of Government at Britain's request in the autumn of 1939, and by the end of 1942, 3,597 loggers had joined its ranks.[167] The unit was commanded by Captain Jack Turner, a veteran of the Royal Newfoundland Regiment, winner of the Military Cross, and, at the time of his appointment, chief forestry officer in the Department of Natural Resources. The Newfoundland foresters were employed, mainly in Scotland, cutting timber that was urgently needed for the war effort. Just as it had done in the Great War, Canada eventually also sent foresters overseas, but unlike their Newfoundland counterparts, who were hastily recruited, they went in uniform.

According to a 1948 Government of Canada report, the number of Newfoundlanders who enlisted in the British, Canadian, and Newfoundland forces to 30 June 1945 was as follows: Royal Navy (including Rescue Tug Service), 3,419; Royal Artillery, 2,343, Royal Air Force, 713; Canadian forces, 1,752; and Newfoundland Regiment, 860. In all, counting the foresters, more than 12,000 Newfoundlanders (the 1945 total population was 321,819) left the country in connection with the war effort. Clearly, the Commission of Government faced a big task to re-absorb into society the many thousands who would be coming home when peace was restored.

Thanks to recruitment for service abroad and military spending and base building at home by Canada and the United States (under the terms of the Anglo-American Leased Bases Agreement of 27 March 1941), Newfoundland boomed during the war. In the process, it soon left British grants-in-aid behind and began making interest-free loans of Canadian dollars (to which the Newfoundland currency was tied) to London. Given this reversal, the British quickly understood that a change vis-à-vis Newfoundland was now required and began planning for constitutional evolution. In September 1942, Clement Attlee, Britain's deputy prime minister and secretary of state for dominion affairs, made a surprise visit to St John's to scout matters out, and the next year London followed up with a parliamentary goodwill mission. In December 1943 it was announced in the British parliament that after the end of the war in Europe, the United Kingdom would provide Newfoundlanders with constitutional machinery whereby they could decide their own constitutional future; Newfoundlanders would decide, but the British would have the last say on what they decided. In what followed, this distinction proved crucial. The United Kingdom had long wanted Newfoundland to be part of Canada, and in 1945 it reached an understanding with Canada on how this objective might be pursued behind the scenes and within the framework of the promise made to Newfoundlanders in 1943. On 11 December 1945, the British government announced that a "National Convention" would be elected in Newfoundland to advise it on choices to be put before the people in a vote on their constitutional future. This body, which was elected on a constituency basis, began meeting at the Colonial Building in St John's (the old legislative building) on 11 September 1946.

While the National Convention was going about its business – this involved much maneouvring and windy debate – Newfoundland's Second World War veterans were participating in a rehabilitation program which the Commission of Government had worked out for them. This program was explained in a radio address on 14 March 1945 by the commissioner for home affairs and education, Albert J. Walsh, a Newfoundlander. The scheme of benefits detailed by him went far beyond what Newfoundland had previously attempted, and it reflected the prosperity of the times. What the Commission of Government had decided, Walsh explained, owed much to Canadian planning for the re-establishment of veterans but took account of Newfoundland's special circumstances, that is to say, the country's "general economy" and its "financial ability." Three principles underpinned the commission's program: "(1) A discharged man should have the opportunity of improving his educational and technical competence with due regard to his abilities and the probability of employment. (2) A discharged man should be encouraged to engage in the country's basic industries. (3) The transition from war service to civil life should be made as easy as possible without financial embarrassment."[168]

To give substance to these principles, the government would provide "maintenance allowances, educational benefits, vocational guidance and training, agricultural assistance for fishermen, assistance for certain small enterprises, unemployment benefits, free medical treatment and employment preference."[169] These benefits would be in addition to the deferred pay, clothing, transportation, discharge furlough, supplementary pension (for United Kingdom pensioners), and employment assistance benefits announced in November 1943. The maintenance allowance would be paid to a veteran taking advantage of one of the opportunities on offer that did not produce immediate earnings, further education being an example. The allowance would be paid on a sliding scale and would take account of marital status and, in the case of married men, their dependants. The allowance would be paid for a fixed number of months according to the requirements of the particular training or other opportunity being pursued. In the case of unemployment, the allowance would be paid for one year.

The new benefits announced by Walsh would apply to servicemen discharged after 1 April 1945 who had served either in the Newfoundland Regiment (the home defence force) or in the armed forces of the United Kingdom. In the case of men who had previously been honourably discharged from the eligible forces, the government would consider on an individual basis what further assistance was appropriate. Walsh's presentation, phrased in the crisp and careful official prose of the commission, put a brave face on the government's plan – indicating that Newfoundland was keeping faith with those who had served the cause of freedom – but glossed over the limitations and the fact that initially the commission had planned to exclude foresters and merchant seamen altogether. The commission's position on the foresters was that they had "been in civilian employment in comparative safety" and that many of them had accumulated "considerable savings."[170] Thus they neither needed nor deserved any special assistance and could return to their usual employment. Those who had volunteered as merchant seamen could likewise be passed over. While it was true that they "had incurred great risk," they had received "high wages"; most had been seamen before the war, and they could continue in their usual line of work. Ultimately, though, about 150 merchant seamen and members of the Rescue Tug Service were given limited assistance under the Newfoundland re-establishment program. Eligible merchant seamen were those recruited in Newfoundland by or on behalf of the British

Ministry of War Transport and who had "signed agreements to undertake service in war zones for the duration of the war."[171] By contrast, the only concession made to ex-members of the Newfoundland Forestry unit was to allow them to participate in a land settlement scheme at Cormack if there were insufficient veteran applicants.[172] Not surprisingly, the letter-of-the-law and cost-saving approach of the government sowed the seeds of much future discontent and public controversy. In varying degrees, foresters, merchant seamen, and rescue tug men were left feeling cheated.

The commission's rehabilitation program was explained in the booklets *When You Come Home* and *Now That You Are Home* and was administered by the Division of Civil Re-establishment.[173] The official in charge was J.A. Cochrane, a former school principal and president of the Newfoundland Teachers' Association.[174] His efforts and those of the commission generally produced mixed reviews from returning servicemen, who had recourse to the GWVA, the Newfoundland Patriotic Association (a wartime civic and military support organization), and the Citizens' Rehabilitation Committee.[175] In May and June 1946, Captain (Gordon) Campbell Eaton, who had served in the Royal Artillery and been awarded the Military Cross, published a series of articles in the St John's *Sunday Herald* that were highly critical of the treatment that ex-servicemen were experiencing, especially in relation to employment and vocational education.[176] Earlier on, the Board of Trade had adopted the slogan "They were behind the guns then – are you behind them now?"[177] This was a question, Eaton cautioned, which every Newfoundland community might now do well to ponder. Just how close he was to the mark was shown on 28 June 1946 when veterans attending the ex-servicemen's school at Fort William, St John's, staged a protest meeting attended by two Great War veterans, W.R. Dawe and Major F.W. Marshall, who were, respectively, president and 1st vice-president of the GWVA.[178] The immediate cause of the protest was the publication of a memorandum by the government limiting educational and vocational training to twelve months; this was a change, the veterans charged, that belied the "fancy clauses" in the booklets they had been given and put them at an "extreme disadvantage."[179] The St John's *Evening Telegram* supported the protesters and called on the government "to give the greatest encouragement" to ex-servicemen who honestly desired to better themselves educationally; there had to be an immediate end to "bumbledom."[180] The commission responded with a more liberal plan for education and employment benefits, but its relations with its veteran clients remained uneasy.[181]

Increasingly, these relations were overshadowed by the evolving debate over the constitutional future of the country. The subject of confederation with Canada was soon introduced into the proceedings of the National Convention and was made a focus of attention in the country, mainly through the efforts of the outspoken and energetic Joseph R. Smallwood, the delegate for Bonavista Centre. Every Newfoundlander had a big stake in this debate, but veterans had particular concerns. For them, the possibility of union with Canada posed obvious and immediate questions. In the event of union, would they be eligible equally with other Canadian veterans for the dominion's benefits? What were those benefits? And would they be better off as Canadians or as Newfoundlanders? If Canada was generous, the veterans' vote in Newfoundland might count at the ballot box in favour of Confederation. Conversely, Ottawa had to think carefully about establishing precedents in negotiations with Newfoundland that might lead to unwanted expenditures elsewhere in the country.

Within the body of Newfoundland's Second World War veterans, those who had served in the Canadian forces constituted a special case and would manifestly benefit from a decision in favour of union. On returning home they were eligible for some but not all Veterans Charter benefits. They were paid gratuities but could use their connected re-establishment credit entitlement only to buy veterans' insurance, and they and were cut off altogether from Canadian out-of-work, temporary incapacity, and awaiting-returns benefits and the benefits available under the VLA.[182] This added up to a very substantial loss of entitlement indeed. The prevailing policy of DVA with respect to Canadian veterans who were resident in Newfoundland was that they were "entitled to exactly the same benefits as any other veterans of the Canadian armed forces who ... [did] not reside in Canada" – no more and no less.[183] The fact that Canada had been allowed to recruit directly in Newfoundland did not affect this situation. It would be impossible to extend the full benefit package to residents of Newfoundland without making similar provision for veterans resident in other countries, and such a general extension of benefits would not be "advisable."[184] Yet another wrinkle in all this was that Newfoundland men who had served in the Canadian armed forces were eligible for some benefits under the Newfoundland re-establishment scheme not covered by their Canadian entitlement, but women who had served alongside them were not.[185]

The formal involvement of DVA with issues arising out of the constitutional future of Newfoundland began in July 1946 when it received a twofold request from the under-secretary of state for external affairs. In view of the interest in Confederation that was developing in Newfoundland, he explained, the government might "some months hence" be faced with the question of whether it was "prepared to admit Newfoundland,

and if so, on what terms."[186] To prepare for this eventuality an interdepartmental committee had been formed under the chairmanship of R.A. MacKay of External Affairs. This committee was compiling information and wanted an estimate from DVA of the cost of extending services to Newfoundland. The committee also wished to know "of any special problems union might raise" for the department. The estimate forthcoming was for an annual cost, low in the event, of $1,704,000.[187] This was based on two assumptions: that there had been 9,100 enlistees from Newfoundland in the armed forces of the United Kingdom (members of the Newfoundland Forestry Unit and merchant marine were purposely excluded); and that "the immediate post-war rehabilitation" would be over "if, as and when union with Newfoundland became a matter of direct concern to the Canadian Government." The department saw no "special problem" in extending its administration to Newfoundland.

In February 1947 the National Convention adopted an omnibus resolution that led eventually to the dispatch of delegations of inquiry, first to London and then to Ottawa.[188] The Ottawa delegation was in the Canadian capital from 24 June to 30 September. During its visit, discussions covered the whole range of issues that Confederation posed. The practical result of the talks was an understanding that was incorporated into a document prepared by the Government of Canada detailing "proposed arrangements" for the union of the two countries "should the people of Newfoundland desire to enter into Confederation."[189] This document, dated 29 October 1947, was submitted by Ottawa, through the governor of Newfoundland, to the National Convention after the return of the delegation to St John's. The subject of "War Service Benefits" was covered in Annex I.[190] Part A of this annex dealt with war veterans and Part B with merchant seamen, who did not have the status of veterans and were offered limited benefits. Under Part A, Canada proposed to extend to Newfoundland veterans a variety of benefits "on the same basis is if these Newfoundland veterans had served in His Majesty's Canadian forces."

Newfoundland veterans of the two world wars would be eligible for Canadian disability and dependants' pensions. Canada would assume Newfoundland's pension liability (which included some merchant marine pensioners), would supplement disability and dependants' pensions paid by the United Kingdom or Allied governments up to Canadian rates, and would pay pensions for disabilities pensionable under Canadian but not British law. Newfoundland veterans would also be eligible for the War Veterans' Allowance and for the free hospitalization and treatment made available to Canadian veterans. Newfoundland veterans of the Second World War would be eligible for benefits under the VLA; for contributions to the national unemployment insurance fund; for veterans' business and professional loans; for veterans' insurance; and for vocational and educational training. In the case of the latter, Canada would "assume from the date of union, the cost of vocational and educational training of Newfoundland veterans on the same basis as if these veterans had served in His Majesty's Canadian Forces." Absent from this list were the popular gratuities and re-establishment credits payable under the War Service Grants Act, but the Canadian offer did note that, at union, Newfoundlanders who had served in the Canadian forces would become eligible for the re-establishment credit benefit, which had an application deadline of ten years from discharge. The re-establishment credit scheme had no Newfoundland equivalent though, on discharge, members of both the Newfoundland Regiment and the British forces were eligible for gratuities. For the Newfoundland Regiment, the terms and amount of the gratuity, together with pension rights, were fixed in regulations published by the Commission of Government in 1944. Newfoundland veterans of the British forces collected their gratuities from the United Kingdom government, but these were far below Canadian rates. Would Canadian rates now apply? And would the Canadian re-establishment credit scheme, which was tied to eligibility for gratuities, be extended to Newfoundland veterans? Qualifying for re-establishment credits would amount to a windfall for Newfoundland veterans. Not surprisingly, therefore, it was the addition of this benefit to what Ottawa had offered in 1947 that spokesmen for Newfoundland veterans identified as the *sine qua non* of equality between them and Canadian veterans.

During the summer of 1948, the stage was set by events in Newfoundland for the resolution of this and the many other complex issues that union posed.[191] In January 1948 the National Convention completed its work and recommended to the British Government that in the referendum to follow, the electorate be offered a choice between "Responsible Government as it existed prior to 1934" and "Commission of Government." The British, who had carefully reserved to themselves the final wording of the ballot, then announced in March that there would be three choices: "Commission of Government for a period of five years"; "Confederation with Canada"; and "Responsible Government as it existed in 1933." They now also ruled that the choice to be followed would need majority support. If the first referendum failed to produce this, there would be a second referendum, which would offer a choice between the two options leading in the first vote. A second ballot was in fact needed, and it was held on 22 July, when "Confederation with Canada" outpolled "Responsible Government as it existed in 1933" by 78,323 (52.3%) to

71,334 (47.7%). After Canada announced that it would proceed on the basis of this result, the Commission of Government appointed a delegation, chaired by Walsh, to go to Ottawa to negotiate the final terms of union. This delegation began talks in the Canadian capital on 6 October.

It was thus with Confederation soon to be a reality that the GWVA, with Herwig in attendance, held its 1948 annual conference at Grand Falls on 13–16 September. A resolution was passed at this gathering which addressed the complaint that the organization was "not represented in any way" on the delegation the government was dispatching to Ottawa.[192] To remedy this situation, a committee was appointed to study the implications of Confederation for Newfoundland veterans and to meet with and make recommendations to the delegation. If the committee found that it would be beneficial to name an adviser to the delegation, this should also be done. The members named to the committee were Marshall (now president of the GWVA), Eaton (now vice-president), W.R. Martin (secretary), and F.G. Harnett. Martin was a Great War Veteran and Harnett a Second World War veteran. Marshall was also president of the Responsible Government League, which had campaigned for "Responsible Government as it existed in 1933" and was now manoeuvring to challenge the legality of the whole constitutional process the United Kingdom government had followed.

When the GWVA's committee met with the delegation headed by Walsh before his group left for Canada, it was agreed that if the veterans' organization sent representatives to Ottawa, meetings could be arranged with the Newfoundland negotiators. On the other hand, the members of the delegation apparently resisted the idea of giving the GWVA a direct role in the pending talks, on the grounds that this would open the door for numerous other groups to claim the same standing. After the delegation began its work in Ottawa, however, it requested the assistance of the GWVA, whereupon Martin and Eaton went there.[193] They were then present at the bargaining table when the final deal on veterans' benefits for Newfoundlanders was struck. Turner, now a Lieutenant-Colonel, also travelled to Ottawa in the autumn of 1948 to be on hand during the negotiations and to represent the interests of the Newfoundland foresters, who had formed their own association in 1944 (he was its first president). Unfortunately, he died in his sleep at the Lord Elgin Hotel on the night of 26 September, soon after arriving in Canada.[194] This left the foresters without a voice at a critical juncture, and to their great detriment, their concerns were ignored in what followed. In effect, they lost their chance to be included in the veteran status group by having their service acknowledged as being equivalent to that of their Canadian counterparts. Of course, it cannot be proved that Turner's presence would have produced this result, but the record of the GWVA participants clearly supports the view that there was a decided advantage in being represented directly in Ottawa.

On the Canadian side, in preparation for the final round of talks, Gregg called for consideration of the anomaly in the 1947 offer to Newfoundland over gratuities and re-establishment credits. The omission of these benefits, he argued, did not accord with the principle of "making available to Newfoundland veterans the benefits still available to Canadian veterans."[195] The truth was, Gregg cautioned, that if Newfoundland veterans were not given these benefits, they would not be treated on the same basis as if they had served in the Canadian armed forces. Subsequently, it was estimated by DVA that the cost of giving eligible Newfoundlanders the gratuity at Canadian rates and the re-establishment credits would be $10,400,780.16.[196]

Within DVA there were two opinions on the issue of gratuities and re-establishment credits. In a memorandum dated 13 October, Garnott Henry Parliament – who had succeeded Burns as director general of rehabilitation in December 1947, having previously been district superintendent of rehabilitation in Toronto – argued that the war service gratuity had been paid "to recompense Canadians who served in the Forces for service rendered to Canada."[197] Therefore it would not "seem logical to extend the same benefit to Newfoundlanders who were not able to render such service." In his view, the Newfoundland side might have "a good point" about the re-establishment credits, but the fact that this benefit was linked in amount to the value of the Canadian gratuity would make its administration difficult. The gratuity paid to members of the British forces, Parliament noted, was small compared with what Canadian ex-service personnel had received. A contrary view on the whole issue, however, was taken in a memorandum prepared for use by the minister in his discussions with the Newfoundland delegation. The conclusion here was "that some concession" would have to be made to the Newfoundland view of gratuities and re-establishment credits if "good relations" were to be maintained.[198]

The issue at hand was joined on 25 October at the second meeting of a subcommittee on veterans' affairs of the main negotiating group.[199] Eaton advanced the Newfoundland claim, whereupon Gregg asked for a brief on the topic from the GWVA representatives. This was duly submitted and made the case to the Canadian authorities, by now familiar to them, that if the War Service Grants Act was not extended in its entirety to the new province, a Newfoundland veteran would "not be treated on the same basis as if he were a veteran of His Majesty's Canadian forces."[200] No final recommendation was made on the submission of the GWVA, but in the final report of the subcommittee, adopted on 27 October, it was agreed that the minister would take the matter up with the government. Gregg likewise agreed to discuss with his colleagues the status of the awaiting-returns benefits available to various categories of Canadian veterans.[201] The GWVA representatives had argued that these should also be extended to Newfoundlanders.

When the subcommittee report was submitted, it was this conciliatory view that prevailed at cabinet level. Thus Canada proposed and Newfoundland agreed that while the Canadian gratuity scheme should not be extended to Newfoundland veterans, re-establishment credits and awaiting-returns allowances should be (DVA's estimate of the cost of extending re-establishment credits on this basis was $4,000,000).[202] The agreement thus made was next incorporated into the final terms of union, which were signed at a ceremony in the Senate chamber on 11 December. The agreement made on veterans' benefits was incorporated as term 38, which provided in part as follows: "A re-establishment credit will be made available to Newfoundland veterans who served in the Second World War equal to the re-establishment credit that might have been made available to them under The War Service Grants Act, 1944, if their service in the Second World War had been service in the Canadian forces, less the amount of any pecuniary benefits of the same nature granted or paid by the Government of any country other than Canada."[203] Merchant seamen were covered in the final document in term 42, which varied the wording of the offer Canada had made in 1947 but was essentially the same.[204]

No doubt, a variety of factors influenced the Canadian decision to accommodate the GWVA negotiators on the re-establishment credit issue. The Newfoundland veterans had made it to the bargaining table, and denying them in face-to-face negotiations would have been tricky. Moreover, Gregg, always a moderate voice, exhibited a fellow feeling for the Newfoundland veterans that encouraged a generous approach. He wanted to do the honourable thing, and with wartime sacrifice still a recent memory, his attitude had force, especially in good times. It was also the case, of course, that the re-establishment credit scheme was still in effect in Canada and that the cost of extending it to Newfoundland veterans would be but a tiny fraction of Canada's total bill for the benefit. Yet another factor may have been the closeness of the vote in Newfoundland in the second referendum. This overshadowed the whole of the negotiations between the two countries and underlined for the Canadian authorities just how important it was to make a good start in Newfoundland. Leaving Newfoundland veterans feeling disgruntled would certainly not have accorded with that approach.

On their return to St John's, Martin and Eaton submitted a report to the executive of the GWVA on what had been accomplished in Ottawa.[205] This summarized events since the 1948 general meeting of the organization and offered a detailed explanation of term 38. The tone of the report was of a good job well done, and certainly Eaton and Martin had reason to be pleased with what they had accomplished in Ottawa. But there were other Newfoundlanders for whom the outcome of the 1948 negotiations was a disappointment. For merchant seamen, the effect of the terms of union was mixed. While it was true that they would enjoy greater benefits as Canadians, it was also the case that they, along with merchant seamen everywhere else in Canada, did not enjoy the status of veteran, with all the benefits that this status conferred. At the same time, two other groups of Newfoundlanders – the members of the Newfoundlander Forestry Unit and the men who had done such dangerous work overseas on rescue tugs – were ignored altogether in the agreement, and they carried grievances with them into their new country.

Following the signing of the terms of union, with official Paul Cross in the lead, DVA stepped up its planning effort to begin operations in Newfoundland after union took effect on 31 March 1949. Earlier that month, the department began distributing to Newfoundland veterans, initially through the GWVA (soon to be the Newfoundland Command of the Canadian Legion) the booklet *Canada's Veterans' Charter: How It Applies in the Province of Newfoundland*.[206] The DVA office in St John's opened on schedule on 1 April, and the first day of business "passed uneventfully."[207] Ten veterans were seen for treatment, twenty-four for re-establishment credits, and twenty-six for war veterans' allowance. Seventeen others made general inquiries. By September 1949, payments to Newfoundland veterans under the re-establishment credit scheme reached $500,000 – a total duly celebrated in a ceremony at DVA's offices and attended by Smallwood, who was now premier of the Province of Newfoundland.[208] By 31 March 1951, 10,750 Newfoundland veterans had received re-establishment credits worth $1,827,627.[209] Of this amount, 60 per cent had been spent on furniture, bringing a bonanza to local retailers. Nor was this all. Although conscripted men who had served only in the Western Hemisphere were ineligible for gratuities and re-establishment credits, Newfoundlanders who had served at home with the Newfoundland Regiment were ruled eligible on the grounds that they had enlisted without territorial limitation.[210]

Years later, Eaton recalled that at one memorable moment in the bargaining in Ottawa in 1948 over this particular benefit, Phil Gruchy of the Newfoundland delegation had said, "Mr. Minister, if we are coming into Confederation we are coming right into your living room, we ain't staying on your back stoop."[211] In truth, for those Newfoundlanders who enjoyed the status of veteran, this objective was achieved by the terms of union. The GWVA representatives had not obtained retroactive supplementation of gratuities to Canadian rates and had not been able to turn the clock back to 1945, but they had obtained satisfaction on every other issue of importance to them. According to one contemporary observer, when Smallwood learned what Newfoundlanders would qualify for under the Veterans' Land Act, he whistled and said, "Heck if I had known about this before, I could have swung Confederation without half the trouble."[212] This spoke for itself about the quality of the bargain that had been struck for veterans in Newfoundland (but not for merchant seamen, foresters, and tugboat men). The Veterans Charter, a flexible instrument of state, had served yet another Canadian national purpose.

8 Conclusion

In 1946 Ian Mackenzie wrote as follows in the foreword he contributed to *The Veterans Charter: Acts of the Canadian Parliament to Assist Canadian Veterans*, the compendium of legislation and regulations published by DVA through the King's Printer: "Not for ten, perhaps twenty, years will it be known how much ex-service men and women have been able to contribute to a Canada at peace as a result of these re-establishment measures. When that accounting is made, I know the program laid down in the VETERANS CHARTER will appear in true perspective as a social investment of unmatched success."[1] No doubt there was much truth in these lofty sentiments. Hundreds of thousands of Canadians benefited in one way or another from the program he extolled. Through the gratuity/re-establishment credit combination, many veterans received the cash they needed to make a fresh start in life, and many families were launched thereby, and the baby boom took hold. Under the VLA, tens of thousands were established, under sensible financial arrangements, on farms and smallholdings. Thanks to the Veterans' Rehabilitation Act, the country quickly augmented its skilled workforce and acquired a new cohort of professionals, many of them from families that had never sent a son or daughter to university before. Canada really did learn from its post–Great War experience and really did do better the second time around.

When Howard Cameron from Sarnia, Ontario, arrived home in 1945 from overseas, he was supported by the Government of Canada to attend medical school at the University of Western Ontario, where all his fellow students but one in the special entering class of January 1946 were veterans. The Latin motto of the Western Meds '50 graduating class translated as "Don't Let the Bastards Wear You Down," but this was eventually changed to "Service Is a Lifetime Commitment."[2] Cameron went on to become a leading orthopaedic surgeon in London, Ontario. In Montreal, André Gadbois, who returned home in September 1945 aboard the crowded troopship *Nieuw Amsterdam*, was assisted to attend the Université de Montréal (from which he already had a baccalaureate) and then McGill, starting out in engineering and then transferring to law. He married Molly (Margaret) Drumm in 1948, and they had five children. On completion

Howard Cameron of Sarnia, Ontario, who enlisted on 6 September 1939, studied medicine at the University of Western Ontario and became an orthopaedic surgeon. (Courtesy of Howard Cameron)

(Gordon) Campbell Eaton (right) and his brother William (Royal Navy), both of St John's. Cam Eaton helped negotiate the terms on which Newfoundland veterans were fitted into the Canadian benefit system in 1949. (Courtesy of Fraser Eaton)

André Gadbois (centre) of Montreal returned from overseas in 1945 on the crowded *Nieuw Amsterdam* and then studied engineering at McGill University. He is shown here with his mother, the painter Louise Gadbois (née Landry), and his grandmother, Blanche Landry (née Lacoste), wife of Brigadier General Joseph Landry. (Courtesy of P. Louise Gadbois)

CONCLUSION

Left: Dante Lenardon of Fernie, British Columbia, a notable humanist, served in the RCAF and then studied at the University of Alberta and the University of Toronto. (Courtesy of Dante Lenardon)

Right: Nonie (Nixon) Ketchum of New Liskeard, Ontario, resumed studies at Queen's University after her service in the WRCNS. (Courtesy of Nonie Ketchum)

of his law studies, he went to work for the Gatineau Power Company, and when that enterprise was taken over by the province during the *révolution tranquille,* he transferred to Hydro-Québec, where he enjoyed a long and productive career. Dante Lenardon, whose parents came to Canada from the Udine area of Italy in 1920 and who grew up in the mining community of Fernie, British Columbia, was assisted under the Veterans' Rehabilitation Act to attend the University of Alberta and then the University of Toronto, where he completed a doctorate in French and Italian. He was a celebrated teacher over many years, and a building was eventually named in his honour at King's University College, London, Ontario. After his quick ascent in the GWVA and his bargaining success in Ottawa, Cam Eaton went on to become a leading businessman and public figure in the new Province of Newfoundland. He was also an inspiration for the youth of the province.

Nora (Nonie) Nixon of New Liskeard, Ontario, volunteered for the WRCNS in 1944, as did two other young women in her Presbyterian congregation, and she went on active service in February 1945. Her church had earlier recognized the men who had joined up since 1939 with a framed list of their names, placed in the choir. When Nonie's father, an elder, noted that the servicewomen's names should now also be added, there was hesitation, revealing just how much having women in uniform challenged attitudes in the country. Eventually, however, the other elders agreed that the names could be added – but in the margin. In 1946, having helped with navy discharge administration in Halifax, Nonie was demobilized and, as a veteran, registered at Queen's University, which she had attended earlier. In 1957 she married Robert Ketchum and joined him at his farm, which had been in the family since 1819, near Port Stanley, Ontario. There they raised three children and were active community volunteers in school activities, youth services, the commemoration of historic events, and the promotion of the visual arts. In all of this, they typified the outlook of the Second World War generation, which exemplified social solidarity.

After the war, CWAC enlistee Susanne Day of Toronto married veteran Leslie Harrison Porter and opted for domestic life. An exact figure cannot be put on the number of veterans who married other veterans, but clearly there were many such couples. Combining benefits facilitated "settling down," forming a household, and having children. Les Porter grew up in Falmouth, Nova Scotia. He and Susanne met by accident in Montreal during the war and corresponded while he was overseas. Les was wounded in the Normandy campaign and arrived back in Canada on 31 December 1945. During his medical examination for discharge, he was found to have tuberculosis and was sent to the hospital at Cornwallis Naval Base, near Deep Brook, Nova Scotia. Susanne visited him there, and they were finally able to marry on 20 September 1947, in Toronto. Les wanted to be a chemical engineer but was told by a counsellor, one of the many gatekeepers of the postwar benefit system, that he was not qualified for this career because of his poor health. Instead, he studied accounting at Shaw Business College in Toronto and then became a teacher there. Eventually, he became principal of the college and later vice-president of the company that ran the enterprise. He and Susanne had three daughters and a son: Susan (1948), Betsy (1951), Donavon (1952), and Catherine (1961) – baby boomers all.

In a January 1944 letter to his mother, Captain Donald Thompson of Saint John, New Brunswick, wondered about the postwar future in these vivid terms: "Arrived home from leave tonight and had a dozen letters and two parcels and one parcel of cigarettes awaiting for me so I sure was lucky. I certainly feel bad about Wink Johnson [killed in action]; he was a good lad and very well liked. I feel very deeply for his father and mother and will write to them right away. Please don't think that there is any note of weariness or anything in my letter at any time because I am always

CONCLUSION

Clockwise: Normandy campaign veteran Leslie Harrison Porter of Falmouth, Nova Scotia, had his postwar career plans delayed by a period in hospital with tuberculosis.
(Courtesy of Betsy Struthers)

CWAC veteran Susanne Day of Toronto met Les Porter in Montreal during the war and visited him in hospital in Nova Scotia. They were married in Toronto on 20 September 1947.
(Courtesy of Betsy Struthers)

Donald M. Thompson of Saint John, New Brunswick, shown here on leave in Scotland in 1943, was wounded in the Normandy Campaign. After the war he became the Canadian Legion's first service officer in New Brunswick and was chairman of the War Veterans' Allowance Board, 1970–86.
(Courtesy of Donald M. Thompson)

happy, but what worries me most is to think of after the war. What are people at home going to do for all these lads and the parents and wives and family of the lads that get it? Will they have the same attitude as after the last war, that they are a lot of bums? Or will they face facts and realize the situation and plan now so that lads will be able to go home to an organized country instead of people worried about paying too many pensions. We all wonder about these things and can you blame us."[3] On his return home Thompson, who was wounded following the D-day landings,

Arthur Patrick Bates of Liverpool, England, who was wounded in Italy, studied social work at the University of Toronto. (Courtesy of Hilary Bates Neary)

indeed found an organized country and was soon able to get ahead in life. He went to work for the Canadian Legion as its first service officer in New Brunswick, rose to become dominion secretary, and in 1970 became chairman of the War Veterans' Allowance Board, serving with distinction in that position until 1986; he was then adviser to the DVA minister for a year. He was a strong advocate for veterans' rights and appeared many times before parliamentary committees.

In 1939 Arthur Patrick Bates,[4] an English clergyman's son born in Barcelona in the Anglican Diocese of Gibraltar, crossed with a chum to do volunteer work for the medical mission founded by Sir Wilfred Grenfell on the coast of Labrador. When the war started, he was unable to get passage back to England and spent the winter of 1939–40 at Cartwright, Labrador. In 1940 he went to St John's, where he took passage for Montreal, with the intention of volunteering for the Canadian army. On this voyage he met Jacob Marcowitz, a Toronto doctor and *bon vivant* (who was later taken prisoner in the fall of Singapore). Having enlisted in the Black Watch, Pat went to Toronto to spend Christmas 1940 with his new friend, Marcowitz. On 31 December he attended a New Year's Eve party given by Margaret (Peggy) deReeder (whose background was even more exotic) and her roommate, who were part of "Marco's" circle. Less than two months later – on the day after Valentine's Day 1941 – Pat and Peggy were married; a son, John Patrick (Jock), was born to them in 1942. Pat then completed officer training and went overseas. He was wounded on the outskirts of Rimini, Italy, in September 1944 and arrived back in Canada in 1945. His son's first memory of his father was seeing him in a bed at Christie Street Hospital. Pat came home to a country in which he had never had a job and to a family from which he had been separated for a long time. Thanks to the Veterans Charter – in later years he could not reconstruct exactly how this happened – he was assisted to attend the University of Toronto, where he completed a course in social work. Two daughters, Hilary and Rosemary, leading-edge baby boomers, were born into the family in 1946 and 1947, respectively. In 1951 the Bates family moved to Point Edward, Ontario, and Pat began work for the Children's Aid Society in Sarnia.

And so it went the length and breadth of Canada, as lives that had been interrupted by military service flowed into different channels and found new meaning and purpose. The personal stories recounted above are ones the author knows well. But many readers of this book will be able to fit their own family histories into the framework of a benefit package with a very long reach indeed. There had never before been a social welfare scheme of such scope and magnitude in Canada, and it unquestionably delivered much to many. The Veterans Charter truly was a nation-building initiative by the Government of Canada.

Above all, it achieved its overarching objectives – to avoid the sort of upheaval that had overtaken the country following the armistice of 1918 and to prevent a return to the economic conditions of the 1930s. As the war progressed, Ottawa made elaborate plans to keep up demand in the economy when peace was restored. The rehabilitation program of the Veterans Charter dovetailed nicely with this basic goal: it spread wealth while keeping public expenditure within predictable limits and for fixed periods of time. Ottawa was well served by a planning process for demobilization and veterans' benefits that began soon after the war started. In the interest of recruitment, the federal government was forced to act in 1941 to equalize the situation of enlistees and civilians vis-à-vis unemployment insurance, and this opening allowed the veterans who ran the Department of Pensions and National Health – experienced administrators all – to lever the package of rehabilitation benefits embodied in PC 7633. These benefits were then perfected through regulation and order-in-council and supplemented by the Reinstatement in Civil Employment Act and the Veterans' Land Act, both put on the statute books in 1942, and by the War Service Grants Act of 1944. To coordinate action on behalf of veterans, DVA was established in 1944. By 1945, Canada had a rehabilitation program in place for veterans that was comprehensive and purposeful, could be seen as honouring the obligation of the country to those who enlisted, was clearly explained to its intended beneficiaries in the mass-circulation pamphlet *Back to Civil Life,* and enjoyed broad public support. The latter was evident in the work of DVA's many citizens' and advisory committees, the generally cooperative approach of business and labour leaders, and the constructive proceedings of the busy postwar House of Commons special committees on veterans' affairs. The cross-party support given to the Veterans Rehabilitation Act of 1945 and the other enactments on behalf of various categories of veterans that soon followed typified the approach of the country's politicians to the Veterans Charter. The guiding principle of Canada's veterans' legislation, Mackenzie explained to Murchison in September 1945, was that "first priority should be given to men who ... [had] served overseas and to pensioners, wherever they ... [might] have served" and second priority "to those whose service was confined to Canada, including N.R.M.A. [conscripts]."[5]

Undoubtedly, Canada's many economic advantages internationally go a long way towards explaining its postwar success, but the careful planning that had gone on during the war also helped shape the course of events. The demobilization of hundreds of thousands of men and women had the potential to destabilize the social order, but, remembering what had happened after the Great War, Ottawa had acknowledged this early on and had acted accordingly. Housing was certainly a big and potentially explosive problem in Canada immediately after the Second World War, but there was no unemployment or labour crisis comparable to what had happened in 1919–21 and no political upheaval. Whereas a decade after the 1914–18 war Canada was headed towards a time of severe economic depression, a decade after VE-day it was well on its way to being part of what native son and economist John Kenneth Galbraith later termed "the affluent society."[6] The contrast is a fundamental reality of Canada's history in the twentieth century. In the expansive decade of the 1950s, Canada doubled its gross national product and enjoyed an unprecedented construction boom in housing and other real estate.[7]

For all its achievements, though, the Veterans Charter had notable limitations. Having been on the scene in Ottawa in the 1930s, the architects of Canada's program for the veterans of the 1939–45 war were cautious in their policy making. Although it brought many changes and had great success, the Veterans Charter maintained a clear distinction between pensioned veterans (to whom the country would have long-term commitments) and non-pensioned veterans, who, following a period of rehabilitation assistance, could be expected to function in the market economy as ordinary Canadians. The Canadian Legion's argument that enlistees should only be discharged to jobs was firmly rejected and was countered by the promise of training for jobs and, through public and private effort, assistance in finding work. This approach, which emphasized self-help and voluntarism, built on the experience of the Depression-era Veterans' Assistance Commission, an organization that was itself the government's answer to another radical Legion idea – that there should be a national program of income support for out-of-work veterans. Just as striking was the omission from the Veterans Charter of an urban housing program. The need for this was well understood within DVA, and Murchison in particular pushed hard for it but to no avail. Except for a small number of houses constructed for veterans by the Wartime Housing Corporation, DVA's own flawed 1945 urban housing effort, and the possibility of using their gratuities and re-establishment credit entitlements for down payments under the National Housing Act, veterans were treated pretty much like everyone else in the urban housing market. With respect to the two material things they most wanted on leaving uniform – jobs and houses – the government acknowledged the need but provided limited help. What would have happened under the Veterans Charter if there had not been a rising economic tide after the war can only be speculated on, but the occupation of the Hotel Vancouver and of a DND building in Ottawa by homeless veterans gives an inkling of how things might have gone.

Yet another striking feature of the Veterans Charter, which emphasized individual choice but was weighted heavily in favour of officialdom, was the inequality of outcomes it produced. Obviously, a veteran who took his or her gratuity and re-establishment credit and went back to work got much less from the program than a veteran who, say, was supported to become an engineer or a medical doctor. By the same token, a veteran who qualified for a two-acre smallholding near a big city in all likelihood stood to gain more in the long run than a veteran who acquired a similar asset near a smaller centre of population. It is impossible to say who among the hundreds of thousands of veterans got the cream of the benefits, because the information needed to make this judgment is buried in individual files; but there can be no doubt that there was a hierarchy of support. Naturally, there was a strong sentiment to the effect that the disabled and those who had served overseas should take precedence. That everyone could qualify for a rehabilitation benefit of some kind made administration easier. Giving everyone something (NRMA conscripts were a special case) meant that some could be given more without calling the overall system into question. Making benefits *alternatives* to one another and fostering a rhetoric of choice doubtless also helped in this regard, as perhaps did the social cohesion and respect for authority fostered by the experience of war. The clincher was the fact that veterans themselves expected to be treated differentially – according to duration and location of service (overseas or at home) and whether they were volunteers or conscripts. The programs of the Veterans Charter balanced these elements and in addition provided for a new group on the Canadian scene, those who served in the women's branches of the fighting forces. Under the War Service Grants Act, gratuities and re-establishment credits were payable to conscripts who were sent overseas beginning in the autumn of 1944, but not to NRMA men who served in the Western Hemisphere only. In *Back to Civil Life*, ex-servicewomen were told that they were "fully eligible" for the benefits on offer.

At root, the Veterans Charter was a big program of government spending to head off more government spending. It did this by providing what Woods called "opportunity with security." Central to this was the belief that what Canadians eventually called the private sector could deliver the jobs the country required. Veterans were assisted for a time in order to re-establish themselves and were then expected to be self-supporting. Behind the Veterans Charter was a vision of a liberal Canada, a country of public-spirited and enterprising people who were community builders but did not look to government for a living. To Woods, for whom less eligibility and moral hazard were abiding economic precepts, it was a "basic truth ... that the great majority of veterans would much rather work than receive relief in any form from the State."[8] Another of his guiding principles was that, given a choice between voluntarism and compulsion, "under a democracy the voluntary way should be tried first."[9] If everybody cooperated – government, opposition, veterans, business, labour, and local communities – the big job of re-establishment would be accomplished in short order and the government's role reduced thereafter to looking after those who could not be expected to look after themselves. Having benefited from the rehabilitation program, the able-bodied would go back to work, provide for themselves and their families, contribute to local communities and organizations, and foster thereby the general well-being of the country. Honour required that there be a coordinated and comprehensive program of veterans' benefits, but the Veterans Charter was also an investment in the young that promised long-term returns. Woods was a deeply conservative thinker, but his understanding of Canada as a country where self-help, individual initiative, and personal responsibility were core values accorded with imagined social reality. In sum, the Veterans Charter, which he had so much influence in shaping, was tailor-made for a country in which work, ambition, get-up-and-go, property holding, and independence were defining norms. Land and home ownership, philosophized Quebec's Veterans' Land Act district superintendent Stéphane Boily in 1947, was "the most stabilizing element in man's struggle for life."[10]

In the 1950s, with mass rehabilitation and re-establishment behind it, DVA settled into its long-term role in relation to the veterans of the two world wars.[11] Its upper ranks were now dominated by Second World War veterans, but in 1968, for the first time, a non-veteran, Jean-Eudes Dubé, was appointed minister. While Hugues Lapointe had been minister (1950–54), the benefits of the Veterans Charter had been extended to those who served in the Special Force sent to fight in Korea at the behest of the United Nations. In 1964, following the report of the Royal Commission on Government Organization, the department began transferring its hospitals to "non-federal agencies" and contracting with them for treatment services. This process eventually left DVA with only one hospital – Ste Anne's Hospital at Ste-Anne-de-Bellevue, Quebec – under its own management. In 1969, having received the report of a three-man committee chaired by Second World War veteran and Saskatchewan Court of Appeal justice Mervyn Woods, the department issued a White Paper on Veterans Pensions. This in turn led to an amending act that improved the pension system generally and made special provision for veterans who had been taken prisoner by the Japanese at the fall of Hong Kong in 1941 and who had been shockingly treated. In 1976, Veterans Affairs Minister Daniel J. MacDonald, a Prince Edward Islander, announced that as part of a federal decentralization initiative, DVA would be moved to Charlottetown, the capital of his home province. Employees began moving there in 1979, and in 1984 a new building was opened in Charlottetown to house the department. It was named after MacDonald, a Second World War amputee and an island hero. A department that existed to administer benefits had itself become a benefit – to the country's smallest province.

Following the move east and while George Hees was minister (he was the last veteran of the world wars to occupy the portfolio), the department introduced an Aging Veterans Program, soon renamed the Veterans Independence Program. This innovative scheme set a standard for the country (but was never followed up by Ottawa with a general program of entitlement for Canadians) and allowed many veterans to navigate the reefs and shoals of old age while continuing to live in their own homes. In 1984 the department was given the "applied title" of Veterans Affairs Canada (VAC), though its legal name in English remained the Department of Veterans Affairs. By this time, the staff was dominated by members who knew about the two world wars only as history. Eventually, as part of another wave of social change in the country, the department moved along to having a female majority, though not in its top positions. (In May 2010, VAC had 3,725 employees, of whom 2,716, or 72.9 per cent, were women.) In the 1990s and the first decade of the twenty-first century, VAC dealt with leftover business under the Veterans Charter, making further provision for Hong Kong prisoners, airmen who had been held at Buchenwald concentration camp in Germany, merchant seamen, Newfoundland foresters (who had slowly clawed their way into the DVA system), various other "civilian groups," First Nations veterans, and military volunteers who had participated in testing during the war at the chemical weapons facility at Suffield, Alberta. (With respect to First Nations veterans – a status group within a status group – good intentions at DVA in the 1940s appear to have been all too often subverted by Indian agents.)[12] On 18 February 2010, John Babcock, the last known surviving Canadian veteran of the Great War, died at the age of 109. By that year also, the average age of surviving Second World War veterans (who numbered about 143,700 in March 2010) was estimated at eighty-seven.[13] The administration of the government's program for them was now clearly in its final phase.

The demographic experience of the Canadian Legion (from 1960 the Royal Canadian Legion) in the second half of the twentieth century mirrored that of DVA. Increasingly, the organization was in the hands of Second World War veterans, but as their numbers eventually began to decline, the Legion had to look for members in the general population. Inevitably, this changed its character and outlook. Former members of the modern Canadian Forces might have formed a natural constituency for the Legion but, until recently, this group played a limited role in its affairs. In 1973 veterans of the Korean campaign formed their own association, and later on Canadian Forces veterans who had served in peacekeeping operations formed two organizations, the Canadian Association of Veterans in United Nations Peacekeeping (1986) and the Canadian Peacekeeping Veterans Association (1991). In 1993 Gulf War veterans likewise launched their own association, known since 1994 as the Gulf War Veterans Association of Canada. How the veterans of the hard war fought in Afghanistan will organize themselves remains to be seen. As the world wars fade into memory, Canada clearly has urgent new business in the field of veterans' affairs.

How does the history of veterans' benefits fit into the larger history of the Canadian welfare state? Through their assertion of rights, it has been argued, the veterans of the Great War fuelled a social revolution and paved the way for "the extension of social, health and life insurance to all citizens."[14] As a result, the Department of Pensions and National Health became, under Mackenzie's leadership, "the cradle of Canada's post-war welfare state."[15] This thesis is persuasive, though it must also be remembered that veterans constituted a status group within the Canadian polity and that, understandably, their organizations first and foremost sought to advance the interests of their own members. Veterans' associations occasionally called for broader social reform (most notably in the Canadian Legion's constructive 1943 submission to the House of Commons Special Committee on Reconstruction and Re-establishment). But this advocacy was incidental to their main business as "economic organizations."[16] By definition, veterans' benefits are not universal entitlements but are particular arrangements made for a particular group that commands and merits support through service and sacrifice. If veterans' benefits prefigured the welfare state, they also set an example of complex eligibility criteria and of coverage based on status rather than citizenship. This, of course, well reflected the individualist outlook of the country. Arguably, the welfare state benefits – whether particular or general – that have succeeded best in Canada are those that mesh with the needs and aspirations of an acquisitive and propertied democracy. Private ownership begets social insurance. Thus Medicare, the country's most impressive and popular program of social insurance, saves individuals with means and in need of care from the dissipation of their personal resources. In effect, it eliminates the fear of foreclosure and bankruptcy and thereby facilitates inheritance. By the same conservative logic, the Veterans Charter helped get tens of thousands of Canadians started in the building of family estates, an objective that was both its purpose and its appeal. In the end, it is not possible to make a *direct* link between veterans' benefits and the basic programs of the Canadian social safety net – unemployment insurance, old age security, the Canada Pension Plan, and Medicare. On the other hand, there is clearly an *indirect* link. The philosophy behind the Veterans Charter was the philosophy that inspired much of the Canadian welfare state. Moreover, veterans stirred the pot in Canadian society, and the benefits provided for them showed what was possible when Ottawa acknowledged an obligation and mobilized resources in support of a needed national social program.

The Canadians who built the cultural institutions and social safety network of the 1950s and 1960s knew what the state could accomplish because they had first-hand experience of its achievements. All over Canada, the successes of the 1945–50 period were remembered fondly by the men and women who had fought and won the war and secured the peace. Veterans' benefits also introduced the country to affirmative action (through the preference given veterans in civil service hiring) and the provision by the government of support for the preparation of claims it might have to meet (through the work of pension advocates who have been assisting individuals in making pension applications since 1930). Veterans' benefits likewise fostered a new understanding of disability, a development with broad social meaning and impact. For all this, Canadians have reason to be grateful, and to honour in particular the many achievements of the Veterans Charter – the product of a fruitful interaction between public servants who were themselves veterans, their old comrades working through the veterans' organizations, and House of Commons special committees that brought together ex-service MPs across party lines. This was the Canadian way in veterans' affairs, and for a broad sweep of the twentieth century it was integral to the country's peace, order, and good government.

On 16 July 1950, having worked for the government for thirty-five years and six months, Woods retired from the civil service and then went to live in Vancouver (he did not want to carry on in Ottawa as one of its superannuated "lonesome ghosts").[17] Thanks to an honorary degree conferred on him on 15 May 1947 by the University of British Columbia, he was now often referred to as "Dr Woods" (he had been made a CMG the previous year).[18] On 6 June 1950, during a debate in the House of Commons on DVA supply, MPs turned away briefly from the business at hand to pay tribute to the long career and many accomplishments of the outgoing deputy minister. Speaking from the CCF benches, H.W. Herridge, who had made the opposition to section 22A of the Veterans' Land Act his personal crusade, said that Woods would "be long remembered by thousands of veterans and their dependents" and that his "first consideration" had always been "to do the best he could for the man who served his country."[19] Progressive Conservative Howard Green, a future secretary of state for external affairs, said that Woods was one of "the biggest men" of the time – "a great friend of the veteran, and ... a great friend of the Canadian people."[20] Extolling Woods as a man with a "realistic and friendly outlook on life," Milton Gregg said that every aspect of the work of DVA had been "immeasurably enriched" by his "patient guidance and clear vision."[21] Plaudits in the House of Commons for a public servant were unusual, and the praise accorded Woods on this occasion was indicative of his influence and standing in official Ottawa. Through grit and merit, he had worked his way to the top in the administration of veterans' affairs in Canada and had been in on every important decision relating to the Veterans Charter. Of the small but determined group that in 1939–40 had taken the first steps to plan a program for Canada's Second World War veterans, he was

CONCLUSION 289

the last man on the job (Mackenzie had died on 2 September 1949) and more than anyone else personified the cause of rehabilitation. A thinker of great practicality, he was a veteran's veteran and an administrator's administrator – a mandarin of distinction in the golden age of Canadian state planning, when experience mattered and politicians listened. To mark his retirement, the government commissioned a portrait of him by Ernest Fosberry, RCA. This was another signal honour. The picture was intended to be hung in a new building under construction at the time to house the department, which was presently in scattered quarters in the capital. At its 1950 Dominion Convention, held in Winnipeg, the Canadian Legion presented Woods with its Meritorious Service Medal, the organization's highest award.

Resettled in Vancouver, Woods kept up his lifetime habit of hard and purposeful work. In 1953, having enjoyed government support in his research effort,[22] he published with the Queen's Printer *Rehabilitation (A Combined Operation)* ("Being a History of the Development and Carrying Out of a Plan for the Re-establishment of a Million Young Veterans of World War II by the Department of Veterans Affairs and Its Predecessor the Department of Pensions and National Health"). This book highlighted his mastery of detail and exemplary grasp of the Queen's English and remains the standard work on the postwar return to civil life. In 1956 he followed up with *The Men Who Came Back: A Book of Memories*, which he published with Ryerson Press. In this autobiographical volume he reflected as follows on the effect the expanding welfare state was having on society: "I think it must be agreed that social protection against unemployment, old age, sickness and so forth, does nothing to encourage the venturesome, who for the sake of his own independence, is prepared to go out to the frontier and, with the pioneer spirit of his forebears, build up a home, and in doing so if necessary face hardship and privation."[23] From a man who had himself presided over such a big program of government spending, these sentiments leap off the page, but in truth it was the philosophy of sturdy self-reliance that had earlier inspired the Veterans Charter, at bottom a conservative program for a conservative country. As Mackenzie told a correspondent in April 1947, "the whole principle of the rehabilitation program" was "to make the veteran self supporting and not dependent upon the paternalism of the Government."[24]

Following his wife Elene's death on 23 January 1960, Woods went into a decline. Then, as fate would have it, he died of pneumonia at Shaughnessy Hospital on 11 November (Remembrance Day) the same year. He is buried in Ocean View Burial Park, Burnaby, far away from the little Somerset town where he was born in another age and two world wars before.

In all likelihood, he knew his fellow British Columbian, Zennosuke Inouye, only as a name in a file. There is no evidence that they ever met, but they manifestly had much in common. They were both immigrants to Canada, one from across the Atlantic and the other from across the Pacific. They both adapted well to their new country and prospered in it. They both enlisted in the Canadian Expeditionary Force, saw action in France, and prided themselves on their military service. They were both veterans, received veterans' benefits, joined the veterans' movement, and died in the same DVA-run hospital. They both prized the value of work, enterprise, thrift, individual responsibility, private ownership, family, and community. Although from remarkably different cultural backgrounds, they were both, each in his own fashion, builders of modern Canada – one of a country of programs and the other of a country of rights.

Appendix

TABLE A1

First World War pensions in force at the end of fiscal years 1918 to 1955

Year ended 31 March	Disability pensions in force	Dependent pensions in force	Total pensions in force	Annual liability in dollars
1918	15,335	10,488	25,823	7,273,728
1919	42,932	16,753	59,685	17,063,785
1920	69,203	17,823	87,026	25,176,288
1921	51,452	19,209	70,661	31,184,838
1922	45,133	19,606	64,739	30,678,772
1923	43,263	19,794	63,057	30,421,766
1924	43,300	19,971	63,271	30,825,049
1925	44,598	20,015	64,613	31,621,205
1926	46,385	20,005	66,390	33,065,471
1927	48,027	19,999	68,026	34,230,649
1928	50,635	19,975	70,610	35,583,853
1929	54,620	20,002	74,622	37,185,308
1930	56,996	19,644	76,640	37,802,510
1931	66,669	19,676	86,345	40,211,726
1932	75,878	19,308	95,186	41,858,377
1933	77,967	18,745	96,712	41,749,318
1934	77,855	18,236	96,091	40,793,425
1935	78,404	18,241	96,645	40,779,021
1936	79,124	18,175	97,299	40,854,474
1937	79,789	18,186	97,975	40,783,023
1938	79,876	18,105	97,981	40,682,055
1939	80,104	17,896	98,000	40,413,665
1940	80,133	18,177	98,310	40,456,252
1941	79,204	17,941	97,145	39,598,180
1942	77,971	17,730	95,701	38,679,159
1943	76,625	17,549	94,174	37,811,877
1944	75,244	17,243	92,487	36,984,872
1945	73,863	17,221	91,084	37,140,669

TABLE A1 (continued)

Year ended 31 March	Disability pensions in force	Dependent pensions in force	Total pensions in force	Annual liability in dollars
1946	72,396	16,982	89,378	37,130,657
1947	70,803	16,799	87,602	36,604,578
1948	69,390	16,510	85,900	36,100,131
1949	67,821	16,272	84,003	44,174,701
1950	67,031	16,163	83,194	44,099,806
1951	65,577	15,945	81,522	43,565,950
1952	64,005	15,671	79,676	57,118,316
1953	61,895	15,358	77,253	55,928,872
1954	59,891	15,221	75,112	54,917,968
1955	57,998	15,095	73,093	54,366,719

Source: Report of the Work of the Department of Veterans Affairs, 1955, 69

TABLE A2

Second World War pensions in force at the end of fiscal years 1941 to 1955

Year ended 31 March	Disability pensions in force	Dependent pensions in force	Total pensions in force	Annual liability in dollars
1941	316	314	630	334,572
1942	1,283	847	2,130	1,049,825
1943	3,862	2,412	6,294	3,106,957
1944	7,145	4,930	12,075	6,227,244
1945	15,341	10,989	26,330	13,418,179
1946	36,138	16,379	52,517	23,031,666
1947	69,701	17,095	86,796	32,209,161
1948	84,762	17,106	101,868	36,270,302
1949	89,078	17,135	106,213	46,657,919
1950	91,801	17,210	109,011	48,476,672
1951	93,162	17,067	110,229	49,555,322
1952	93,848	16,998	110,846	64,911,337
1953	94,827	17,117	111,944	66,788,340
1954	96,094	17,297	113,391	68,143,019
1955	97,512	17,443	114,955	69,508,131

Source: Report of the Work of the Department of Veterans Affairs, 1955, 90

TABLE A3
Number of veterans approved for the receipt of an allowance under the Veterans Rehabilitation Act, fiscal years 1941–42 to 1951–52[1]

Fiscal Year	Out-of-work allowances		Vocational training allowances		Awaiting-returns allowances		Temporary incapacity allowances		University training allowances		Total	
	Men	Women[2]	Men	Women[2]	Men	Women[2]	Men	Women[2]	Men	Women[2]	Men	Women[2]
1941–42	974	–	238	–	24	–	328	–	2	–	1,566	–
1942–43	1,071	–	783	–	63	–	1,293	–	21	–	3,231	–
1943–44	946	–	1,497	–	135	–	691	–	77	–	3,346	–
1944–45	3,022	206	3,943	1,042	713	3	280	131	1,044	29	9,002	1,411
1945–46	39,176	436	16,166	1,763	3,477	16	276	11	27,885	945	86,980	3,171
1946–47	98,055	1,983	40,652	5,722	31,563	137	952	42	18,691	1,349	189,913	9,233
1947–48	15,561	350	6,137	843	10,107	59	680	25	2,398	343	34,973	1,620
1948–49	873	10	526	61	1,940	23	43	1	562	60	3,944	155
1949–50	142	–	416	18	1,232	21	1	–	266	35	2,057	74
1950–51	4	–	296	6	978	5	–	–	74	7	1,352	18
1951–52	–	–	48	2	560	12	–	–	19	1	627	15
Total	159,914	2,985	70,702	9,457	50,792	276	4,544	210	51,039	2,769	336,991	15,697

1 Each veteran is reported under the allowance for which first approved. The extent to which veterans received more than one allowance is as follows: the 336,991 male veterans reported received 381,347 awards; the 15,697 female veterans reported received 17,716 awards.

2 Separate records for female veterans were not available prior to 1944–45.

Source: *Report of the Work of the Department of Veterans Affairs*, 1952, 21

TABLE A4

Activity under the Veterans' Business and Professional Loans Act, to 31 March 1951

Purpose	Number	Amount
Purchase of business	1,501	3,392,591
Purchase of interest in partnership	1,638	3,426,595
Purchase of tools, equipment, etc.	1,134	1,641,798
Repair of tools, equipment, etc.	35	47,062
Construction or repair of building	651	1,271,461
Purchase of motorized unit	1,133	1,451,229
Totals	6,092	11,230,736

Source: Woods, *Rehabilitation (A Combined Operation)*, 182

TABLE A5
Application for qualification under the Veterans' Land Act, to 31 March 1951

	British Columbia	Alberta	Saskatchewan	Manitoba	Western Ontario	Eastern Ontario	Quebec	Maritimes	Total
Number of applications received	28,962	22,559	23,717	15,491	26,395	32,960	16,811	18,988	185,883
Number of applications received, part 2	266	380	121	279	297	503	398	130	2,374
Number dealt with by regional advisory committee	23,038	18,908	19,834	13,802	23,029	28,272	12,700	16,368	155,951
Number declined qualification	2,438	2,552	3,143	1,849	2,678	4,318	2,294	3,672	22,944
Number qualified as full-time farmers	2,877	9,456	12,296	6,673	3,871	3,835	1,905	3,339	44,252
Number qualified as smallholders	16,913	3,458	1,523	4,270	16,186	19,545	7,564	8,090	77,549
Number qualified as commercial fishermen	310	29	15	94	45	23	142	950	1,608
Number qualified for crown lands	261	3,090	2,753	621	2	136	529	159	7,551
Number qualified, part 2	123	240	74	143	174	298	196	55	1,303

TABLE A5 (continued)
Application for qualification under the Veterans' Land Act, to 31 March 1951

	British Columbia	Alberta	Saskatchewan	Manitoba	Western Ontario	Eastern Ontario	Quebec	Maritimes	Total
Certificates cancelled: farmers	814	3,122	4,104	2,016	776	1,143	550	1,271	13,796
Certificates cancelled: smallholders	5,992	1,467	573	1,791	5,698	8,468	3,321	3,481	30,791
Certificates cancelled: fishermen	75	10	2	42	12	8	44	303	496
Certificates cancelled: crown lands	65	627	1,058	181	2	28	121	33	2,115
Certificates cancelled: part 2	5	34	27	14	8	13	9	3	113
Acreage involved	205,232	2,028,705	3,035,405	1,091,138	292,635	358,418	190,653	339,578	7,541,764

Source: Report of the Work of the Department of Veterans Affairs, 1955, 58

APPENDIX

TABLE A6
Hospitals operated by DVA during the fiscal year 1946–47

Halifax District
Camp Hill Hospital, Halifax
Veterans' Home, Halifax
Veterans' Hospital, Sydney
Veterans' Hospital, Cornwallis

Saint John District
Lancaster Hospital, Saint John
Veterans' Hospital, Sussex
Veterans' Home, Saint John
Ridgewood Health and Occupational Centre, Saint John

Quebec District
Savard Park Hospital, Quebec
Veterans' Hospital, Quebec

Montreal District
Ste Anne's Hospital, Ste-Anne-de-Bellevue
Veterans' Hospital, Lachine
Veterans' Health and Occupational Centre, Huntingdon
Veterans' Hospital, St. Hyacinthe
Queen Mary Veterans' Hospital, Montreal

Ottawa District
Ottawa Civic Veterans' Pavilion
Rideau Health and Occupational Centre, Ottawa
Veterans' Hospital, Ottawa

Kingston District
Veterans' Hospital, Kingston
Veterans' Hospital, Peterborough

Toronto District
Christie Street Hospital, Toronto
Veterans' Home, Toronto
Lyndhurst Lodge, Toronto
Sacrboro Hall, Toronto
Veterans' Convalescent Hospital, Malton
Sunnybrook Hospital, Toronto
Toronto East General, Veterans' Pavilion
Divadale Health and Occupational Centre, Leaside

Hamilton District
Veterans' Hospital, Hamilton

London District
Westminster Hospital, London
Veterans' Hospital, Crumlin
Veterans' Health and Occupational Centre, London

Winnipeg District
Deer Lodge Hospital, Winnipeg
Veterans' Home, Winnipeg
Veterans' Hospital, Brandon
Veterans' Health and Occupational Centre, Portage la Prairie

Regina District
Veterans' Convalescent Hospital, Regina
Regina General Hospital, Veterans' Pavilion

Saskatoon District
Veterans' Hospital, Saskatoon

TABLE A6 (continued)
Hospitals operated by DVA during the fiscal year 1946–47

Calgary District
Colonel Belcher Hospital, Calgary
Veterans' Home, Calgary
Veterans' Convalescent Hospital, Calgary

Edmonton District
Veterans' Home, Edmonton
University Hospital Veterans' Pavilion, Edmonton

Vancouver District
Shaughnessy Hospital, Vancouver
Veterans' Home, Vancouver
Veterans' Health and Occupational Centre, Victoria

Source: *Report of the Work of the Department of Veterans Affairs*, 1947, 6, 49–50, 63–4.

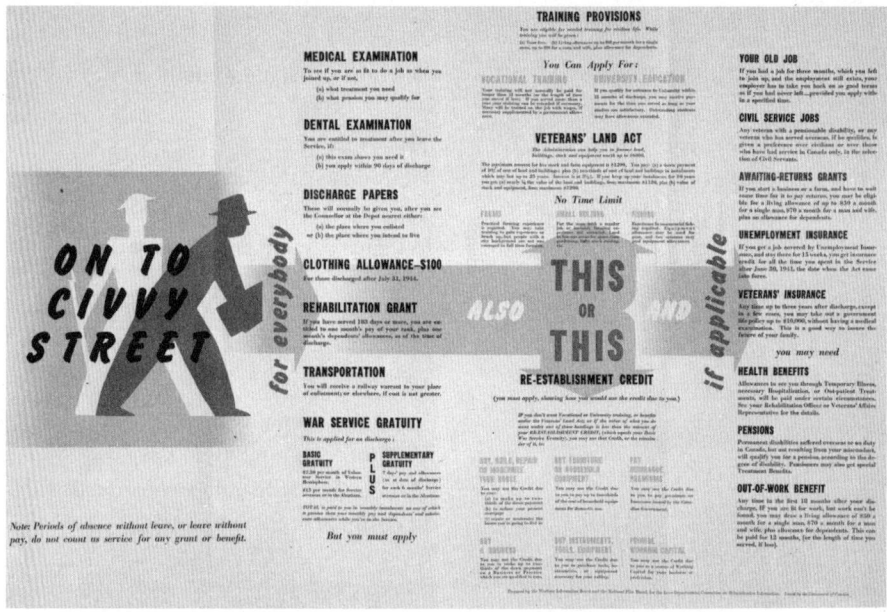

LAC, C-087457

TABLE A7
Walter Wood's 1953 table of benefits

Second World War	General service	N.R.M.A.[1]	Allied veterans	Fire fighters (overseas)	Supervisors (overseas)	Merchant seamen	WRNS, SA Nurses[2]	RAF Transport Command[3]	Special Operators	Overseas welfare workers (CRC and STJA)[4]
Gratuities	YES	YES For service outside Western Hemisphere	YES Domiciled before and after discharge	A gratuity of $15 for every 30 days' service	YES	War Service Bonus plus 10% Special Bonus	Yes Domiciled before and after discharge	NO	YES	NO
Re-establishment credits	YES	Same as above	YES Same as above	NO	YES	NO	YES Same as above	NO	YES	NO
Veterans Rehabilitation Act	YES	YES	YES Same as above	Vocational training	YES	Vocational training under certain conditions	YES Same as above	NO	YES	NO
Veterans' Land Act	YES	YES	YES Same as above	YES (if in receipt of pension)	YES	YES (if in receipt of pension)	YES Same as above	NO	YES	NO
War Veterans' Allowance	YES Basic conditions	YES[5]	YES Same as above	NO	YES[6]	NO	YES Same as above	–	YES	NO
Pension	YES (CPA)[6]	YES (CPA)[6]	YES (CPA)[6] Same as above	YES (CWPAA)[7]	YES[6]	YES (CWPAA)[7] For enemy action or counter action	YES Same as above (CPA)[6] Supplementation	YES (CWPAA)[7] For enemy action or counter action	YES (CPA)[6]	YES (CWPAA)[7] For enemy action or counter action

TABLE A7 (continued)
Walter Wood's 1953 table of benefits

Second World War	General service	N.R.M.A.[1]	Allied veterans	Fire fighters (overseas)	Supervisors (overseas)	Merchant seamen	WRNS, SA Nurses[2]	RAF Transport Command[3]	Special Operators	Overseas welfare workers (CRC and STJA)[4]
Veterans Insurance Act	YES	YES	NO	YES	YES	YES (if in receipt of either bonus)	YES	NO	YES	NO
Business and Professional Loans Act	YES[8]	YES[8]	YES	NO	YES	NO	Same as above	NO	YES	NO
Civil Service Preference	YES	YES	Same as above	NO	YES	NO	YES	NO	YES	NO
Reinstatement in Civil Employment Act	YES	YES	YES	YES	YES	YES	Same as above	NO	YES	NO
U.I.C. benefits	YES	YES	Same as above	YES	YES	YES	YES	NO	YES	NO
			Same as above				Same as above			
Treatment	Full benefits subject to certain conditions	Full benefits subject to certain conditions	Limited benefits	Limited benefits	Full benefits subject to certain conditions	Limited benefits	Limited benefits	Limited benefits	Full benefits subject to certain conditions	Limited benefits

1 National Resources Mobilization Act (applies to conscripted men)
2 Women's Royal Naval Service, South African Nurses
3 Royal Air Force Transport Command
4 Canadian Red Cross, St John Ambulance
5 Service in a theatre of war or in receipt of a pension of 5% or more
6 Canadian Pension Act
7 Civilian War Pensions and Allowances Act
8 Veteran must be in receipt of a war service gratuity in order to qualify under this act.

Source: Adapted from Woods, Rehabilitation (A Combined Operation), 247

Notes

CHAPTER ONE

1 The account of Woods's life that follows is based on his *The Men Who Came Back: A Book of Memories*.
2 Ibid., 5.
3 Ibid., 3.
4 Provincial Archives of Alberta, Heritage Division, Vital Statistics Register, GR1987.0385/510.
5 Woods, *The Men Who Came Back*.
6 Ibid., 45.
7 Library and Archives Canada (hereafter LAC), Record Group (hereafter RG) 150, Records of the Ministry of the Overseas Military Forces of Canada, box 10566-11, accession 1992–93/166, Walter S. Woods file.
8 Woods, *The Men Who Came Back*, 54.
9 Ibid., 57.
10 Ibid., 60.
11 Ibid., 61.
12 Woods, *Rehabilitation (A Combined Operation)*, 461; England, "Veterans' Rehabilitation."
13 Morton and Wright, *Winning the Second Battle: Canadian Veterans and the Return to Civilian Life, 1915–1930*.
14 LAC, MG 28-I298, Royal Canadian Legion fonds, vol. 3, "Constitution, By-Laws, Rules and Regulations," the Great War Veterans' Association of Canada, Article I (microfilm A2207).
15 LAC, MG 28-I298, vol. 3, "Minutes of the Annual Convention of the Great War Veterans' Association of Canada held in Winnipeg April 10th to 12th, 1917," 11–15 (microfilm A2207).
16 Quoted in Canada, House of Commons, *Debates* (hereafter *Debates*), 1944, 3816.
17 Carrigan, ed., *Canadian Party Platforms, 1867–1968*, 77.
18 Canada, *Public General Acts* (hereafter *Acts*), 1901, c. 17, 101–7; Canada, House of Commons, *Soldiers' Pensions: Proceedings of the Special Committee ...*, House of Commons, *Journal*, 1916, app. 4, v (see Dunbar), 59.
19 England, "Veterans' Rehabilitation," 10:225.
20 Canada, House of Commons, *Pensions and Pension Regulations: Proceedings of the Special Committee ...*, House of Commons, *Journal*, 1919, app. 3, iv. For the scale of pensions effective 1 September 1914, see *Debates*, 1916, 4140–42.
21 Woods, *Rehabilitation*, 461; England, "Veterans' Rehabilitation," 226.

22 England, "Veterans' Rehabilitation," 225.
23 Ibid.
24 House of Commons, *Journal*, 1916, 355-9.
25 House of Commons, *Debates* (hereafter *Debates*), 1916, 4132.
26 *Pensions and Pension Regulations*, iv.
27 *Debates*, 1919, 4209.
28 *Acts*, 1919, c. 43, 275-94.
29 *Pensions and Pension Regulations*, vii.
30 Ibid. The statistics for beneficiaries and costs cited here vary somewhat from those given in my appendices.
31 England, "Veterans' Rehabilitation," 226; *Debates*, 1918, 611–12.
32 *Acts*, 1918, c. 42, 137–8.
33 *Report of the Work of the Department of Soldiers' Civil Re-establishment* (Dec. 1919), House of Commons, Sessional Paper 14, 1920, 7.
34 Ibid., 11–30.
35 Ibid., 9–10.
36 Ibid., 10.
37 Ibid., 31–2.
38 Ibid., 33.
39 For his career and the history of Canada's war blinded, see Durflinger, *Veterans with a Vision: Canada's War Blinded in Peace and War*.
40 Veterans Affairs Canada, records of the Department of Veterans Affairs (DVA), 1205-6, vol. 1, "Pensions and Other Post-War Benefits Granted by Canada to Ex-Members of the Forces," Department of Pensions and National Health, 15 June 1935, 1.
41 Ibid., 2.
42 England, "Veterans Rehabilitation," 226. For details of gratuity administration, see, DVA, VLA, V-25-6, "Brief Summary of the Work of the Repatriation Committee – 1918," enclosed in England to Jones, 22 November 1940.
43 DVA, 1205-6, vol. 1, "Pensions and Other Post-War Benefits," 14.
44 Ibid.; England, "Veterans Rehabilitation," 226.
45 DVA, 1205-6, vol. 1, "Pensions and other Post-War Benefits," 14; England, "Veterans Rehabilitation," 226.
46 DVA, 1205-6, vol. 1, "Pensions and Other Post-War Benefits," 25–6.
47 *Acts*, 1920, c. 54, 327-33.
48 DVA, 1205-6, vol. 1, "Pensions and Other Post-War Benefits," 15.
49 England, "Veterans' Rehabilitation," 226.
50 *Acts*, 1917, c. 21, 123–6.
51 *Debates*, 1919, 255.
52 Ibid., 255–6.
53 *Acts*, 1919, c. 71, 627-61.
54 *Debates*, 1919, 256.
55 Ibid.

56 Ibid.
57 England, "Soldier Settlement: Revising the Oldest Rehabilitation Prospectus," 294.
58 See Carter, *Lost Harvests: Prairie Indian Reserve Farmers and Government Policy* and "'An Infamous Proposal': Prairie Indian Reserve Land and Soldier Settlement after World War I," 9–21.
59 This section and the passages that follow about Zennosuke Inouye draw variously on my "Zennosuke Inouye's Land: A Canadian Veterans Affairs Dilemma," *Canadian Historical Review* 85, no. 3 (2004): 423–50. I acknowledge gratefully the assistance of the University of Toronto Press.
60 *British Columbian*, 10 July 1920.
61 Woods, *The Men Who Came Back*, 62.
62 Ibid., 63.
63 *Debates*, 1919, 245.
64 Ibid., 242.
65 Ibid., 242–3.
66 Ibid., 1749.
67 *Report of the Work of the Department of Soldiers' Civil Re-establishment* (Dec. 1920), House of Commons, Sessional Paper 14, 1921, 164–5.
68 DVA, 65-31, "Re: The Issue of Unemployment Relief to Former Members of the Forces," 6 April 1932.
69 Fedorowich, *Unfit for Heroes: Reconstruction and Soldier Settlement in the Empire between the Wars*, 81.
70 Ibid., 99.
71 England, "Soldier Settlement," 295.
72 Royal Commission on Pensions and Re-establishment, *Report on First Part of Investigation*, House of Commons, Sessional Paper 154, 1923; *First Interim Report on Second Part of Investigation*, Sessional Paper 154a, 1923; *Second Interim Report on Second Part of Investigation*, Sessional Paper 203, 1924; and *Final Report on Second Part of Investigation*, Sessional Paper 203a, 1924.
73 *Acts*, 1923, c. 62, 409–15; 1924, c. 60, 205–8.
74 *Acts*, 1920, c. 62; 1921, c. 45; 1922, c. 38; 1923, c. 62; 1924, c. 60; 1925, c. 49; 1927, c. 65; 1928, c. 38; 1930, c. 35; 1931, c. 44; 1932–33, c. 45; 1934, c. 58; 1935, c. 8, 45; 1936, c. 44; and 1939, c. 32.
75 DVA, 1033-85/R5, vol. 1, *Report of the Proceedings of the National Unity Conference and Draft Constitution*, 15.
76 For this event, see Vance, "'Today They Were Alive Again': The Canadian Corps Reunion of 1934."
77 *Debates*, 1928, 1908; *Acts*, 1928, c. 39, 173–9.
78 Canada, *Reports, Proceedings, and Evidence of the Special Committee on Pensions and Returned Soldiers' Problems* (3 March–23 May 1930), House of Commons, *Journal*, 1930, app. "Pensions and Returned Soldiers' Problems," Minutes of Evidence, 27 March 1930, 1.

CHAPTER TWO

1 This chapter draws variously on my "'Without the Stigma of Pauperism': Canadian Veterans in the 1930s," *British Journal of Canadian Studies* 22, no. 1 (2009): 31–62. I acknowledge gratefully the assistance of Liverpool University Press.
2 Dickson and Allen, "Marching on History."
3 *Acts*, 1930, c. 48, 349-53.
4 The other members of the committee were Major A.M. Wright (chairman) and Dr Fred S. Burke (see Woods, *Rehabilitation*, 385–6).
5 *Acts*, 1930, c. 35. 289–300.
6 *Acts*, 1933, c. 45, 231–49.
7 DVA, 1205-6, vol. 1, "Pensions and Other Post-War Benefits Granted by Canada to Ex-Members of the Forces," 29.
8 DVA, 65-31, "Re: The Issue of Unemployment Relief to Former Members of the Forces," 6 April 1932.
9 DVA, GS 1032-01-1, vol. 1, Brereton to Prime Minister, 14 January 1935.
10 DVA, 1033-85/R5, vol. 5, Canadian Legion of the BESL Manitoba Command, Eighth Provincial Convention, 21–23 June 1937, Secretary's Report, 5.
11 DVA, GS 1032-01-1, vol. 1, E.H. Scammell memorandum, 14 February 1935.
12 LAC, MG 28-I298, vol. 7, Legion Circular no. 31/2/12, 18 June 1931.
13 LAC, MG 28-I298, vol. 7, "Report of the Unemployment Committee."
14 LAC, MG 28-I298, vol. 7, Legion Circular no. 31/2/34, 18 September 1931.
15 DVA, 65-31, "The Genesis of Distribution of Relief to Unemployed Pensioners."
16 LAC, MG 28-I298, vol. 7, Legion Circular no. 32/2/36, 26 July 1932.
17 Ibid.
18 DVA, 65-31, Herwig to McKee, 29 August 1933.
19 DVA, 65-31, "Subject: Soldiers' Relief Work," 16 July 1934.
20 LAC, MG 28-I298, vol. 75, Fifth Dominion Convention, "Address of the Dominion President," 6.
21 Ibid., 7.
22 DVA, 65-31, "Supplementary submission by the Canadian Legion of the British Empire Service League touching measures for the relief of unemployed ex-service men and particularly disabled and handicapped ex-service men," January, 1935.
23 LAC, RG 38, Records of Veterans Affairs, vol. 190, 65-668, Ross to Sutherland, 7 June 1935.
24 DVA, 65-31-1, *Report of the Committee Appointed to Carry Out an Investigation into the Existing Facilities in Connection with Unemployment of Ex-Service Men and Care and Maintenance While Unemployed, and to Report Thereon with Such Suggestions and Recommendations as May Be Deemed Advisable* (Ottawa: King's Printer, 1935).
25 Ibid., 4.
26 Ibid., 5.
27 Ibid., 7.

28 Ibid., 16–18.
29 DVA, 65-31-1, Wodehouse to District Administrators, 12 July 1935.
30 DVA, 65-31-1, *Report of the Committee Appointed to Carry Out an Investigation into the Existing Facilities in Connection with Unemployment of Ex-Service Men*, 13.
31 DVA, 65-31, "Unemployment Assistance."
32 LAC, RG 38, vol. 190, 65-668, vol. 1, memorandum by E.H. Scammell, "Re: The Report of the Hyndman Committee," 18 November 1935.
33 LAC, RG 38, vol. 190, 65-668, vol. 1, Ross to Sutherland, 5 June 1935.
34 LAC, MG 28-1298, vol. 8, statement attached to Legion Circular no. 35/8, 13 June 1935.
35 LAC, RG 38, vol. 190, 65-668, vol. 1, Ross to Sutherland, 7 June 1935.
36 LAC, MG 28-1298, vol. 8, Legion Circular no. 35/8, 13 June 1935, and statement attached.
37 Ibid.
38 Canada, House of Commons, *Debates*, 2 July 1935, 4159.
39 LAC, MG 28-1298, Legion Circular no. 35/4/6, 11 September 1935.
40 LAC, MG 28-1298, Legion Circular no. 36/2/2, 20 January 1936.
41 *Debates*, 1937, 2670. Power told the House of Commons that he had given up his pension "to meet the so-called public clamour of those who say that if you are disabled to some extent you should not hold such a position" [i.e., that of minister].
42 *Debates*, 1937, 2670.
43 Ibid.
44 *Debates*, 16 March 1936, 1097–8.
45 House of Commons, *Journal*, 1936, 438–43.
46 Canada, House of Commons, Special Committee on Pensions and Returned Soldiers' Problems, *Minutes of Proceedings and Evidence*, 1936.
47 House of Commons, *Journal*, 1936, 439; *Acts*, 1936, c. 44, 307–22.
48 House of Commons, *Journal*, 1936, 441; *Acts*, 1936. c. 48, 349–51.
49 House of Commons, *Journal*, 1936, 441.
50 *Acts*, 1936, c. 47, 345–8.
51 LAC, MG 28-1298, vol. 8, Legion Circular no. 36/9, 25 June 1936.
52 LAC, MG 28-1298, vol. 8, "Memorandum submitted by the Dominion President to the Dominion Executive Council of the Canadian Legion as to the situation in regard to unemployment," 23 January 1937, attached to Legion Circular no. 37/4/1, 28 January 1937.
53 Ibid.
54 Ibid.
55 *Report of the Veterans' Assistance Commission*, 1937, 7.
56 LAC, MG 28-1298, vol. 8, "Memorandum submitted by the Dominion President ... as to the situation in regard to unemployment," 23 January 1937, attached to Legion Circular no. 37/4/1, 28 January 1937.
57 Ibid.
58 Ibid.
59 *Debates*, 1937, 96–7.

60 LAC, MG 28-1298, vol. 8, "Memorandum submitted by the Dominion President ... as to the situation in regard to unemployment," 23 January 1937, attached to Legion Circular no. 37/4/1, 28 January 1937.
61 LAC, MG 28-1298, vol. 8, Legion Circular no. 37/4/1, 28 January 1937.
62 DVA, 1033-85/R5, vol. 4, Mackenzie to Power, 1 February 1937.
63 DVA, 1033-85/R5, vol. 4, Legion Circular no. 37/1, 28 January 1937.
64 Ibid.
65 LAC, MG 28-1298, vol. 8, Legion Circular no. 37/5, 16 February 1937. See also DVA, 1033-85/R5, vol. 4, "The 'Bonus' Bogey," *Canadian Veteran*, March 1937.
66 LAC, MG 28-1298, vol. 8, Legion Circular no. 37/10, 12 March 1937.
67 Veterans' Assistance Commission, *Interim Report*, 27 January 1937, House of Commons, Sessional Paper 220, 1937.
68 Ibid., 9–10.
69 Ibid., 10–11.
70 Ibid., 11.
71 Ibid.
72 Ibid., 3.
73 Ibid., 11–12.
74 Ibid., 17.
75 Ibid., 18–22.
76 Ibid., 22.
77 Ibid., 25.
78 Ibid., 28.
79 LAC, MG 28-1298, vol. 8, "Memorandum ... Concerning the First Interim Report of the Veterans' Assistance Commission," 15 March 1937, enclosed in Legion Circular no. 37/12, 16 March 1937.
80 LAC, MG 28-1298, vol. 8, Legion Circular no. 37/12, 16 March 1937.
81 LAC, MG 28-1298, vol. 8, Bowler to Power, 5 April, 1937, enclosed in Legion Circular no. 37/2/9, 5 April 1937.
82 *Debates*, 1937, 2669.
83 Ibid., 2672.
84 Ibid., 2673.
85 Ibid., 2671.
86 Ibid.
87 Ibid., 2672.
88 Ibid., 2675.
89 Ibid., 2671.
90 Ibid.
91 Ibid., 2675.
92 LAC, MG 28-1298, vol. 8, Ross to Power, 12 April 1937, enclosed in Legion Circular no. 37/4/4, 27 April 1937.
93 *Report of the Veterans' Assistance Commission*.
94 Ibid., 40.

95 Ibid.
96 Ibid.
97 Ibid.
98 Ibid., 69.
99 LAC, MG 28-I298, vol. 8, enclosure in Legion Circular no. 37/34, 28 December 1937.
100 LAC, MG 28-I298, vol. 8, Legion Circular no. 39/3/2, 5 May 1939.
101 LAC, MG 28-I298, vol. 8, Legion Circular no. 38/5, 21 April 1938; *Debates*, 1938, 1042.
102 LAC, MG 28-I298, vol. 8, Legion Circular no. 38/5, 21 April 1938; *Acts*, 1938, c. 16, 41–3.
103 LAC, MG 28-I298, vol. 8, Legion Circular no. 38/3, 23 March 1938.
104 His letter, dated 21 March 1938, is in ibid.
105 LAC, MG 28-I298, vol. 8, "Memorandum of submissions made ... to members of the cabinet," September 1938, enclosed in Legion Circular no. 38/4/4, 10 September 1938.
106 LAC, MG 28-I298, vol. 8, Legion Circular no. 38/3/3, 13 December 1938.
107 Ibid. and MG 28-I298, vol. 8, Power to Foster, 4 May 1939, attached to Legion Circular no. 39/17, 19 May 1939.
108 LAC, MG 28-I298, vol. 8, Legion Circular no. 38/3/3, 13 December 1938.
109 LAC, MG 28-I298, vol. 8, Legion Circular no. 39/3/2, 5 May 1939; Legion Circular no. 39/17, 19 May 1939.
110 LAC, MG 28-I298, vol. 8, Legion Circular no. 39/3/2, 5 May 1939.
111 Ibid.
112 LAC, MG 28-I298, vol. 8, enclosure in Legion Circular no. 39/17, 19 May 1939.
113 Ibid. and LAC, MG 28-I298, vol. 8, "Information re pensions, treatment, and certain recommendations of Veterans' Assistance Commission."
114 LAC, MG 28-I298, vol. 8, attachment to Legion Circular no. 39/17.
115 This account of Mackenzie's career is based on his file in LAC, RG 150, box 6972-27, accession 1992-93/166, and on information from Professor Patricia Roy, University of Victoria.
116 LAC, MG 26-J, William Lyon Mackenzie fonds, diary, 18 September 1939, 1056. Online at http://www.collectionscanada.gc.ca/databases/king/001059-119.02-e.php?&page_id_nbr=20753&interval=20&&&&&&&&&&PHPSESSID=r98s6mgd93s51p15d7qam53661.
117 *Globe and Mail*, 3 September 1949, 3.

CHAPTER THREE

1 For the enlistment total given here, see Woods, *Rehabilitation (A Combined Operation)*, 461. This chapter draws variously on my "'A Great Stride Forward': The Post-Discharge Re-establishment Order (PC7633) of 1October 1941," *British Journal of Canadian Studies* 23, no. 2 (2010): 207–32. I acknowledge gratefully the assistance of Liverpool University Press.

2 Granatstein, *Canada's War: The Politics of the Mackenzie King Government, 1939–1945*, 373. For the social history of the war period, see Keshen, *Saints, Sinners, and Soldiers: Canada's Second World War*.
3 Figures from Directorate of History, Department of National Defence.
4 Canada, House of Commons, Special Committee on the Pension Act and the War Veterans' Allowance Act, *Minutes of Proceedings and Evidence*, no. 10, 4 April 1941, 274.
5 Ibid., 273.
6 Woods, *Rehabilitation (A Combined Operation)*, 5.
7 LAC, RG 38, vol. 185, file 65-34-9, vol. 1, Woods to McDonald, 27 September 1940; *Debates*, 6 December 1940, 782.
8 LAC, RG 38, vol. 185, file 65-34-9, vol. 1, McDonald to Woods, 10 October 1939.
9 Brown, "Re-establishment and Rehabilitation: Canadian Veteran Policy, 1933–1946," 9.
10 LAC, MG 27 III B5, Ian Mackenzie fonds, vol. 56, file 527-10(1), Mackenzie to King, 30 October 1939.
11 Ibid., King to Mackenzie, 1 November 1939.
12 Woods, *Rehabilitation (A Combined Operation)*, 463.
13 LAC, RG 38, vol. 185, file 65-34-9, vol. 3, attachment to Woods to Mackenzie, 25 September 1943.
14 LAC, RG 38, vol. 185, file 65-34-9, vol. 1, attachment to memorandum for General Administrative file, Demobilization and Rehabilitation, 18 September 1940.
15 For his career, see *Living, Learning, Remembering: Memoirs of Robert England*.
16 LAC, MG 27 III B5, vol. 56, file 527-10(2), attachment to England memorandum to Minister, 24 November 1940.
17 *Debates*, 6 December 1940, 785–6.
18 Woods, *Rehabilitation (A Combined Operation)*, 7.
19 *Proclamations and Orders in Council Passed under the Authority of the War Measures Act*, vol. 1, 30–1. Publication ordered by PC 108, 13 January 1940.
20 LAC, MG 27 III B5, vol. 57, 527-10F, letter to Byron Woods, 13 April 1946.
21 Woods, *Rehabilitation (A Combined Operation)*, 451.
22 *Debates*, 6 December 1940, 781.
23 LAC, RG 38, vol. 185, file 65-34-9, vol. 1, Woods to McDonald, 27 September 1940.
24 Ibid.
25 LAC, MG 27 III B5, vol. 57, file 527-11, Woods to McDonald, 23 October 1940.
26 LAC, MG 27 III B5, vol. 57, file 527-11, Woods to Mackenzie, 20 November 1940.
27 DVA, 1033-85/R5, appendix A of "Memorandum Concerning the Welfare of Ex-Service Men, Men Now Serving and Their Dependents," March 1940.
28 Hale, *Branching Out: The Story of the Royal Canadian Legion*, 60–1. For an

earlier history of the Legion, see Bowering, *Service: The Story of the Canadian Legion, 1925–1960*.
29 LAC, MG 28-I298, Royal Canadian Legion fonds, vol. 75, Address of the Dominion President, Brigadier W.W. Foster.
30 Ibid.
31 Ibid.
32 LAC, MG 28-I298, vol. 75, Report of the General Secretary, Eighth Dominion Convention.
33 DVA, 1033-85/R5.
34 LAC, MG 28-I298, vol. 8, Legion Circular no. 40/4/5, 9 March 1940.
35 Canada, House of Commons, Special Committee on the Pension Act and the War Veterans' Allowance Act, *Minutes of Proceedings and Evidence*, no. 14, 6 May 1941, appendix B, 530–43.
36 DVA, 14-4-3, vol. 1, Report of the Committee on Rehabilitation.
37 DVA, 14-4-3, vol. 1, Legion Circular no. 40/41, 26 November 1940.
38 *Debates*, 6 December 1940, 782.
39 *Debates*, 6 December 1940, 781-88.
40 Ibid., 783.
41 *Proclamations and Orders in Council*, vol. 3, 139-41.
42 LAC, RG 38, vol. 185, file 65-34-9, vol. 1, "Precis of Conference with Provincial Departments of Labour or Unemployment Relief."
43 Special Committee, *Minutes of Proceedings and Evidence*, no. 1, 28 February and 11 March 1941, iii.
44 Ibid., no. 22, 5, 10, 11 June 1941, 815.
45 Ibid., no. 14, 6 May 1941, 500–19.
46 Ibid., no. 22, 5, 10, 11 June 1941, 817.
47 DVA, 14-4-3, vol. 1, Legion Circular no. 41/15, 20 June 1941.
48 Special Committee, *Minutes of Proceedings and Evidence*, no. 10, 4 April 1941, 276.
49 LAC, MG 27 III B5, vol. 57, file 527-11, enclosure in Duguid to Chairman, GACDR, 2 July 1940.
50 Special Committee, *Minutes of Proceedings and Evidence*, no. 10, 4 April 1941, 275, 278.
51 LAC, MG 27 III B5, vol. 57, file 527-14(2), McDonald memorandum to Minister, 23 July 1941.
52 LAC, MG 27 III B5, vol. 57, file 527-14(2), "Re: Proposed Post Discharge Benefit Fund," enclosed in McDonald memorandum to Minister, 23 July 1941.
53 LAC, MG 27 III B5, vol. 56, file 527-10(4), Woods to Minister, 25 July 1941.
54 LAC, MG 27 III B5, vol. 57, file 527-14(2), Mackenzie to King, 28 July 1941, and Heeney to Mackenzie, 31 July 1941.
55 LAC, MG 27 III B5, vol. 57, file 527-14(3), memorandum to McDonald, "Re Negotiations with Unemployment Insurance Commission as to Post-Discharge Re-Establishment Order Draft."

56 LAC, MG 27 III B5, vol. 57, file 527-14(3), memorandum, "Being a Brief Review of Post-Discharge Re-establishment (Draft) Order, as reported by the Committee, Sept. 29, 1941," 12.

57 Ibid., 12–13.

58 LAC, MG 27 III B5, vol. 57, file 527-14(2), MacNamara to Phelan, 9 September 1941.

59 LAC, MG 27 III B5, vol. 57, file 527-14(2), McDonald to England, 5 September 1941.

60 LAC, MG 27 III B5, vol. 57, file 527-14(3), memorandum to McDonald, "Re Negotiations with Unemployment Insurance Commission as to Post-Discharge Re-Establishment Order Draft."

61 LAC, MG 27 III B5, vol. 57, file 527-14(3), Watson to Mackenzie, 25 September 1941.

62 LAC, MG 27 III B5, vol. 57, file 527-14(3), GACDR minutes, 29 September 1941.

63 LAC, MG 27 III B5, vol. 57, file 527-14(3), memorandum, "Being a Brief Review of Post-Discharge Re-establishment (Draft) Order, as reported by the Committee, Sept. 29, 1941," 14–15.

64 *Proclamations and Orders in Council*, vol. 5, 184–90.

65 LAC, MG 27 III B5, vol. 57, file 527-14(3), DPNH, information leaflet, "The Post-Discharge Re-establishment Order."

66 LAC, MG 27 III B5, vol. 57, file 527-14(3), memorandum, "Being a Brief Review of Post-Discharge Re-establishment (Draft) Order, as reported by the Committee, Sept. 29, 1941," 11.

67 *Acts*, 1942, 135–8.

68 LAC, MG 27 III B5, vol. 57, file 527-14(3), "Statement by the Honourable Ian Mackenzie, Minister of Pensions and National Health, and Chairman of the Cabinet Committee on Demobilization and Re-establishment."

69 LAC, MG 27 III B5, vol. 57, file 527-14(3), Mackenzie to Atkinson, 1 October 1941.

70 LAC, MG 27 III B5, vol. 57, file 527-14(3), document submitted by Bowler to Minister, 2 October 1941.

71 LAC, MG 27 III B5, vol. 57, file 527-14(3), MacNamara to McDonald, 6 October 1941.

72 LAC, MG 27 III B5, vol. 57, file 527-14(3), Department of Pensions and National Health, C.L # 2811.

73 England, *Living, Learning, Remembering*, 122-23.

74 DVA, 65-10-2-1, "Report of the General Advisory Committee (Inter-Departmental) on Demobilization and Rehabilitation," enclosed in Woods to Mackenzie, 25 September 1943.

75 England, *Living, Learning, Remembering*, 125.

76 Woods, *Rehabilitation (A Combined Operation)*, 16.

77 DVA, 65-14, vol. 1.

78 LAC, MG 27 III B5, vol. 56, file 527-10(6), enclosure in Woods memorandum to Minister, 15 April 1942.

CHAPTER FOUR

1 The statistics given in this paragraph are from LAC, MG 27 III B5, vol. 60, file 527-61(2), Murchison to Mackenzie, 13 January 1942, and Special Committee on the Pension Act and the War Veterans' Allowance Act, *Minutes of Proceedings and Evidence*, no. 20, 30 May 1941, 752-4, 802.
2 LAC, MG 27 III B5, vol. 60, file 527-61A(2), Keep to Mackenzie, 16 February 1944.
3 The account of his career given here is based on information in LAC, RG 150, box 6497-20, accession 1992–93/166, and RG 32 (Records of the Public Service Commission), series C-2, vol. 203, 1889.11.12. Part of an unpublished memoir (covering his life to the 1930s) is online at http://www.rootsweb.ancestry.com/~skkinder/GordonMurchison/Chapter6-StartingAgain.html.
4 LAC, RG 150, vol. 6497-20, accession 1992–93/166, attestation paper.
5 Ibid., "Medical History of an Invalid."
6 LAC, RG 32, series C-2, vol. 203, 1889.11.12, Civil Service of Canada, "Application Form for Special Positions."
7 LAC, MG 27 III B5, vol. 60, file 527-61(3A), Senior to Mackenzie, 13 December 1944.
8 DVA, VLA, V-25-1, vol. 1, "Report of Sub-Committee on Colonel Duguid's Plan for Voluntary Community Settlements or Villages," 22 August 1940.
9 Ibid.
10 DVA, VLA, V-25-3, District Superintendent to Murchison, 12 April 1941.
11 DVA, VLA, V-25-1, vol. 1.
12 LAC, MG 27 III B5, vol. 57, file 527-11.
13 DVA, VLA, V-25-1, vol. 2, Meeting of Sub-Committee on Land Settlement, 3 April 1941; Special Committee on the Pension Act and the War Veterans' Allowance Act, *Minutes of Proceedings and Evidence*, no. 20, 30 May 1941, 751–6, and no. 21, 4 June 1941, 801–13.
14 DVA, VLA, V-25-1, vol. 2, Report of the Sub-Committee on Land Settlement.
15 DVA, VLA, V-25-1, vol. 2, Murchison to Crerar, 22 December 1941.
16 *Debates*, 1942, 1768.
17 Ibid., 1769.
18 Ibid., 1771.
19 Ibid., 1819.
20 Ibid., 1872.
21 Ibid., 2002, 3301, 3975, 4325.
22 Canada, House of Commons, *Journal*, 1942, 260.
23 Canada, House of Commons, Special Committee on Land Settlement of Veterans of the Present War, *Minutes of Proceedings and Evidence*, no. 6, 4 June 1942, evidence of J.C.G. Herwig, Acting General Secretary of the Canadian Legion, 98.
24 Ibid.
25 *Debates*, 4383–435.
26 *Acts*, 1942, c. 33, 161–77.

27 *Debates*, 1942, 4385.
28 LAC, MG 27 III B5, file 527-61(2), Murchison to Woods, 15 January 1942.
29 DVA, 5401-01-1, vol. 1, England memorandum to McDonald, 29 April 1942.
30 DVA, 5401-01-1, vol. 1, Woods to McDonald, 29 April 1942.
31 LAC, MG 27 III B5, vol. 60, 527-61(4), *Second report of the Veterans' Land Act for the fiscal year ended March 31, 1944*, 219.
32 Ibid., 222.
33 Ibid.
34 The statistics that follow are from the second report.
35 Canada, House of Commons, Standing Committee on Public Accounts, *Minutes of Proceedings and Evidence*, no. 8, 20 May 1947, evidence of Gordon Murchison, 182–3.
36 LAC, RG 117 (Records of the Custodian of Enemy Property), file 8788, microfilm C-9386, Inouye to Custodian's Office, Vancouver, 27 May 1944.
37 LAC, RG 117, file 8788, microfilm C-9386, Inouye to Custodian's Office, 30 July 1943.
38 LAC, RG 117, file 8788, microfilm C-9386, Shears to Inouye, 5 August 1943.
39 There is a copy of the WD1 form in DVA, 65-14. See also, in the same file, Wright to Deacon, 3 December 1941.
40 DVA, 65-14, vol. 1, "Regulations Governing Order in Council PC 7633 entitled 'The Post-Discharge Re-establishment Order.'"
41 Ibid.
42 Ibid.
43 Ibid.
44 Ibid.
45 DVA, 65-14, vol. 1, Woods to Boyd, 23 October 1941.
46 DVA, 65-14, vol. 1, Woods to Fenton, 31 October 1941.
47 DVA, 65-15, vol. 1, DPNH Confidential Letter no. 11.
48 DVA, 65-15, vol. 1, DPNH Confidential Letter no. 16.
49 DVA, 65-14, vol. 1, DPNH Confidential Letter no. 29, 15 August 1944.
50 DVA, 65-28, vol. 2, Woods to Isnor, 9 February 1944. There is a copy of the booklet in LAC, MG 30-C181 (Robert England fonds), vol. 2, GACDR file.
51 DVA, 65-28, vol. 1, Woods to Green, 6 March 1943.
52 DVA, 65-4-4, minutes, 18 November 1942.
53 DVA, 65-14, vol. 2, DPNH Confidential Letter no. 46.
54 DVA, 65-14, vol. 2, Woods memoranda to Minister, 17 February 1943 and 8 February 1944.
55 DVA, 65-14, vol. 2, DPNH Confidential Letter no. 46.
56 DVA, 65-14-1, Woods memorandum to Minister, 8 February 1944.
57 DVA, 65-14-1, Woods memorandum, 5 April 1943.
58 DVA, 66-15, Woods to Minister, 16 July 1943.
59 Woods, *The Men Who Came Back*, 134.
60 Ibid., 135.
61 DVA, 66-15, Woods to Minister, 23 September 1943.
62 DVA, 32-3, vol. 1, Woods to Hundevad, 29 September 1943.

63 DVA, 66-15, McNaughton to Woods, 13 September 1943.
64 For Weir's career, see *The Canadian Who's Who*, 1948, 979, and Francis, ed., *Encyclopedia of British Columbia*, 759.
65 There is a copy in the library of Veteran Affairs Canada, Charlottetown.
66 DVA, 65-14, vol. 2, Woods memorandum to Minister, 17 February 1943.
67 Weir, "Survey of Rehabilitation (Interim Report)," 23.
68 Ibid.
69 Ibid.
70 DVA, 65-9-1, vol. 2, Walker to Woods, 16 April 1943.
71 DVA, 65-9-1, vol. 2, Sub-Committee on Employment, minutes, 9 April 1943.
72 DVA, 65-9-1, vol. 2, Woods to Walker, 13 April 1943.
73 DVA, 65-9-1, vol. 2, Walker to Woods, 16 April 1943. For Herwig's attitude, see, in the same file, England memorandum to Woods, 13 April 1943.
74 There is a copy of the speech in DVA, 65-10.
75 *Free Press*, London, 4 June 1943, 8.
76 This section and the passages that follow about women veterans draw variously, on my (with Shaun Brown), "The Veterans Charter and Canadian Women Veterans of World War II," *British Journal of Canadian Studies* 9, no. 2 (1994): 249–77; reprinted in Neary and Granatstein, eds., *The Good Fight: Canadians and World War II*. I acknowledge gratefully the assistance of Liverpool University Press and Nelson Education.
77 There is a copy of PC4/7635 in DVA, 5431-03-4, vol. 1.
78 DVA, 5431-03-4, vol. 1, Wright to Woods, 27 October 1941.
79 See, for example, PC49/8817 of 11 November 1941, dealing with reinstatement in civil employment, and PC8880 of 18 November 1941, dealing with the payment of rehabilitation grants (copies in DVA, 5431-03-4, vol. 1).
80 DVA, 5431-03-4, vol. 1, England to Wright, 24 October 1941.
81 See PC1965 (copy in DVA, 5431-03-4, vol. 1).
82 Under PC7633, "discharged person" was defined as follows: "any person who, having been in receipt of either active service rates of pay or of Permanent Force rates of pay while serving in the Naval, Military or Air Forces of Canada during the present war, subsequent to July 1, 1941, is discharged or retired from, or ceases to serve on active service in, the said forces."
83 DVA, 5431-03-4, vol. 1, McDonald to Woods, 26 November 1941.
84 DVA, 5431-03-4, GACDR, Sub-Committee on Post-Discharge Benefits for Members of the Canadian Women's Army Corps and the Canadian Women's Auxiliary Air Force, minutes, 29 December 1941.
85 Ibid.
86 DVA, 5431-03-4, vol. 1, Woods to McDonald, 3 January 1942.
87 Ibid., memorandum to Minister of Pensions and National Health, 25 March 1942, from chairman, Sub-Committee on Post-Discharge Benefits for Members of the Canadian Women's Army Corps and the Canadian Women's Auxiliary Air Force. There is a copy of PC1965 in this file. The revised definition of "discharged person" in the amended PC7633 was as follows: "any person who, subsequent to July 1st, 1941, has been discharged or retired

from, or has ceased to serve on active service in any of the following Forces or Corps; (i) the Naval, Military or Air Forces of Canada, in respect of this class, that such person was in receipt of either active service rates of pay or of Permanent Force rates of pay while serving in the said Forces during the present war, or (ii) the Canadian Women's Army Corps, established by Order in Council, PC6289, dated the 13th day of August, 1941, or (iii) the Royal Canadian Air Force (Women's Division), established by Order in Council, PC790, dated the 3rd day of February, 1942, or (iv) the Military, Naval or Air Forces of His Majesty other than His Majesty's Canadian Forces, provided in respect to this class, that such person was domiciled in Canada at the time of his enlistment therein in the present war" (Woods, *Rehabilitation*, 467).

88 By PC56/6755 (copy in DVA, 5431-03-4, vol. 1).
89 DVA, 5431-03-4, vol. 2, Woods to National Secretary, Imperial [Order] Daughters of the Empire, 27 October 1943.
90 *Debates*, 24 July 1943, 5357–8.
91 DVA, 5431-03-4, vol. 1, Woods to McDonald, 24 January 1942.
92 DVA, 5431-03-4, vol. 1, minutes, Sub-Committee on Post Discharge Benefits for Members of the Canadian Women's Army Corps and the Royal Canadian Air Force (Women's Division), 24 March 1942.
93 Veterans Affairs Canada, Canadian Pension Commission, list 8167, box 80, minutes, Sub-Committee on the Special Problems of Discharged Women, 19 June 1942.
94 The interim report is in the same box and is attached to the minutes of the meeting of 23 June 1942.
95 There is a copy in DVA, 5431-03-4, vol. 2.
96 There is a copy in the same file.
97 See copy in the library of Veterans Affairs Canada, Charlottetown.
98 Ibid., P157.
99 See 212–26.
100 See ibid.
101 This section and the passages that follow about universities draw variously on my "Canadian Universities and Canadian Veterans of World War II," in Neary and Granatstein, eds., *The Veterans Charter and Post–World War II Canada*, 110–48.
102 NCCU, *Report of the National Conference of Canadian Universities on Post-War Problems*, 5. There is a copy in DVA, 66-27-3.

CHAPTER FIVE

1 For the work of this committee, see Robert A. Young, "Reining in James: The Limits of the Task Force." England served as secretary of the committee in its initial phase see his *Living, Learning, Remembering*, 123.
2 *Debates*, 1942, 1573, 1643, 2002, 4376, 5194; 1943, 1074, 3927, 5225, 5433.
3 Canada, House of Commons, Special Committee on Reconstruction and

NOTES TO PAGES 118–26   315

Re-establishment, *Minutes of Proceedings and Evidence*, no. 1, 9, and 23 February 1944.

4   LAC, MG 28-1298, vol. 75, *Report of the General Secretary*, Tenth Dominion Convention.
5   LAC, MG 28-1298, vol. 75, *Report of the Dominion President*, Tenth Dominion Convention.
6   *Debates*, 1944, 2102.
7   Ibid., 4256.
8   Ibid., 1638.
9   Ibid., 3916.
10 Ibid., 2117.
11 Ibid., 3914, 3941.
12 Ibid., 3980, 4382.
13 Ibid., 3877.
14 Ibid., 2112–13.
15 Ibid., 3914.
16 Ibid., 3917.
17 *Acts*, 1944, c.19, 62.
18 *Canada Gazette*, 21 October 1944, 4451.
19 Woods, *Rehabilitation (A Combined Operation)*, 477–94.
20 DVA, 65-14, vol. 3, Woods to Ronson, 7 July 1944.
21 Ibid.
22 DVA, 65-13, Woods to Weir, 25 July 1944.
23 Ibid.
24 DVA, 65-13, Kilpatrick to Woods, 24 July 1944.
25 DVA, 65-13, Woods to Kilpatrick, 27 July 1944.
26 LAC, MG 27 III B5, vol. 65, file 527-154, "Re: War Service Gratuity," 8 September 1943.
27 *Debates*, 1944, 4.
28 LAC, MG 27 III B5, vol. 65, file 527-154, Woods to Minister, 23 February 1944.
29 LAC, MG 27 III B5, vol. 65, file 527-154, Woods to Minister, 21 March 1944.
30 DVA, box 247m 65-24, Glass to Goldstone, 15 January 1944.
31 Slater (with two chapters by R.B. Bryce), *War Finance and Reconstruction: The Role of Canada's Department of Finance 1939–1946*, 212–15.
32 DVA, W5810-03-00, "War Service Gratuities and Rehabilitation Grants," 17 July 1944. Slater (*War Finance*, 214) attributes the 17 July memorandum to Deputy Minister of Finance W.C. Clark, but in his unpublished endnotes (copy supplied by Robert Wardhaugh) he writes that the memo was "almost certainly by W.C. Clark." My source for attributing the memorandum to Mackintosh is another memorandum, dated 8 August 1944, by E.B. Armstrong in RG 19, vol. 303, file 101-53-113 (the Finance file on war service gratuities). "I am inclined," Armstrong wrote, "to the view that the principles outlined in Dr. Mac[k]intosh's memorandum offer the best solution."
33 LAC, MG 27 III B5, vol. 65, file 527-154, Woods to Minister, 26 July 1944.

34 LAC, R10383-0-6-E, diary, 10 August 1944, 760. Online at http://www.collectionscanada.gc.ca/databases/king/001059-119.02-e.php?&page_id_nbr=26581&interval=20&&PHPSESSID=38h04ql6bs13b9qs906sk8lgr6.
35 *Debates*, 1944, 6199-200.
36 DVA, VLA, V-11-1, vol. 1, Wiiliamson to Crerar, 11 April and 12 May 1944; Mackenzie to Murchison, 5 September 1945.
37 *Debates*, 1944, 6225.
38 *Acts*, 1944, c. 51, 460.
39 *Debates*, 1944, 6278-308, 6311-29.
40 *Acts*, 1944, c.49, 457-63.
41 *Debates*, 1944, 6308.
42 Ibid., 6287.
43 Ibid., 6308.
44 Ibid., 6314.
45 LAC, MG 27 III B5, vol. 65, file 527-154, Herwig to Ralston, 21 August 1944.
46 LAC, MG 27 III B5, vol. 65, file 527-154(2), Williamson to Mackenzie, 7 April 1945.
47 LAC, MG 26-J, diary, 10 August 1944, 760. Online at http://www.collections-canada.gc.ca/databases/king/001059-119.02-e.php?&page_id_nbr=26576&interval=20&&&PHPSESSID=lugqbveq6o1em1rt9hv8caaov6.
48 Ibid., 9 August 1944, 758.
49 *Report of the Work of the Department of Veterans Affairs*, 1944-45 (hereafter DVA report, 1944-45 [etc.])
50 Woods, *Rehabilitation*, 43.
51 LAC, MG 27 III B5, vol. 65, file 527-154(2), England to Woods ("Re-establishment Credits, Part II, The War Service Grants Act, 1944"), 8 February 1945.
52 Ibid.
53 For his career, see his military service record file at LAC; *Canadian Who's Who*, 1948, 788; *New York Times*, 23 July 1973, 34; and *Toronto Star*, 23 July 1973, 58.
54 DVA report, 1944-45, 28-9.
55 Ibid., 28; *Debates*, 1944, 6329.
56 Reprinted in Neary and Granatstein, eds., *The Veterans Charter and Post–World War II Canada*, 246-90.
57 *Acts*, 1944, c. 49 ("An Act to Provide for the Insurance of Veterans by the Dominion of Canada"), 443-51. This act, cited as the Veterans Insurance Act, received assent on 15 August 1944.
58 DVA report, 1944-45, 28-9.
59 Ibid., 129.
60 Ibid., 13.
61 Ibid.
62 Tremblay, "Going Back to Main Street: The Development and Impact of

Casualty Rehabilitation for Veterans with Disabilities, 1945–1948," in *The Veterans Charter and Post-World War II Canada*, ed. Neary and Granatstein, 162.
63 Ibid., 163.
64 Ibid., 162.
65 DVA report, 1944–45, 12.
66 Ibid.
67 This account draws on my paper (with Shaun Brown), "The Veterans Charter and Canadian Women Veterans of World War II," in *The Good Fight: Canadians and World War II*, ed. Granatstein and Neary, 387–415.
68 Veterans Affairs Canada, Canadian Pension Commission, list 8167, box 80, Sub-Committee on the Special Problems of Discharged Women, minutes of the meeting of 23 June 1942; and Interim Report of the Sub-Committee on the Special Problems of Discharged Women, 2–3.
69 The account of her career that follows is based on LAC, Olive Ruth Russell fonds, MG 31 K13, vol. 1, file 1, "Dr. Olive Ruth Russell Occupies Important Post," *Evening Citizen*, Ottawa, 15 August 1946; vol. 1, file 4, T.J. Rutherford letter, "To Whom It May Concern," 30 April 1947; vol. 2, file 14, "Dr. Russell – Rehabilitation," draft article by Florence E. Whyard intended for *Saturday Night*; and Susan Ruth Swallow, "Olive Ruth Russell: A 20th Century Canadian Progressive," MA thesis, University of Western Ontario, 1996. For another account of her career with DVA, see Pierson and Cohen, "Educating Women for Work: Government Training Programs for Women before, during, and after World War II," in *Modern Canada 1930-1980s*, ed. Cross and Kealey, 208–43.
70 LAC, MG 31 K13, vol. 2, file 15, Russell to Whyard, 19 June 1946.
71 LAC, MG 31 K13, vol. 2, file 15, Russell to Coffey, 24 July 1945.
72 LAC, MG 31 K13, vol. 1, file 11, "Women To-morrow."
73 LAC, MG 31 K13, vol. 1, file 11, "Proposed Film, Project and Training in Homemaking and Family Living," 1. The report is attached to Russell to Burns, 25 September 1945.
74 LAC, MG 31 K13, vol. 2, file 14, "Rehabilitation of Women of the Armed Forces."
75 For an account of Hardy's life, see *Ottawa Citizen*, 21 June 1963, 11.
76 *Maclean's*, 15 January 1945, "Dames at Desks," 10.
77 The account that follows draws on my "Canadian Universities and Canadian Veterans of World War II," in *The Veterans Charter and Post-World War II Canada*, ed. Neary and Granatstein, 110–48.
78 DVA, 66-27-3, NCCU, Committee on Post-War Problems, minutes of meeting of 3-5 January 1944.
79 DVA, 66-27-3, Fennell to Jamieson, 24 May 1944; Thomsen to Jamieson, 8 June 1945.
80 NCCU, *Report of the National Conference of Canadian Universities on Post-War Problems*, 1.
81 Ibid.,, 7.

82 Ibid., 29.
83 Ibid., 32.
84 Ibid., 30.
85 Ibid., 36.
86 DVA, 66-38-2, vol. 1.
87 Ibid.
88 Ibid.
89 There is a copy in DVA, 66-38-2, vol. 1.
90 DVA, 66-38-2, vol. 1.
91 Ibid.
92 DVA, 66-38-2, vol. 1, Jamieson to James, 10 May 1945.
93 DVA, 66-38-2, vol. 1.
94 DVA, 66-38-2-1, Minutes of the Advisory Committee on University Training for Veterans, 28 May 1945, 1.
95 DVA, 66-38-2, vol. 1, Woods to Clark, 23 May 1945.
96 The statistics in this paragraph are taken from DVA report, 1944–45, 47–8, 50–1.
97 LAC, MG27 III B5, vol. 60, 527-61(3), Murchison speech, 13 December 1944.
98 LAC, MG 27 III B5, vol. 60, 527-61(4), "Veterans' Land Act Administrative Policy-1945," 2 January 1945.
99 LAC, MG 27 III B5, vol. 60, 527-61(4), "Staff Directive re Veterans' Land Act," 2 January 1945.
100 LAC, MG 27 III B5, vol. 60, 527-61(3), MacDonell to Mackenzie, 8 November 1944.
101 LAC, MG 27 III B5, vol. 60, 527-61(3), Mackenzie to MacDonell, 8 December 1944.
102 LAC, MG 27 III B5, vol. 60, 527-61(3A), Purnell memorandum, 20 February 1945.
103 *Acts*, 1942, c. 33, 172–3.
104 LAC, MG 27 III B5, vol. 60, 527-61(3A), Laidlaw to Crerar, 27 November 1944.
105 Ibid.
106 LAC, MG 27 III B5, vol. 60, 527-61(3A), Mackenzie to Laidlaw, 4 December 1944.
107 LAC, MG 27 III B5, vol. 60, 527-61(3A), Purnell to Mackenzie, 25 January 1945.
108 LAC, MG 27 III B5, vol. 60, 527-61(3A), Murchison to Mackenzie, 6 March 1945.
109 LAC, MG 27 III B5, vol. 60, 527-61(3A), Roebuck to Senior, 2 January 1945; Williamson to Mackenzie, 24 January 1945; Murchison to Mackenzie, 6 March 1945.
110 DVA, 5401-01-1, vol. 2, Wartime Information Board, "Housing and Community Planning," 20 June 1944.
111 DVA, 5401-01-1, vol. 2, "Address at Montreal City Improvement League Luncheon on May 3rd, 1944."

112 DVA, 5401-01-1, vol. 2, Woods to Nicholls, 27 March 1944.
113 LAC, MG 27 III B5, vol. 56, 527-10(10), Woods to Minister, 17 April 1944.
114 DVA, 5401-01-1, vol. 2, Sub-Committee on Housing, minutes, 18 April 1944.
115 *Debates*, 1944, 5638–9, 6013.
116 DVA, 5401-01-1, vol. 2, Woods to minister, 13 July 1944.
117 DVA, 5401-01-1, vol. 2, Sub-Committee on Housing, minutes, 3 July 1944.
118 DVA, 5401-01-1, vol. 2, Senior memorandum, 17 July 1944.
119 Ibid.
120 Ibid.
121 DVA, 5401-01-1, vol. 2, Woods to Minister, 2 August 1944.
122 There is a copy of the draft in DVA, 5401-01-1, vol. 2.
123 Canada, House of Commons, Special Committee on Reconstruction and Re-establishment, *Minutes and Proceedings of Evidence*, no. 15, second report, 29 July 1944, 480.
124 DVA, 5401-01-1, vol. 2, Woods to Piggott, 5 July 1944, and Piggott to Woods, 7 July 1944. For the history of this organization, see Wade, *Wartime Housing Limited, 1941–1947: An Overview and Evaluation of Canada's First National Housing Corporation*.
125 *Acts*, 1944, c. 46 ("An Act to Promote the Construction of New Houses, the Repair and Modernization of Existing Houses, the Improvement of Housing and Living Conditions, and the Expansion of Employment in the Postwar Period"), 390–422.
126 DVA, 5401-01-1, vol. 2, Senior to Woods, 25 July 1944.
127 The text is in DVA, 32-3-3.
128 The information in this paragraph comes from *Soldier Settlement: An Explanation of Concessions and Policy*.
129 Ibid., 4.
130 Ibid., 7.
131 There is a copy of the submission in DVA, 65-10-5, vol. 5.
132 DVA, VLA, V-17-1, vol. 2, Standing Committee file, 1964.
133 LAC, RG 117, microfilm C-9386, file 8788, Inouye to Custodian's Office, Vancouver, 27 January 1944.
134 There is a copy of his letter in file 8788.
135 LAC, RG 38, vol. 404, file 12, Murchison to Inouye, 7 October 1944. Inouye's letter to Murchison, dated 29 September 1944, is also in this file.
136 LAC, RG 117, microfilm C-9386, file 8788, Shears to Inouye, 18 October 1944. For Inouye's $14,000 estimate, see ibid., Shears to McPherson, 18 October 1944.
137 Quoted in *Montreal Standard*, "Man of the Week," 4 November 1944 (copy in DVA, 32-3-2, vol. 2).
138 DVA, 32-3-3, Woods to Minister, 8 September 1944.

CHAPTER SIX

1 Granatstein and Neary, eds., *The Good Fight*, 334–6.
2 Ritchie, *The Siren Years*, 207.

3 In February 1946, Captain F.W. Park of the Wartime Information Board reported that the colloquial French equivalent of "Back to Civvy Street" was "Dans le Civil." Subsequently, consideration was given within the government to promoting the usages "Rue de la Paix" and "Chez les Pékins." See DVA, 65-10-3, vol. 1, minutes, Demobilization and Rehabilitation Information Committee, 28 February and 7 March 1945. For the history of demobilization, see Oliver, "Canadian Military Demobilization in World War II," *The Good Fight*, ed. Granatstein and Neary, 367–86.
4 Woods, *Rehabilitation (A Combined Operation)*, 462.
5 This account of the discharge procedure is based on the information given in the third edition (1 April 1946) of *Back to Civil Life*. See Neary and Granatstein, eds., *The Veterans Charter and Post-World War II Canada*, 253–4.
6 Woods, *Rehabilitation (A Combined Operation)*, 43.
7 Ibid., 42.
8 DVA, 65-10-5, vol. 1, Cabinet Committee on Demobilization and Re-establishment, minutes of meeting of 24 October 1945.
9 DVA, 65-10-5, vol. 1, B.F. Wood, "Memorandum on Status of Committees Related to Cabinet Committee on Demobilization and Re-establishment," 20 October 1945.
10 Woods, *Rehabilitation (A Combined Operation)*, 19-20.
11 Canada, House of Commons, Special Committee on Veterans Affairs, *Minutes of Proceedings and Evidence*, no. 1, 12 October 1945, 44–5.
12 DVA, 65-10-5, vol. 1, Cabinet Committee on Demobilization and Re-establishment, minutes of meeting of 24 October 1945.
13 Ibid.
14 Special Committee on Veterans Affairs, *Minutes of Proceedings and Evidence*, no. 1, 11 October 1945, 4–35, and 12 October 1945, 37–60.
15 *Debates*, 1945, 8.
16 DVA, W5810-03-00, "War Service Gratuities and Rehabilitation Grants."
17 The full title was "An Act to Provide Federal Government Aid for the Readjustment in Civilian Life of Returning World War II Veterans" (*United States Statutes at Large*, 58 Stat. 284).
18 Willenz, *Women Veterans: America's Forgotten Heroines*, 168–79.
19 House of Commons, *Journal*, 4 December 1945, 376–84. For the progress of the Special Committee, see *Debates*, 1945, 467, 826–27, 2180, 2487, 2952, 3406.
20 *Debates*, 1945, 3290–302. A resolution preliminary to the introduction of the bill had been moved by Mackenzie on 7 December 1945 (see *Debates*, 1945, 3135, 3290).
21 *Debates*, 1945, 3291.
22 Ibid.
23 Ibid.
24 *Debates*, 1945, 3292.
25 Ibid., 3294.

26 Ibid.
27 *Debates*, 1945, 3553; *Acts*, 1945, c.35, 225-34.
28 Special Committee on Veterans Affairs, 1946, *Minutes of Proceedings and Evidence*, no. 1, 26 March 1946, 22–64.
29 Ibid., 6.
30 *Debates*, 1946, 4056 (quotation) and 255, 585, 1848, 1876, 2319, 2590, 2798, 3037, 3155, 3260, 3391, 3485, 3604, 3722, 3785, 3944 (tabling of reports).
31 Ibid., 4054-5.
32 *Acts*, 1946, c.62 (401–16), c.63 (417–27), c.70 (477–80), c.71 (481–4), c.72 (485), and c.74 (495–8).
33 Ibid., c.69 (469–75) and c.75 (499–509).
34 *Debates*, 1946, 4057.
35 *The Veterans Charter: Acts of the Canadian Parliament to Assist Canadian Veterans*, 297; *Acts*, 1946, c.36 (141–3), c.52 (243–5), c.64 (429-30), and c.66 (437–8).
36 *The Veterans Charter*, 297–98; *Acts*, 1946. c.43 (187-203).
37 *Acts*, 1946, c.58, 343–58.
38 *Acts*, 1946, c.34, 137–8.
39 DVA *Report of the Work of the Department of Veterans Affairs* (DVA report), 1945–46, 43; DVA, 32-6, Reid to Asst. Director of Re-establishment Credits, 15 October 1945.
40 LAC, MG 27 III B5, vol. 56, 527-10(9), Woods memorandum re discussion with General Frank T. Hines and Major Clark, 1 November 1943.
41 Ibid.
42 There is a copy in DVA, 65-10-3, vol. 1.
43 The minutes of the committee are in DVA, 65-10-3, vol. 1. Dunton was later president of the CBC and president of Carleton University.
44 DVA, 65-10-3, vol. 1, "Rehabilitation: Civilian Interest and Knowledge."
45 England, *Living, Learning, Remembering*, 128.
46 A number of these were submitted by Mackenzie to the 1945 House of Commons Special Committee on Veterans Affairs (see *Minutes of Proceedings and Evidence*, 11 October 1945, 34-5, and 12 October 1945, 59–60).
47 DVA, 67-11, Counsellors' Training Course, no. 5.
48 LAC, MG 27 III B5, vol. 59, 527–51(3), "Report to the Rehabilitation Information Committee on CBC Re-establishment Programmes," 17 October 1945.
49 DVA report, 1945–46, 43; *Back to Civil Life*, 3rd edn., no. 18.
50 LAC, MG 27 III B5, vol. 64, 527-148, Report of Proceedings.
51 There are copies in LAC, MG 27 III B5, vol. 64, 527-148.
52 There is a copy of this pamphlet in DVA, 67-11.
53 DVA, 67-11.
54 *Back to Civil Life*, 3rd edn., no. 11.
55 Ibid., no. 13.
56 Ibid., no. 11.

57 There is a copy of the handbook in DVA, 65-45-MO.
58 DVA, 66-18, Woods memorandum, 31 January 1945.
59 DVA, 65-45-VA, Dowler to Russell, 29 April 1945.
60 DVA, 65-10-5, vol. 2, Burns to Woods, 31 January 1946, memorandum re "Accommodation – Rehabilitation Centres – Toronto, Winnipeg and Montreal."
61 *Globe and Mail*, 10 April 1945, 8.
62 Brokaw, *The Greatest Generation*.
63 Woods, *Rehabilitation (A Combined Operation)*, 136. See also *Report of the Department of Labour for the Fiscal Year Ending March 31, 1947*, 73.
64 DVA report, 1945–46, 20.
65 DVA report, 1946–47, 34.
66 DVA, 65-10-5, vol. 1, memorandum to the cabinet (Minister of National Defence), 5 November 1945.
67 DVA, 65-10-5, vol. 3, Woods memorandum to Chairman, Cabinet Committee on Demobilization and Re-establishment, 30 May 1946.
68 DVA report, 1946–47, 34.
69 DVA report, 1947–48, 26.
70 Woods, *Rehabilitation (A Combined Operation)*, 114, 117.
71 Ibid., 136.
72 Ibid., 117.
73 Ibid., 124.
74 Ibid., 119.
75 DVA report, 1952, 21.
76 Woods, *Rehabilitation (A Combined Operation)*, 127.
77 Ibid., 127.
78 Ibid.
79 Ibid., 129.
80 Ibid., 128.
81 Ibid., 180–1.
82 Ibid., 182.
83 Ibid.
84 Ibid., 183.
85 Ibid.
86 Stevenson, "National Selective Service and Employment and Seniority Rights for Veterans, 1943-1946," in *The Veterans Charter and Post-World War II Canada*, ed. Neary and Granatstein, 98.
87 Ibid., 96–7.
88 Ibid., 98–9.
89 Ibid., 99.
90 Ibid., 99; DVA, 65-12, vol. 1, Crawford memorandum to Woods, 21 April 1943.
91 Stevenson, "National Selective Service," 99–100; DVA, 65-12, vol. 1, Canadian Legion "Memorandum on the Employment of Veterans in Unionized Industry."

92 DVA, 65-12, vol. 1, Mosher to Herwig, 14 March 1944, and Bengough to Herwig, 31 May 1944.
93 Ibid., 100.
94 Ibid.
95 Ibid.
96 Ibid.
97 Ibid.; DVA, 65-12, vol. 1, MacNamara to Woods, 23 January 1946.
98 DVA, 65-12, vol. 1, minutes of meeting of Committee on Seniority and Priority Rights of Veterans, 22 January 1945.
99 Stevenson, "National Selective Service," 95; DVA, 65-12, vol. 2, "Model Contract Clause re Veterans Seniority" adopted by UAW District Council, 28–29 October 1944.
100 DVA, 65-12, vol. 1, "Report of the Sub-Committee re Seniority Rights for Veterans in Employment," 10 September 1945.
101 DVA, 65-12, vol. 1, Shoults memorandum to Advisory Committee on Rehabilitation and Re-establishment, 13 September 1945. For Mosher's reasoning, see minutes of meeting of Committee on Seniority and Priority Rights of Veterans, 22 January 1945.
102 Stevenson, "National Selective Service," 104.
103 DVA, 65-12, vol. 1, Maclean to MacNamara, 27 December 1945.
104 DVA, 65-12, vol. 1, MacNamara to Mackenzie, 23 January 1946.
105 There is a copy of the agreement in DVA, 65-12, vol. 1, enclosed in Harris to Burns, 15 March 1944.
106 *Globe and Mail*, 6 June 1946, 5.
107 Stevenson, "National Selective Service," 106.
108 DVA, 65-12, vol. 2, Stacey to Burns, 19 August 1946.
109 DVA, W5810-03, minutes, 14 August 1944.
110 DVA, W5810-03, Derby memorandum, 17 August 1944.
111 DVA, W5810-03, Barrow circular letter, 21 October 1944.
112 There is a copy in DVA, 53-5-7-1.
113 DVA, 53-5-7-1, "Re-establishment Credit Advisory Committee."
114 Ibid.
115 DVA, 53-5-7-1, Woods circular letter.
116 There is a copy of the form in DVA, 67-7.
117 This document is in DVA, 53-5-7-1.
118 There is a copy in DVA, 67-13.
119 DVA, W5810-03-00, England memorandum, 8 February 1945.
120 The other chairmen were "A" District (Montreal), E.P. Fitzgerald; "B" District (Charlottetown), A.W. Hyndman; "C" District (Ottawa), Colonel C.M. Edwards; "D" District (Toronto), H.L. Rous; "E" District (Quebec City), Arthur Lagueux; "F" District (London), Gordon Thompson; "G" District (Winnipeg), C.A. Clendening; "H" District (Saskatoon), L.C. Brown; "I" District (Calgary), S.J. Patterson; "I" District "(Edmonton), Colonel H.A. Dyde; "J" District (Victoria), A.J. Watson; "K" District (Saint John), F.M. Myles; and "L" District (Hamilton), H.S. Thurstans.

121 See DVA, 32-6, Reid to Woods, 18 December 1944.
122 Vol. 58, no. 6, 55.
123 There is a copy in DVA, 32-6.
124 DVA, 32-6.
125 Copy in DVA, 32-6.
126 DVA, 67-15, Sutton to Hogan, 20 March 1945.
127 *Winnipeg Tribune*, 20 April 1945, "Racketeers Prey on Veterans, Says Local Business Bureau" (copy in DVA, 67-15).
128 *Winnipeg Tribune*, 21 April 1945, "Veterans Watch Your Wallets" (copy in DVA, 67-15).
129 DVA, 67-15, Haskell to Bryers, 16 July 1945; "Royal Chinchilla"; and Herbert to Director General of Rehabilitation, 3 July 1945.
130 DVA, 67-15, attachment to Herbert to Director General of Rehabilitation, 18 July 1945.
131 DVA, 32-6, attachment to District Supervisor (Calgary) to Hogan, 30 July 1945.
132 DVA, 67-15, Greene to Director General of Rehabilitation, 18 August 1945.
133 "3 More Arraigned on Racket Counts," Montreal *Gazette*, 21 August 1945 (copy in DVA, 67-15).
134 DVA, 67-15, attachment to Fenton to Assistant Deputy Minister, 18 June 1947.
135 Ibid.
136 Woods, *Rehabilitation (A Combined Operation)*, 64, 69.
137 Ibid., 69.
138 Ibid., 70–1.
139 See DVA, 67-16, Barrow circular re "Compensating Adjustment under Section 10 of The War Service Grants Act, 1944, in relation to The Veterans' Land Act, 1942"; 67-20-1, PC4211, 17 October 1947; 67-20, PC625, 17 February 1948; 53-5-7, "Re-establishment Credit Payments Refunded to Qualify for V.L.A. Benefits."
140 Calculated using total budgetary expenditure figures given in Leacy, ed., *Historical Statistics of Canada*.
141 See information in DVA, 65-45-MO.
142 Woods, *Rehabilitation (A Combined Operation)*, 95–7. Section 13 provided as follows: "In determining the amount of an allowance to be paid to a veteran under this Act, the Minister may take into account any prospective wages, salary, pension or other income of the veteran and his dependents, if any, for the period with respect to which the allowance is or may be paid" (*Acts*, 1945, c.35, 231).
143 Woods, *Rehabilitation (A Combined Operation)*, 92–3.
144 Ibid.
145 Ibid.
146 Ibid., 90–1.
147 *Report of the Department of Labour*, 1945–46, 6, 67.
148 Ibid., 68.

149 Ibid., 69.
150 Ibid.
151 Ibid.
152 Ibid.
153 Ibid., 71.
154 There is a copy of the announcement of the opening in DVA, 66-13-3 (see Crawford to District Administrators, 27 August 1948).
155 For the history of the commission, see the finding aid to its records on the LAC website.
156 20th Parliament, 1st Session, unpublished sessional papers, 117A; House of Commons, *Debates*, 1945, 1568.
157 *Debates*, 1946, 2874. The report is filed with sessional paper 117A.
158 Woods, *Rehabilitation (A Combined Operation)*, 107.
159 DVA, 66-38-2-2, vol. 1.
160 Urquhart and Buckley, eds., *Historical Statistics of Canada*, 601.
161 DVA, 66-38-2-1, Minutes of the Advisory Committee on University Training for Veterans (hereafter Minutes), 12 November 1946, 4, and "Summary of Enrolments of Veterans in Receipt of Allowances, as Furnished by D.V.A. District Offices as of November, 1946."
162 Minutes, 20 November 1948, appendix A, Superintendent's Report, 2.
163 Minutes, 6 February 1950, Superintendent's Report, 1. According to this same source, the equivalent United States figure was 40 per cent.
164 Minutes, 25 February 1946, Confidential Letter no. 154.
165 Minutes, 13 November 1945, 9.
166 Minutes, 6 February 1950, Superintendent's Report, 3.
167 Ibid.
168 Ibid.
169 Minutes, 9 February 1951, Superintendent's Report, 7.
170 Ibid., and Minutes, 6 February 1950, Superintendent's Report, 9.
171 Minutes, 25 February 1946, appendix I, "Data re Veterans in Receipt of University Training Allowances."
172 Minutes, 20 November 1948, Superintendent's Report, 2. See also Minutes, 6 February 1950, Superintendent's Report, 1.
173 Thompson, *The University of Saskatchewan: A Personal Memoir*, 133.
174 Ibid., 133-4.
175 Minutes, 25 February 1946, 5.
176 Minutes, 13 November 1945, 6.
177 Ibid.
178 There is a copy of PC7129 in DVA, 66-38-2, vol. 1.
179 DVA, 66-38-2, vol. 1, "Interim Report of Committee on University Requirements," 1.
180 Ibid., 2.
181 Ibid.
182 Ibid.
183 Ibid.

184 Ibid., appendix 2, "Notes on University Accommodation for Veterans," 1.
185 Ibid.
186 Ibid., 2. This college should not be confused with the later College d'enseignement général et professionnel of the same name (see Frost, *McGill University for the Advancement of Learning*, 2:240.)
187 DVA, 66-38-2, vol. 1, "Interim Report of Committee on University Requirements," appendix "Notes on University Accommodation for Veterans," 2.
188 There is a copy of PC7224 attached to Minutes, 25 February 1946.
189 Minutes, 19 November 1947, 3.
190 Ibid.
191 Ibid.
192 Minutes, 20 November 1948, appendix A, Superintendent's Report, 5.
193 Ibid.
194 Ibid.
195 Ibid.
196 Minutes, 12 November 1946, 6.
197 Minutes, 17 March 1947, appendix H.
198 Minutes, 6 February 1950, appendix, Superintendent's Report, 5.
199 Minutes, 20 November 1948, appendix A, Superintendent's Report, 5.
200 Minutes, 6 February 1950, appendix, Superintendent's Report, 5.
201 For the relevant section of PC4059, see Minutes, 17 March 1947, 2.
202 Minutes, 9 February 1951, Superintendent's Report, 1.
203 Ibid.
204 Minutes, 13 November 1945, 9.
205 Minutes, 12 November 1946, 3.
206 Ibid.
207 Minutes, 17 March 1947, 5–6, and 16 January 1948, 2.
208 Minutes, 12 November 1946, 3.
209 Minutes, 17 March 1947, 4.
210 Ibid., 5.
211 Minutes, 19 November 1947, 6.
212 Minutes, 20 November 1948, 2.
213 Ibid.
214 Minutes, 6 February 1950, 3. England was a Guggenheim Foundation Fellow in 1945.
215 Minutes, 17 March 1947, 3.
216 Ibid., 3.
217 Ibid., 4.
218 Ibid.
219 Minutes, 19 November 1947, 2.
220 Ibid.
221 Minutes, 6 February 1950, 2.
222 Ibid., 3.
223 Ibid.
224 Ibid.

225 Minutes, 20 November 1948, 6.
226 Ibid., 7.
227 Ibid.
228 Minutes, 12 November 1946, 3. See also appendix C, "Survey of Professionally Trained Persons."
229 Ibid.
230 Minutes, 17 March 1947, 30.
231 Ibid.
232 Minutes, 19 November 1947, 4.
233 DVA, 66-27-4, vol. 1, Jackson to Mackenzie, 9 December 1945.
234 DVA, 66-27-4, vol. 1, memorandum attached to Plommer to Woods, 7 December 1945. A.G. Plommer was president of the University of New Brunswick Veterans' Club.
235 DVA, 66-27-4, vol. 1, memorandum by Burns to Woods, 29 December 1945.
236 Ibid.
237 Ibid.
238 DVA, 66-27-4, vol. 1, "Report of the National Conference of Student Veterans Montreal Quebec December 27–29th 1945." The others named to the council were G.P. Lagenière, Université de Montréal; J. Testart, University of Western Ontario; G.E. King, Ontario Training and Re-establishment Institute, Toronto; N.E. Wright, University of Manitoba; W. Rorkem, University of Alberta; and A.E. Hart, Dalhousie University.
239 DVA, 66-27-4, vol. 1, "Brief to the Dominion Government Submitted by the National Conference of Student Veterans."
240 DVA, 66-27-4, vol. 1, memorandum by Riches to Rutherford, 30 November 1946.
241 DVA, 66-27-4, vol. 1, memorandum by Jamieson to Rutherford, 2 January 1947.
242 DVA, 66-27-4, vol. 1, "Report of National Conference of Student Veterans McGill University, Montreal December 27–29th, 1946," 1.
243 Beaufoy, ed., *A Report on the Second National Conference of Student Veterans*, 17. Beaufoy, of the Canadian Vocational Training Centre no. 8, Red Deer, Alberta, attended the 1946 conference. The report was printed at the School of Printing Trades, Red Deer. There is a copy in DVA, 66-27-4, vol. 1. See also, "Communist Pressure on Campus Charged," *Globe and Mail*, 13 December 1946.
244 DVA, 66-27-4, vol. 1, "Report of National Conference of Student Veterans McGill University, Montreal December 27–29th, 1946," 7.
245 In an introductory letter to "the final brief covering the sessions held in Montreal December 27th to 29th, 1946," Schierbeck wrote: "An alien philosophy knocks at our door. During the past quarter century it has had a hearing from the Canadian people and they want nothing of it; now it grows insistent and uses those cherished privileges which we believe to be the right of every law abiding Canadian to exercise, to attack us from within. The next twenty years will show whether we can unite in determination to

exclude this insidious venom and at the same time offer every Canadian those same material advantages which it holds out to attract the unwary. We can do this only if [we] unremittingly undertake to expose the disastrous consequences of dictatorship in the community where we work and live. That, we believe, is one way in which Student Veterans can in some measure repay Canada the debt they owe for what they have received" (enclosure in DVA, 66-27-4, vol. 1, Schierbeck to Jamieson, 17 March 1947).
246 DVA, 66-27-4, vol. 1, copy attached to memorandum by Jamieson, 10 March 1947.
247 Minutes, 17 March 1947, 6.
248 Minutes, 25 February 1946, 4.
249 For PC4060, see Minutes, 12 November 1946, appendix E.
250 Minutes, 12 November 1946, 3.
251 Minutes, 16 January 1948, 1–2.
252 Ibid., 3; Minutes, 20 November 1948, appendix A, Superintendent's Report, 1.
253 Woods, *Rehabilitation (A Combined Operation)*, 107.
254 Martin O'Malley, Good! By Judy," *Globe and Mail*, 6 December 1969, magazine, 4 (there is a copy in DVA).

CHAPTER SEVEN

1 LAC, MG 31 K31, vol. 2, file 14, Salter to Russell, 28 November 1944.
2 There is a copy of the 15 September 1945 "Manual of Instructions Women's Rehabilitation" in DVA, 65-45, vol. 1.
3 DVA, 65-45, vol. 1, "Proceedings Training Conferences on Women's Rehabilitation," 1.
4 Ibid., 47.
5 Ibid.
6 Ibid., 48.
7 Ibid.
8 Ibid., 49.
9 Ibid.
10 Ibid.
11 Ibid.
12 Ibid.
13 Ibid., 50.
14 A number of her articles were collected in "Rehabilitation of Women Veterans in Canada," Ottawa, August 1946. There is a copy in LAC, MG 31 K13, vol. 1, file 9.
15 There is a transcript of this interview in ibid., vol. 1, file 1.
16 Ibid.
17 Olive Ruth Russell, "Women Veterans and Their Rehabilitation," *Echoes*, summer 1946, 7.
18 Hodgetts et al., *The Biography of an Institution: The Civil Service of Canada, 1908–1967*, 487.

19 LAC, MG 31 K13, vol. 2, file 14, Burns to Woods, 5 December 1945.
20 See DVA, 65-45-W1, memorandum "Re: Report of Visit of Superintendent of Women's Rehabilitation to Vancouver District, 11–13 February 1947."
21 See DVA, 65-45-W1, Russell to Rumball, 3 April 1946; DVA, 65-45-CA, Salter to Sutton, 23 April 1946.
22 DVA, 65-45, vol. 2, Rutherford to Woods, 4 January 1947, and Rehabilitation Branch Instruction, 15 January 1947.
23 DVA, 65-45, vol. 2, Hunt to Rutherford, 26 August 1947.
24 DVA, 65-45, vol. 2, "Re: Final Report of Supt. of Women's Rehabilitation," Salter to Burns, 12 July 1946.
25 DVA, 65-45, vol. 2, "Re: Report of Superintendent of Women's Rehabilitation – August, 1946 to November, 1947," Hunt to Wright, 25 November 1947.
26 DVA, 65-45, vol. 2,, "Women's Rehabilitation as of December 31, 1948," Rider to Mann, 31 January 1949.
27 DVA, 65-45, vol. 2, Russell to Woods, 6 November 1947.
28 DVA, 65-45, vol. 2, Woods to Minister, 27 July 1946, and Woods to Russell, 30 November 1946.
29 LAC, MG 31 K13, vol. 1, file 4, Russell to MacNamara, 23 July 1947.
30 See DVA, 65-45, vol. 2, "Re: Final Report of Supt. of Women's Rehabilitation," Salter to Burns, 12 July 1946; Hunt to Rutherford, 23 December 1946; Russell to Elliott, 14 April 1947; "Re: Report of Superintendent of Women's Rehabilitation – August, 1946 to November, 1947," Hunt to Wright, 25 November 1947.
31 Calculated from Woods, *Rehabilitation (A Combined Operation)*, appendix A, 461.
32 LAC, MG 27 III B5, vol. 53, Mackenzie to McNaughton, 30 January 1945.
33 For Warner's career, see LAC, MG 27 III B5, vol. 53, Warner to Woods, 6 February 1945.
34 LAC, MG 27 III B5, vol. 53, "Re: Confidential Report by Brigadier W.P. Warner," 26 February 1945.
35 DVA, 5000-00, vol. 2, Warner to Cutler, 20 October 1945.
36 Ibid.
37 LAC, MG 27 III B5, vol. 53, Woods to Minister, 19 April 1945; DVA, 5097-01, vol. 1, Warner to District Administrators, 17 August 1945. For a chronology of events see, DVA, 5097-01, vol. 1, Warner memorandum, 23 May 1946.
38 LAC, MG 27 III B5, vol. 53, News Release no. 139, 18 October 1945.
39 LAC, MG 27 III B5, vol. 53, Mackenzie to Woods, 26 September 1945.
40 LAC, MG 27 III B5, vol. 53, Mackenzie to Gibson, 14 January 1946.
41 LAC, MG 27 III B5, vol. 53, Warner to McClung, 1 August 1946.
42 There is a copy of the order in DVA, 1-500, vol. 2. See also in the same file "Departmental Hospitals and Institutions," 5 December 1946.
43 DVA, 8-15, vol. 1, Warner to Deputy Minister, 9 December 1946.
44 DVA, 8-15, vol. 1, Graham to Warner, 11 August 1947.
45 DVA, 5097-01, vol. 1, Warner to District Administrators, 17 August 1945.

46 DVA, 5097-01, vol. 1, Woods to Routley, 2 January 1946; Woods to Secretary, Treasury Board, 22 February 1945.
47 There is a copy of the order in DVA, 5097-01, vol. 1. See also in this source Warner to Woods, 21 May 1946, and Kelly to Warner, 14 August 1946.
48 DVA, 5097-01, vol. 2, Woods circular letter, 28 November 1946.
49 Canada, House of Commons, Special Committee on Veterans Affairs, 1945, *Minutes of Proceedings and Evidence*, no. 1, 12 October 1945, 42.
50 DVA, 5000-00, vol. 5, "Summary of Treatment Classification under Treatment Regulations," 18 May 1948.
51 LAC, MG 27 III B5, vol. 53, Padwick to Mackenzie, 25 March 1947.
52 LAC, MG 27 III B5, vol. 53, Mackenzie to Padwick, 14 April 1947.
53 LAC, MG 27 III B5, vol. 53, Woods memorandum, "Re: 'Means Test' – for Hospitalization," 10 June 1947.
54 LAC, MG 27 III B5, vol. 53, Harron to Mackenzie, 18 October 1947.
55 For accounts of his life, see *Canadian Parliamentary Guide*, 1964–71, and *Globe and Mail*, 7 January 1981, 11.
56 DVA, 5401-01, script for address delivered during intermission of Metropolitan Opera broadcast, 24 February 1945.
57 DVA, 5401-01, "Precis of Speech on the Work of the Casualty Section," 24 January 1945.
58 DVA *Report of the Work of the Department of Veterans Affairs* (DVA report), 1947, 28.
59 There is a copy in DVA, 65-10-8, vol. 1.
60 There is a copy of the conference proceedings in DVA, 65-10-8, vol. 3.
61 There is a copy in DVA, 65-10-8, vol. 9.
62 For Counsell's career, see Tremblay, "Lieutenant John Counsell and the Development of Medical Rehabilitation and Disability Policy in Canada," in *Disabled Veterans in History*, ed. David A. Gerber, , 322-46.
63 For the history of this facility, see Reaume, *Lyndhurst: Canada's First Rehabilitation Centre for People with Spinal Cord Injuries, 1945–1998*.
64 Tremblay, "The Canadian Revolution in the Management of Spinal Cord Injury," 141. For detailed accounts of DVA's treatment and rehabilitation services in the immediate postwar period, see also her "Going Back to Main Street" and "The Right to the Best Medical Care: Dr. W.P. Warner and the Canadian Department of Veterans Affairs, 1945–1955." Mary Tremblay died in 2009, and there is a collection of her papers at McMaster University, Hamilton, Ontario.
65 DVA report, 1947, 29.
66 Ibid.
67 LAC, MG 28-I298, vol.10, Legion Circular no. 44/25.
68 LAC, MG 28-I298, vol. 75, Report of the General Secretary, 1946, 17; 1948, 15.
69 LAC, MG 28-I298, vol.75, Report of the Dominion President, 1946.
70 Hale, *Branching Out: The Story of the Royal Canadian Legion*, 90.
71 Ibid., 95.

NOTES TO PAGES 241–8 331

72 Ibid., 99.
73 Ibid., 97.
74 For the membership, see DVA, 5000-00, vol. 4, submission to Special Committee on Veterans Affairs, 1948.
75 LAC, MG 28-I298, vol. 10, Walker to King, 18 July 1945.
76 There is a copy of his address in DVA, VLA, V-20-1, vol. 1.
77 DVA, 5401-01-1, vol. 3, enclosure in Herwig to Senior, 22 October 1945. For the history of the Veterans' Land Act, see DVA, VLA, V-39-27-5, "General Summary of the History and Operation of The Veterans' Land Act, 1942," enclosed in McCracken to Deputy Minister, 17 August 1951; DVA, VLA, V-39-27-1, "History of VLA," Pawley to District Superintendents, 3 December 1964; and Harris and Shulist, "Canada's Reluctant Housing Program: The Veterans' Land Act, 1942–75."
78 DVA, 65-25-1, vol. 1, Murchison to Mackenzie, 5 March 1945.
79 DVA, 65-25-1, vol. 1, PC3409; vol. 2, minutes of first meeting, Interdepartmental Housing Committee; DVA, VLA, V-39-27-5, "General Summary of the History and Operation of The Veterans' Land Act, 1942," enclosed in McCracken to Deputy Minister, 17 August 1951.
80 DVA, 65-15-1, vol. 1, Murchison to Baldwin, 14 May 1945.
81 For campaign details, see the records in DVA, 5401-01-1, vol. 3.
82 DVA, 5401-01-1, vol. 3, attachment to Reid memorandum to Woods, 23 November 1945.
83 DVA, 5401-01-1, vol. 3, Murchison to Woods, 5 November 1945.
84 DVA, 65-10-5, vol. 2, minutes, Cabinet Committee on Demobilization and Re-establishment, 9 November 1945.
85 Ibid., 12 November 1945.
86 There are copies of the relevant orders in council, PC7499 and PC7502, in DVA, 65-25-1, vol. 1.
87 For this episode, see Wade, *Houses for All: The Struggle for Social Housing in Vancouver, 1919–50*, 143–7.
88 *Debates*, 29 April 1946, 985.
89 *Debates*, 22 July 1946, 3672–3.
90 Ibid., 3673.
91 For the text, see DVA, VLA, V-43-11, vol. 1, Circular Letter no. 103-1946.
92 LAC, MG 28-I298, vol. 10, file 10-7, Legion Circular no. 46/2/5, 10 September 1946. For the Ottawa occupation, see *Globe and Mail*, 3 September 1946, 3.
93 DVA, 5401-01-1, vol. 3, Legion brief attached to Reid to Burns, 11 October 1946.
94 DVA, 5401-01-1, vol. 3, Reid to Burns, 11 October 1946.
95 DVA, VLA, V-43-11, vol. 1, statement by Mackenzie, 17 October 1946.
96 DVA, VLA, V-39-27-5, "General Summary of the History and Operation of The Veterans' Land Act, 1942," enclosed in McCracken to Deputy Minister, 17 August 1951.
97 LAC, MG 28-I298, vol. 10, file 10-9, Woods to Minister, 18 March 1947.

98 DVA, VLA, V-43-1, vol. 1, Murchison to Scott, 19 August 1947.
99 See http://www.owensoundsuntimes.com/ArticleDisplay.aspx?archive=true&e=770928.
100 Harris and Shulist, "Canada's Reluctant Housing Program," 276.
101 *Acts*, 1954, c.66, 761-78.
102 DVA report, 1960, 48.
103 DVA, VLA, V-39-27, vol. 6, Chaput to Brice, 5 November 1974.
104 LAC, RG 117, microfilm C-9399, file 10396, Anderson to Shears, 16 August 1945; Anderson to Inouye, 9 January 1946.
105 LAC, RG 117, "Report on Evacuated Japanese Property," 13 July 1942; microfilm C-9386, file 8788, Iverson to Inouye, 1 October 1945.
106 LAC, RG 117, microfilm C-9386, file 8788, Iverson to Inouye, 1 October 1945.
107 LAC, RG 117, microfilm C-9386, file 8788, Iverson to Robinson, 1 October 1945.
108 LAC, RG 117, microfilm C-9386, file 8788, Robinson to Iverson, 5 October 1945.
109 LAC, RG 117, microfilm C-9386, file 8788, Inouye to Iverson, 15 October 1945.
110 Ibid., 28 October 1945.
111 LAC, RG 117, microfilm C-9386, file 8788, Iverson to Robinson, 19 October 1945.
112 Japanese Canadian National Museum (hereafter JCNM), Burnaby, British Columbia, Zennosuke Inouye Papers (hereafter ZIP), Inouye to Pickersgill, 28 November 1945.
113 JCNM, ZIP, unsigned letter by Inouye.
114 JCNM, ZIP, Inouye to Foster, 5 June 1947.
115 JCNM, ZIP, Foster to Inouye, 19 June 1947.
116 LAC, MG 28-I298, vol. 63, file 50, Backhus to LaFlèche, 26 October and 17 December 1926.
117 LAC, MG 28-I298, vol. 63, file 50, McKee to Thomas, 19 March 1942.
118 Ibid.
119 LAC, MG 28-I298, vol. 63, file 50, Aitken to Sutton, 21 March 1946.
120 Ibid.
121 Ibid.
122 JCNM, ZIP, McIntosh to Inouye, 8 July 1947.
123 JCNM, ZIP, Murchison to Anderson, 29 July 1947, enclosed in Anderson to McIntosh, 6 August 1947. The copy of Murchison's letter is incomplete.
124 JCNM, ZIP, quoted in Murchison to Anderson, 29 July 1947.
125 Reid had been an anti-Japanese crusader since he was first elected to Parliament in 1930. His chief concern was fisheries.
126 JCNM, ZIP, Inouye to Reid, 4 December 1947.
127 JCNM, ZIP, Reid to Inouye, 10 December 1947.
128 JCNM, ZIP, Reid to Morrow, 9 December 1947.
129 DVA, 48, Mackenzie memorandum, 20 May 1948.

130 LAC, RG 38, vol. 404, file 12, memorandum to the Minister, 23 May 1946. PC 5973 of 14 September 1945, amended PC 946 of 5 February 1943, and on 17 April 1946 was explained by W.G. Gunn as follows: "This Order in Council in general prohibits the acquisition or holding of land or growing crops in Canada by persons of the Japanese race. It provides, however, that the Minister of Labour may grant a license to persons of the Japanese race to acquire or hold land if he deems it in the public interest." By Order no. 1 (New Series), Gunn further noted, the Minister of Labour required "all persons of the Japanese race to obtain a travel permit from the Royal Canadian Mounted Police for certain purposes," but the Minister had also issued a directive "exempting a person of the Japanese race who has served as a member of the naval, military or air forces of His Majesty in the present war or who served in a similar capacity in the 1914–18 war" from the operation of Order no. 1. This exemption also extended "to the wife and dependent children under 16 years of age of each such person." This was "the first relaxation of regulations in favour of a veteran of Japanese origin" (DVA, 48, Gunn to Woods, 17 April 1946).
131 LAC, RG 38, vol. 404, file 12, Murchison to MacNamara, 6 June 1946.
132 LAC, RG 38, vol. 404, file 12, MacNamara to Murchison, 14 June 1946.
133 LAC, RG 38, vol. 404, file 12, memorandum from Private Secretary, 25 June 1946.
134 LAC, RG 38, vol. 404, file 12, Murchison to MacNamara, 30 July 1946.
135 The terms of reference of the royal commission were specified in PC 1819 of 18 July 1947, as amended by PC 3737 of 17 September 1947 and PC 242 of 22 January 1948. The terms of reference as amended are given in the report that Bird submitted on 6 April 1950 (tabled as House of Commons, Sessional Paper 185A, 13 June 1950, 21st Parliament, 2nd Session). The investigation began in Vancouver on 3 December 1947 and was completed on 3 March 1950; 1,434 claims were filed with the commission. The report had two appendices, explained as follows: "Appendix I is a 32 page irregular shaped (13" by 18") tabulation in limp cover of the names of claimants, location of real property (urban, rural, etc.,), kinds of personal property (motor vehicles, boats and gear, nets and gear and other miscellaneous chattels) together with amounts under each head, recommended for payment. Appendix II is a bound volume consisting of 299 foolscap pages between stiff covers. The Commissioners found, in the early stages of the work, that many of the claims could be more conveniently dealt with if placed in categories. Counsel for the claimants and the Crown agreed and proceeded to do so. In this Appendix the Commissioner has given his reasons for judgment, based on decisions of the courts in those 'special cases' which did not fall within any of the 7 categories."
136 For Mackenzie's exit from cabinet, see LAC, MG 26-J, diary, 14 January 1948, 63–4. Online at http://www.collectionscanada.gc.ca/databases/king/001059-119.02-e.php?&page_id_nbr=30589&interval=20&&&&&&&&&&&&&&&&&&&&&&&PHPSESSID=4dlgema5odojl6avvt1dqrfgto.

137 LAC, RG 117, microfilm C-9386, file 8788, Inouye to Watson, 28 January 1948.
138 LAC, RG 33 (Records of Federal Royal Commissions), 69, vol. 8, file 142, "Inouye, Zennosuke (Vernon)."
139 LAC, RG 33, 69, vol. 8, file 142, Proceedings at Hearing, Vernon, 16 February 1948, 1–2.
140 LAC, RG 38, vol. 404, file 12, Bird to Gregg, 23 July 1948.
141 LAC, RG 38, vol. 404, file 12, Bird to Gregg, 23 October 1948.
142 LAC, RG 38, vol. 404, file 12, Superintendent, Secretarial Section, to District Superintendent, Vancouver, 22 January 1949. In a memorandum dated 16 February 1950, T.J. Rutherford, Murchison's successor as director of the Veterans' Land Act, noted that in addition to Inouye, five (this revised Bird's number) other Japanese Canadian veterans were candidates for restoration of property. Two of them were Great World soldier settlers and three were veterans of World War II. To date, the only action taken had been in relation to Inouye (LAC, RG 38, vol. 404, file 12).
143 LAC, RG 33, 69, vol. 8, file 142, Gregg to Bird, 17 November 1948.
144 LAC, RG 38, vol. 404, file 12, Superintendent, Secretarial Section, to District Superintendent, Vancouver, 22 January 1949.
145 LAC, RG 117, microfilm C-9386, file 8788, Miller to Hunter, 11 March 1949.
146 LAC, RG 38, vol. 404, file 12, minute of Treasury Board, 18 May 1949.
147 LAC, RG 117, microfilm C-9386, file 8788, McMaster to Bird, 11 March 1950, and Shears to Inouye, 6 March 1951. Inouye had earlier been given a claims award of $217.84 (Shears to Inouye, 20 February 1951).
148 LAC, RG 117, microfilm C-9386, file 8788, "Special Report," "Claim no. 142 – Zennosuke Inouye."
149 Inouye sold land to David Dorosewich on 15 July 1949 for $3,000; to Henry Hadley Beers, Francis Xavier Le Clair, and Lawrence Le Clair on 12 September 1949 for $1,500; to Austin Grant Beers on 12 September 1949 for $600; to Peter John Martens and Tina Martens on 27 October 1949 for $1,250; to his son Arthur Rizo Inouye on 19 July 1950 for $7,000; and to Henry Niessen on 31 August 1950 for $2,700. I am grateful to Ruth Brookshaw of the Land Title Office, Ministry of the Attorney General, New Westminster, British Columbia, for this information.
150 This information about Inouye is from Province of British Columbia, Department of Health and Welfare, Division of Vital Statistics, Registration of Death, 57-09-006580.
151 LAC, MG 27 III B5, vol. 26, file 67-25(6), note on Mitchell to Mackenzie, 18 July 1946.
152 LAC, MG 27 III B5, vol. 26, vol. 26, file 67-25(7). The petitioners did not condemn outright the wartime actions of the government in relation either to themselves or to Japanese Canadians generally, but made their case on the grounds that the time had now come for action on their behalf.

153 Ito, *We Went to War: The Story of the Japanese Canadians Who Served during the First and Second World Wars*, 279, 294, 296.

154 This section draws variously on my "How Newfoundland Veterans became Canadian Veterans: A Study in Bureaucracy and Benefit," in *Twentieth-Century Newfoundland: Explorations*, ed. Neary and Hillier, 195–237. I acknowledge gratefully the assistance of Breakwater Books.

155 For Newfoundland's role in the Great War, Murphy, "Newfoundland's Part in the Great War"; Nicholson, *The Fighting Newfoundlander*; Noel, *Politics in Newfoundland*; O'Brien, "The Newfoundland Patriotic Association: The Administration of the War Effort, 1914–1918"; and Parsons, *Pilgrimage: A Guide to the Royal Newfoundland Regiment in World War One* and *The Best Small-Boat Seamen in the Navy: The Newfoundland Division, Royal Naval Reserve, 1900–1922*.

156 See *Acts of the General Assembly of Newfoundland*, 1919, 95.

157 *Evening Telegram* and *Daily News*, St John's, 20 August 1918; *The Great War Veterans' Association of Newfoundland Constitution and By-Laws, 1918*. This item was published by the association. There is a copy in the Centre for Newfoundland Studies, Queen Elizabeth II Library, Memorial University, St John's.

158 Archives and Special Collections Division, Queen Elizabeth II Library, Memorial University, St John's, John G. Higgins Collection, COLL-087, 4.04.003, GWVA, A message to the men who served in the present war (St John's 1945).

159 Higgins Collection, COLL-087, 4.05.001, typescript of radio address, "The Necessity for the Newfoundland Patriotic Association."

160 For the history of Newfoundland in the 1930s and 1940s, see my *Newfoundland in the North Atlantic World, 1929–1949*.

161 Ibid., 16.

162 Ibid., 37.

163 For Newfoundland's role in the Second World War, see LAC, RG 24 (Records of the Department of National Defence), vol. 10995, file 290-NFD-013-(D1), A.M. Fraser, "History of the Participation by Newfoundland in World War II"; Neary, *Newfoundland in the North Atlantic World*; and Nicholson, *More Fighting Newfoundlanders: A History of Newfoundland's Fighting Forces in the Second World War*.

164 *Documents on Relations between Canada and Newfoundland*, ed. Bridle, 1, 839–51.

165 DVA, SECTY-6517-45/V2, "Acts: Union of Newfoundland," vol. 1, McDonald to Chant, 30 July 1945.

166 This was the official name. The unit is, however, commonly referred to as "the Newfoundland Overseas Forestry Unit" or, sometimes, "the Newfoundland (Overseas) Forestry Unit." The rationale for these variations is self-evident.

167 Neary, *Newfoundland in the North Atlantic World*, 118.

168 *Evening Telegram*, 15 March 1945.
169 Ibid.
170 Neary, *Newfoundland in the North Atlantic World*, 242.
171 *Now That You Are Home* (St John's, 1946), 37. See also DVA, 34-NF, vol. 3, report by M.G. Chambers, 1 January 1948; SECTY-6517-45/V2, vol. 1, Cross to Deputy Minister, 29 September 1948, 3. I am grateful to J.R. Walsh for a copy of *Now That You Are Home*.
172 Curran, *They Also Served: The Newfoundland Overseas Forestry Unit, 1939–1946*, 95–6.
173 *Evening Telegram*, 29 June 1946.
174 For his career, see Cuff et al., eds., *Dictionary of Newfoundland and Labrador Biography*, 225.
175 The monthly report for July 1946 of the Citizens' Rehabilitation Committee is in the Higgins Collection COLL-087, 4.04.004. See also *Evening Telegram*, 26 January 1946.
176 For Eaton's career, see Cuff et al., eds., *Dictionary of Newfoundland and Labrador Biography*, 97.
177 *Sunday Herald*, St John's, 19 May 1946.
178 *Evening Telegram*, 29 June 1946. For the general approach of the GWVA, see also ibid., 1 December 1945. For the GWVA executive at the time see ibid., 22 September 1945.
179 *Evening Telegram*, 29 June 1946.
180 Ibid., 2 July 1946.
181 See ibid., 27 July 1946.
182 DVA, SECTY-6517-45/V2, vol. 1, Woods to Under-Secretary of State for External Affairs, 16 May 1946.
183 Ibid.
184 Ibid.
185 DVA, 67-28, 'Re-establishment Credits: Newfoundland," Hogan to Director General, Veterans' Welfare Services, 4 April 1949; SECTY-6517-45/V2, vol. 1, Cole to Russell, 17 July 1945.
186 DVA, SECTY-6517-45/V2, vol. 1, Robertson to Deputy Minister, 16 July 1946.
187 DVA, SECTY-6517-45/V2, vol. 1, Woods to Under-Secretary of State for External Affairs, 31 July 1946.
188 For these events in the National Convention, see Neary, *Newfoundland in the North Atlantic World*, 295–8.
189 *Proposed Arrangements for the Entry of Newfoundland into Confederation*.
190 Ibid., 11–12.
191 For these events, see Neary, *Newfoundland in the North Atlantic World*, 313–24.
192 Higgins Collection, COLL-087, 4.04.006, "Report of the Great War Veterans' Association Delegation to Ottawa," enclosed in Martin to Editor, *Newfoundlander*, 17 January 1949.
193 I am grateful to the late Cam Eaton for this information and for letting me read a diary he kept in Ottawa.
194 *Evening Telegram*, 28 September 1948.

195 DVA, SECTY-6157-45/V2, vol. 1, Gregg to Pearson, 15 December 1948.
196 DVA, SECTY-6157-45/V2, vol. 1, Parliament to Woods, 4 October 1948.
197 DVA, SECTY-6157-45/V2, vol. 1, Parliament to Deputy Minister, 13 October 1948.
198 DVA, SECTY-6157-45/V2, vol. 1, "Memorandum for Use by the Minister in Discussing Proposal No. 12 of the Memorandum Submitted by the Newfoundland Delegation, October 1948."
199 The minutes of the meeting are in DVA, SECTY-6157-45/V2, vol. 1.
200 DVA, SECTY-6157-45/V2, vol. 1, "Memorandum re War Service Gratuities and Rehabilitation Credits from the Great War Veterans' Association Newfoundland."
201 The minutes of the 27 October meeting and the report of the subcommittee are also in DVA, SECTY-6157-45/V2, vol. 1.
202 *Documents on Relations between Canada and Newfoundland*, ed. Birdle, vol. 2, pt. 1, 1183; Woods, *Rehabilitation (A Combined Operation)*, 248–9; DVA, SECTY-6157-45/V2, vol. 1, "Memorandum for Use by the Minister in Discussing Proposal No. 12 of the Memorandum Submitted by the Newfoundland Delegation, October 1948."
203 *Documents on Relations between Canada and Newfoundland*, ed. Birdle, vol. 2, pt. 1, 1255–6.
204 Ibid., 1257.
205 Higgins Collection, COLL-087, 4.04.006, "Report of the Great War Veterans' Association Delegation to Ottawa," enclosed in Martin to Editor, *Newfoundlander*, St John's, 17 January 1949.
206 I am grateful to J.R. Walsh for a copy of this booklet.
207 DVA, SECTY-6157-45/V2, vol. 1, tel., Elliott to Cross, 2 April 1949.
208 *Evening Telegram*, 10 September 1949; DVA, 34-NF, vol. 5, Woods to Gregg, 21 Sept. 1949.
209 Woods, *Rehabilitation (A Combined Operation)*, 250.
210 DVA, 67-28, Gunn to Woods, 2 April 1949.
211 Unpublished speech by Cam Eaton to St John's Rotary Club (in possession of author).
212 *Daily News*, 15 January 1949.

CHAPTER EIGHT

1 *The Veterans Charter: Acts of the Canadian Parliament to Assist Canadian Veterans.*
2 Information obtained in telephone conversations with Dr Cameron, 31 May and 1 June 2010.
3 *Honouring Canada's Commitment: "Opportunity with Security" for Canadian Forces Veterans and Their Families in the 21st Century*, Veterans Affairs Canada – Canadian Forces Advisory Council, March 2004, 36–7.
4 The author's late father-in-law.
5 DVA, VLA, V-11-1, vol. 1,
6 The title of his celebrated 1948 book.
7 See Careless and Brown, eds., *The Canadians, 1867–1967*, 314–15.

8   Woods, *Rehabilitation (A Combined Operation)*, 5.
9   DVA, 65-6, vol. 1, Woods "Notes for Address to Joint Meeting of the Kiwanis Rehabilitation Council of Greater Toronto and the Toronto Rehabilitation Committee on January 18th, 1944."
10 DVA, 67-20, Boily to Director, 25 June 1947.
11 This paragraph draws on *The Origins and Evolution of Veterans Benefits in Canada, 1914–2004*, Veterans Affairs Canada – Canadian Forces Advisory Council, March, 2004.
12 For this history, see Sheffield, *A Search for Equity: A Study of the Treatment Accorded to First Nations Veterans and Dependents of the Second World War and the Korean Conflict.*
13 Information provided by David Pedlar, VAC, 1 June 2010.
14 Morton and Wright, *Winning the Second Battle: Canadian Veterans and the Return to Civilian Life, 1915–1930*, 118.
15 Ibid., 222.
16 Ibid., 65.
17 Woods, *The Men Who Came Back*, 167; LAC, RG 32, series C-2, vol. 257, 1884.07.16 (Walter S. Woods file).
18 See http://www.library.ubc.ca/archives/hdcites/hdcites2.html.
19 *Debates*, 6 June 1950, 3263.
20 Ibid.
21 Ibid., 3264.
22 Under PC45/3304 (there is a copy in LAC RG 32, series C-2, vol. 257, 1884.07.16 (Walter S. Woods file).
23 Page 89.
24 LAC, MG27 III B5, vol. 53, draft letter to Padwick, 5 April 1947.

Bibliography

ARCHIVAL SOURCES

ARCHIVES AND SPECIAL COLLECTIONS DIVISION, QUEEN ELIZABETH II
    LIBRARY, MEMORIAL UNIVERSITY, ST JOHN'S, NEWFOUNDLAND
John G. Higgins Collection, COLL-087

BRITISH COLUMBIA ARCHIVES, VICTORIA, BRITISH COLUMBIA
Records of the Department of Health and Welfare, Division of Vital Statistics

JAPANESE CANADIAN NATIONAL MUSEUM, BURNABY, BRITISH COLUMBIA
Zennosuke Inouye Papers

LIBRARY AND ARCHIVES CANADA, OTTAWA, ONTARIO
MG 27-III B5, Ian Mackenzie fonds, R4742
MG 28-I298, Royal Canadian Legion fonds, R2966
MG 30-C181, Robert England fonds, R5347
MG 31-K13, Olive Ruth Russell fonds, R4197
MG 26-J, William Lyon Mackenzie King fonds, R10383
Military Service records
RG 24, Records of the Department of National Defence
RG 32, Records of the Public Service Commission
RG 33, Records of Federal Royal Commissions
RG 38, Records of Veterans Affairs
RG 19, Records of the Department of Finance
RG 117, Records of the Custodian of Enemy Property
RG 150, Records of the Ministry of the Overseas Military Forces of Canada

PROVINCIAL ARCHIVES OF ALBERTA
Heritage Division, Vital Statistics Register

VETERANS AFFAIRS CANADA, CHARLOTTETOWN, PRINCE EDWARD ISLAND
Records of the Canadian Pension Commission
Records of the Department of Veterans Affairs (this collection has now been
    deposited in Library and Archives Canada)

GOVERNMENT PUBLICATIONS

Canada. Annual Reports of Department of Labour, Department of Mines and Resources,
Department of Pensions and National Health, Department of Veterans Affairs
– House of Commons. *Debates*
– House of Commons. *Journals*
– *Public General Acts*

House of Commons, Special and Standing Committees

Canada. House of Commons. *Pensions and Pension Regulations: Proceedings of the Special Committee Appointed to Consider the Questions of Pensions and Pension Regulations, and All Matters Pertaining Thereto, and to Prepare a Bill Dealing with Pensions for the Consideration of the House.* House of Commons, *Journal* 1919, app. 3
– *Reports, Proceedings and Evidence of the Special Committee on Pensions and Returned Soldiers' Problems, Comprising Amendments to the Pension Act, Soldiers' Insurance Act, Land Settlement Act, the Establishment of a Pension Tribunal and a Pension Appeal Court for War Veterans, also Evidence Respecting Bill 119, An Act to Provide for War Veterans' Allowances* (3 March – 23 May 1930). House of Commons, *Journal* 1930, app: "Pensions and Returned Soldiers' Problems"
– *Soldiers' Pensions: Proceedings of the Special Committee Appointed to Consider and Report upon the Rates of Pensions to Be Paid to Disabled Soldiers and the Establishment of a Permanent Pension Board.* House of Commons, *Journal* 1916, app. 4
– Special Committee on Land Settlement of Veterans of the Present War. *Minutes of Proceedings and Evidence*, no. 1–11. Ottawa: King's Printer, 1942
– Special Committee on Pensions and Returned Soldiers' Problems. *Minutes of Proceedings and Evidence*, no. 1–22. Ottawa: King's Printer, 1936
– Special Committee on Reconstruction and Re-establishment. *Minutes of Proceedings and Evidence*, no. 1–13 (1942), 1–36 (1943), 1–15 (1944). Ottawa: King's Printer, 1942–44
– Special Committee on the Pension Act and War Veterans' Allowance Act (1941). *Minutes of Proceedings and Evidence*, no. 1–22. Ottawa: King's Printer, 1941
– Special Committee on Veterans Affairs. *Minutes of Proceedings and Evidence*, no. 1–34 (1945). Ottawa: King's Printer, 1945
– Special Committee on Veterans Affairs. *Minutes of Proceedings and Evidence*, no. 1–51 (1946). Ottawa: King's Printer, 1946
– Standing Committee on Public Accounts (1947). *Minutes of Proceedings and Evidence*, no. 1–22. Ottawa: King's Printer, 1947

Royal Commission Reports

Royal Commission on Pensions and Re-establishment. *Report on First Part of Investigation.* House of Commons, Sessional Paper 154, 1923; *First Interim Report on*

BIBLIOGRAPHY 341

Second Part of Investigation. Sessional Paper 154a, 1923; *Second Interim Report on Second Part of Investigation*. Sessional Paper 203, 1924; *Final Report on Second Part of Investigation*. Sessional Paper 203a, 1924.
Royal Commission on Veterans' Qualifications. First and second interim reports. House of Commons, Sessional Paper 117a, 1945; third report, Sessional Paper 124h, 1946
Royal Commission to Investigate Complaints of Canadian Citizens of Japanese Origin Who Resided in British Columbia in 1941. That Their Real and Personal Property Had Been Disposed of by the Custodian of Enemy Property at Prices Less Than the Fair Market Value. House of Commons, Sessional Paper 185a, 1950

Other Official Publications and Reference Sources

The Directory of Dominion and Provincial Agencies of Demobilization and Rehabilitation Documents on Relations between Canada and Newfoundland, edited by Paul Bridle. Vol. 1: *1935–49*, introduction by R.A. MacKay. Ottawa: Information Canada, 1974. Vol. 2 (in two parts): *1940–49*, introduction by Paul Bridle. Ottawa: Supply and Services Canada, 1984
Handbook on Rehabilitation. Ottawa: King's Printer, 1945
Honouring Canada's Commitment: "Opportunity with Security" for Canadian Forces Veterans and Their Families in the 21stCentury. Veterans Affairs Canada, Canadian Forces Advisory Council, March 2004
The Origins of the Evolution of Veterans Benefits in Canada, 1914–2004. Veterans Affairs Canada, Canadian Forces Advisory Council, March 2004
Proclamations and Orders in Council Passed under the Authority of the War Measures Act. 7 vols. Ottawa: King's Printer, 1940–42
Proposed Arrangements for the Entry of Newfoundland into Confederation. Ottawa: King's Printer, 1948
Reference Manual on Provincial Rehabilitation Measures. Ottawa: Wartime Information Board, 1945
Reference Manual on Rehabilitation. Ottawa: King's Printer, 1945
Report of the Committee Appointed to Carry Out an Investigation into the Existing Facilities in Connection with Unemployment of Ex-Service Men and Care and Maintenance While Unemployed, and to Report Thereon with Such Suggestions and Recommendations as May Be Deemed Advisable. Ottawa: King's Printer, 1935
Report of the Work of the Department of Soldiers' Civil Re-establishment (Dec. 1919). House of Commons, Sessional Paper 14, 1920; (Dec. 1920), Sessional Paper 14, 1921
Report of the Veterans' Assistance Commission. Ottawa: King's Printer, 1937
Second Report of the Veterans' Land Act, for the Fiscal Year Ended March 31, 1944. Ottawa: King's Printer, 1945. Reprinted from *Report of the Department of Mines and Resources*, 218–31. Ottawa' King's Printer, 1945
Soldier Settlement: An Explanation of Concessions and Policy. Ottawa: King's Printer, 1944

Veterans' Assistance Commission. *Interim Report.* House of Commons, Sessional Paper 220, 1937

The Veterans Charter: Acts of the Canadian Parliament to Assist Canadian Veterans. Ottawa: King's Printer, 1947

White Paper on Veterans Pensions: Pensions for Disability and Death Related to Military Service. Ottawa: Queen's Printer, 1969

Canada and Newfoundland: Information for Veterans

Back to Civil Life. First issued by the Department of Pensions and National Health, 1 June 1944. It was then revised to 25 August 1944, 15 October 1945, and 1 April 1946. The third edition (revised to 1 April 1946 and issued by the Department of Veterans Affairs), is reprinted in *The Veterans Charter and Post-World War II Canada*, ed. Neary and Granatstein, 246–89.
Canada's Veterans' Charter: How It Applies in the Province of Newfoundland
The Common-Sense of Re-establishment
The Community and Re-establishment: Suggestions for Activities of Citizens' Committees
Dismiss – But What of a Job?
Employers Guide – An Aid for Employing Former Members of the Royal Canadian Air Force
A Farm on R.R. no. 1
A Home on Civvy Street
Future for Fighters (written for the Wartime Information Board by Dr E.A. Corbett)
It's Your Money
The Machinery of Re-establishment
Naval Rates – Their meaning for Employers
Now That You Are Home (Newfoundland)
The Role of Information
Veterans Affairs
Vocational Training on Civvy Street
What Will I Do When the War Is Won?
What's Ahead
When You Come Home (Newfoundland)
Vocational Training on Civvy Street
Your Own Business on Civvy Street

NEWSPAPERS AND MAGAZINES

British Columbian (New Westminster)
Calgary Herald
Canada Gazette
Canadian Veteran
Daily News (St John's)
Echoes (Imperial Order Daughters of the Empire)
Edmonton Bulletin
Evening Citizen (Ottawa)

BIBLIOGRAPHY

Evening Telegram (St John's)
Globe and Mail (Toronto)
Gazette (Montreal)
Halifax Mail
London Free Press
Maclean's
Montreal Standard,
New York Times
Newfoundlander (St John's)
Ottawa Citizen
Sunday Herald (St John's)
Windsor Daily Star
Toronto Star
Winnipeg Tribune

SECONDARY SOURCES

Barrow, Frederick Lyon. *A Post-War Era: A Study of the Veterans Legislation of Canada, 1950–1963*. Ottawa: Queen's Printer, 1964
Beaufoy, S. Roger G., ed. *A Report on the Second National Conference of Student Veterans*. Red Deer, AB: School of Printing Trades [1946]
Bowering, Clifford H. *Service: The Story of the Canadian Legion, 1925–1960*. Ottawa: Canadian Legion, 1960
Broadfoot, Barry. *The Veterans' Years: Coming Home from the War*. Vancouver & Toronto: Douglas & McIntyre, 1985
Brokaw, Tom. *The Greatest Generation*. New York: Random House, 1998
Brown, Shaun R.G. "Re-establishment and Rehabilitation: Canadian Veteran Policy, 1933–1946." PHD thesis, University of Western Ontario, 1995
Burke, F.S., "Deaths among War Pensioners." *Canadian Medical Association Journal*, Nov. 1939, 457–65
Campbell, Lara. "'We Who Have Wallowed in the Mud of Flanders': First World War Veterans, Unemployment, and the Development of Social Welfare in Canada, 1929–1939.'" *Journal of the Canadian Historical Association*. New series, 11 (2000): 125–49
Campbell, Marjorie Wilkins. *No Compromise: The Story of Colonel Baker and the CNIB*. Toronto: McClelland & Stewart, 1965
Canadian Parliamentary Guide. Ottawa
The Canadian Who's Who. Toronto: Trans-Canada Press, 1948
Careless, J.M.S., and R. Craig Brown, eds. *The Canadians, 1867–1967*. Toronto: Macmillan, 1967
Carrigan, D. Owen. ed. *Canadian Party Platforms, 1867–1968*. Toronto: Copp Clark, 1968
Carter, Sarah. *Lost Harvests: Prairie Indian Reserve Farmers and Government Policy*. Montreal & Kingston: McGill-Queen's University Press, 1990

- "'An Infamous Proposal': Prairie Indian Reserve Land and Soldier Settlement after World War I." *Manitoba History* 37 (Spring/Summer 1999): 9–21
CCF. *Marching Home to What? CCF Post-war Program for Canada's Fighting Men and Women.* Ottawa: CCF, 1944
Christie, Nancy. *Engendering the State: Family, Work, and Welfare in Canada.* Toronto: University of Toronto Press, 2000
Cuff, Robert H., Melvin Baker, and Robert D.W. Pitt, eds., *Dictionary of Newfoundland and Labrador Biography.* St. John's: Harry Cuff Publications, 1990
Curran, Tom, *They Also Served: The Newfoundland Overseas Forestry Unit, 1939–1946.* St John's: Jesperson, 1987
Dick, Lyle. "Sergeant Matsumi Mitsui and the Japanese Canadian War Memorial." *Canadian Historical Review* 91 (2010): 435–63
Dickson, Paul, and Thomas B. Allen. "Marching on History." *Smithsonian* 33 (Feb., 2003): 84–94
Durflinger, Serge M. *Lest We Forget: A History of the Last Post Fund, 1909–1999.* Montreal: The Last Post Fund, 2000
- *Veterans with a Vision: Canada's War Blinded in Peace and War.* Vancouver: UBC Press, 2010
England, Robert, *The Central European Immigrant in Canada.* Toronto: Macmillan, 1929
- *The Colonization of Western Canada: A Study of Contemporary Land Settlement (1896–1937).* London: P.S. King, 1936
- "Civil Re-establishment in Canada." *Public Welfare* (Journal of the American Public Welfare Association), 1 (Sept. 1943): 268–78
- *Discharged: A Commentary on Civil Re-establishment of Veterans in Canada.* Toronto: Macmillan, 1943
- "Soldier Settlement: Revising the Oldest Rehabilitation Prospectus." *Journal of Land and Public Utility Economics* 20 (Nov. 1944): 285–98
- "Disbanded and Discharged Soldiers in Canada Prior to 1914." *Canadian Historical Review* 47 (1946): 1–18
- *Twenty Million War Veterans.* London: Oxford, 1950
- "Veterans' Rehabilitation." In *Encyclopedia Canadiana*, 10:225–6. Toronto: Grolier, 1957
- *Living, Learning, Remembering: Memoirs of Robert England.* Vancouver: Centre for Continuing Education, University of British Columbia, 1980
Fahrni, Magda. *Household Politics: Montreal Families and Postwar Reconstruction.* Toronto: University of Toronto Press, 2005
Fedorowich, Kent, *Unfit for Heroes: Reconstruction and Soldier Settlement in the Empire between the Wars.* Manchester: Manchester University Press, 1995
Francis, Daniel, ed. *Encyclopedia of British Columbia.* Madeira Park, BC: Harbour Publishing, 2000
Frost, Stanley Brice. *McGill University for the Advancement of Learning.* 2 vols. Kingston & Montreal: McGill-Queen's University Press, 1980–84
Gardam, John, ed. *The Commissionaires: An Organization with a Proud History.* Burnstown, ON: General Store Publishing House, 1998

Gerber, David A. "Disabled Veterans, the State, and the Experience of Disability in Western Societies, 1914–1950." *Journal of Social History* 36 (2003): 899–916

Granatstein, J.L. *Canada's War: The Politics of the Mackenzie King Government, 1939–1945*. Toronto: Oxford, 1975

Granatstein, J.L., and Peter Neary, eds. *The Good Fight: Canadians and World War II*. Toronto: Copp Clark, 1995

The Great War Veterans' Association of Newfoundland Constitution and By-Laws, 1918. Published by the association

Hale, James. *Branching Out: The Story of the Royal Canadian Legion*. Ottawa: Royal Canadian Legion, 1995

Harris, Richard. *Creeping Conformity: How Canada Became Suburban, 1900–1960*. Toronto: University of Toronto Press, 2004

Harris, Richard, and Tricia Shulist. "Canada's Reluctant Housing Program: The Veterans' Land Act, 1942–75." *Canadian Historical Review* 82 (June 2001): 253–82

Hodgetts, J.E., William McCloskey, Reginald Whitaker, and V. Seymour Wilson. *The Biography of an Institution: The Civil Service of Canada, 1908–1967*. Montreal & London: McGill-Queen's University Press, 1972

Humphries, Mark. "War's Long Shadow: Masculinity, Medicine and the General Politics of Trauma, 1914–1939." *Canadian Historical Review*, 91 (2010): 503–31

Ito, Roy. *We Went to War: The Story of the Japanese Canadians Who Served during the First and Second World Wars*. Etobicoke: S-20 and Nisei Veterans Association, 1984

Keshen, Jeff, *Saints, Sinners and Soldiers: Canada's Second World War*. Vancouver: University of British Columbia Press, 2004

Leacy, F.H., ed. *Historical Statistics of Canada*. 2nd edn. Ottawa: Statistics Canada, 1983

McDonald, John. "Soldier Settlement and Depression Settlement in the Forest Fringe of Saskatchewan." *Prairie Forum* 6 (Spring 1981): 35–55

McIntosh, Dave. *Hell on Earth: Aging Faster, Dying Sooner. Canadian Prisoners of the Japanese during World War II*. Toronto: McGraw-Hill Ryerson, 1997

Morgan, E.C. "Soldier Settlement in the Prairie Provinces." *Saskatchewan History* 21 (Spring 1968): 41–55

Morton, Desmond. "'Noblest and the Best': Retraining Canada's War Disabled, 1915–23." *Journal of Canadian Studies* 16 (Fall-Winter 1981): 75–85

– "Resisting the Pension Evil: Bureaucracy, Democracy, and Canada's Board of Pension Commissioners, 1916–33." *Canadian Historical Review* 68 (1987): 199–224

– *Fight or Pay: Soldiers' Families in the Great War*. Vancouver & Toronto: University of British Columbia Press, 2004

Morton, Desmond, and Glenn Wright. "The Bonus Campaign, 1919–21: Veterans and the Campaign for Re-establishment." *Canadian Historical Review* 64 (1983): 147–67

– *Winning the Second Battle: Canadian Veterans and the Return to Civilian Life, 1915–1930*. Toronto: University of Toronto Press, 1987

Murchison, Gordon. "Gordon Murchison Memoirs." Online at http://www.roots web.ancestry.com/~skkinder/GordonMurchison/Chapter6-StartingAgain.html
Murphy, Captain Leo C., "Newfoundland's Part in the Great War." In *The Book of Newfoundland*, ed. J.R. Smallwood, 1:351–451. St John's: Newfoundland Book Publishers, 1937
National Conference of Canadian Universities. *Report of the National Conference of Canadian Universities on Post-War Problems*. Toronto: NCCU, 1944
Neary, Peter. *Newfoundland in the North Atlantic World, 1929–1949*. Montreal & Kingston: McGill-Queen's University Press, 1988
– "How Newfoundland Veterans Became Canadian Veterans: A Study in Bureaucracy and Benefit." In *Twentieth-Century Newfoundland: Explorations*, ed. James Hiller and Peter Neary, 195–237. St John's: Breakwater, 1994
– "Zennosuke Inouye's Land: A Canadian Veterans Affairs Dilemma." *Canadian Historical Review* 85 (Sept. 2004): 423–50
– "'Without the Stigma of Pauperism': Canadian Veterans in the 1930s." *British Journal of Canadian Studies* 22, no. 1 (2009): 31–62
– "'A Great Stride Forward': The Post-Discharge Re-establishment Order (PC7633) of 1 October 1941." *British Journal of Canadian Studies* 23, no. 2 (2010): 207–32
Neary, Peter, and J.L. Granatstein, eds. *The Veterans Charter and Post–World War II Canada*. Montreal & Kingston: McGill-Queen's University Press, 1998
Nicholson, G.W.L. *The Fighting Newfoundlander*. St John's: Government of Newfoundland, 1964
– *More Fighting Newfoundlanders: A History of Newfoundland's Fighting Forces in the Second World War*. St John's: Government of Newfoundland and Labrador, 1969
Noel, S.J.R. *Politics in Newfoundland*. Toronto: University of Toronto Press, 1971
O'Brien, Patricia. "The Newfoundland Patriotic Association: The Administration of the War Effort, 1914–1918." MA thesis, Memorial University, 1981
Oliver, Dean F. "Canadian Military Demobilization in World War II." In *The Good Fight*, ed. J.L. Granatstein and Peter Neary, 367–86: Toronto: Copp Clark, 1995
Parsons, W. David, *Pilgrimage: A Guide to the Royal Newfoundland Regiment in World War One*. St John's: Creative, 1994
– *The Best Small-Boat Seamen in the Navy: The Newfoundland Division, Royal Naval Reserve, 1900–1922*. St John's: DRC Publishing, 2009
Pierson, Ruth Roach. *"They're Still Women After All": The Second World War and Canadian Womanhood*. Toronto: McClelland and Stewart, 1986
Pierson, Ruth Roach, and Marjorie Cohen. "Educating Women for Work: Government Training Programs for Women before, during, and after World War II." In *Modern Canada, 1930–1980s*, ed. Michael S. Cross and Gregory S. Kealey, 208–43. Toronto: McClelland & Stewart, 1984.
Reaume, Geoffrey. *Lyndhurst: Canada's First Rehabilitation Centre for People with Spinal Cord Injuries, 1945–1998*. Montreal & Kingston: McGill-Queen's University Press, 2007
Ritchie, Charles. *The Siren Years*. London: Macmillan, 1974

Schecter, Jack. "The Achievements of Trooper Mulloy." *Canadian Military History* 11 (Winter 2002): 71–9

Schull, Joseph. *Veneration for Valour: An Assessment of the Veterans Charter, Its Impact on Canadian Veterans and on Canada as a Whole.* Ottawa: Department of Veterans Affairs, 1973

Segsworth, Walter E. *Retraining Canada's Disabled Soldiers.* Ottawa: King's Printer, 1920

Senior, C.N. *When the Boys Come Home: Their Post War Opportunities in Canada.* Toronto: Collins, 1944

Sheffield, R. Scott. *A Search for Equity: A Study of the Treatment Accorded to First Nations Veterans and Dependents of the Second World War and the Korean Conflict.* National Round Table on First Nations' Veterans' Issues, 2001

Slater, David W. (with two chapters by R.B. Bryce). *War Finance and Reconstruction: The Role of Canada's Department of Finance, 1939–1946.* Ottawa: David W. Slater, 1995. Robert Wardhaugh kindly supplied me with the unpublished endnotes to this volume.

Stevenson, Michael D. "National Selective Service and Employment and Seniority Rights for Veterans, 1943–1946." In *The Veterans Charter and Post–World War II Canada*, ed. Peter Neary and J.L. Granatstein, 95–109. Montreal & Kingston: McGill-Queen's University Press, 1998

– *Canada's Great Wartime Muddle: National Selective Service and the Mobilization of Human Resources during World War II.* Montreal & Kingston: McGill-Queen's University Press, 2001

Struthers, James. "'They Suffered With Us and Should be Compensated': Entitling Caregivers of Canada's Veterans." *Canadian Journal on Aging* 26, supplt. 1 (2007): 117–32

– "'Comfort, Security, Dignity': Home Care for Canada's Aging Veterans, 1977-2004." In *Essays in Honour of Michael Bliss: Figuring the Social*, ed. E.A. Heaman, Alison Li, and Shelley McKellar, 315–48. Toronto: University of Toronto Press, 2008

Sunahara, Ann Gomer. *The Politics of Racism: The Uprooting of Japanese Canadians during the Second World War.* Toronto: Lorimer, 1981

Swallow, Susan Ruth, "Olive Ruth Russell: A Twentieth Century Canadian Progressive." MA thesis, University of Western Ontario, 1996

Swift, Diana, and Jack Jarvie, *The Royal Canadian Legion.* Toronto: Discovery Books, 1985

Thompson, W.P. *The University of Saskatchewan: A Personal Memoir.* Toronto: University of Toronto Press, 1970

Tremblay, Mary. "The Canadian Revolution in the Management of Spinal Cord Injury." *Canadian Bulletin of Medical History* 12 (1995): 125–55

– "Going Back to Main Street: The Development and Impact of Casualty Rehabilitation for Veterans with Disabilities." In *The Veterans Charter and Post–World War II Canada*, ed. Peter Neary and J.L. Granatstein, 160–78. Montreal & Kingston: McGill-Queen's University Press, 1998

- "The Right to the Best Medical Care: Dr. W.P. Warner and the Canadian Department of Veterans Affairs, 1945–1955." *Canadian Bulletin of Medical History* 15 (1998): 3–25
- "Lieutenant John Counsell and the Development of Medical Rehabilitation and Disability Policy in Canada." In *Disabled Veterans in History*, ed. David A. Gerber, 322–46. Ann Arbor: University of Michigan Press, 2000
Urquhart, M.C., ed., and K.A.H. Buckley, asst. ed. *Historical Statistics of Canada.* Toronto: Macmillan, 1965
Vance, Jonathan F. "'Today They Were Alive Again': The Canadian Corps Reunion of 1934." *Ontario History* 87 (Dec. 1995): 327–44
Wade, Jill. *Wartime Housing Limited, 1941–1947: An Overview and Evaluation of Canada's First National Housing Corporation.* Vancouver: UBC School of Community and Regional Planning, 1984
- *Houses for All: The Struggle for Social Housing in Vancouver, 1919–50.* Vancouver: University of British Columbia Press, 1994
Warner, W.P. "Policy of Treatment Services, Department of Veterans' Affairs." *Canadian Medical Association Journal* 54 (June 1946): 564–68
- "Treatment Services for Canadian Veterans." *Health*, 14 (Sep.–Oct. 1946): 8, 25
- "Relationship between Government Medical Services and the Canadian Medical Profession." *Canadian Medical Association Journal* 61 (October 1949): 383–8
- "The New D.V.A. Treatment Plan for Non-entitled Veterans." *Legionary* 25 (May 1950): 46–7
- "The New Concept of D.V.A. Treatment Services." *Legionary* 26 (July 1950): 32–5
Warner, W.P., and C.C. Misener. "If Sickness Strikes … The New D.V.A. Treatment Plan for Non-Pensioned Veterans." *Legionary*, 29 (August 1954): 20–1
Willenz, June A. *Women Veterans: America's Forgotten Heroines.* New York; Continuum, 1983
Woods, Walter S. *Rehabilitation (A Combined Operation).* Ottawa: Queen's Printer, 1953
- *The Men Who Came Back: A Book of Memories.* Toronto: Ryerson Press, 1956
Young, Robert A. "Reining in James: The Limits of the Task Force." *Canadian Public Administration* 24 (Winter 1981): 596–611

Index

Abbott, Douglas, 214
Advisory Committee on Rehabilitation and Re-establishment, 161; subcommittee on seniority rights for veterans, 184–5
Afghanistan veterans, 286
Aging Veterans Program, 285
Air Raid Precautions workers, 119, 166
Aleutian Islands, 128
Allen, Robert, 169
Allied Benefits Act, 165
Allward, Walter Seymour, 43
Amulree, William Warrender Mackenzie, 1st Baron, 262
Amyot, J.A., 24, 27–8
Anderson, T.D., 254
Andrew, G.C., 167
Armstrong, E.B., 125, 164
Army and Navy Veterans in Canada (later Army and Navy and Air Force Veterans in Canada), 23–4, 242
Army Show, 169
Arthnes, L.L., 15
Athlone, Alexander Augustus Cambridge, 1st Earl of, 162
Atkinson, J.E., 83
Atlantic Charter, 108, 162
Attlee, Clement, 264
Ault, Orville, 211
Auxiliary Service personnel, 165

Babcock, John, 286
Back to Civil Life, 133, 135, 137, 138, 142, 154, 160, 166, 174, 225, 282, 284. *See also* Post-Discharge Re-establishment Order (PC7633)
Bain, Donald, 98
Bain, T.D., 137

Baker, Edwin Albert (Eddie), 14, 235
Baker, H.C., 156
Baldwin, J.R., 244
Barclay, R.G., 109
Barrow, F.L., 131, 164, 187
Bates, Arthur Patrick, 280–1
Bates, Hilary, 281
Bates, John Patrick, 280
Bates, Rosemary, 281
Baxter, Lionel, 242
Beamish, Royd, 169
Beecroft, G.W., 226
Bell, H.M., 175–6
Bengough, Percy, 182
Bennett, R.B., 27, 28
Bird, Henry Irvine: chairs royal commission, 257; recommendation re properties of Japanese Canadian veterans sold to VLA, 258; recommends additional payment to Inouye, 259
Bland, C.H., 75
Bloc populaire canadien, 159
Board of Pension Commissioners (Canada). *See* pensions
Board of Pension Commissioners (Newfoundland), 261
Boily, Stéphane, 285
"Bonus Army" (United States), 25, 32
Borden, Robert, 7, 9; on gratuity, 20
Botterell, (Edmund) Harry, 238
Bovey, Wilfrid: chairs Royal Commission on Veterans' Qualifications, 202; director Canadian Legion Educational Services, 66; foreword by, 171; on "last chance" of free enterprise, 176–8
Bowler, J.R. (Reg), 39, 49, 75, 76; on Chubby Power, 40; death of, 110;

general secretary Canadian Legion, 31
Braefoot Estate (Victoria), 248
Brereton, A.L., 28–9
British Columbia Command, Canadian Legion, 43, 54
British Columbia Security Commission, 97, 99
Brokaw, Tom, 178
Brooks, A.J., 161, 163
Bryce, R.B., 205
Burgess, A.L., 161
Burns, Eedson Louis Millard (Tommy): addresses student conference, 211–12; director general of rehabilitation, 164; employment of married women in public service, 220; on Montreal rehabilitation centre, 176; on seniority rights for veterans, 186

Cabinet Committee on Demobilization and Re-establishment, 160–1, 185; on Demobilization and Rehabilitation, 63
Calder, James: on GWVA proposals, 20–1
Cameron, Howard, 275
Cameron, K.M., 152
Canada's Veterans' Charter: How It Applies in the Province of Newfoundland, 273
Canadian Active Service Force: demography, 61–2; extension of preference to, 69
Canadian Adult Education Association, 66
Canadian Army Medical Corps, 61
Canadian Association of Real Estate Boards, 151
Canadian Association of Veterans in United Nations Peacekeeping, 286
Canadian Bar Association, 210
Canadian Broadcasting Corporation, 66, 158, 169; radio programs re demobilization, rehabilitation, and re-establishment, 169, 170

Canadian Chamber of Commerce, Post-War Planning Committee of, 108
Canadian Congress of Labour, 182–3
Canadian Corps, 6, 23; reunion of, 24
Canadian Corps Association, 24, 104, 130, 151, 242
Canadian Corps of Commissionaires, 51, 55
Canadian Expeditionary Force (CEF), 5, 6, 8, 10, 14, 18, 61, 65, 69, 89, 280
Canadian Farm Loan Board, 90
Canadian Japanese Volunteer Corps, 18
Canadian Legion Educational Services, 66, 70, 106, 145, 202, 242
Canadian Legion of the British Empire Service League: advocacy re unemployed veterans in 1930s, 30–5, 56; Branch 9, Vancouver, 253–4, 261; on civil service preference for veterans, 242; constitution and organization of, 23; conventions, 30, 33, 40, 50–1, 118, 241; criticism by British Columbia Command of national leadership, 54; on DND relief camps, 3; Imperial Division of, 23; on Inouye, 254; launched at 1925 unity conference in Winnipeg, 23; on membership of NRMA men with overseas service, 241–2; memo to government 1 Sept. 1939, 69; memo to party leaders, 70; policy of retarded demobilization, 72–3, 76–7, 104; postwar history of, 241–3, 286–7; on postwar housing situation, 243, 257; professional and business loans for veterans, 154; reform legislation (1930), 25; renamed Royal Canadian Legion, 286; response to Hyndman committee report, 38–9, 40; response to PC 7633, 84; role of *Legionary* in, 23; Ross memo on rehabilitation and re-establishment, 71–2; on seniority rights for veterans, 182–4; Sir Arthur

INDEX

Currie branch (Montreal), 179; Special Unemployment Committee, 30–1; standard uniform of, 242; support for conscription, 69–70; "They served till death! Why not we?" 23; on Veterans' Assistance Commission, 48–9, 52–5; wartime services, 70; on War Veterans' Allowance, 40
Canadian Legion War Services, 70, 165, 242
Canadian Manufacturers' Association, 15, 186
Canadian Medical Association, 229, 231
Canadian National Council of Women, 142
Canadian National Institute for the Blind, 235, 238
Canadian Overseas Fire Fighters, 165
Canadian Paraplegic Association, 238, 242
Canadian Patriotic Fund, 21
Canadian Peacekeeping Veterans Association, 286
Canadian Pension Commission. *See* pensions
Canadian Pensioners' Association of the Great War, 24, 242
Canadian Red Cross, 166
Canadian Retail Federation, 193
Canadian Soldiers Non-Pensioned Widows' Association, 136
Canadian Women's Army Corps (CWAC), 61, 112–13, 114
Canadian Women's Auxiliary Air Force, 61, 11. *See also* Royal Canadian Air Force Women's Division
Canadian Vocational Training, 198, 201, 221
Carmichael, Dougall, 131
Carter, Sarah, 18
Central European Immigrant in Canada, The (Robert England), 66
Central Mortgage and Housing Corporation, 245–6

Chant, Sperrin N.F.; background, 131; chairs committee on university veterans advisers, 208; head, Department of Philosophy and Psychology, UBC, 208–9; report for DVA Advisory Committee on University Training, 208–9; represents DVA on research subcommittee of Demobilization and Rehabilitation Information Committee, 167; seconded to DPNH as director general of rehabilitation, 164
Charlottetown, 285
Christie Street Hospital, 137, 236, 281
Churchill, Winston, 108
Citizens' Rehabilitation Committee (Newfoundland), 266
citizens' war services co-ordinating committees, 171
Civil Re-establishment Committee (Newfoundland), 261
Civil Service Commission, 63, 110, 211, 220, 228; preference for veterans, 15–16, 137, 225–6
Civilian War Pensions and Allowances Act, 165–6
Clark, W.C., 315n32
Clement, Fred M., 259
Cochrane, J.A., 266
Colonization of Western Canada: A Study of Contemporary Land Settlement (1896–1934), The (Robert England), 66
Committee Appointed to Carry Out an Investigation into the Existing Facilities in Connection with Unemployment of Ex-Service Men... *See* Hyndman committee
Committee on Priority and Seniority Rights of Veterans, 182–3, 184
Committee on Reconstruction, 117, 152
Committee on University Requirements, 205, 214
Common, Frank B., 212
Conroy, Pat, 183–4

Co-operative Commonwealth Federation (CCF), 58, 119, 164
Corbett, E.A., 167
Cornellier, Philippe, 204
Corps of (Civilian) Canadian Fire Fighters, 165
Coulthard, R.W., 14
Counsell, John Gibbons, 137, 238
Cowan, Andrew G., 169
Crerar, T.A., 92
Currie, Arthur, 23-4, 33-4
Custodian of Enemy Property, 97, 148, 257; Vancouver office of, 99, 156, 242, 251

Davis, E.G., 14
Dawe, W.R., 266
Day, Susanne, 278
Demobilization and Rehabilitation Information Committee, 167
Department of Defence (Newfoundland), 263
Department of Finance: 17 July 1944 memorandum, 125-6, 162
Department of Labour, 73, 142, 174-5, 215, 216, 252, 258
Department of Militia (from 1906 Department of Militia and Defence), 10, 13; Pensions and Claims Board, 10
Department of National Defence (DND), 62; auxiliary services, 62-3, 70; relief camps, 28, 32
Department of National Health and Welfare, 141, 229, 230
Department of Natural Resources (Newfoundland), 263
Department of Pensions and National Health (DPNH): appointment of associate deputy minister responsible for rehabilitation administration and planning, 74; attitude to relief and unemployment, 26-8, 30, 31; formation and work of, 24; insurance administration, 24; introduction of 1940 rehabilitation grant, 74; Toronto Orthopaedic Division, 137; veterans' welfare division (1940), 73-4. *See also* Post-Discharge Re-establishment Order (PC7633); relief; treatment services
Department of Reconstruction, 154
Department of Soldiers' Civil Re-establishment (DSCR): formation and purpose, 13; Information and Service Branch, 14; medical and rehabilitation operations, 14-15, 18. *See also* relief
Department of Veterans Affairs (DVA): Advisory Committee on University Training for Veterans, 147, 161, 204-5, 207-11, 214; "applied title" of Veterans Affairs Canada, 285; benefit statistics, 178-81; bill 83 introduced and passed, 118-20; casualty rehabilitation, 232-6, 238-41; citizens' committees, 171-3; Committee on University Requirements, 205-6, 214; counselling initiatives and services, 137, 169, 171, 197; employment of married women, 220-1; housing campaign, 244; moved to Charlottetown, 285; Newfoundland policy and administration, 267-8, 273; organization, 131-2; policy re universities, 146-7, 148; proposal for creation of department, 118; public relations initiatives, 133-5, 166-7; rehabilitation centres, 137, 174-5; role of women in administration, 286; terms of 1944 act, 120-1; *See also* treatment services
Dependents' Allowance Board, 104
Dependents' Board of Trustees, 107
deReeder, Margaret, 280
Disablement Fund, 171
Division of Civil Re-establishment (Newfoundland), 266
Dixon, A.J., 131
Dominion Bureau of Statistics, 92, 211

Dominion Government Annuities, 190
Drope, H.E., 191
Drumm, Molly (Margaret), 275
"dual service" veterans, 161
Dubé, Jean-Etudes, 285
Duguid, A.F., 90–1
Dunlop, Edward Arunah: background, 232–3; executive secretary, Canadian Arthritis and Rheumatism Society, 236; later political and business career, 236; lecture established in his honour, 236; national conference on rehabilitation, 236; philosophy re disability, 233–5; publishes national action plan (1958), 236; "The Rehabilitation Needs of the Crippled and Disabled in Canada" (1947), 236
Dunton, A. Davidson, 167
Dupuis, Hector, 202
Dymond, J.R., 210

Eaton, (Gordon) Campbell: GWVA (Newfoundland) executive, 270; later career, 277; military record, 266; newspaper articles, 266; Ottawa negotiations, 270–3, 274
Eaton, Fraudena, 217–18
Edward VIII, 43
Elliott, O.C., 104
Employment of veterans: preference for, 109–10; seniority issue, 182–7
Employment Service of Canada, 14, 109–10. 174, 182
England, Robert: background, 65–6, 85, 171; books by, 66; chairs Committee on University Requirements, 205; on draft PC7633, 79, 81; executive secretary GACDR, 63, 85; on gratuity payment, 123; re-establishment credits administration, 132; "Ventures in Citizenship," broadcasts, 66
Everest & Jennings self-propelled wheelchairs, 137

Fadiman, Clifton, 158

Farmers' Creditors Arrangements Act, 88
Fawk, Elene Lucille, 19, 289
Fedorowich, Kent, 22
Fennell, A.B., 116, 144
Finlayson, G.D., 40
Fire Fighters Service Benefits Act, 165
First Nations veterans, 286
Ford strike, 184–6
Fosberry, Ernest, 289
Foster, William Wasbrough: background, 34; director, DND auxiliary services, 70; elected president of Canadian Legion, 52; exchange with Inouye, 253; radio address, 69; on unemployment, 34, 53–5
"future wife," 16

Gadbois, André, 275
Galbraith, John Kenneth, 282
Gartshore, John, 137
General Advisory Committee on Demobilization and Rehabilitation (GACDR), 63, 161; on gratuity, 77; report, 85; subcommittees of, 66, 80, 88, 90, 92, 94–5, 112, 113–16, 137, 152–3, 182
George VI, 59
G.I. Bill of Rights, 125, 162, 203
Gibson, Colin, 229
Gillis, Clarence (Clarie), 164
Glass, K.G., 124
Gordon, Walter, 239
Gowan, Elsie Park, 169
Graham, Duncan, 230
Graham, Marion, 221
gratuity (Great War), 15, 20, 77, 83, 84, 86
gratuity (Second World War). See War Service Grants Act
Great War Veterans' Association of Canada (GWVA): "Aims and Objects," 8; bonus campaign, 20–1; on enemy aliens, 9; on gratuity, 20; on land settlement, 9; origins, 7–9; out-

look, 8–9; on public service jobs, 9 ; Vancouver convention, 20
Great War Veterans' Association of Newfoundland, 261–2, 266, 270–3
Green, Howard C., 43, 165, 288
Gregg, Milton F.: appointed minister of veterans affairs, 257; decision re Inouye property, 258; Newfoundland veterans, 271–2; on Woods, 288
Grier, Margaret, 216
Grierson, John, 169
Grucy, Phil, 274
Gulf War Veterans Association of Canada, 286
Gunn, W.G., 131

Hardy, Laura (Taylor), 142
Harnett, F.G., 270
Harvey, A.R., 150
Hazen, J.D., 10, 12
Hees, George, 285
Herridge, H.W., 248, 288
Herwig, J.G.C.: attends Newfoundland GWVA convention, 270; attends student conference, 211; becomes Canadian Legion general secretary, 110; on postwar housing crisis, 247; on preference and seniority for veterans, 182–3; Royal Commission on Veterans' Qualifications, 202; on Second World War veterans and Canadian Legion, 241; on War Service Grants Act, 130
Higa, Harry (Sargeant), 254
Higman, Jack, 137
Hodgkin, J.O., 187
Hogan, J.H., 131, 191, 192, 195
Holland, Laura, 114
Hong Kong prisoners, 285, 286
Homuth, Karl, 129
Hoover, Herbert, 25
Hori, Kachichi, 98
Hotel Vancouver: occupation of, 246, 283
House of Commons special committees: land settlement (1942), 93; Pension Act and War Veterans' Allowance Act (1941), 75, 78, 92, 109; pensions (1916 and 1919), 10–13; pensions and returned soldiers' problems (1930 and 1936), 24, 40; reconstruction and re-establishment (1942–44), 117, 154; soldiers' civil re-establishment (1919), 12–13; veterans affairs (1945, 1946, 1948), 156, 161–2, 164
House of Commons Standing Committee on Public Accounts, 157
Housing: consideration of by GACDR, 95–6, 152–3; National Housing Act (1938), 95; postwar situation, 243–6
Howe, C.D., 182, 246, 247
Hundevad, John, 106
Hunt, Helen, 21, 222, 224–5
Hunter, J.W.G., 258
Hyndman, J.D., 35
Hyndman committee: government response to recommendations, 37, 40; membership, 35; purpose, 34–5; report and recommendations, 35–7; sessions, 35; on War Veterans' Allowance, 38–9

Ilsley, J.L., 44, 245
Imada, Tom, 258
Imperial Economic Conference, 32
Imperial Order Daughters of the Empire, 113, 219
Imperial Veterans in Canada, 23
Inouye, Arthur, 99
Inouye, Beverley (Kiyoko), 99
Inouye, Mary (Yasuko), 99
Inouye, Robert, 99
Inouye, Tom, 99
Inouye, Zennosuke: beginnings, 18; case before Bird royal commission, 258; death and interment, 259; demobilization and re-establishment as soldier settler, 18–19; efforts to recover property, 99–100, 156–7, 251–

INDEX 355

5; letter to Mackenzie King (4 Oct. 1944), 156–7; marries Hatsuno Morikawa, 19; New Westminster *British Columbian* on, 19; relocation and loss of property, 97–9; restored to property, 258
Inter-departmental Advisory Committee on Professionally Trained Persons, 210
Interdepartmental Committee on Government Medical Services, 230
interdepartmental committee on veterans' affairs, 164
Inter-departmental Co-ordinating Committee on Rehabilitation, 182
Interdepartmental Housing Committee, 244
Invalided Soldiers' Commission, 13
Iverson, W.J., 252

Jackson, Barbara E., 211
Jackson, Kathleen, 169
James, F. Cyril, 117, 152, 202, 209
Jamieson, Harold Williams, 144, 147, 207, 208, 212
Japanese Canadians: Great War service, 18; relocation of and sale of properties, 96–7, 148
Johnson Wax radio program, 158
Johnson, Wink, 278
Jones, Albert John, 98
Jones, Dennis Cecil, 98
Jones, Denzil Lester, 98
Jousse, Albin T., 238

Kent, Katherine, 143
Ketchum, J.D., 167
Ketchum, Robert, 278
Khaki University, 66, 144
Kidner, T.B., 14
Kildare barracks, 247
Kilpatrick, G.G.D.: on means testing, 122
King, J.H., 24
King, Margery, 208

King, William Lyon Mackenzie: on demobilization and rehabilitation planning, 62–3; promise re conscription, 60; unflattering jokes about, 159; on War Service Grants Act, 128–9, 130
Kinoschita, Seichi, 258
Kinross, Cecil John, 3
Knights of Columbus, 165
Knowles, Stanley, 119
Korean War veterans, 286

Lacombe, Liguori, 119
Laflèche, Léo Richer, 25, 27
land settlement (Great War): administration by director, 90; agricultural qualification committees, 17; consequences for First Nations peoples, 18; economic downturn of 1920s, 22; effect of Great Depression, 27, 88–9; end of scheme, 156; last settler in arrears refuses payment, 156; legislation, 17; number of settlers, 18, 27; Second World War changes, 155–6; Soldier Settlement Board, 17–18, 20, 26, 90; submission by Soldier Settlers' Association of Canada, 156
LaMarsh, Judy, 215, 216
Lapointe, Hugues, 161
Legionary, 23, 106
Lenardon, Dante, 277
Lethbridge, Citizens' Rehabilitation Committee of, 254
Lett, Sherwood, 191
Line, William, 208
Lougheed, James: approach to vocational education, 14; minister of soldiers' civil re-establishment, 13
Lyndhurst Lodge (Toronto), 238
Lyons, D.S., 202

MacArthur, Douglas, 25
MacDonald, Daniel J., 285
McDonald, Donald, 169
McDonald, Harold French: background, 63–4; on Canada's Great

War re-establishment effort, 64–5; on Canadian Legion, 78; chairman of Canadian Pension Commission, 64; chairman of GACDR, 63; death of, 85; on PC7633, 80–1, 87
Macdonald, R.H., 99, 252
MacDonell, Andrew, 150
McGill Student Veterans' Society, 211, 212
McIntosh, F.K., 254
MacKay, R.A., 268
Mackenzie, A.A., 74–5
Mackenzie, Ian Alistair: background and appointment as minister of pensions and national health, 57–9; becomes first minister of veterans affairs, 131; on "Canada's rehabilitation belief," 134; chairs cabinet committee re draft PC7633, 79; convenor of cabinet committee on demobilization and rehabilitation, 63; death of, 289; on gratuity and re-establishment credit, 77, 130; on history of veterans' affairs, 119–20, 282; House of Commons speech of 6 December 1940 on pension and rehabilitation policy, 63; on Inouye, 256–7; on Japanese Canadians, 59, 96, 255–7, 260; leaves cabinet and appointed to Senate, 257; meets provincial labour and relief officials, 74; names interdepartmental committee on veterans' affairs, 164; on national health insurance, 232; on objective of rehabilitation program, 117, 135, 289; presentation to 1945 special committee on veterans' affairs, 161–2; relationship with Mackenzie King, 257; on special committee (1946), 164–5; on treatment services, 229, 232; on Veterans Charter, 275; visits Washington, 166
Mackenzie, N.A.M., 116, 144, 209
MacKinnon, J.A., 63
Mackintosh, W.A., 125–6, 152

MacLaren, Murray, 32
Maclean, M.M., 182, 184
McMaster, R.J., 258
Macmillan, Cyrus, 75, 93
MacNamara, Arthur: chairs Advisory Committee on Rehabilitation and Re-establishment, 161; on Inouye, 256–7; on PC7633, 80, 84; on veterans with overseas service, 182
McNaughton, A.G.L., 105
McNeill, W.E., 145
Macnicol, Robert, 43, 48
Machum, J.R., 191
Mansur, David, 249
Marcowitz, Jacob, 280
Marshall, F.W., 226, 270
Martigny, Hugues Le Moyne de, 42, 48
Martin, W.R., 270, 273
Massey, Vincent, 105
Mathers, A.W., 152
Matsui, Masumi, 260
Matthews, Thomas H., 144
Meighen, Arthur, 7
Melville, J.L., 131
Men Who Came Back: A Book of Memories, The (Woods), 289
Merchant Seamen Compensation Act, 166
Military Hospitals Commission, 13, 24
Military Pension Act, 10
Military Service Act, 6
Millar, Ross, 32, 104
Millard, C.H., 183
Mills, L.J., 205
Ministry of War Transport (UK), 265–6
Misener, C.C., 231
Mitchell, Humphrey, 202
Moore, A.E., 30
Morikawa, Hatsuno, 19, 99
Morrow, C.W., 255
Morton, Desmond, 8, 22
Mosher, A.R., 182
Murchison, Gordon: background, 89–90; becomes director of soldier settlement, 89; becomes director of

VLA, 94; becomes superintendent of farm settlement, 249; clashes with real estate agents, 150–1; general supervisor of real estate division, CMHC, 249; on Inouye property, 157, 256–7; on National Housing Act, 243–4; proposal for veterans' land and housing act, 244–5; on proposals re land settlement, 1940–41, 91–2; submits draft bill, 92; on urban housing for veterans, 152; visits United Kingdom, 95

National Advisory Committee on the Rehabilitation of Disabled Persons, 236
National Conference of Canadian Universities (NCCU): on admission of medical and dental students, 209–10; agrees to participate in DVA advisory committee on university affairs, 147; committee on postwar prospects, 116; findings of report on postwar problems, 144–6
National Conference of Student Veterans, 211
National Council of Student Veterans, 212, 213
National Council of Veteran Associations in Canada, 242
National Employment Commission, 53
National Film Board, 133, 141; films on rehabilitation and re-establishment, 169
National House Builders Association, 152
National Housing Act (1938), 95
National Housing Act (1944), 154, 190, 197, 244, 245
National Resources Mobilization Act, 60–1, 122, 128, 274
National Selective Service, 138, 216, 217
National Society for the Deaf and Hard of Hearing, 235

Newfoundland: Commission of Government, 262–3; National Convention, 264, 267, 268–9; negotiations with Canada, 270–2; policy re veterans, 264–6; political and military history, 261–4; referendums, 269–70; terms of union, 38, 42, 272
Newfoundland Forestry Unit, 263, 266, 268, 273, 286
Newfoundland Patriotic Association, 266
Newfoundland Regiment (Second World War), 263, 265, 269, 273–4
Nichol, J.R., 129
Nicholls, F.W., 152
Nickle, W.F., 13
Nielsen, Dorise, 117
Nixon, Nora (Nonie), 277–8
No. 1 Canadian Neurosurgical Hospital, 238

O'Neil, Moira, 217
Ontario Association of Real Estate Boards, 150–1
Ontario Soldiers' Aid Commission, 14
Ord, Jack, 213
Orders-in-Council: PC2491 (2 Sept. 1939), 67; PC4068½ (8 Dec. 1939), 63; PC1971 (21 May 1940), 67; PC5421 (8 Oct. 1940), 63; PC204-6613 (18 Nov. 1940), 73; PC6282 (27 Nov. 1940), 73; PC7521 (19 Dec. 1940), 73–4; PC4798 (2 July 1941), 61; PC6289 (13 Aug. 1941), 61; PC7633 (1 Oct. 1941), 82; PC4/7635 (1 Oct. 1941), 111; PC1965 (13 Mar. 1942), 113; PC 56/6755 (31 July 1942), 61; PC10472 (19 Nov. 1942), 155; PC818 (5 Feb. 1943), 115; PC946 (5 Feb. 1943), 333n130; PC1003 (17 Feb. 1944), 183; PC4465 (12 June 1944), 136; PC5210 (13 July 1944), 121, 198; PC8096 (17 Oct. 1944), 167; PC8404 (1 Nov. 1944), 188;

PC165 (18 Jan. 1945), 191; PC3206 (3 May 1945), 147; PC3342 (8 May 1945), 202; PC4383 (20 June 1945), 161; PC215/4940 (13 July 1945), 148; PC5973 (14 Sept. 1945), 333n130; PC7129 (4 Dec. 1945), 205; PC7224 (4 Dec. 1945), 207; PC746 (2 Mar. 1946), 231; PC2486 (10 Apr. 1946), 201–2; PC1513 (16 Apr. 1946), 246; PC3724 (12 Sept. 1946), 246; PC4059 (1 Oct. 1946), 208; PC4060 (1 Oct. 1946), 214; PC1819 (18 July 1947) 333n135; PC3737 (17 Sept. 1947), 333n135; PC3799 (23 Sept. 1947), 214; PC242 (22 Jan. 1948), 333n135; PC45/3304 (6 July 1950), 338n22; PC3799 (23 Sept. 1947), 214; PC943 (6 Mar. 1948), 214. *See also* Post-Discharge Re-establishment Order (PC7633)
Oshiro, Yasue, 254
overseas welfare workers, 166

Padwick, W.R., 232
Parkinson, N.F., 14
Parliament, G.H., 271
Parrish, Charles E., 248
Patullo, T. Dufferin, 107
pensions, 104, 111, 120; benefits extended to Second World War enlistees, 67; Board of Pension Commissioners, 12, 22–3, 26; Canadian Pension Commission created, 26; "due to service" ("compensation") and "insurance" principles, 67–8, 88, 136, 165; extension of benefits to Second World War enlistees, 67; Federal Appeal Board, 23; income tax on, 26; Military Pension Act, 10; number of disability and dependent pensioners, 31 Mar. 1919, 13; Pension Act and amendments, 23, 25, 41; Pension Appeal Court, 26, 35, 40; Royal Commission on Pensions and Re-establishment, 22–3; special committees (1916, 1919, 1930), 10–13, 24; Veterans' Bureau and pension advocates, 26, 40, 131
"pension widow," 12
Phelan, V.C., 80
Picking, F.J., 32
Porter, Betsy, 278
Porter, Catherine, 278
Porter, Donavon, 278
Porter, Leslie Harrison, 278
Porter, Susan, 278
Post-Discharge Re-establishment Order (PC7633): administration under, 100–6; background, 77; debate over within government, 79–80, 81–2; definition of "discharged person" under, 112–13, 313n82 and n87; draft, 77–8; eligibility of women for benefits, 112; explained in *Back to Civil Life*, 133–6, 160; first regulations under, 84–5; means testing under, 109, 121, 128; referred to cabinet committee, 79; reissued as PC5210, 121; significance, 85–7; terms and effect of, 82–3
potential recruits disabled in training, 166
Power, Charles Gavan (Chubby): background, 39–40; own disability pension, 40, 305n41; response to findings of Veterans' Assistance Commission, 49–50, 53, 54–5; speech at Legion's 10th anniversary banquet, 40
Price, C.B., 35, 52, 53, 242
Price, J.L., 152
Prowse, Harper, 196
Purvis, Arthur, 53
Putnam, J.H., 107

RAF Transport Command: Canadian civilian air crew of, 166

Ralston, J.L.: chairs Royal Commission on Pensions and Re-establishment, 22; in 1930s, 39; War Service Grants Act, 126, 129
Rand, Ivan, 185
Rattray, John Grant, 42, 43, 48
Re-establishment credit(s). *See* War Service Grants Act
Rehabilitation (A Combined Operation) (Woods), 289
Reid, Emerson Baker (Tim): background, 133; on postwar housing situation, 247; represents DVA on Demobilization and Rehabilitation Information Committee, 167; work with citizens' committees, 171–3
Reid, Tom, 255
Reinstatement in Civil Employment Act (1942), 136, 165, 182, 281
relief: in 1920s, 21–2; in 1930s, 27–8, 31; name changed to "unemployment assistance," 35; recommendations of Hyndman committee, 35–8; Second World War decline in payments, 105; situation of single unemployed in Manitoba, 29; statistics, 35–6
Report of the National Conference of Canadian Universities on Post-War Problems, 144
Rescue Tug Service, 263, 265
Richards, Gerald, 196
Ritchie, Charles, 159
Robertson, Gideon, 31
Robinson, H.C.W. (Colin), 251–2
Roebuck, A.W., 151
Rogers, Norman, 39, 44, 54
Ronson, W.C., 121
Roosevelt, Franklin, 108
Roper, John S.: background, 31–2; confronts MacLaren, 32; on relief and unemployment, 33
Roscoe, B.W., 48
Ross, Alexander: background, 34; on bonus movement, 45–6; chairs committee on treatment regulations, 136–7; elected Canadian Legion president, 34; on Hyndman committee report, 39; memos on rehabilitation and re-establishment, 71–2 (1936), 41; on Veterans' Assistance Commission, 42, 51–2
Ross, Steward R., 202
Rowell, N.W., 12
Royal Canadian Air Force Women's Division, 61
Royal Canadian Legion. *See* Canadian Legion of the British Empire Service League
Royal Canadian Mounted Police, 99; special constables, 165–6
Royal Commission on Dominion-Provincial Relations, 51, 75
Royal Commission on Government Organization, 285
Royal Commission on Pensions and Re-establishment. *See* pensions
Royal Commission on Veterans' Qualifications, 201–2, 204–5
Royal Commission to Investigate Complaints of Canadian Citizens of Japanese Origin Who Resided in British Columbia in 1941 ..., 257, 333n135
Russell, Olive Ruth: background, 138; on career choices of women veterans, 218–19, 227; on counselling of women veterans, 142; on homemaking, 141; named executive assistant to director general of rehabilitation, 138; on postwar employment prospects of women, 142–4; on rehabilitation and postwar role of women, 139–41; on Woods, 224
Rutherford, F.S., 202
Rutherford, Thomas John, 249
Ryerson Institute of Technology, 201

Ste Anne's Hospital, 285

St John Ambulance Brigade, 166
St Laurent, Louis, 178
Salter, Mary Dinsmore (later Ainsworth), 216, 221–2, 224, 225–6
Salvation Army, 165
Scammell, Ernest H.: on Brereton claims, 30; secretary of DSCR, 24; secretary of Hyndman committee, 35
Schierbeck, John, 213, 327–8n245
Segsworth, W.E., 14
Senior, C.N., 152, 154, 171
Servicemen's Readjustment Act of 1944. *See* G.I. Bill
Sharp, Mitchell, 135
Shaughnessy Hospital, 18, 259, 289
Shears, F.G., 100, 157
Shimotakahara, Kozo, 99
Shoji, George Yasuzo, 258
Shoulds, A.M., 184–5
Shuster, Frank, 169
Sibley, Alfred J., 156
Simpson's, 193–4
Sir Arthur Pearson Club for Blinded Sailors and Soldiers, 23, 235, 242
Slater, David, 315n32
Smallwood, Joseph R., 267, 273, 274
Smelts, F.S., 202
Smith, Frank, 98
Smith, Sidney, 209, 213
Smith, Tom, 20
Soldier settlement. *See* land settlement (Great War)
Soldier Settlers' Association of Canada, 156
soldiers' insurance, 24, 25
South African Military Nursing Service, 166
Speakman, Alfred, 38
Special Force (Korea), 285
Special Operators War Service Benefits Act, 165
Special Unemployment Committee, 30
Starkey, Len, 212, 213
Stewart, R.M., 20
Styran, Betty, 219

Sunnybrook Hospital, 137
Supervisors War Service Benefits Act, 165
Sutherland, Donald, 38–9

Thompson, Donald, 278–80
Thompson, John, 26
Thompson, R.S., 104
Thomson, James S., 146–7
Toronto and District Ex-Servicemen's Advisory Committee, 232
Toronto Better Business Bureau, 193, 195
Toronto Veterans Rehabilitation Committee, 179
Tosland, A.L., 164
Trades and Labor Congress, 76, 78, 182–3
treatment services: consolidation of regulations (1944), 136–7; "Doctor of Choice" program, 228–31; one-year general benefit under Veterans Charter, 136–7; PC204–6613 (18 Nov. 1940), 73; postwar reform, 227–31; regulatory change, 1937, 54–5; wartime expansion of hospital facilities, 137
Tremblay, Mary, 238
Tubercular Veterans' Association, 23
Tucker, Walter A., 161
Tufts, Robert, 169
Tupper, Charles Hibbert, 233
Tupper, Dorothy Joyce, 233
Turgeon, J.G., 117
Turner, Jack, 263, 270–1

Unemployed Ex-Servicemen's Association, 28
Unemployment and Farm Relief Act, 31
Unemployment Insurance Commission, 78, 80–1, 83, 84, 103, 136, 179, 217
Union government: formation of, 7; pledge re service in Great War, 9

United Auto Workers, 184–5
United Farmers of Alberta, 151
United Nations Charter, 162, 220
United Steelworkers of America, 183
universities and colleges: Alberta, 203, 208, 215, 277; British Columbia, 66, 106, 116, 144, 147, 191, 203, 205, 215, 288; Carleton, 147; Columbia, 138; Dalhousie, 139; Edinburgh, 138; Laval, 147, 215; McGill, 66, 106, 117, 147, 202, 203, 206–7, 211–12, 213, 215, 275; McMaster, 144; Manitoba, 203, 215; Montréal, 147, 208, 215, 275; New Brunswick, 147; Ottawa, 205; Queen's, 65, 125, 145, 147, 203, 205, 212, 278; Ryerson, 201; Saskatchewan, 146, 147, 203, 204, 215; Toronto, 116, 138, 147, 203, 205, 208, 209, 212, 213, 215, 228, 233, 277, 281; Western Ontario, 275
University Veterans' Advisory Service, 208
University Women's Club (Dalhousie University), 139
"unmarried wives," 13

Vancouver Real Estate Exchange, 150
Veterans Affairs, 166, 218
Veterans Affairs Canada, 285. *See also* Department of Veterans Affairs
Veterans' Assistance Commission: established by 1936 act, 40–2; honorary committees, 50, 55, 68; lessons of, 57, 283; members, 42; model for future PC7633, 86; philosophy of training, self-help, and voluntarism, 57; proposal for, 35, 38; recommends "provisional economic allowance," 51; reports, 46–8, 50; sets limit on benefits, 57; Veterans' Bureau, 26, 131. *See also* pensions
Veterans' Business and Professional Loans Act, 165, 181
Veterans Charter: achievements of, 215, 281–2, 287–8; benefit package of 1 Apr. 1946, 135–6; and Canadian welfare state, 287; compared to programs of other countries, 166; directive approach of, 191; extension to Special Force, 285; legislative completion, 165–6; limitations of, 95, 250, 282–3; origin of term, 125; philosophy of, 226; promised in 1945 Throne Speech, 162; rhetoric of service, 176; role in keeping up demand, 197; summarized in 1947 DVA publication, 166
Veterans Charter: Acts of the Canadian Parliament to Assist Canadian Veterans, The, 166, 275
Veterans Guard of Canada, 70
Veterans Housing Registry, 173
Veterans Independence Program, 285
Veterans Insurance, 16, 190
Veterans' Land Act: administration and statistics, 95–6, 97, 148–52, 244–5; "Build Your Own Home" program, 250; consideration of and approval by Parliament, 92–3; controversy over regulation 22A, 246, 248, 250; controversy with real estate agents, 150–1; formation of veterans' co-operative housing associations under, 250; house building initiative, 151, 244, 248; introduction of Part II ("Home Construction Assistance"), 250; land settlement subcommittee of GACDR, 89, 92, 94–5; Murchison memo of July 1940 on land settlement, 91; terms of legislation, 93–4
Veterans Rehabilitation Act: administration and statistics, 176; bill introduced and passed, 163–4; means testing under, 197–8; university training under, 202–4; vocational training under, 198–201
Voluntary Aid Detachments, 166

Walker, Alex: background, 71; elected

president of Canadian Legion, 71; on employment of aliens, 110; overseas visit of, 242; philosophy of advocacy, 118; on postwar housing situation, 242–3; presentation to House of Commons 1941 special committee, 76
Wallace, John, 213
Wallace, R.C., 205, 209
Walsh, Albert J., 264–5, 270
War Amputations of Canada, 23, 85, 235, 242
Wardhaugh, Robert, 315n32
War Emergency Training Programme, 78, 83, 101, 104
War Measures Act, 82
Warner, Wilfred Parsons: background, 227–8; named director general of treatment services, 228; publications by, 231; reform program of, 228–31
War Service Grants Act: background 122–3; bill 194 introduced and passed, 129; Finance memo of 17 July 1944, 125–6; and NRMA men, 128; prevention of rackets under, 193–6; resolution approved, 128 ; response of Canadian Legion and Canadian Corps Association to legislation, 130; war service gratuity and re-establishment credits under, 122, 128–30, 154, 175–6, 187–93, 223, 225, 275n283
Wartime Bureau of Technical Personnel, 210
Wartime Housing Ltd, 154
Wartime Information Board, 246
Wartime Prices and Trade Board, 246
War Veterans' Allowance: act (1930) and 1936 and 1938 amendments, 25–6, 41–2 52–5; administration by War Veterans' Allowance Committee (from 1937 War Veterans' Allowance Board), 25, 40, 41, 131; dubbed, "burnt-out pension," 26; extension of benefits to Second World War veterans, 136; extension of benefits to select widows of Great War veterans, 136; fact-finding committee, 26; number of beneficiaries, 1934–35, 26; reduction in number of beneficiaries during Second World War, 105
Watson, W.D., 81
Watts, Alf, 242
Wayne, Johnny, 169
WD forms and leaflet, 100, 103; WD12 (service interview summary), 160
Weir, George M.: background, 106–7; on means testing, 121–2; on PC7633, 107–8; presentation to House of Commons special committee on reconstruction and re-establishment, 117–18; "Survey of Rehabilitation (Interim Report)," 107–9
White Paper on Veterans Pensions (1969), 285
Whitworth, F.E., 211
Whitton, Charlotte, 114
Winning the Second Battle: Canadian Veterans and the Return to Civilian Life, 1915–1930 (Morton and Wright), 22
Winnipeg Better Business Bureau, 193, 195
Women's Advisory Committee of the United States Manpower Commission, 220
Women's Airforce Service Pilots (US), 162
Women's Army Auxiliary Corps (US), 162
Women's Army Corps (US), 162
Women's Royal Canadian Naval Service, 61
Women's Royal Naval Service, 166
Women veterans: *Back to Civil Life* on, 138. 284; evolution of policy towards, 111–16; findings of "Survey of Rehabilitation (Interim Report)," 115–16, 117–18; progress and outcome of rehabilitation program for, 216–17; training conferences re,

216–18; work of GACDR Sub-Committee on the Special Problems of Discharged Women, 113–16, 138
Wood, Lewis, 238
Woods, Ben, 5
Woods, Byron F., 178
Woods, Elizabeth (Barnes), 3
Woods, Frank, 5
Woods, Mervyn, 285
Woods, Rose Nancy, 5
Woods, W.B., 25
Woods, Walter Edwin Sainsbury: beginnings, 3; belief in "opportunity with security," 86, 106, 284; books by, 289; *Canadian Veteran* assessment of, 158; death and interment, 289; demobilization and re-establishment, 6, 19–20; early life in Canada, 3–5; on fact-finding committee, 26; on Finance memo of 17 July 1944, 126–8; on gratuity payment, 124; Great War service, 5–6; on "guiding principle" in administration of training benefits, 176; on housing for veterans, 128, 153–4; marries Elene Lucille Fawk, 19; on means testing, 122; named associate deputy minister DPNH, 74; named chair of War Veterans' Allowance Committee (later Board) and moves to Ottawa, 26; named deputy minister of veterans affairs, 131; named director of DPNH Veterans' Welfare Division, 74; named vice-chairman Advisory Committee on Rehabilitation and Re-establishment, 161; named vice-chairman and chairman of GACDR, 63, 85; on national health insurance, 232; philosophy of voluntarism, 110–11, 182, 284; portrait of, 289; on professional and business loans for veterans, 153–4; on radio broadcast hosted by Clifton Fadiman, 158; receives Canadian Legion Meritorious Service Medal, 289; recruiting trip overseas, 160; retires, 288; role in Calgary GWVA, 19; role in making of PC7633, 78–9; secretary, Vimy Pilgrimage Committee, 59; soldier settlement official, 20; speeches and radio addresses, 103, 111–12, 154–5, 244; suggests title of *Back to Civil Life*, 133; tours country re rehabilitation planning (Oct.–Nov. 1940), 68; tours country with England to explain PC7633 (Nov.–Dec. 1941), 85; visits United Kingdom (1943), 105–6; visits Washington (1943), 166; on War Service Grants Act, 154–5; on welfare state, 289; on work versus dependence, 180, 284
Woods, William, 5
Woods, William Sainsbury, 3
Wright, A.M., 104, 131
Wright, Glenn, 8, 22

YMCA, 19, 165

"zombies," 60